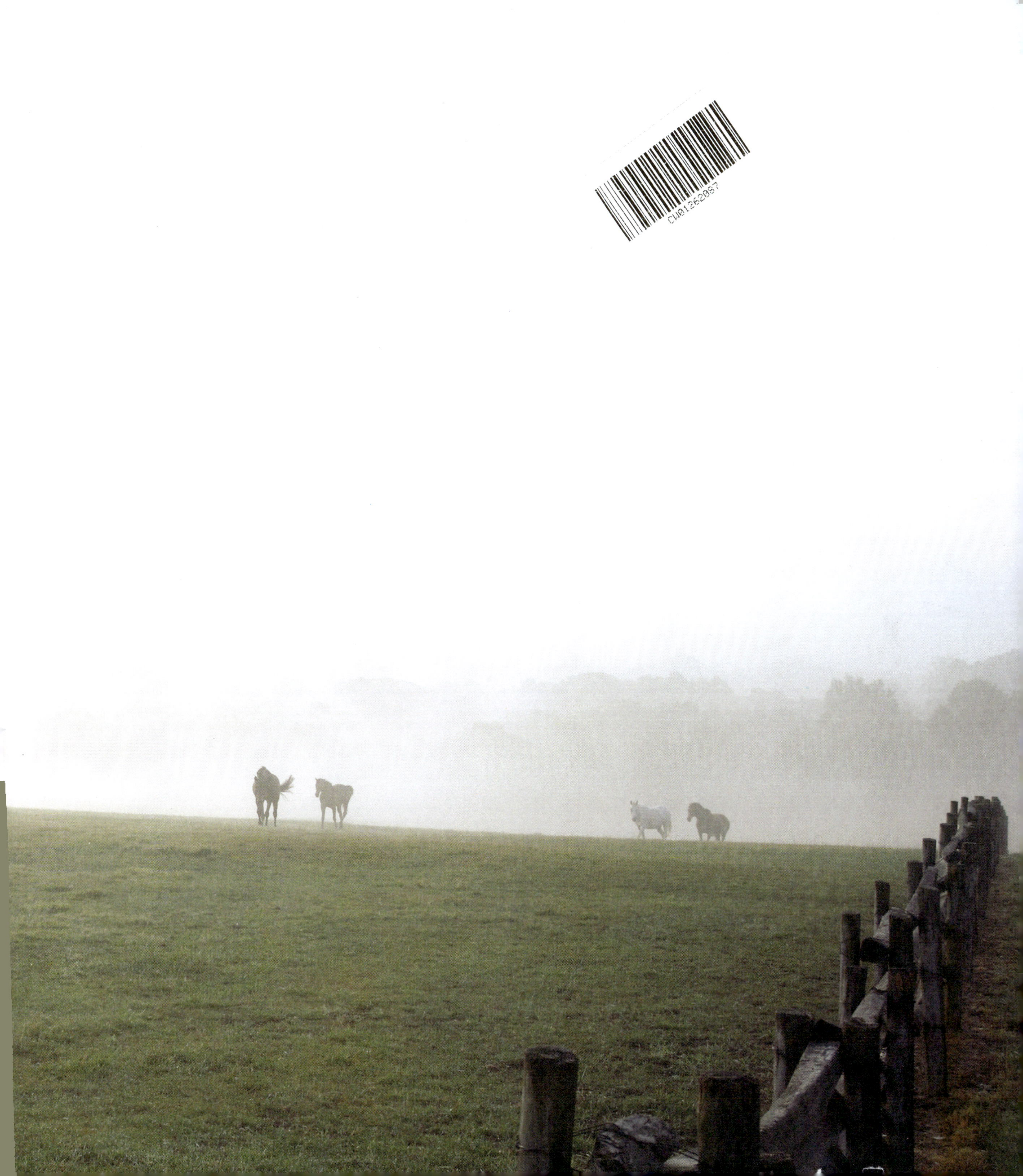

HUNT
COUNTRY
STYLE

HUNT COUNTRY STYLE

KATHRYN MASSON

Photography by PAUL ROCHELEAU

RIZZOLI
NEW YORK

First published in the United States of America in 2008 by
RIZZOLI INTERNATIONAL PUBLICATIONS, INC.
300 Park Avenue South, New York, NY 10010
www.rizzoliusa.com

ISBN-10: 0-8478-2949-9
ISBN-13: 9-780-8478-2949-1
Library of Congress Control Number: 2007907646

© 2008 Rizzoli International Publications, Inc.
Text © 2008 Kathryn Masson
Photographs (unless otherwise indicated below
or throughout book) © 2008 Paul Rocheleau

All rights reserved. No part of this publication may be
reproduced, stored in a retrieval system, or transmitted
in any form or by any means, electronic, mechanical,
photocopying, recording, or otherwise, without prior
consent of the publisher.

FRONT COVER *Formal east parlor in Old Keswick (p. 50).*

BACK COVER *Hickory House in the moonlight (p. 102).*

ENDPAPERS *Horses in Virginia's hunt country.*

PAGE 1 *A Staffordshire figurine sits on a Federal mahogany drop-leaf table under a window in the main parlor in West View (p. 158). The view is of the barn and stables.*

PAGES 2–3: *Members of the Old Dominion Hounds enjoy breathtaking scenery in their hunt territory that comprises approximately 100 square miles in Rappahannock and Fauquier Counties. Photo by Kathryn Masson.*

PAGES 6 *At Hickory House (p. 102), a kitchen garden adjacent to the house is enclosed with a picturesque white picket fence.*

PAGES 252–253 *Photo by Kathryn Masson.*

Designed by ABIGAIL STURGES

Printed and bound in China
2008 2009 2010 2011 2012 2013/ 10 9 8 7 6 5 4 3 2 1

CONTENTS

8 INTRODUCTION

32 OAKLAND GREEN FARM
Loudoun County
c.1730, c.1740, c.1790, 1978

40 CASTLE HILL
Albemarle County
1764, 1824, 1830, 1844, 1910, 1945

50 OLD KESWICK
Albemarle County
c.1764, 1818, 1832, 1970s

60 WELBOURNE
Loudoun County
c.1770, 1833, 1840s, 1850s, 1870s, 1880s, 1910

70 THE TANNERY
Fauquier County
c.1790, 1831, 1850, 1955, 1985, 2005

80 SEVEN SPRINGS FARM
Loudoun County
c.1790, 1818, c.1890, 1955, 1970s

90 EDGEWOOD
Fauquier County
c.1790, 1938, 1955, 2005

102 HICKORY HOUSE
Fauquier County
c.1795, c.1920, 1970s, 1980s

114 CHAPEL HILL FARM
Clarke County
1826, 1941, 2002

124 LLEWELLYN
Clarke County
c.1825, 1930s, 1975, 1986, 2003

134 OVOKA FARM
Fauquier County
c.1830s, c.1840s, c.1860s, 1930s, 1950s, 2004, 2006

146 KINROSS FARM
Fauquier County
1830, 1960, 1996, 1999, 2000, 2002

158 WEST VIEW
Fauquier County
1831, 1910

166 FOXHALL FARM
Rappahannock County
c.1840s, 1970s

176 GREENVILLE
Culpeper County
1854, 1900, c.1960, 1998, 1999, 2002, 2003

186 WOODLAWN
Orange County
Mid-1800s, 1930, 2005

196 MORROWDALE FARM
Albemarle County
c.1880s, c.1970s, 1999

210 WHILTON
Albemarle County
1914, 1936, 1988, 2004

226 FARM IN NORTHERN VIRGINIA
Loudoun County
c.1920, 1986

242 HENCHMAN'S LEA
Fauquier County
1941, 1992

254 ACKNOWLEDGMENTS

255 RESOURCES

256 INDEX

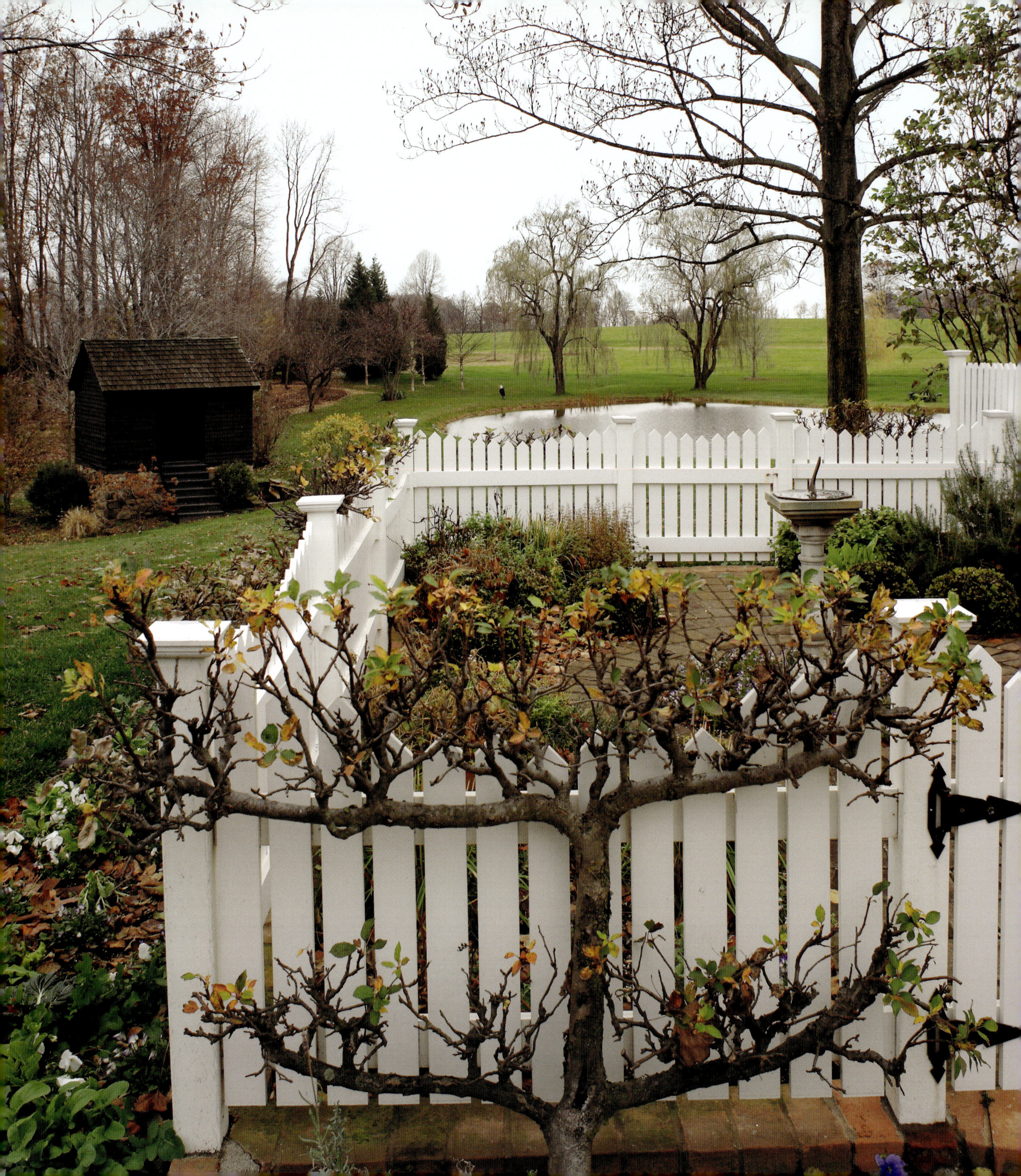

To my grandfather,
SAM JACK MUSICK, *1880–1928*
Heathcote, Keswick, Virginia

and

To those in Virginia's numerous conservation organizations who love and help to conserve and protect the incomparable beauty and important historical resources of the Piedmont countryside, especially Christopher Miller, president of the Piedmont Environmental Council, his staff, board of directors, and the organization's members.

Also, to the memory of those who gave generously of their time and talents to further the work of P.E.C., most notably Eve Fout, G. F. Steedman Hinckley, George L. Ohrstrom, Jr., Paul Mellon, Julian Scheer, and Ambassador Charles Whitehouse.

And for all of the Virginia Piedmont's landowners who preserve and protect the irreplaceable rural beauty of this part of our American heritage.

INTRODUCTION

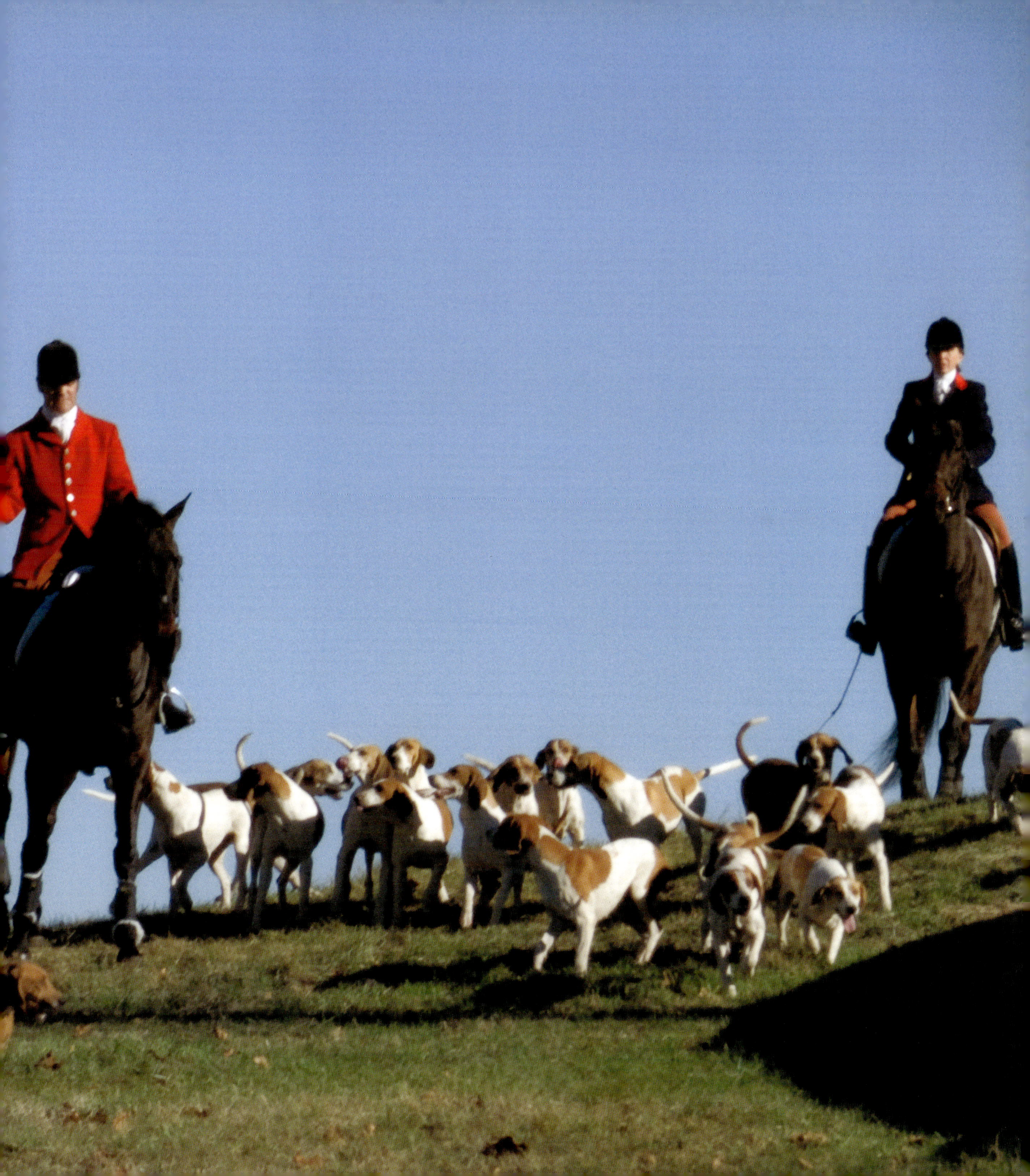

In a land of overwhelming beauty, of rolling hills and green forested countryside, where eighteenth- and nineteenth-century architecture constructed of indigenous materials endures, where local history extends to the very origins of our American heritage, where a culture based on a dependence upon animals and an enthusiasm for horse sports persists, a unique American lifestyle has evolved and survived. Today there are a few places that contain these qualities and embrace this lifestyle, but possibly no place in America is better known for all of these reasons than the Piedmont of Virginia, or as it is often called, Hunt Country.

The historical, cultural, and natural resources of the Hunt Country of Virginia constitute an ongoing American legacy. Preservation of historic architecture, conservation of open land, protection of an economy supported by agriculture and the equine industry, and a passion for horse sports are of the utmost importance. Hunt Country has a mystique about it and a quality that is at the core of our shared heritage. Virginia Hunt Country style is all about open land, the love of the horse, and evocative and often historic architecture.

Virginia Hunt Country is centered in the Piedmont, which extends from Alabama to New York, from the western edge of the Coastal Plain at the fall lines of the rivers westward to the Appalachian Mountains. In Virginia the point at which upstream navigation becomes impossible due to suddenly rugged topography of the Potomac, Rappahannock, York, and James rivers denote the Piedmont's eastern boundary and the Blue Ridge Mountains the western. In between is some

PRECEDING PAGES *Hounds move out to the crack of the Huntsman's whip. Photo by Kathryn Masson.*

RIGHT *The National Sporting Library in Middleburg is open to the public as an unequalled resource on turf and field sports. Its world class collections include more than 16,000 rare and historic books and current publications, as well as art. Established in 1954 by George L. Ohrstrom, Sr., and Alexander Mackay-Smith, the library's growing collections were relocated in 1999 to a new building, designed by architect Tommy Beach as a carriage house to architecturally complement the adjacent historic house of Ivy Hill. At the entrance stands Tessa Pullan's bronze statue that honors Civil War cavalry horses, given by the late Paul Mellon. The library hosts lectures, exhibitions, and special events throughout the year.*

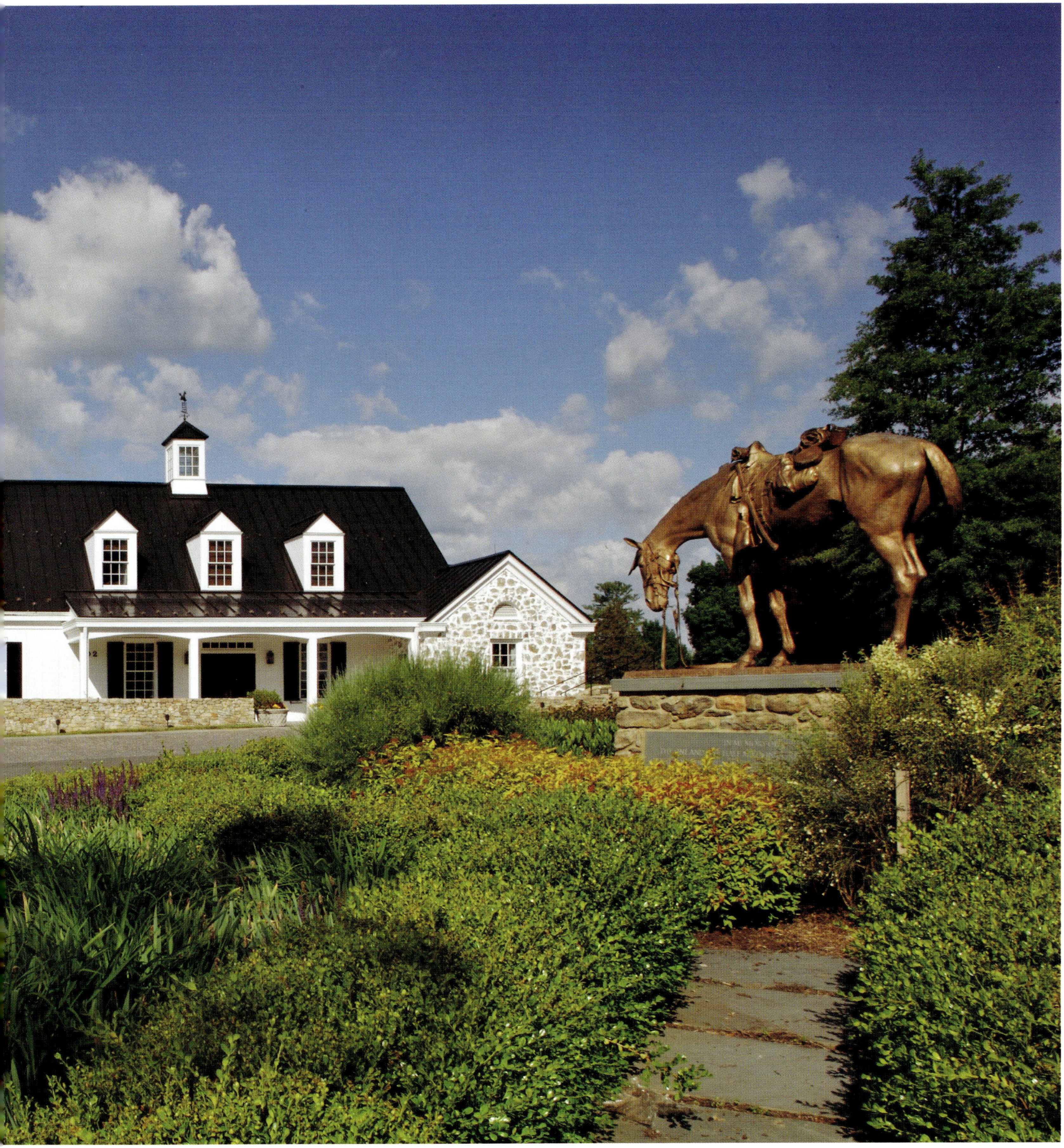

of the most beautiful countryside in America. The climate is mild compared to the harsh New England winters or the unrelenting heat of the far southern states. The landscape is mostly rolling hills with fertile soil amid outcroppings of blue, green, or brown basalt, pale limestone, Short Hill Mountain granite, and Bull Run Mountain quartzite. This soil was farmed and these stones were prominently used in eighteenth century construction of houses and barns, as well as to form the miles of stone walls that characterize the countryside, bordering farms and designating pastures.

Native Americans had resided in the Piedmont for centuries and had done much to shape its landscape. Their hunting trails and trade routes became the main roads of early transportation and some have developed into today's modern thoroughfares and highways. But from the early eighteenth century these Native American tribes migrated or were displaced to the north, south, and west and the preeminence of their culture was replaced with that of the European settlers. The Virginia Piedmont was part of the six-million-acre Proprietary of the Northern Neck, the 1719 inheritance of Thomas 6th Lord Fairfax (1693–1781). Although there had been some European exploration of lands in northern Virginia as early as the mid-seventeenth century, there was not a steady flow of inhabitants until a succession of three important political and legal events took place. First, in 1722 the Iroquois ceded their lands south of the Potomac River and east of the Blue Ridge Mountains, then in 1748 the highway act was passed that created better-maintained roads, and finally in 1749 English courts confirmed Lord Fairfax's legal title to his inheritance of nearly six million acres of Virginia. Lord Fairfax granted vast tracts of land to speculators and developers, often descendants of Virginia's first families of English gentry. He also granted smaller parcels of 150 to 200 acres to small independent farmers. Planters from the Tidewater region moved west-

ABOVE *Ever-present in Virginia's hunt country landscape are its walls of local fieldstone, masterfully built since the eighteenth century to line pastures, property boundaries, and roads.*

ABOVE *Scenic Goose Creek runs through Fauquier and Loudoun counties, draining a portion of the northern Piedmont of Virginia into the Potomac River. Since 1970 efforts of the Goose Creek Association have helped to preserve and protect this important natural and historic resource.*

ward for fertile land, having depleted the soil with continuous planting of tobacco over the decades. Also, because the land of the Coastal Plain had been completely settled, small farmers migrated west. Others came from colonies north.

Hardwood forests covered the region, save for clearings of grasslands where Native Americans had practiced seasonal burns in order to prevent the regrowth of forests, create openings for agriculture, and to encourage wild game populations. Settlers continued to labor to clear the forests to allow the cultivation of tobacco and grain such as wheat, corn, and barley and to breed cattle and horses. The walls that define pastures and farm boundaries were built from stones painstakingly gathered from the fields and stacked by early farmers, indentured servants, and slaves.

During his Virginia residency from 1747 to 1781 Thomas, Sixth Lord Fairfax, administered the granting of his land first from Belvoir on the Potomac River, then from the office he established at his Greenway Court estate in what would later become Clarke County. Fairfax hired sixteen-year-old George Washington in 1748 to survey his western lands and to serve as a commissioner, with Robert Burwell and Fielding Lewis, to substantiate the deeds of sale of much of this property. Washington's leadership skills, his capabilities as an explorer and surveyor, and familiarity with the western frontier lands were largely responsible for his significant roles in the French and Indian War.

In his first visits to Lord Fairfax's estate in the western frontier (of what was then Frederick County) Washington was exposed to foxhunting, a sport for which Fairfax was extremely passionate. It is believed that Fairfax had chosen to live in the far western region of his lands not only because it was a better location from which to administer them, but because of its perfect foxhunting terrain of rolling hills, meadows, and plentiful deer and game. He had imported English

ABOVE *The Aldie Mill, in the Aldie Historic District near Middleburg, was built 1807–1809 and is owned by the Virginia Outdoors Foundation. The mill, now fully restored and open to the public, is one of the most outstanding examples of a water-powered corn and wheat mill in Virginia. One of the many neighboring landowners who used the mill was James Monroe.*

OPPOSITE *The entry hall at Seven Springs Farm (p. 80).*

hounds in 1747 at about the time that it is believed that Thomas Walker, a planter in Albemarle County, hunted with his private pack of hounds at his estate Castle Hill. Foxhunting was a major venue for socializing among the proprietors of huge estates and has, since the mid-eighteenth century, been integral to life in the Northern Piedmont. Washington, who would become famous for his excellent horsemanship, hunted often with Lord Fairfax and other gentry and in 1767 established an outstanding pack of his own at Mt. Vernon. It included both colonial and English hounds, and later powerful French hounds sent to him as a gift by the Marquis de Lafayette. Washington continued to foxhunt whenever he could for the four decades that led up to his presidency.

George Washington and members of his extended family purchased large parcels of this land. Washington owned, among other land, 2,712 acres

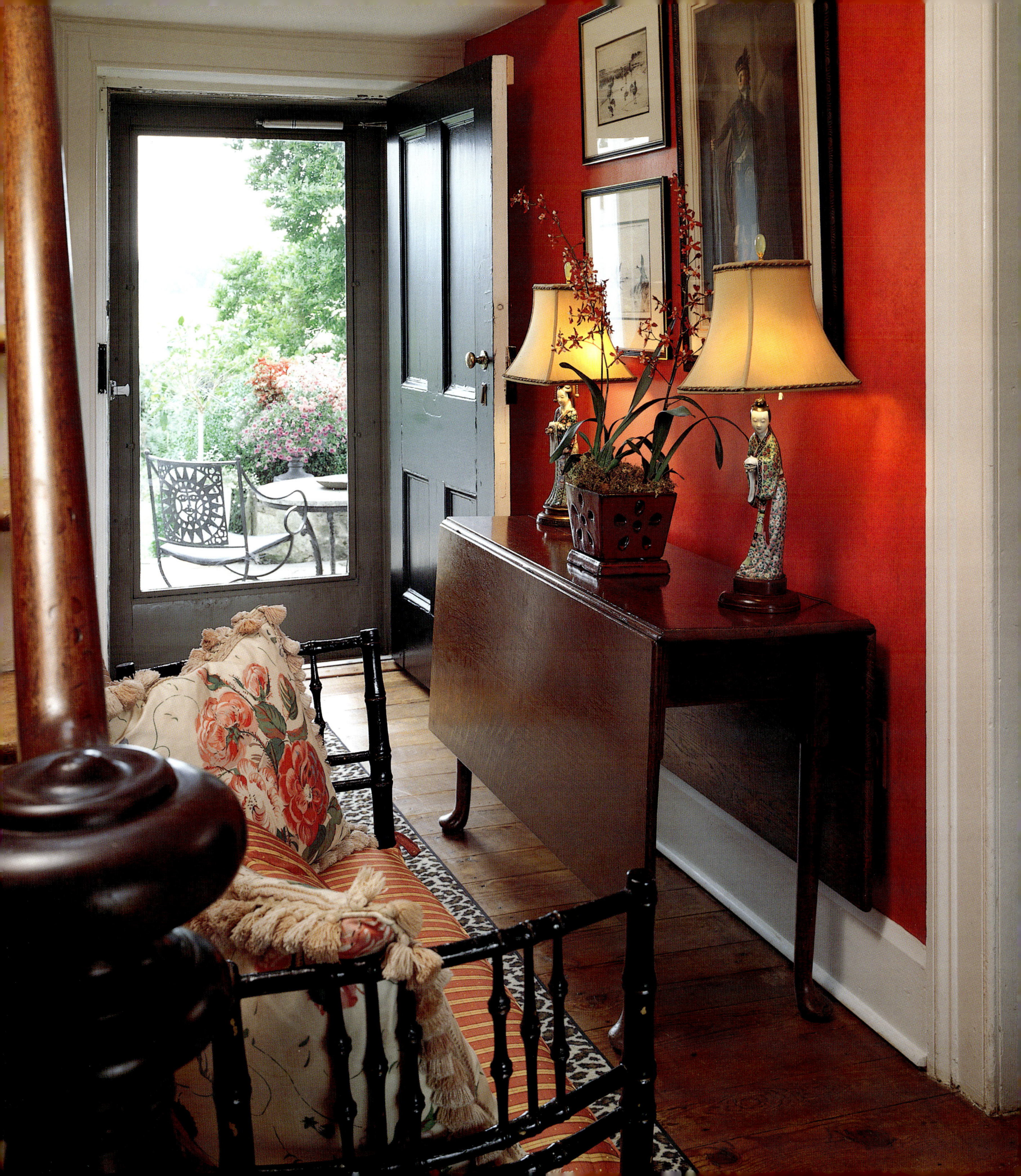

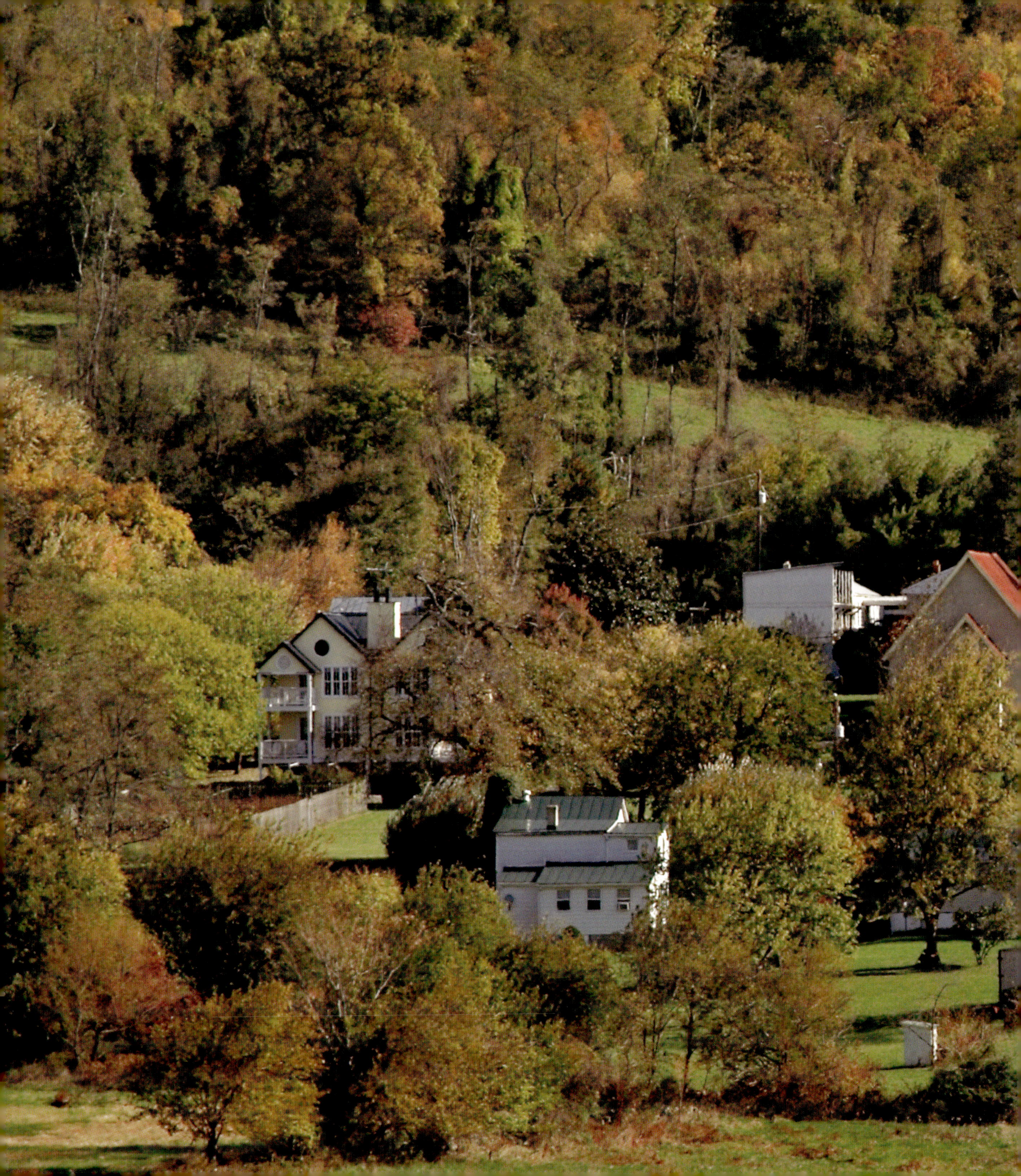

Paris, near the borders of Loudoun, Fauquier, and Clarke Counties, is one of the most picturesque hamlets in Virginia's rural countryside. It was renamed Paris to honor the Marquis de Lafayette on his celebratory farewell tour of the United States in 1824–1825.

near Ashby's Gap, a pass through the Blue Ridge Mountains dividing the Shenandoah Valley from the Piedmont, not far from Greenway Court. His brothers, Samuel and Charles, purchased and settled land just west of the Blue Ridge. After his first venture in 1748 Washington continued involvement with the area, often staying in the homes of relatives and friends during his seasonal trips.

The sophisticated brick architecture of the landed gentry of Tidewater Virginia was familiar to the new settlers, but as bricks were costly and the labor to use them intensive, such brick houses were rare in the early days of frontier settlement. Rather, farmers built in vernacular styles that met the needs required in a frontier environment and constructed with the raw materials at hand using the man-powered tools available. The earliest dwellings were simple log houses. Logs were hand-adzed or cut with a two-man pit saw until the early 1800s, at which time water-powered sawmills sped up the production of lumber, resulting in construction of frame houses with weatherboard siding. The "Virginia house," as the type came to be known, was either one room or two, with a high-pitched roof for an attic or loft space, and either one or two end chimneys. Well-to-do planters and successful farmers built new houses of local fieldstone. These manor houses, designed with a center hall and flanking two-over-two rooms, projected the owner's social status and financial solidity. This typically English plan was adapted in various forms to suit the Virginia climate and the frontier life. By the early to mid-nineteenth century, prosperity had allowed many landowners on the developing frontier to construct larger homes of brick, limestone, or wood. In eighteenth-century towns such as Charlottesville, Warrenton, Leesburg, and Culpeper, brick construc-

Montpelier was the lifelong home of President James Madison, "Father of the Constitution," and his wife Dolley Madison, the nation's first first lady. The house is situated on 2,650 acres in Orange County, in the Virginia Piedmont, with lush gardens, a landmark forest, and is within view of the Blue Ridge Mountains. A newly restored Montpelier, after having undergone an extensive four-year restoration by The Montpelier Foundation, will be unveiled on Constitution Day (September 17), 2008. The mansion is being returned to the classically inspired 1820s home to which James and Dolley returned after his presidency. Photo by Peggy Seiter Vaughn, courtesy of The Montpelier Foundation.

tion was used as well as frame construction. It is predominately the brick structures that have survived until today. And as early as 1769 Thomas Jefferson used brick when beginning the construction of the first phase of Monticello, his new home in Albemarle County. The material was also used by Jefferson later in the eighteenth century and early nineteenth century as he continued to design some of the most architecturally significant and majestic structures in America. He effectively began a national architectural movement with his Neoclassical styling of designs for Monticello, the original University of Virginia campus in Charlottesville, the State Capitol Building in Richmond, and various friends' houses, often incorporating Palladian elements.

The Civil War destroyed the way of life on many northern Virginia farms. Houses and barns were burned, livestock was confiscated or destroyed, and personal belongings were stolen. The area was worn down with continual movement of both Confederate and Union troops, huge encampments on private property, and numerous battles, including the largest cavalry

Monticello, now owned by the Thomas Jefferson Foundation, Inc., is Thomas Jefferson's home in Albemarle County that he redesigned to incorporate major Palladian architectural features after his return from France in 1789. Recognition of the importance of this building, along with Jefferson's original structures for the University of Virginia, the State Capitol in Richmond, and various friends' residences instigated a national architectural movement featuring Neoclassical design. Photo courtesy of Virginia Department of Historic Resources.

encounter of the war at Brandy Station, Culpeper County. But though the devastation was widespread, many structures survived. New residents, many of them wealthy Northerners who moved to the area in the latter part of the nineteenth century, purchased, restored, and remodeled the eighteenth-century farmhouses and created large farms for their Thoroughbred breeding operations, sporting pursuits, and a lifestyle unavailable to them elsewhere.

In 1905 a well publicized foxhunting event, the International Foxhound Match or The Great Hound Match, brought widespread recognition to Virginia and put it on the map for American horse sports enthusiasts, foxhunters in particular. Harry Worcester Smith, master of foxhounds (M.F.H.) of the Grafton Hunt in Massachusetts, who had been visiting the Dulany family in Upperville and hunting with an American pack of hounds, from stock bred for many generations in this country, and A. Henry Higginson of Middlesex, Massachusetts, who hunted with his pack of English hounds, held a ten-day foxhunting event that pitted the wits and abilities of their hounds against one another to

The historic and architecturally significant Farmington Country Club and its residential community are situated on nearly 1,000 acres in Albemarle County. Originally a 4,365-acre plantation, Farmington was comprised of various auxiliary buildings that have since been renovated and converted for modern usage. The c.1780 manor house that received a two-room octagonal addition designed by Thomas Jefferson in 1803 is now the main clubhouse and centerpiece of the country club complex. Photo courtesy of Farmington Country Club.

end their long public debate and determine which breed was superior. Victory went to the American hounds. Smith was enticed to move to the Middleburg-Upperville area and later became M.F.H. of the Piedmont Hunt and changed foxhunting in America thereafter by establishing the Masters of Foxhounds Association in 1907. The renown of Piedmont Virginia's Hunt Country grew and horse sports, especially Thoroughbred racing and foxhunting, became even more popular.

Again in the 1920s, a surge of Northerners, among them wealthy industrialists and socialites, seeking open land for Thoroughbred breeding farms and foxhunting in a better climate and rolling terrain moved to Hunt Country. They purchased small farms and adjoining properties and created what are still famous estates today. They also established the Orange County, Middleburg, and Warrenton Hunts.

To live in the countryside has long held an appeal for modern Americans. Perhaps it is that from the beginning of European settlement here we were indelibly bound to the land. Perhaps it is the desire to leave modern urban culture behind and return to a pastoral environment. Or it may be an aesthetic imperative that calls us to be surrounded by natural beauty. Whatever it is, many Americans are determined to enjoy the calming rural landscape first hand and to live in houses that are either actual eighteenth-century structures or based

The rotunda and the other buildings of his "academical village" in Charlottesville were designed by Thomas Jefferson. The institution was established in 1819 and is the origin of the University of Virginia. Photo courtesy of Virginia Department of Historic Resources.

on the American designs of their prototypes, English country houses. In effect, we desire to live the English country life, where an interdependence among man, horse, and land creates a thriving lifestyle and a daily *raison d'être*.

Traditional styles abound today in residential architecture and interiors. We aspire to capture the warmth and charm of country life in our homes. For many this is an effortless task. Family heirlooms, antique furniture with exceptional provenance, mementos of the hunting field or race track, and horse-themed art fill the houses, endowing a timeless quality. The interiors are sometimes elegant, sometimes casual, even rustic, but always comfortable, and appear as if to have evolved over time.

The horse has always been central to the Virginian's way of life, whether as an indispensable farm animal, a means of transportation for business, a focus of a breeding enterprise, or an integral part of a social life that includes all horse sports. In Virginia horses are a way of life that crosses all class, age, and economic barriers. When descendants of Virginia's first families began to move west into the Piedmont, they brought their English customs, their fine Thoroughbred horses, their love of horse racing and foxhunting, and their need for open space. From Albemarle County north through Greene, Orange, Culpeper, and Rappahannock to Loudoun and Fauquier Counties in the Piedmont and Clarke County just over the Blue Ridge in the Shenandoah Valley,

ABOVE *Morven Park, owned by The Westmoreland Davis Memorial Foundation, Inc., is located just outside downtown Leesburg. The impressive mansion was built in stages, with the oldest part dating to the 1750s and the latest construction in the 1880s. It was purchased in 1903 as the residence for Mr. Davis, later Governor of Virginia and master of foxhounds of the Loudoun Hunt, and his wife. The 1,100-acre grounds include the Morven Park International Equestrian Center, the extraordinary antique carriages and coaches of the Winmill Carriage Collection, and the Museum of Hounds and Hunting North America, and is open to the public. The institution hosts equestrian events such as polo matches, steeplechase races, Pony Club events, the Virginia Foxhound Club's Hound Show, and in 2007, the Masters of Foxhounds Association Centennial Celebration. Photo by Cathy Hill, courtesy of The Westmoreland Davis Memorial Foundation, Inc.*

LEFT *Morven Park stable yard.*

OPPOSITE *The library at the Farm in Northern Virginia (p. 226) is a modern take on Palladian grandeur. Fine collections of English and American art, English and European porcelain, and pristine eighteenth-century furnishings decorate the room.*

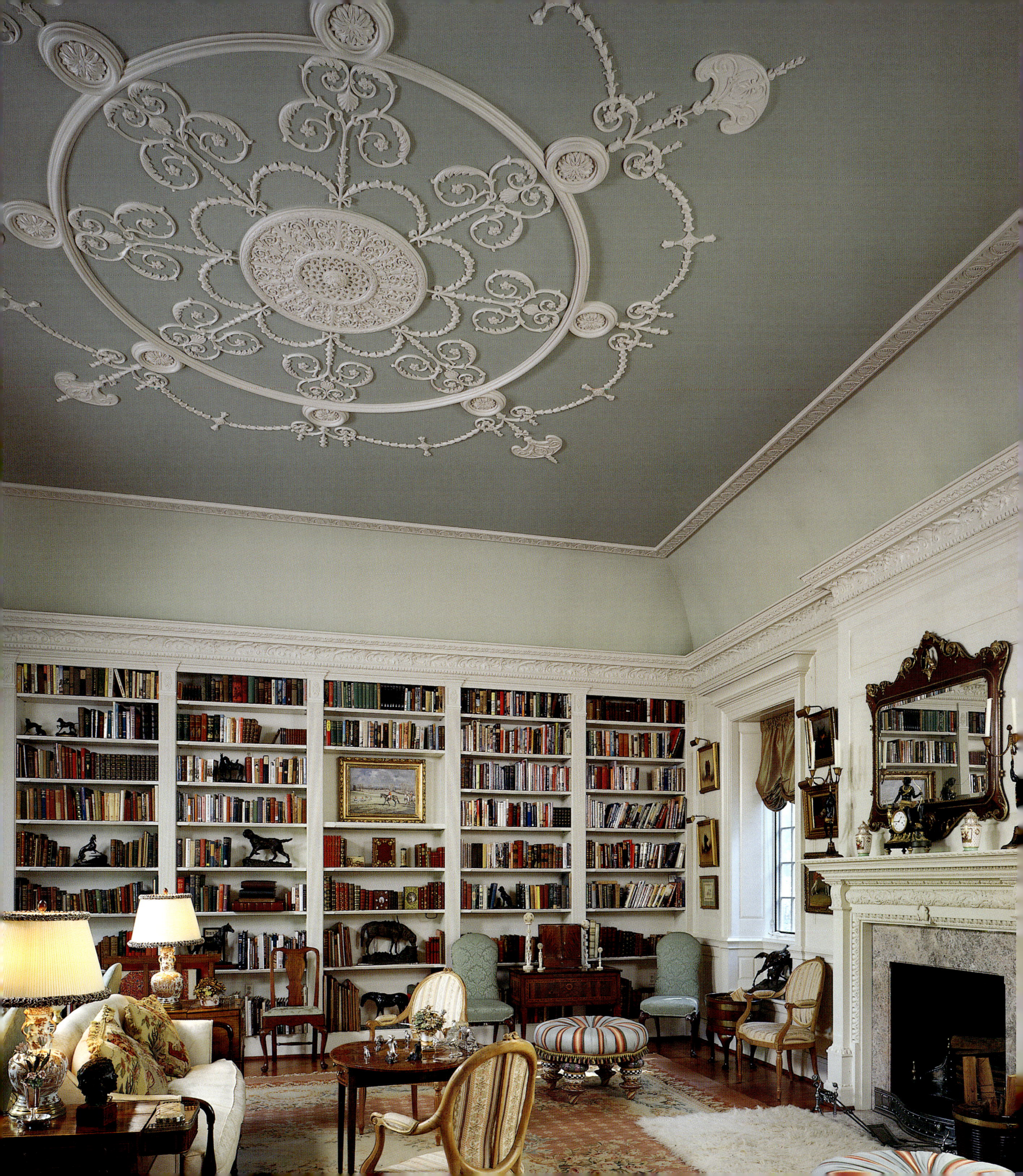

ABOVE *The Casanova Hunt is based in Casanova, Virginia, in Fauquier County. Hounds are followed by, front, left to right: Gaylord Hoisington, honorary whipper in; Jeanne Fendley Clark, honorary whipper in and master of foxhounds; and Tommy Lee Jones, huntsman. Immediately behind, left to right: Joyce Fendley, master of foxhounds (directly behind Jeanne Clark); Robert Johnson, honorary whipper in; Kay Blassic, honorary whipper in; and the field (riders). Photo by Douglas Lees.*

people enjoy living with a scenic rural landscape, historic homes, small villages and quaint hamlets, and myriad opportunities to enjoy horses.

Equestrian events abound. The change of seasons brings horse shows, foxhunting, trail riding, eventing, coaching and carriaging events, polo, and steeplechases as large as the Virginia Gold Cup or as intimate as a hunt point-to-point. There are riding clinics for every equestrian discipline and farm and stable tours. Hunt breakfasts and hunt balls, and special events that raise funds to support such organizations as the Middleburg Humane Foundation or the Piedmont Environmental Council, as well as festivals such as the Beasty Bazaar at Ayshire Farm, are always well-attended. Historic Grace Episcopal Church in Keswick observes

24 INTRODUCTION

ABOVE *Displayed in the tack room at the Farm in Northern Virginia (p. 226) are some of the owner's silver trophies, equestrian memorabilia, and specialized collections of various types of saddles, bridles, stirrups, and over a thousand bits.*

an annual Blessing of the Hounds, and prayers are offered for hounds, horses, and their mounts at opening hunt meets. Piedmont farms may be modest homes, impressive professional operations such as Kinross Farm, or historic horse breeding farms such as Keswick Stables or Hickory Tree Farm. Young riders as well as world-class athletes and Olympic medalists live in the Piedmont. Civil War encampments and cavalry reenactments educate the public about the heroic Confederate Col. John Singleton Mosby and the Mosby Heritage Area Association works today to protect the region in which he operated. Everywhere, the horse culture permeates life. Important equestrian-oriented organizations in the Piedmont include the National Sporting Library in Middleburg, a world-class research center dedicated to preserving some of the rarest manuscripts and art of all types of equestrian and field sports, the headquarters for *The Chronicle of the Horse* magazine, established in 1937, a nationally renowned weekly publication that reports on all of the horse events in America, the offices of *Covertside*, a publication of the Masters of Foxhounds Association of America, the Museum of Hounds & Hunting North America, the Virginia Steeplechase Association, and the Virginia Thoroughbred Breeders Association.

Most recently, people have moved to the Piedmont because it is one of the most beautiful areas in the country. Although development is encroaching at an ever-increasing rate, villages and small towns still exist, and there is a large community of preservationists and

25

LEFT *The long line of a pendant lantern complements the upward sweep of the graceful curved stair rail at Henchman's Lea (p. 242).*

OPPOSITE *In the front entry hall at Hickory House (p. 102), an English hat rack holds traditional English walking sticks and sturdy felt hats at the ready beside an English wood bin and a pair of fox-head oil paintings by Wallace Nall, an ode to the sporting life of the homeowners.*

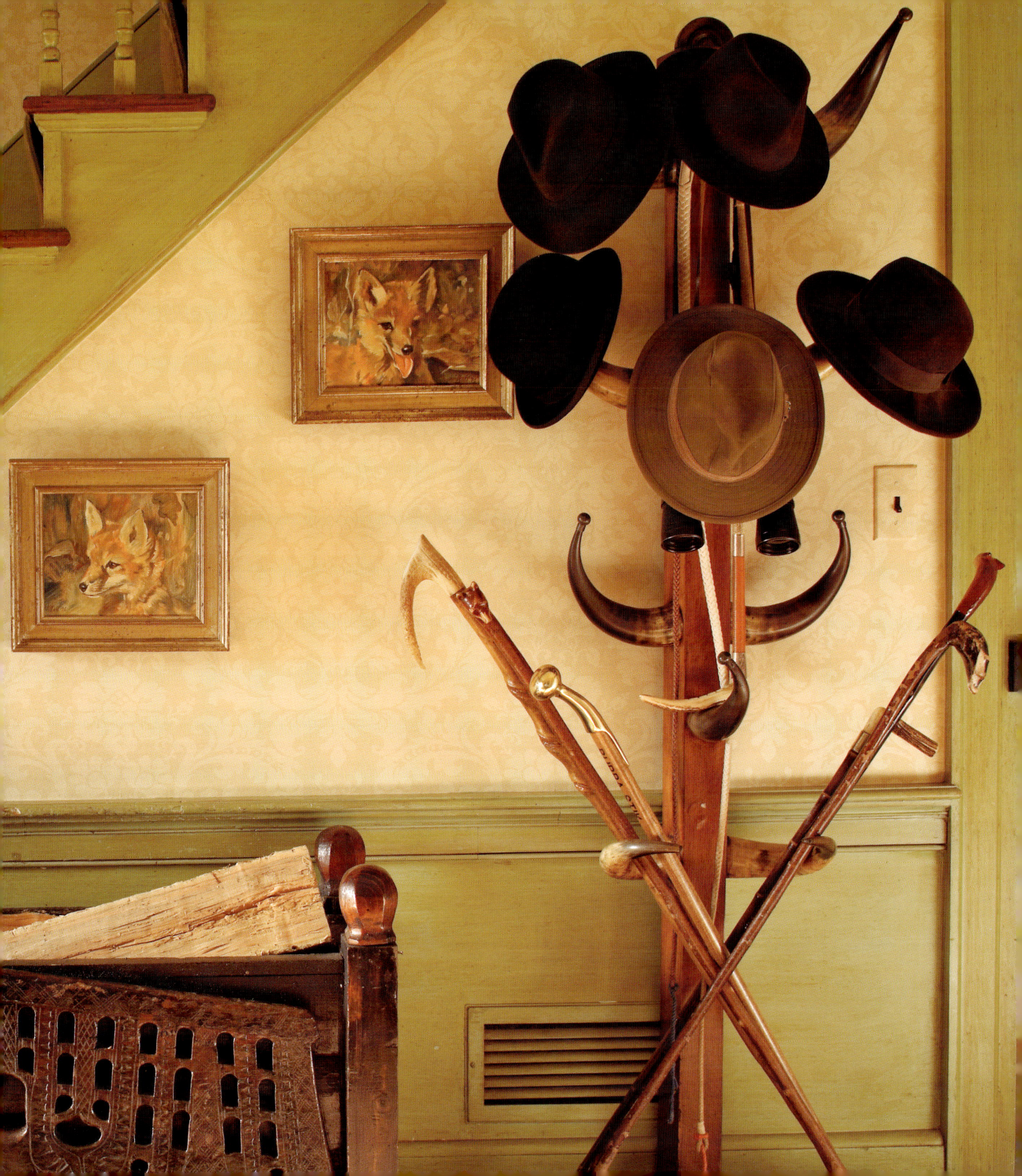

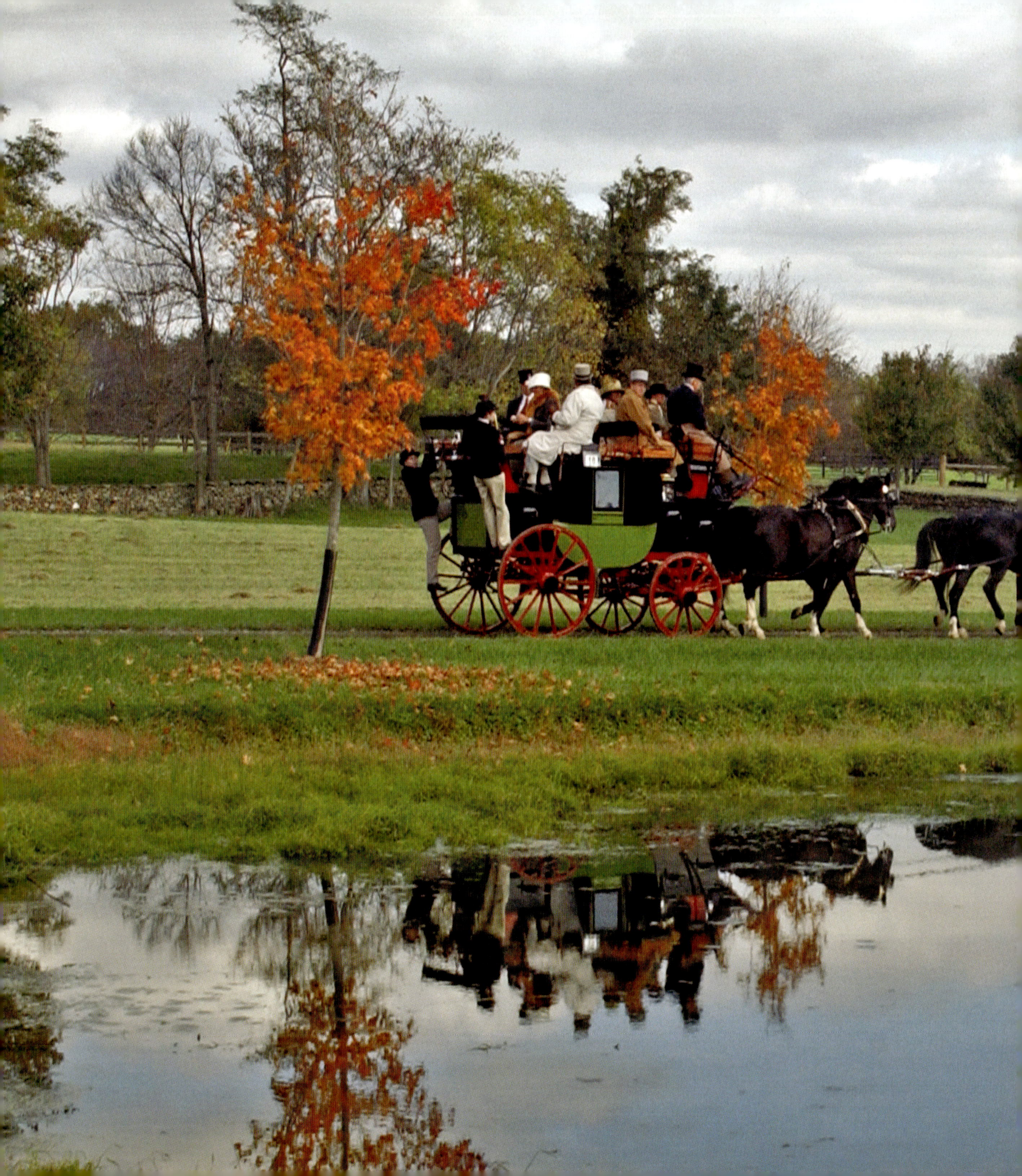

LEFT *One of the spectacular coaches featured in the National Sporting Library's 2004 coaching drive through the countryside surrounding the Llangollen estate in Upperville, Virginia, was the apple-green 1895 Brewster & Co. private coach drawn by a team of Hackney horses. The park drag's provenance includes ownership by the Vanderbilt and Rothchild families. The current owners, Joe and Karen Jennings of Allentown, New Jersey, have restored the coach over the past twenty years. Photo by Robert Jennings.*

conservationists who are passionate about protecting their natural and historic resources. In the Piedmont of Virginia, the largest towns are Charlottesville, Leesburg, and Warrenton. The historic cores of these towns as well as small towns such as Culpeper, Berryville, Orange, Greene, Madison, and Middleburg remain intact, and smaller villages and hamlets, such as the Quaker settlements of Waterford and Lincoln in Loudoun County, Little Washington in Rappahannock County, and Millwood in Clarke County, all established in the eighteenth century, dot the rural landscape and continue to be the centers of community life.

More than three centuries have passed since the Northern Piedmont first saw European settlers. The fertile soil that drew them and sustained them, along with the equine industry that began with them, are still important contributors to the economy today. Much of the rural countryside has been protected with easements and retains its beauty. Vernacular architecture that charms us today because of its design, materials, and setting in the landscape is valued for its cultural and historic significance. Northern Virginia residents have become passionate preservationists. The most prominent organization whose goal is the permanent protection of the Piedmont's exceptional resources is the Piedmont Environmental Council, founded in 1972. Its focus of concern is the nine counties featured in this book, in which it educates and promotes the importance of protecting open space and natural resources with land easements. To date, easements have been donated on over 250,000 acres in the Piedmont. Included in the rich and varied heritage that must be protected are the area's historical resources, paramount of which is the eighteenth- and nineteenth-century architecture. Altogether, the protection of the open rural landscape and the region's irreplaceable historic sites and support of the horse sports that dominate the way of life in Virginia's Piedmont will result in the continued enjoyment of the scenic beauty and equine culture that affords a style of life for all who live in and love the area.

LEFT *The Red Fox Inn in Middleburg was established in 1728 and is famous as one of the region's most evocative stone structures as well as one of its oldest. Located on Rt. 50 an equal distance from two of the region's busiest towns during the westward expansion of the eighteenth century, Winchester and Alexandria, it served as an important way station for early travelers and was an instrumental site for Confederate headquarters during the Civil War. Today it is still a popular restaurant and inn.*

OPPOSITE *The Warrenton headquarters of the Piedmont Environmental Council (P.E.C.) are located in a late-eighteenth-century house built by the Horner family and donated and restored by the late George L. Ohrstrom, Jr. P.E.C., one of the most important and active conservation-oriented non-profit organizations in Virginia, has been instrumental in helping to preserve and protect the natural, cultural, and historic resources in nine counties in the northern Virginia Piedmont.*

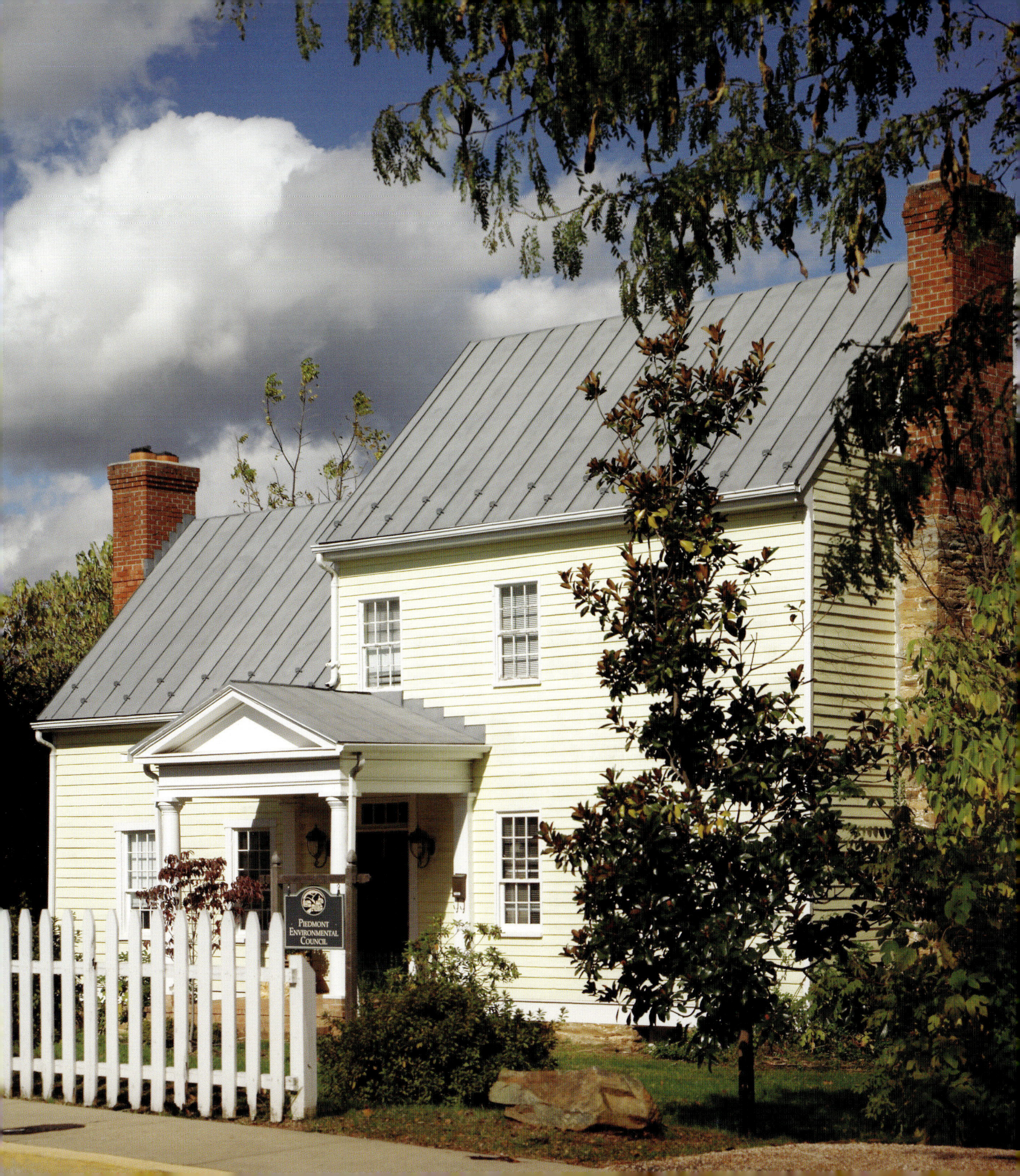
Piedmont Environmental Council

OAKLAND GREEN FARM

Residence of Jean Brown
Original log house c.1730; stone addition c.1740;
brick addition c.1790
Kitchen and family room addition, 1978,
designed by Bill and Jean Brown

The farmhouse of Oakland Green and its voluminous weatherboard and stone bank barn were built near the early-eighteenth-century Quaker settlement of Lincoln. Looking much as it did almost three hundred years ago, Lincoln shares a Quaker heritage with a cluster of villages in Loudoun County. The oldest of these settlements is Waterford, established in 1733 and America's first community to be designated a National Historic Landmark District. A few miles from Waterford, Lincoln was established between 1736 and 1738 as a Quaker settlement that was originally known as Goose Creek but later renamed for President Abraham Lincoln to entice the U.S. government to install a post office there.

Oakland Green, now home to a tenth generation Brown family member, reveals the evolution of a quin-

ABOVE AND RIGHT *Oakland Green Farm is one of the earliest residences built near the quaint village of Lincoln, established as a Quaker settlement in the early 1730s. It is now a bed and breakfast. The main house's architecture tells the story of generations of ownership by the Brown family, from its log structure beginnings in the early 1730s, to its fieldstone structure in the 1740s and hand-made brick addition in the 1790s, to its most recent addition to the back of the house in 1978.*

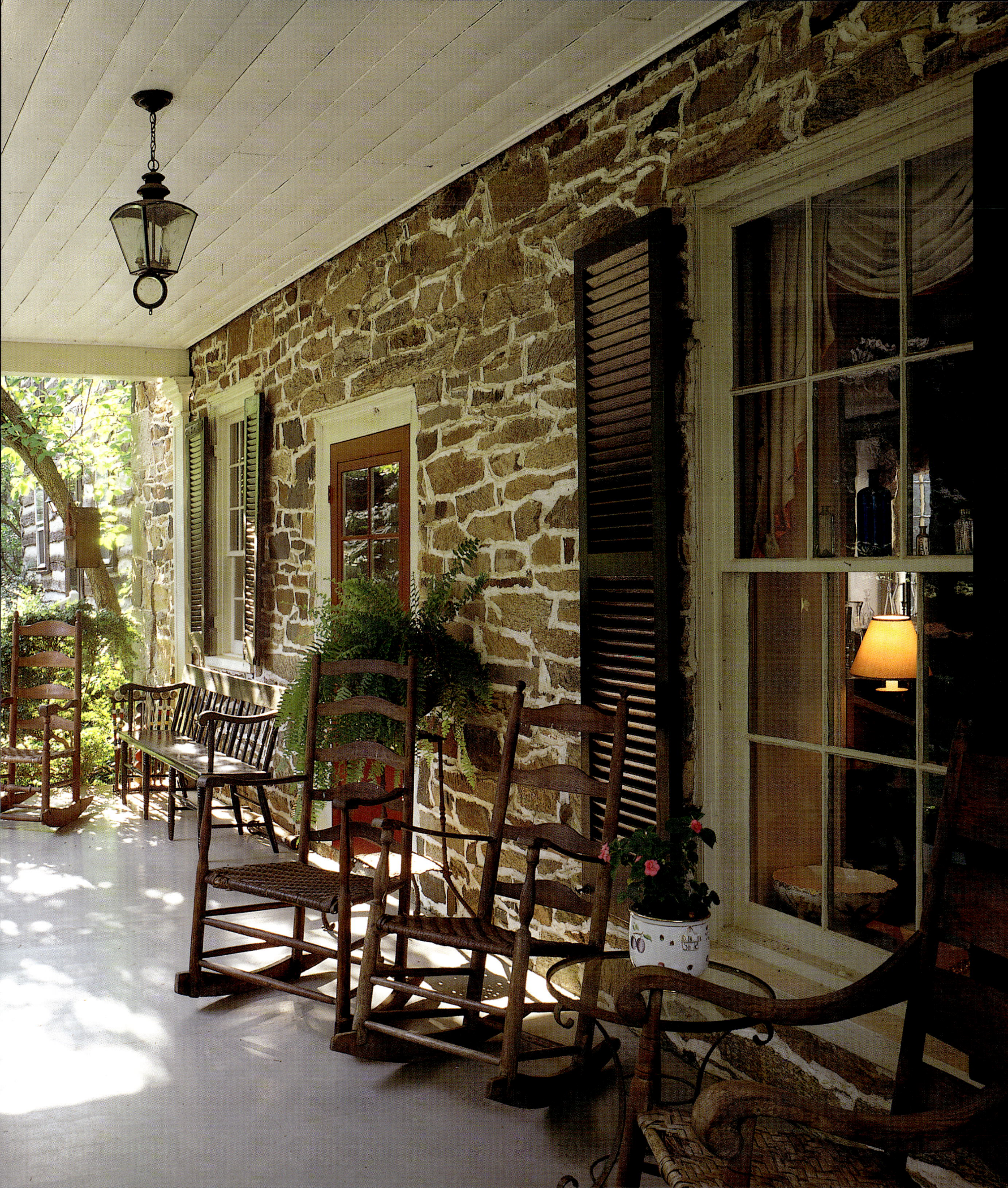

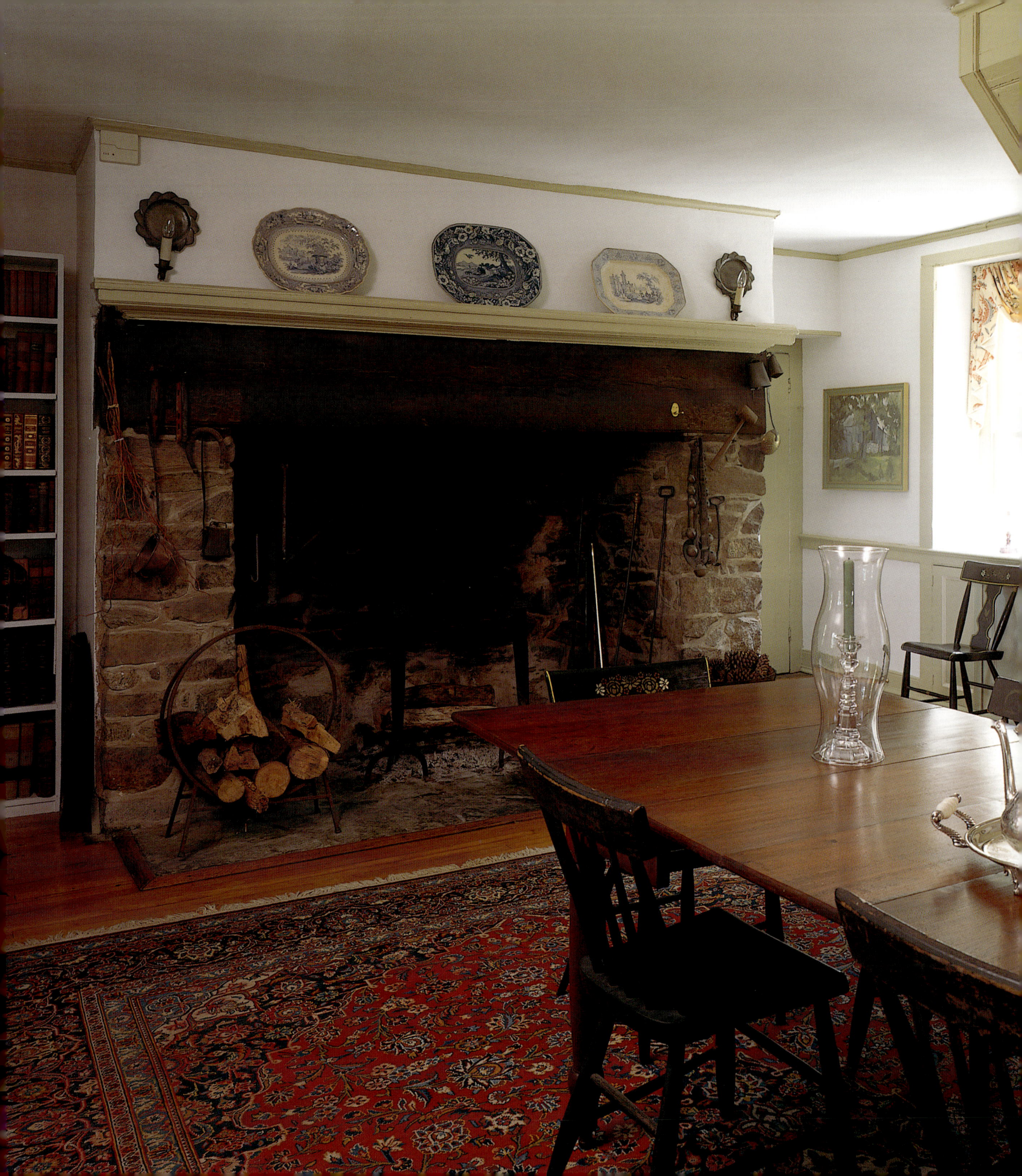

The central portion of the house consists of the two-story addition built in the 1740s with fieldstone gathered from the surrounding land. It was not attached to the original log structure until 1969, and contains a large space with an immense stone hearth as well as a bedroom upstairs. The door at the bottom of the staircase is a typical Quaker design for shutting out the cold drafts from the upstairs. The mid-nineteenth century walnut dining room table was made from trees harvested on the property.

tessential Virginia homestead, from a small log house to a multi-phased country house, constructed with indigenous building materials of hand-hewn logs, local limestone, and locally fired brick. The oldest portion, a log house with a huge fieldstone fireplace and chimney, was built in the 1730s by Quaker settler Richard Brown on his 505-acre tract. A farm that size was then considered small enough to be managed by one family with no slaves, as Quakers would not own slaves. Through the centuries the Brown family has expanded the house, adding a stone structure in the 1740s, one of brick in the 1790s, and in 1978 a new kitchen and family room whose design reflects the original house in style and materials.

The interior of the farmhouse contains many original family furnishings. The evocation of the past could

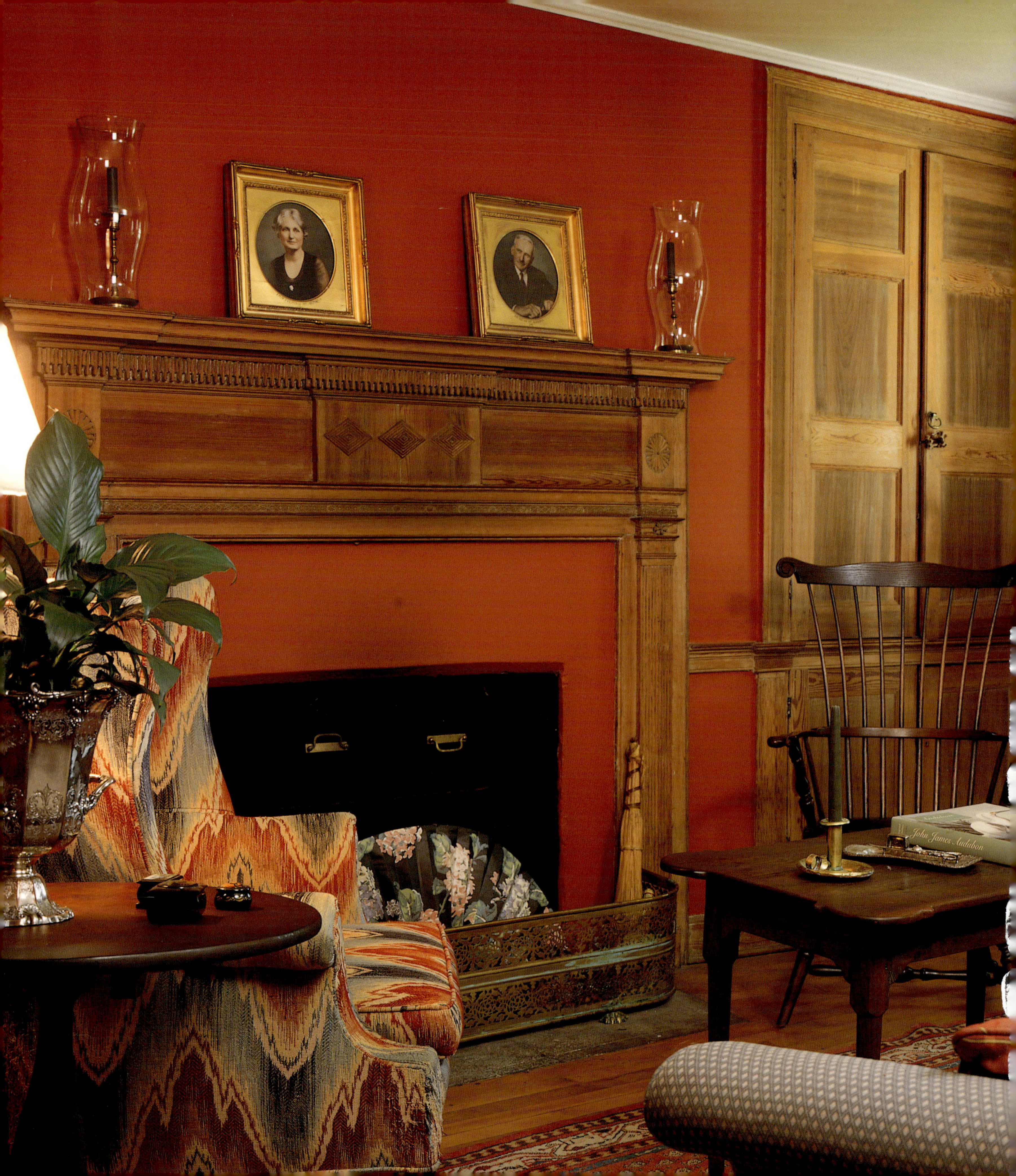
John James Audubon

The third addition that is now attached to the c.1740s stone structure creates a cohesive elongated design for the house. The addition is two stories, with one room downstairs and originally two small rooms upstairs. It is built of bricks fired on the property in the 1790s. It serves today as the formal parlor, with fine Federal detailing.

not be stronger or more fascinating. The family has taken great care through the centuries to preserve its heirlooms, prized among which is the original grant deed to Richard Brown signed by Thomas, Sixth Lord Fairfax, in 1741 (after the original dwelling was built). Other notable interior features include fine and unusual pieces of eighteenth and nineteenth century American furniture and family porcelain, silver, and glass, which are used daily. These items and the farmhouse, with the original log house, restored and structurally retrofitted by owner Bill Brown in the 1969, are not only the legacy of the Brown family, but are a living history of the Quaker culture that filled the region.

The late William Holmes Brown—assistant parliamentarian beginning in 1958 and then chief parliamentarian of the U. S. House of Representatives from

TOP AND ABOVE *Mature landscaping now surrounds the historic house and opens to the pastures of the 200-acre cattle farm. A loose stone driveway leads down to the 40-by-60-foot weatherboard bank barn with its fieldstone foundation.*

RIGHT *The back of the house, which may have once been the front, reveals the three chimneys and differing building materials that denote the phases of construction of this extraordinary house. The 1978 addition is set at a right angle to the elongated house, so as not to compromise the integrity of the front facade or the plan of the historic structure.*

1974 to 1994—and his family raised cattle on the 200 acres that remained of the estate and ran the house as a bed and breakfast. His wife, Jean, a savvy political and conservation activist, and their daughter and son-in-law continue to raise cattle and manage the bed and breakfast and event site and open the grounds periodically for Historic Garden Week in Virginia. Committed to preserving this important and beautiful part of Loudoun County history and their own, the Brown family has given visitors a rare look back into our American beginnings.

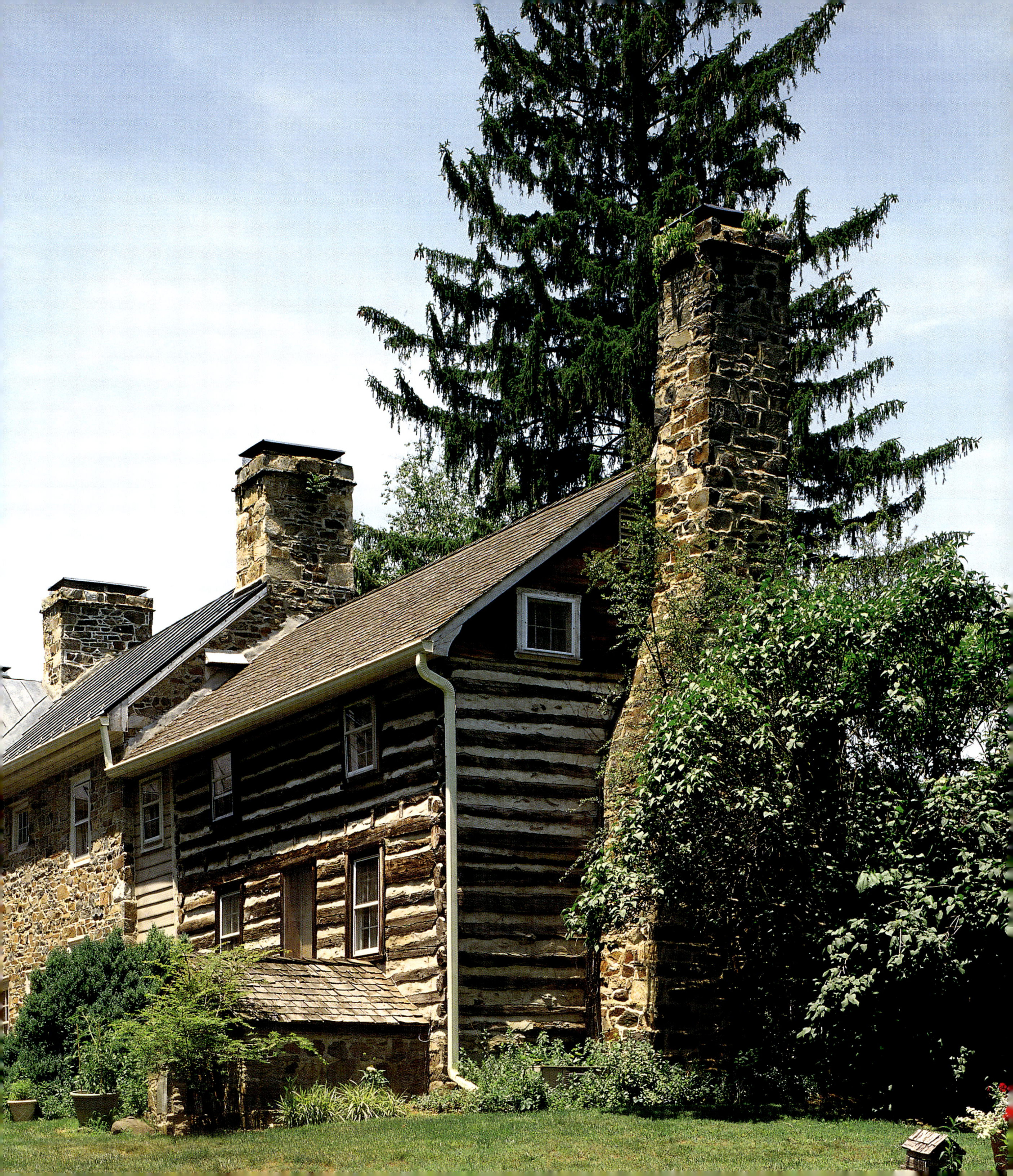

CASTLE HILL

Virginia Historic Landmark
Listed on the National Register of Historic Places
Original wood frame dwelling and plantation outbuildings, 1764
Other outbuildings, c.late 1700s and early mid-1800s
Main brick house addition, 1824; John M. Perry, master builder
Conservatories, 1844; William B. Phillips, master builder
Room additions and remodeling; 1830, 1910, 1945

Castle Hill is one of the most magnificent and historically significant plantations in Virginia. It is located in Keswick on what was one of the first land grants in Albemarle County. In the early 1700s Nicholas Meriwether II was granted nearly 18,000 acres that included much of the Southwest Mountain range, now designated as a Historic District on the National Register of Historic Places. Today Castle Hill consists of

ABOVE *The front door of Castle Hill is finished with impressive faux bois painting. The fanlight and sidelights allow light into the entry foyer and long, deep central hall.*

RIGHT *Castle Hill is historically and architecturally significant for Albemarle County, Virginia, and America, as a fully intact early-eighteenth-century plantation. The classically styled, two-story brick portion of Castle Hill became the main house when it was built in 1824. In 1844 Classical Revival–style orangeries added at each side by the owners Senator and Mrs. William Cabell Rives (Judith Walker Rives) gave the house its impressive front facade (as shown). The brick masons were two of Thomas Jefferson's best.*

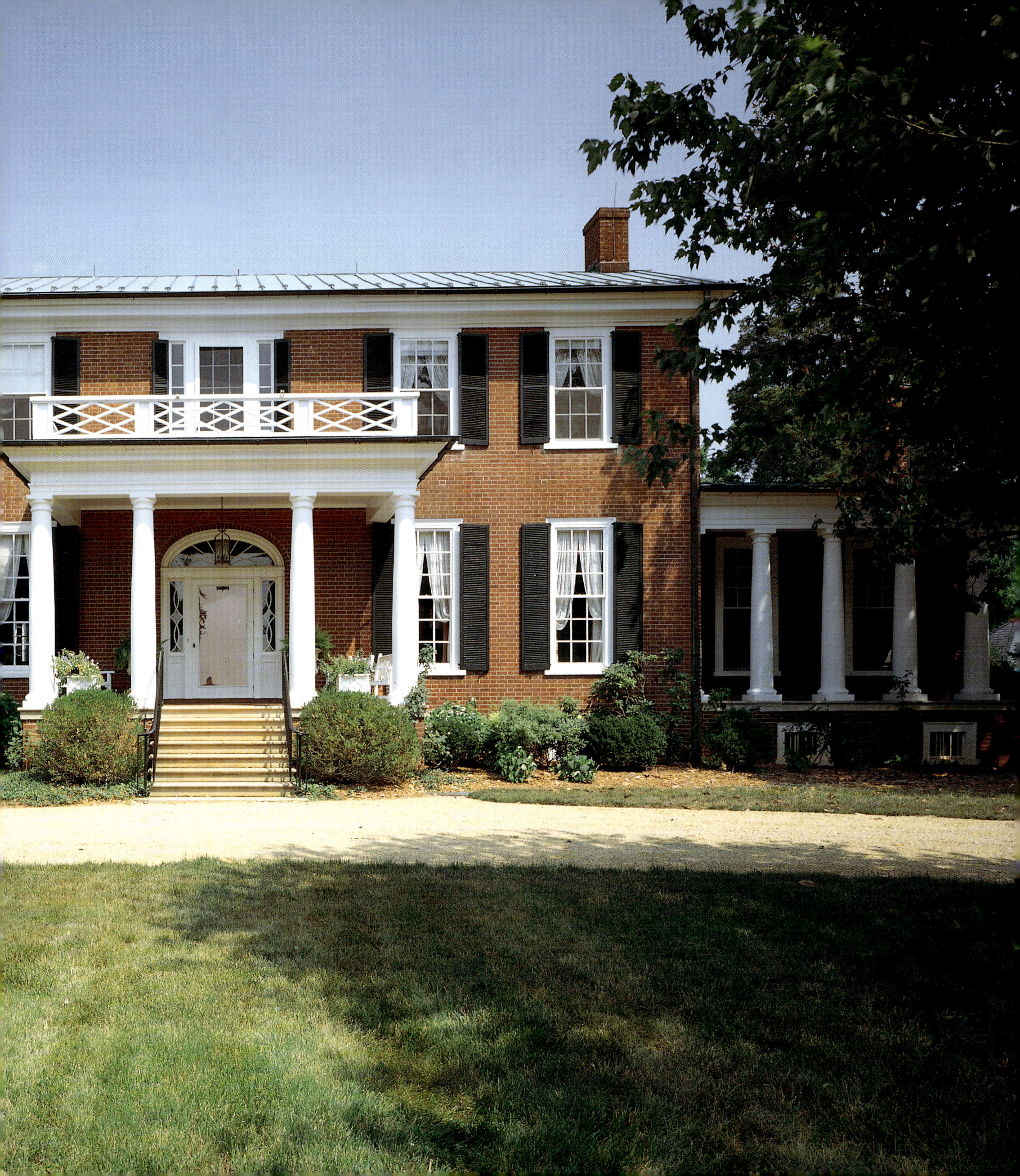

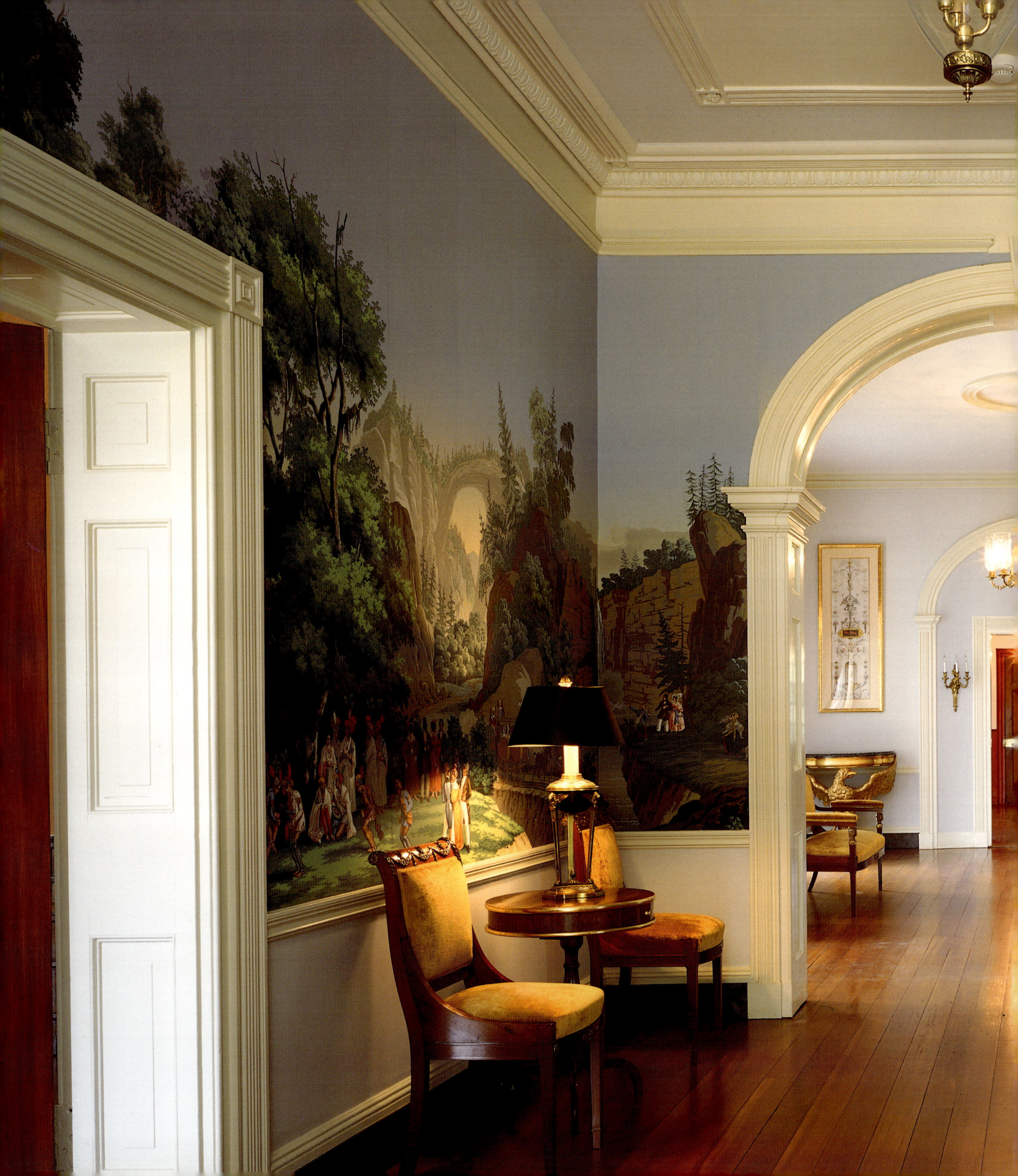

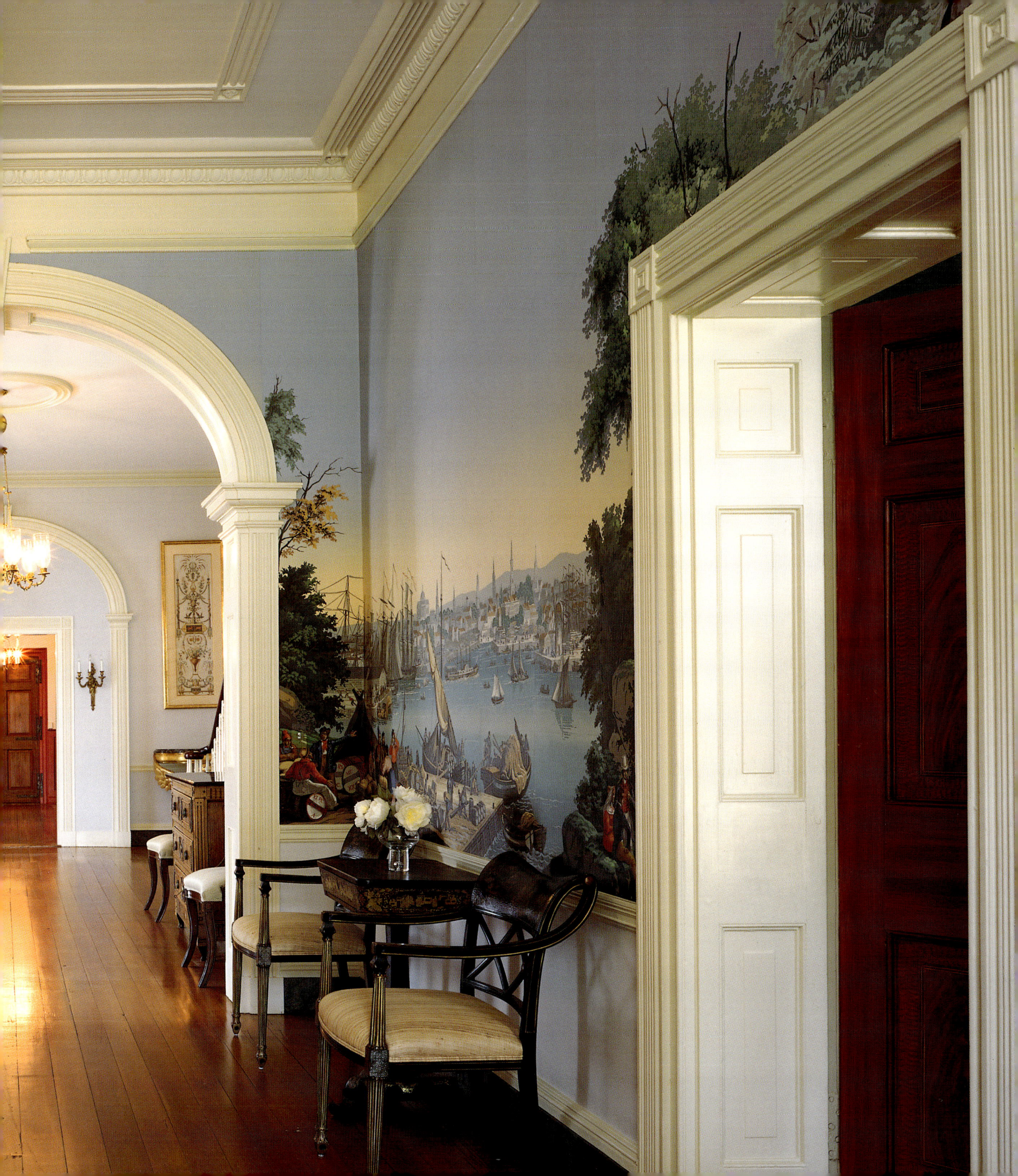

PRECEDING PAGES *The voluminous central hall that connects the two main structures of Castle Hill serves as a double foyer with generous proportions that create a majestic space. It runs the length from the front door of the large brick mansion addition to the back door of the c.1764 frame plantation house and creates one wholly new H-shaped house. During the nineteenth century residency of the William Riveses the hall was used often as a dance floor and gathering place.*

ABOVE *Matching wings were added to either side of the main brick house in 1844. Each wing currently has a colonnaded open front porch and a room in back of that area (here the current music room). Originally the columns had triple-hung sash windows between or behind them that formed an enclosed space that was used as an orangerie. The orangerie interiors were originally painted white to reflect the sunlight onto the collection of indoor plants.*

RIGHT *Exquisite French wallpaper and the finely crafted Federal-style woodwork of the door trim create a substantial entry into the front drawing room. The room is grandly scaled, as is the rest of the brick mansion, with twelve-foot ceilings and ornamental detailing throughout. On the black marble mantel, a fittingly dramatic element for the room, rest a pair of candelabra with winged figures brought from France by Judith Walker Rives in the early 1820s. The portrait above the mantel is of Mrs. Rives.*

44 CASTLE HILL

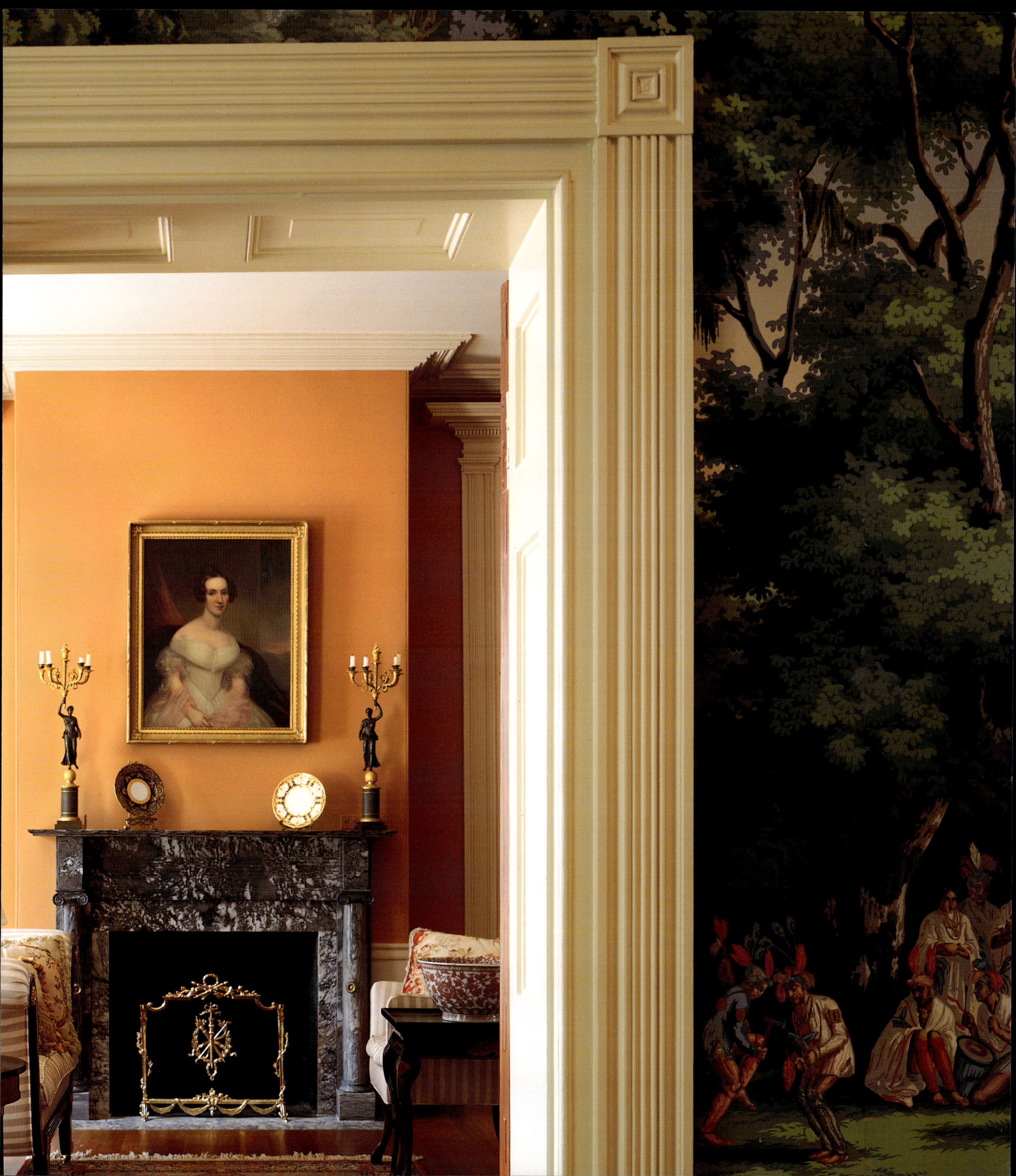

ABOVE *The barn and stables are built on their original foundations and are located in the lower portion of the 1,100-acre grounds with access to the road through fields where tobacco and grain used to be grown and others where cattle and horses grazed.*

RIGHT *The original entrance and original front facade to Castle Hill, built by Dr. Thomas Walker in 1764, is the centerpiece of a complex of auxiliary buildings (not shown) that include a smoke house, a springhouse, a gardener's house, servants' quarters, and a carpenter's workshop on Walker's 18,000-acre plantation.*

1,100 acres of farmland and forests. To maintain its integrity, the owners have protected the former tobacco plantation with its stately brick Federal mansion and fourteen dependency buildings, a Virginia Historic Landmark, and over 600 acres that include the viewshed of the Southwest Mountains with a conservation easement.

In 1741 a 26-year-old Dr. Thomas Walker acquired a majority of the huge estate by marriage and lived at Castle Hill with his young bride. The earliest existing dwelling, however, is a Georgian-style frame house built in 1764. In this small house, this extraordinary man, who was one of the first to explore what would become Kentucky, and his wife raised twelve children. Walker, less well known in American history than his celebrated neighbor Thomas Jefferson, was nonetheless a major force in the development of Albemarle County in its formative years. Twenty-eight years older and godfather to Thomas Jefferson, Walker would serve with him in the House of Burgesses, while he was also a successful tobacco planter, merchant, trader, and sought-after negotiator with chiefs of Native American tribes. A local legend claims that in 1781 the

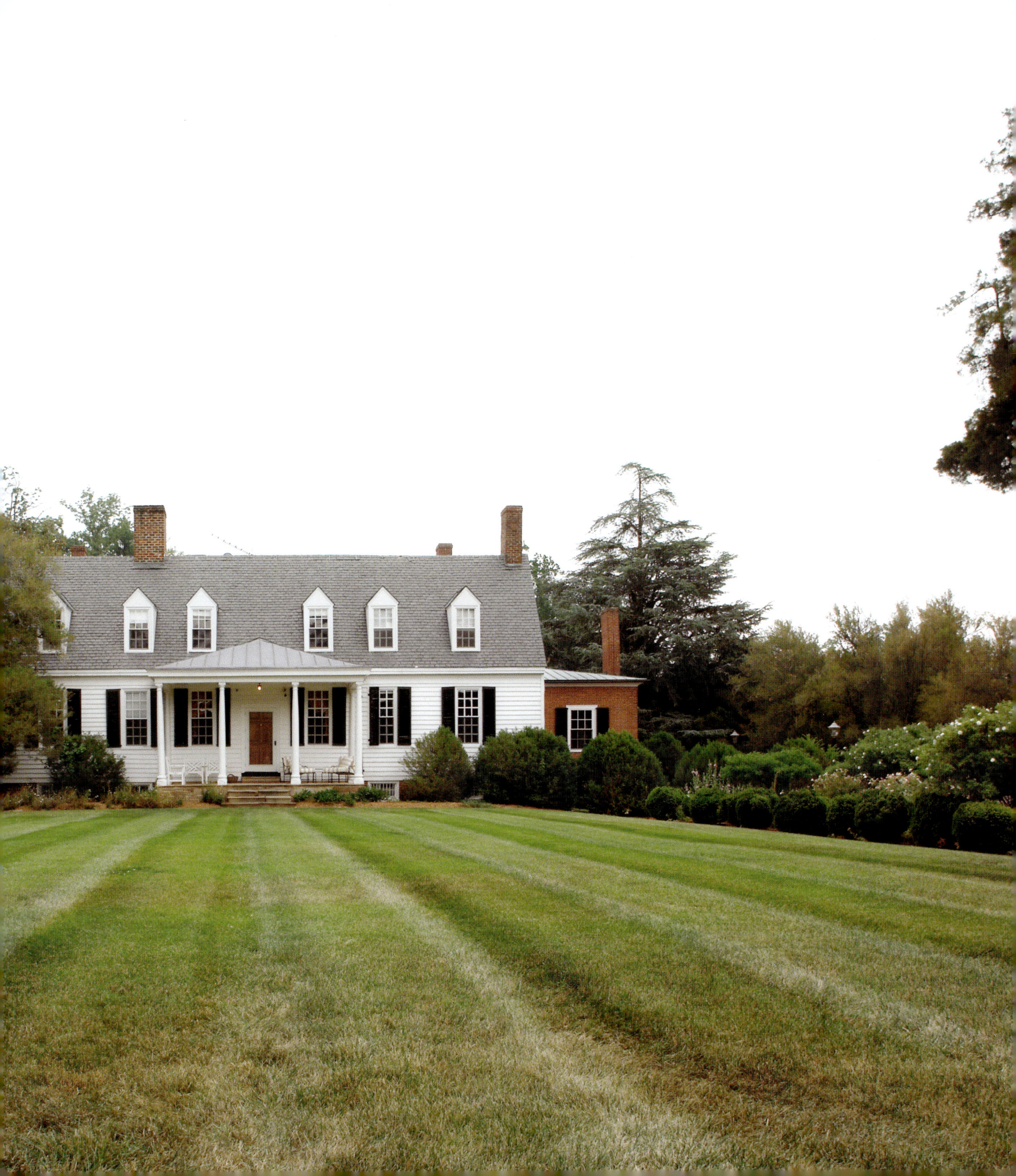

View from the entrance to the grand nineteenth-century brick mansion of Castle Hill faces an 800-foot-long slipper-shaped lawn surrounded by a drive lined with tall 180-year-old boxwoods. Cedar, red maple, white pine, mimosa, white ash, sycamore, spruce, American holly, hemlock, and ginkgo, many planted by Judith Walker Rives, accent the expansive lawn and create the mature landscape that immediately surrounds Castle Hill.

Walkers thwarted an attempt by the British to capture then Governor Jefferson and legislators who had fled Richmond. Tipped off by patriot Jack Jouett during his ride to warn the politicians who had convened in Charlottesville, the Walkers stalled British General Tarleton and his men at Castle Hill with Virginia hospitality that included mint juleps, allowing the politicians to escape just a mere 6 miles up the road.

In subsequent years the plantation was owned by Dr. Walker's granddaughter Judith Page Walker and her distinguished husband William Cabell Rives, who served three terms as a U. S. senator and twice as minister to France. In 1824, the Riveses added a new grandly scaled two-story Federal-style brick house to the earlier dwelling and reoriented the front entrance so that the Southwest Mountains served as a dramatic backdrop to the mansion. In 1844, they expanded Castle Hill further by attaching at each side Classical Revival-style conservatories or orangeries—colonnaded wings with triple-hung sash windows between the columns—creating an even more impressive front facade.

The property was later inherited by their granddaughter, Amelie Rives, an international socialite and popular novelist who married Russian Prince Pierre Troubetzkoy, a painter whose studio at Castle Hill became a gathering place for early twentieth-century artists and writers. In 1947 owners Col. and Mrs. Clark J. Lawrence restored the plantation house, dependency buildings, and gardens, which are maintained in their entirety today to present an uncommon view into a

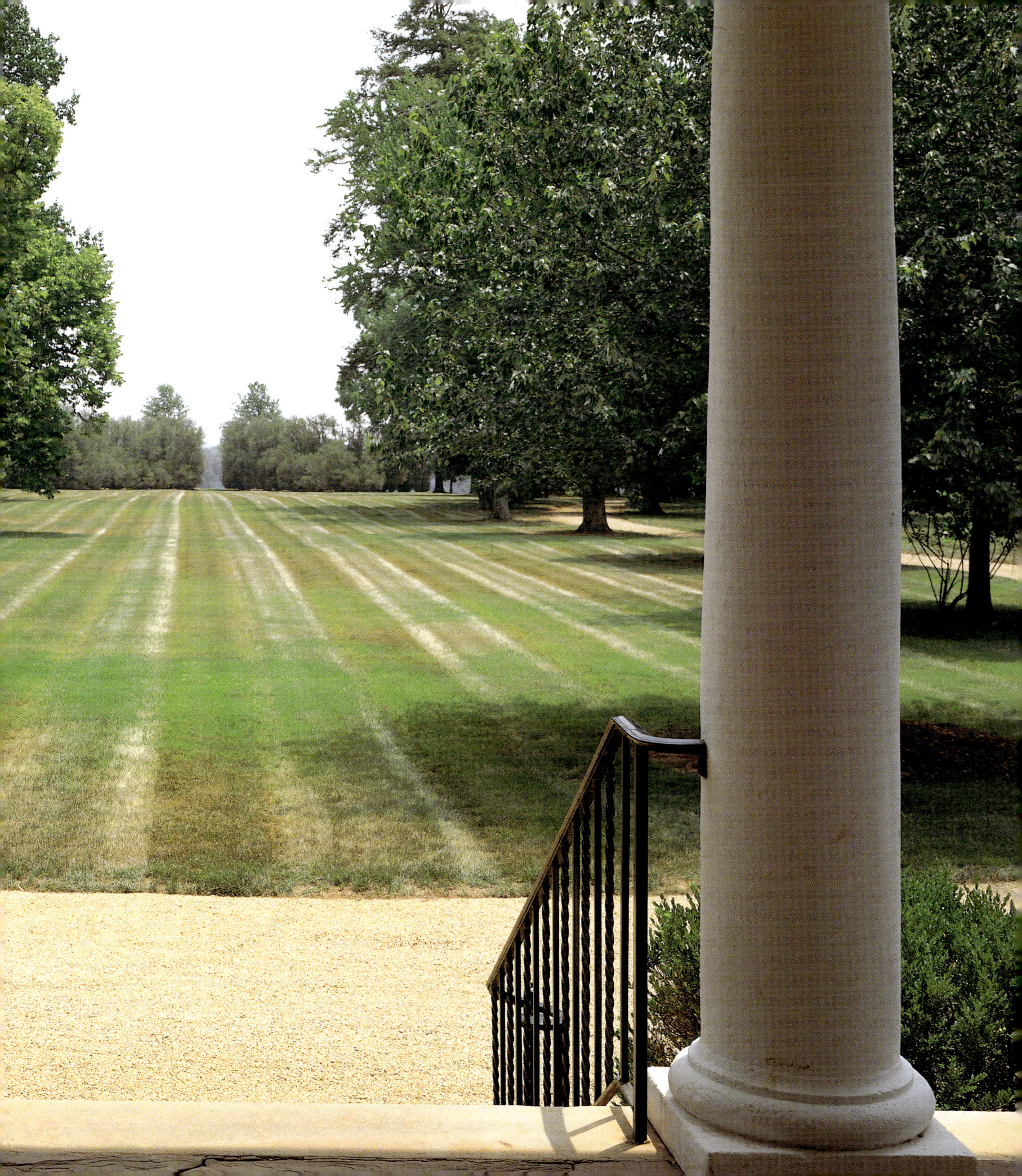

OLD KESWICK

Original kitchen (now guest house), possibly pre-1818
Two-story log house (section of main house), possibly pre-1764, 1764, or c.1818
One-and-a-half-story wood frame house and one-story hyphen connection, c.1832, possibly Thomas R. Blackburn, architect
Master suite addition, 1970s

Old Keswick is one of the earliest houses in an exclusive area, outside Charlottesville, famed for its large horse farms and the Keswick Hunt. A rambling driveway begins at an entrance marked by two low fieldstone columns and winds past barns and stables, a stone springhouse, and pastures for finely bred horses, leading to a white weatherboard farmhouse hidden among trees. It is a rare piece of Virginia history.

Thomas Walker was a young doctor in the late 1730s when he moved to what would become Albemarle County, and in 1741 married the young heiress and widow of Col. Nicholas Meriwether, III, Mildred Thornton. Mildred brought to her second marriage a major portion of the largest original land grant, nearly 18,000 acres that included much of the eastern side of the Southwest Mountain range, granted to Nicholas Meriwether II by Lord Fairfax in 1727. In 1764 the Walkers built Castle Hill, a Georgian frame house on their estate of the same name. At this time or earlier

ABOVE AND RIGHT *Old Keswick is one of Keswick's earliest farmhouses, which possibly began as a hunting lodge on the northern region of the vast Castle Hill estate of Dr. Thomas Walker. Old Keswick is an H-shaped plan residence constructed of painted weatherboard with brick steps leading to its porticos.*

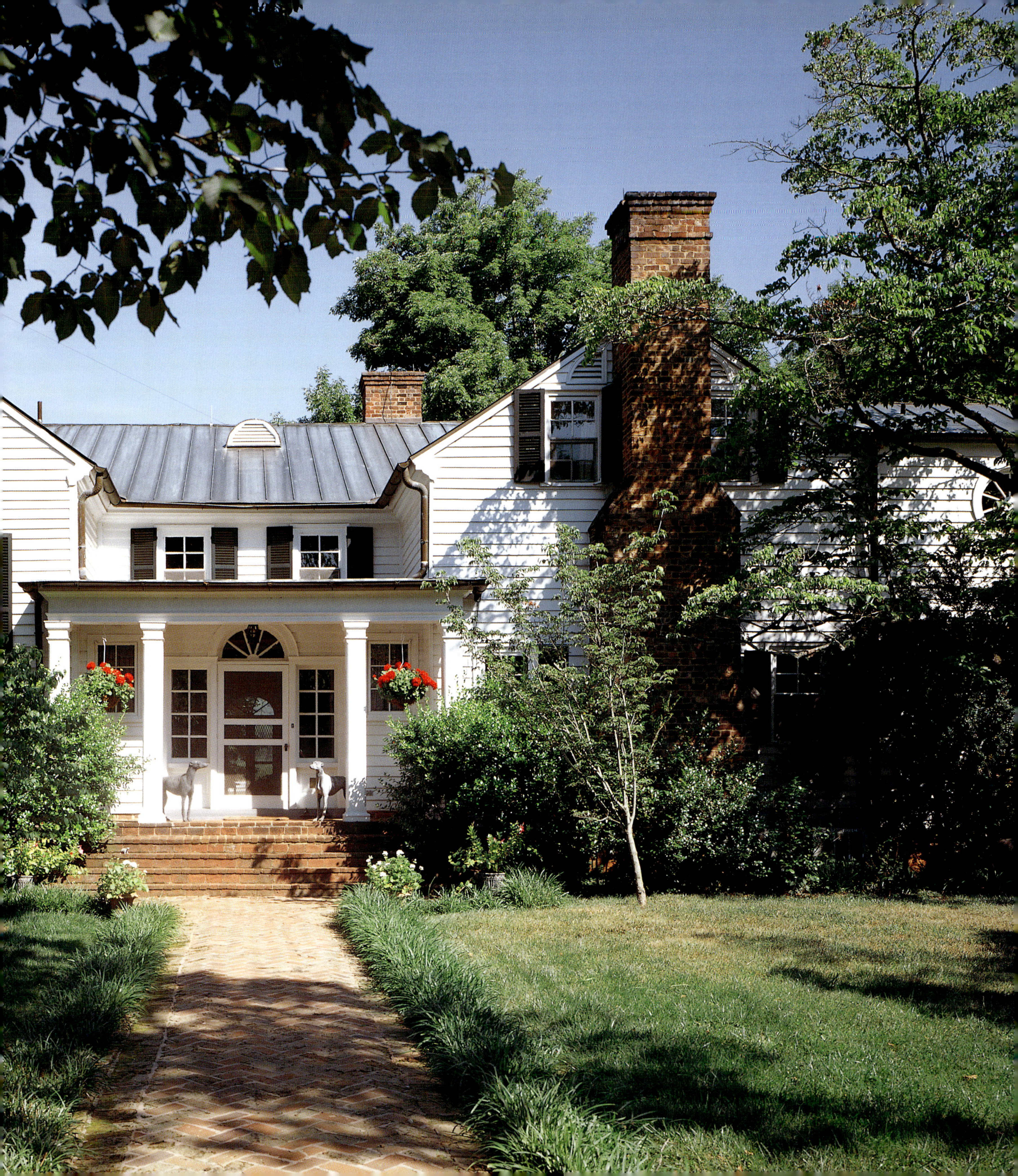

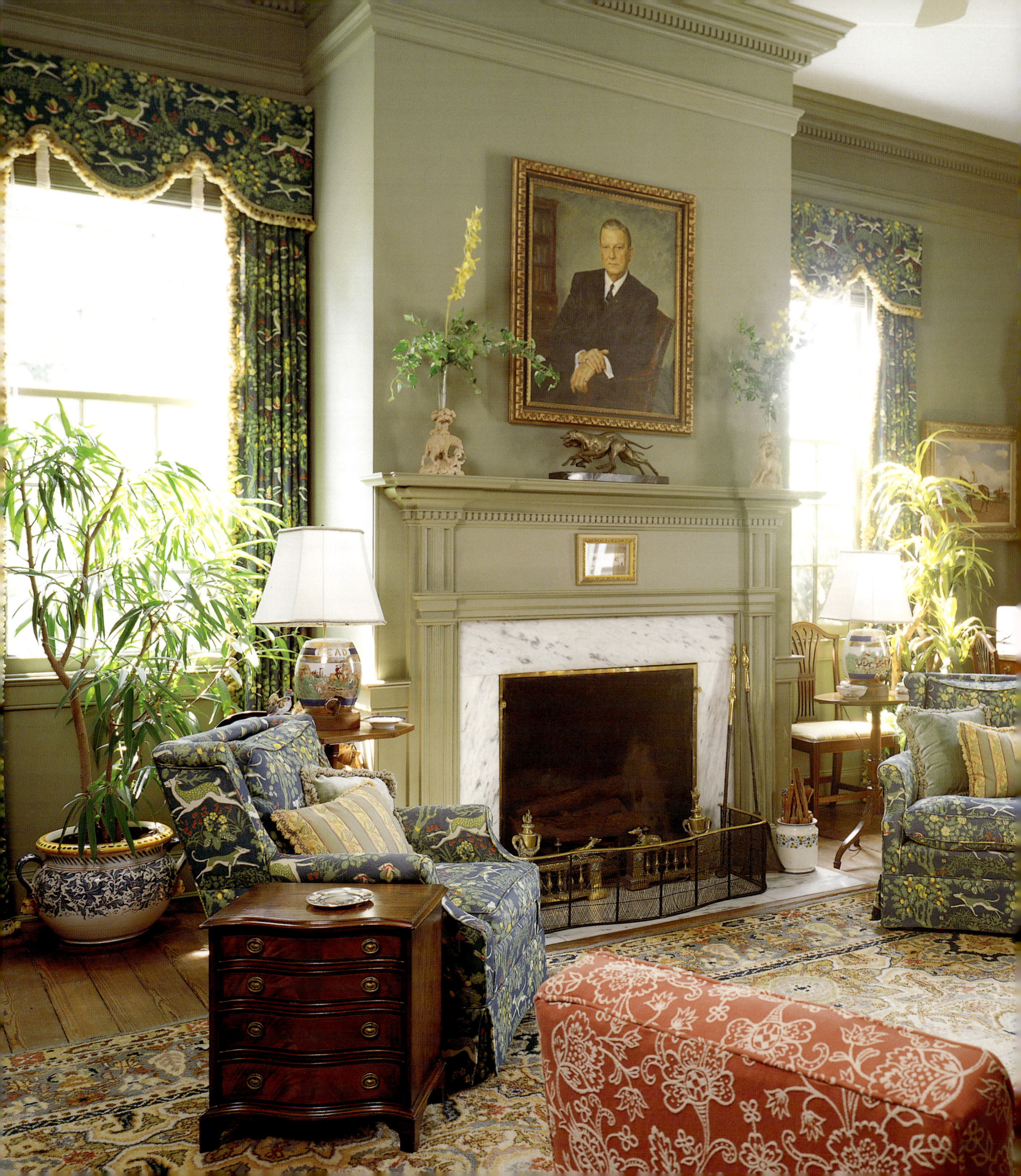

In 1832 a wood frame house with two matching parlors and a hallway was added to the original wood structure, along with a wide one-story "hyphen" that connected this new addition to the older wood portion. The formal parlors' elegant proportions of 16-by-23 feet with 12-foot ceilings are augmented with Federal-style carved wood trim. In the east parlor (left) one of the owner's prize-winning orchids is prominently displayed among family antique furnishings.

they built a hunting lodge on a northern portion of the lands, which ultimately became known as Keswick.

This simple hunting lodge evolved through three building phases into the Old Keswick of today. When Dr. Walker's granddaughter, Jane Frances Walker, inherited her portion of the Castle Hill estate in 1818, she and her husband Dr. Mann Page changed the look of the original structure completely. In 1832 they added a one-and-a-half-story frame house comprised of two 16-by-23-foot parlors with 12-foot ceilings and a central hall, along with a single-story hyphen that connects the two houses, resulting in a farmhouse of considerably greater size.

Keswick Stables has been a renowned Thoroughbred operation since the mid 1950s. At that time the current owner's mother began a Thoroughbred breeding operation with the purchase of half interest in three brood mares, one of which would become the granddam of famed stallion Northern Dancer. She also sold the world record yearling filly in 1963, as did her daughter in 1983. Champion show hunters were also trained at Keswick Stables in the 1950s and 1960s. And since the late 1950s the farm has seen a succession of top stakes-winning Thoroughbreds.

TOP *The office is in the original wood structure of Old Keswick that was on the property when Judith Walker Page (Mrs. Mann Page) inherited it in 1818. The building's walls are constructed of hand-adzed heart pine boards that run its full length. Trophies and ribbons commemorate the multitude of wins over the decades for Keswick Stables.*

ABOVE *The dining room furnishings include a rare nineteenth-century American cherrywood sideboard with serpentine apron and tapered legs, a large rare set of twelve tiger maple Sheraton dining chairs that sit at the tiger maple dining table, a late-Sheraton American piece of Southern origin. The owner had the corner cabinet custom made of tiger maple. The magnificent early-nineteenth century mirror has a gilded molded oval girandole frame decorated with a crouching eagle at the crest and pineapple-shaped side sconces.*

RIGHT *A wide hall that divides the formal parlors served in the nineteenth century as the main entrance on the south.*

54 OLD KESWICK

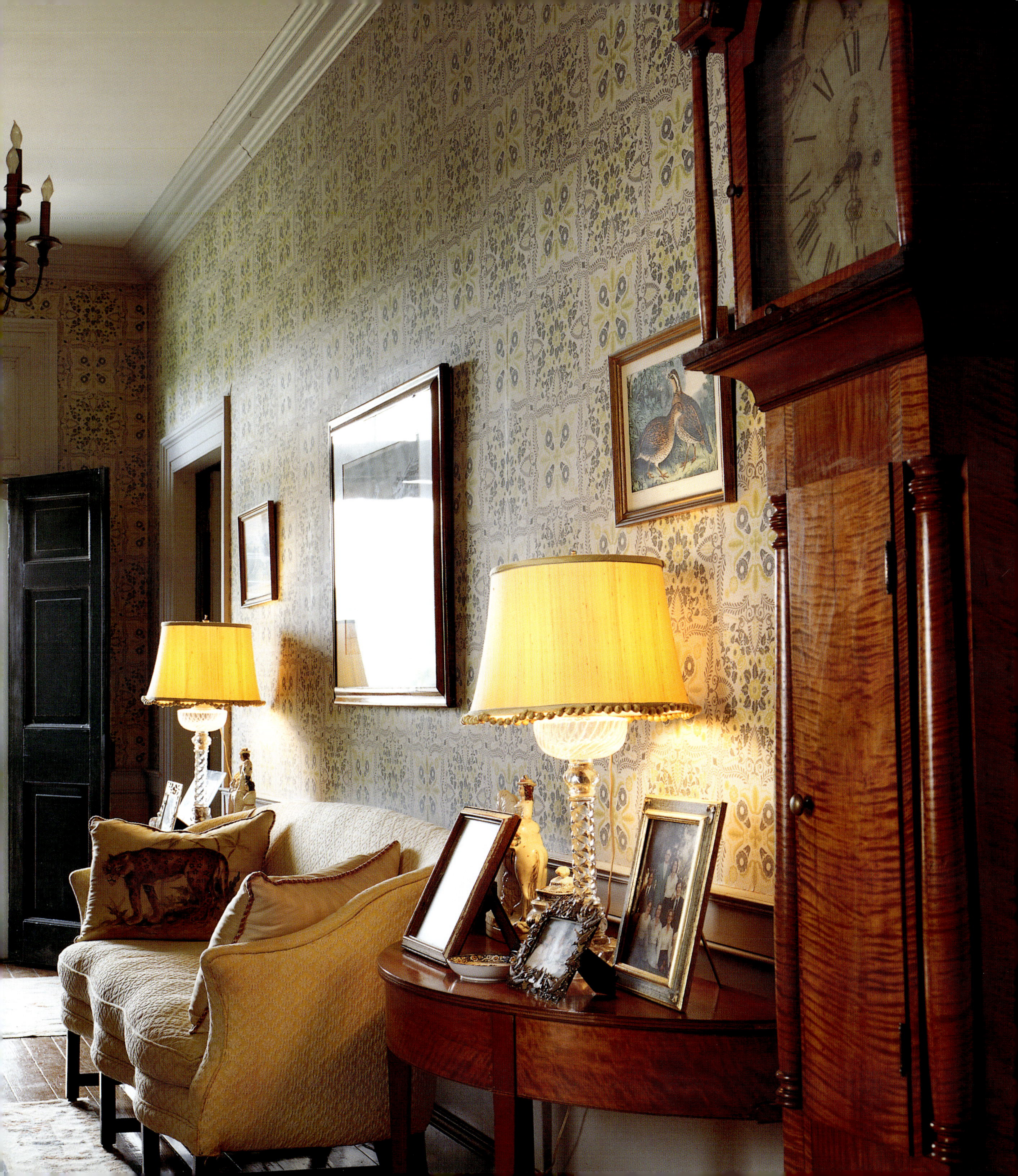

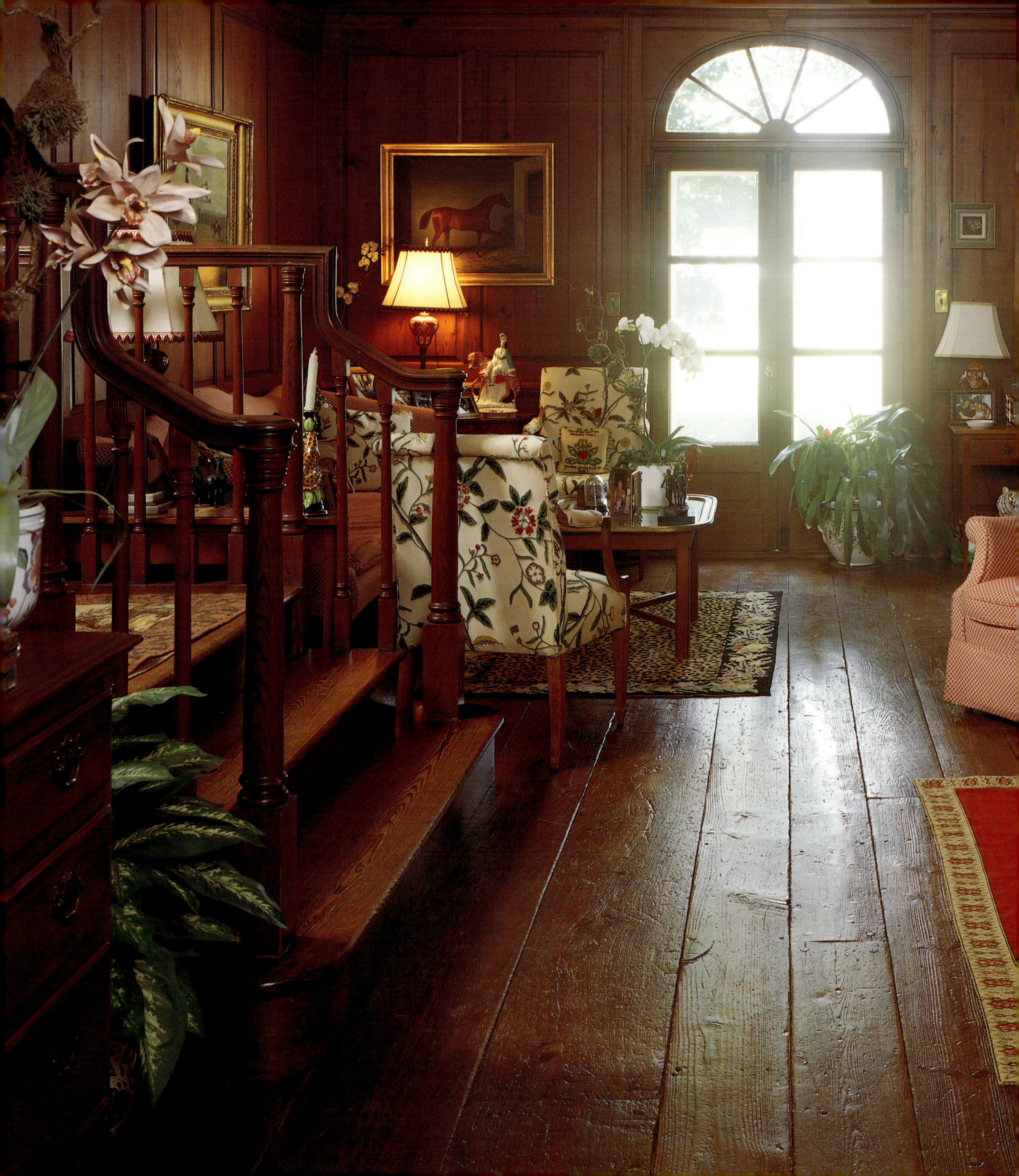

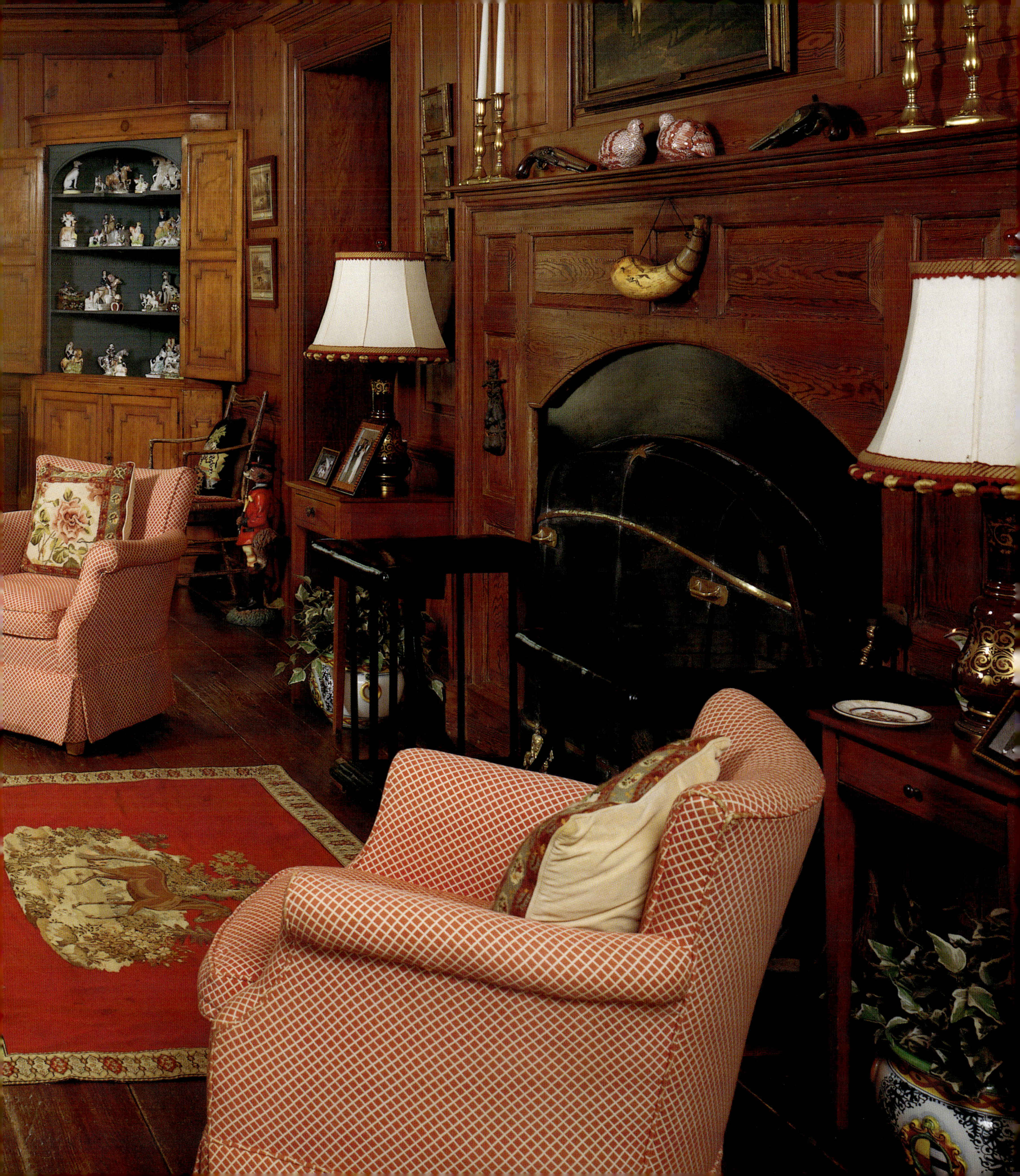

PRECEDING PAGES *The house's reception room is the "hyphen" that connects the pre-1818 log structure to the 1832 wood frame house addition. The room is paneled in warm heart pine. Evocative of its early history and rural setting, the reception room contains a large masonry fireplace with a carved wood mantel. On it are a pair of late-eighteenth-century English dueling pistols and a c.1800 scrimshaw powder horn decorated with "The Chase." Fine antiques such as a late-eighteenth-century American hickory and ash armchair and a late-eighteenth-century American corner cabinet are combined with newer traditional upholstered pieces. The petit point rug is English c.1875.*

ABOVE AND OPPOSITE *Keswick Stables is a 500-acre Thoroughbred breeding and training farm whose renown reaches back to the 1950s and 60s. The current owner, her mother, and Keswick Stables are honored by recognition in the Virginia Thoroughbred Association Hall of Fame.*

The owner of Old Keswick successfully competed as a rider of show hunters during the 1950s and 1960s, and has also continued to breed outstanding Thoroughbreds, building upon her family's legacy. She and her horses have competed internationally, and today she is honored in four halls of fame and, together with her late mother and Keswick Stables, are in the Virginia Thoroughbred Association Hall of Fame.

Having enjoyed a career as one of America's foremost Thoroughbred breeders and rider of champion show hunters, the owner of Old Keswick has now turned her attention toward raising prize orchids and is involved in environmental and philanthropic causes that include the Piedmont Environmental Council, for which she has served many years as a board member, and the Thoroughbred Retirement Foundation.

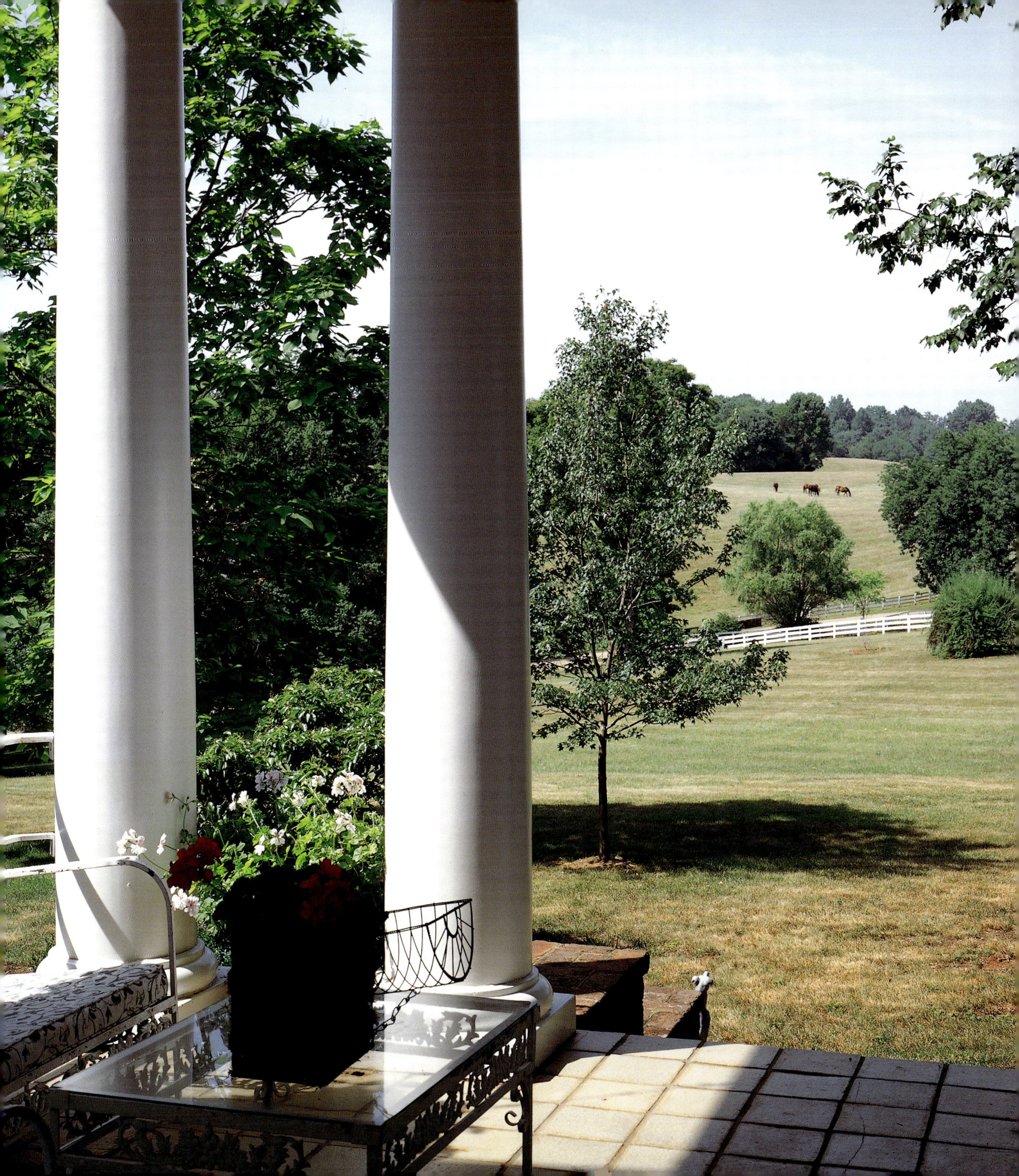

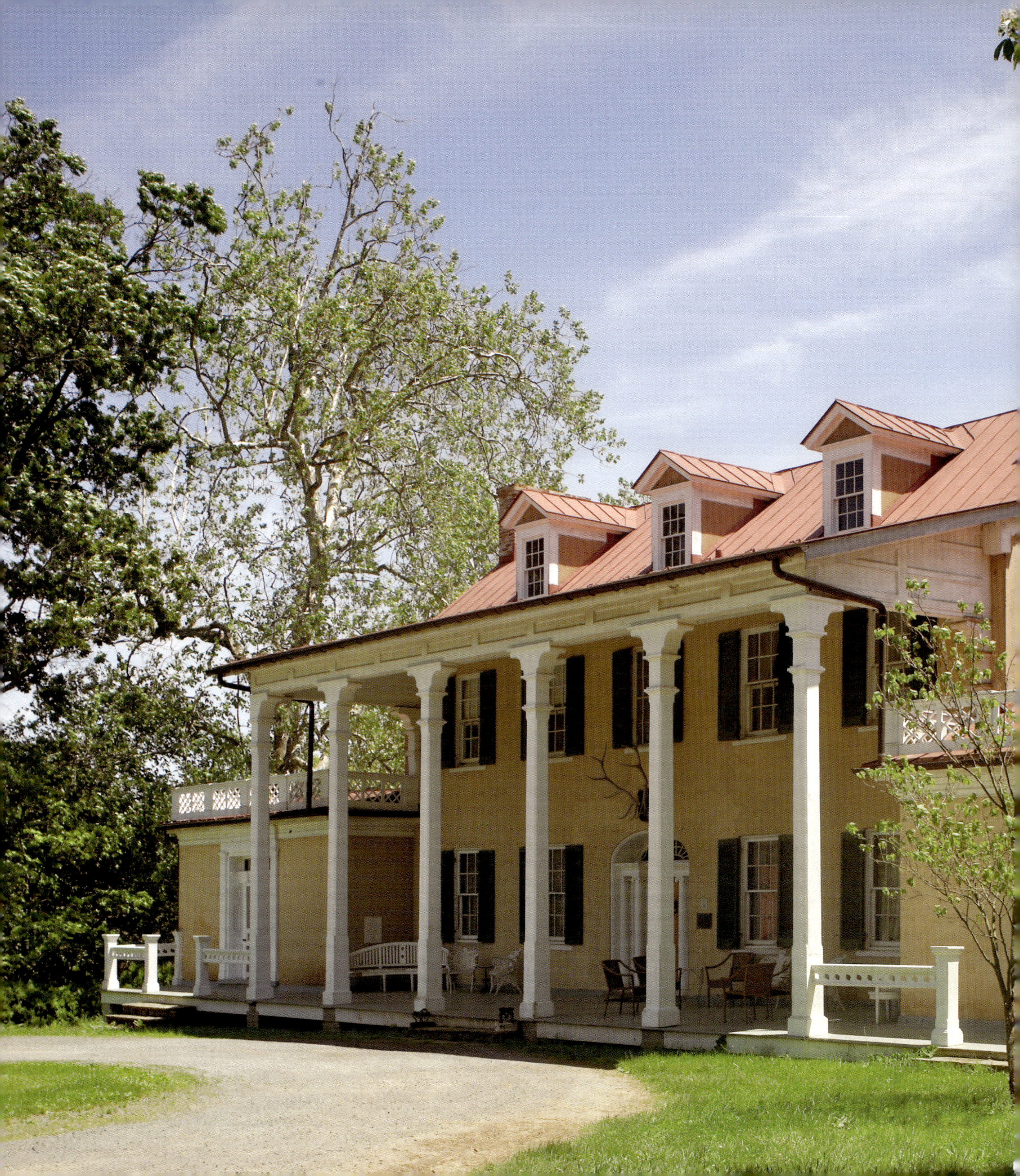

WELBOURNE

Residence of Mr. and Mrs. Nathaniel Holmes Morison III
Virginia Historic Landmark
Listed on the National Register of Historic Places
First stone house, c.1770; additions, 1833, 1840s, 1850s, 1870s
Three backyard cottages: one possibly c.1760, the second c.1830, the third c.1880
Smoke house, c.1830
Greenhouse, pre-1860s; converted into a guesthouse, 1880s
Coach barn, c.1830; cattle barn, c.1910

Welbourne is one of the most beloved houses in the northern Piedmont. Its history is renowned, as are the people who have owned and lived in it. The past is present at Welbourne and the endearing quality of faded glory in its architecture, interiors, and history imbues it with an incomparable

LEFT AND ABOVE *For nearly two centuries Welbourne has been an essential part of life in the northern Piedmont's hunt country. This Virginia Historic Landmark is now a country inn and horse retirement boarding farm. To protect the property further, the current owners, Nat and Sherry Morison, have placed the house and its immediate ten acres into a historic easement and 510 acres into a scenic land easement.*

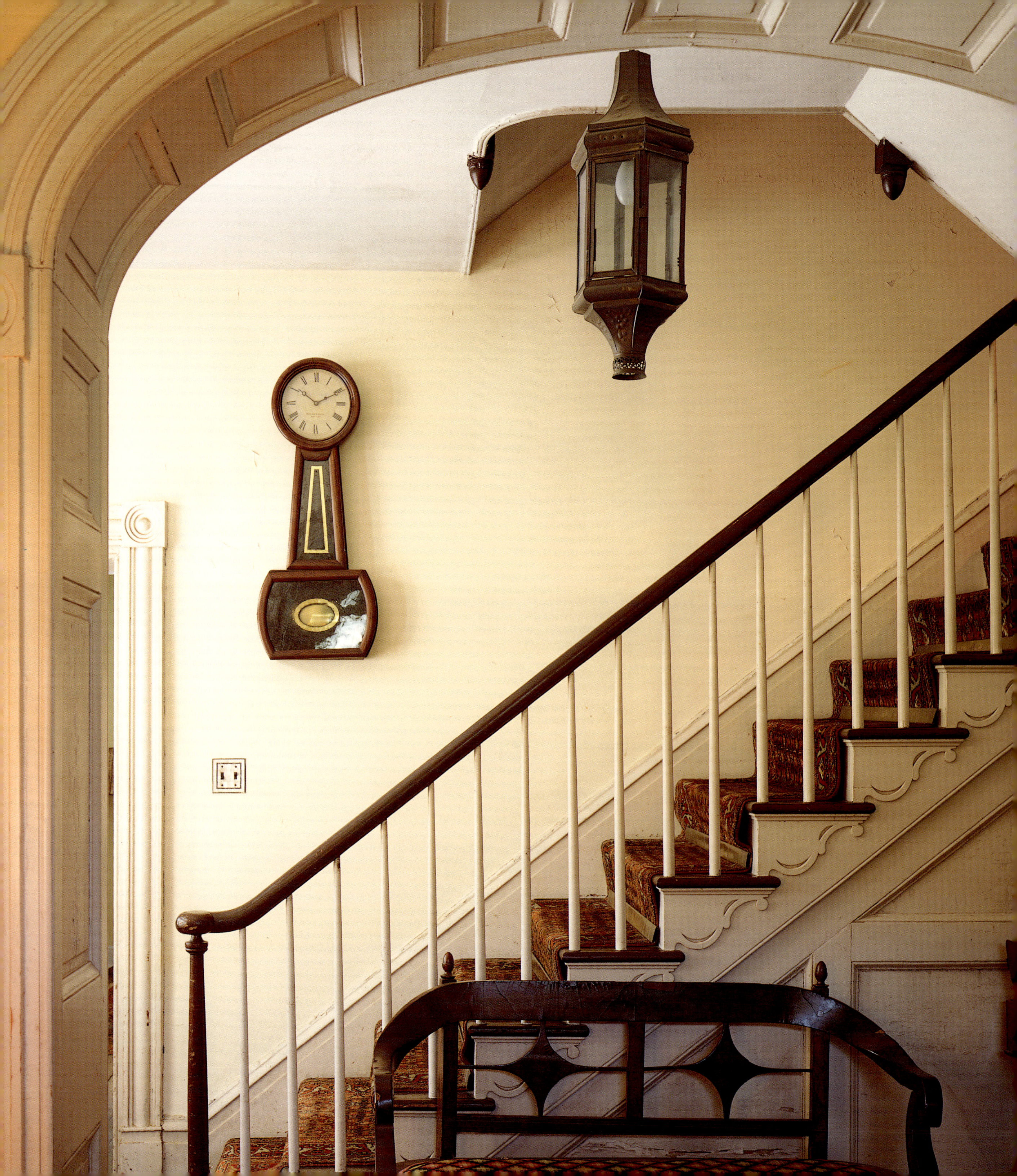

The interiors hold family treasures, art, and furnishings that are as much a part of the history of Welbourne as its ambiance. Original mid-nineteenth-century woodwork and flooring as well as carved mantels and large double-hung windows complement the bygone atmosphere. A plaque prominently displayed in the entry hall commemorates the masters of The Piedmont Hunt (now the Piedmont Fox Hounds), whose founder was Colonel Richard Henry Dulany, C.S.A. The Piedmont Fox Hounds hunt meets are still held at Welbourne.

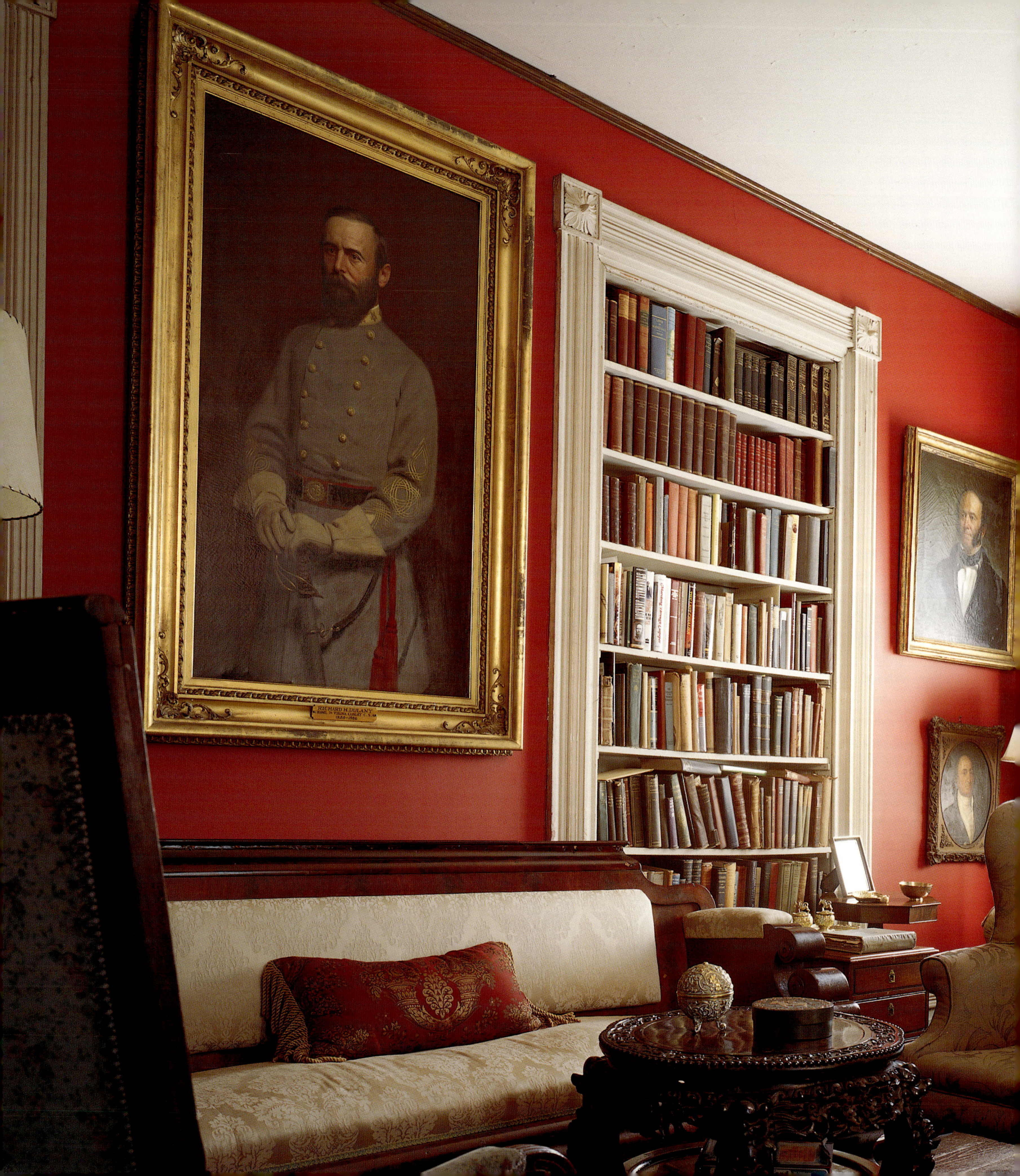
RICHARD H. DULANY

LEFT AND ABOVE *In the west parlor there are two original portraits of a celebrated early owner of Welbourne, Colonel Richard Henry Dulany, 7th Virginia Cavalry, C.S.A. (1820–1906). His integrity was that of a true Virginia gentleman. He was widowed in 1858 with five children, but through the following decades he provided for them, his aging father, and assorted relatives and others at Welbourne. The current owner of Welbourne, Nathaniel Holmes Morison III, is Colonel Dulany's great-great grandson.*

charm. Seemingly untouched by time, this historical treasure is a Virginia Historic Landmark and is listed on the National Register of Historic Places. To preserve the farm for perpetuity, its owners, Nat and Sherry Morison and family, have placed Welbourne's structures and the ten acres immediately surrounding them into a historic preservation easement and have protected the farm from future subdivision by placing 510 acres, the size of the original farm, into a scenic land easement.

From its modest beginning as a simple stone and frame farmhouse erected in the 1770s to its present incarnation as a country inn and horse retirement boarding farm, this family estate remains true in form and spirit to the essence of hunt country. It is the setting for hunt breakfasts, hunt meets, and other gatherings of family and friends where the owners' respect for the traditions of the past and code of Virginia hospitality gives everything a special charm.

Welbourne is currently owned by Nat Morison and his family, the eighth generation of owners since 1833,

RIGHT *The intimate dining room is one of the original rooms of the small c.1770 stone and frame house that existed on the Welbourne property when John Peyton Dulany purchased the farm in 1833. Silver pieces, the imported French china containing the Morison family crest, original portraits, and other family heirlooms attest to decades of care and consideration by their owners.*

FOLLOWING PAGES *In the early evening, Welbourne's serenity is felt in the silence of the stately aged mansion and the quiet, unbothered land that surrounds it. The sweeping front porch creates a scene that recalls a slower, calmer, more genteel time. The manor house, as we see it today, is much as it was in the mid-1800s.*

when John Peyton Dulany came to live with his wife in Welbourne's original small eighteenth-century stone house and to farm the rich Virginia soil. To this simple stone and frame structure Dulany added a two-over-two-room Georgian mansion with an elegant center hall. The house was enlarged through the next decades with two single-story wings, large front and back porches, and another two-story section. John Peyton's son, Colonel Richard Henry Dulany, 7th Virginia Cavalry C.S.A., of whom current owner Nat Morison is a great-great grandson, is the estate's most famous owner. He became one of Virginia's wealthiest gentlemen, expanded the acreage of Welbourne in the 1850s and ran it as a prosperous corn and wheat plantation and Thoroughbred breeding farm. Colonel Dulany was an accomplished horseman and passionate horse enthusiast who, before the Civil War, founded two of the area's most important equestrian organizations that still exist today. He established the first organized hunt in Northern Virginia in 1840 with the Piedmont Hunt, now the Piedmont Fox Hounds, and in 1853 organized and sponsored the Upperville Colt & Horse Show, the oldest horse show in America.

Welbourne has been visited by famous American writers, artists, and politicians, among them Scribner's editor Maxwell Perkins. He was a friend of Colonel Dulany's grand-daughter Miss Elizabeth (Beth) Lemmon, with whom he corresponded for many years. Perkins thought the house so exceptional that he sent his authors F. Scott Fitzgerald and Thomas Wolfe to visit and experience it for themselves. Welbourne has always elicited a passionate response from visitors, and so each writer immortalized the charming mansion in a story, capturing the solid and steady Southern beauty for posterity. Welbourne has a unique place in the region's history. The exploits of its famed owners and the mythological character of the mansion continue to be celebrated today.

66 WELBOURNE

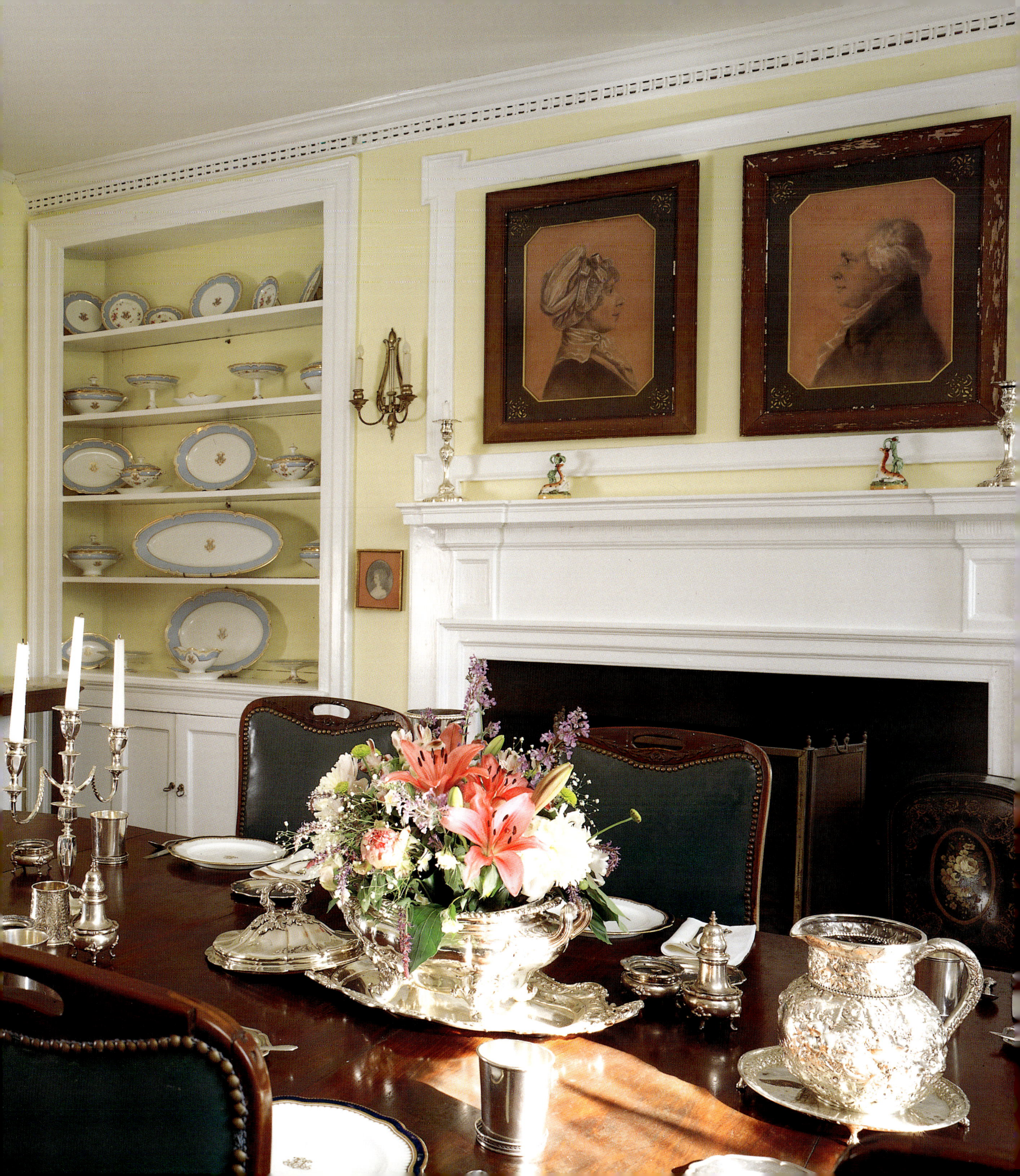

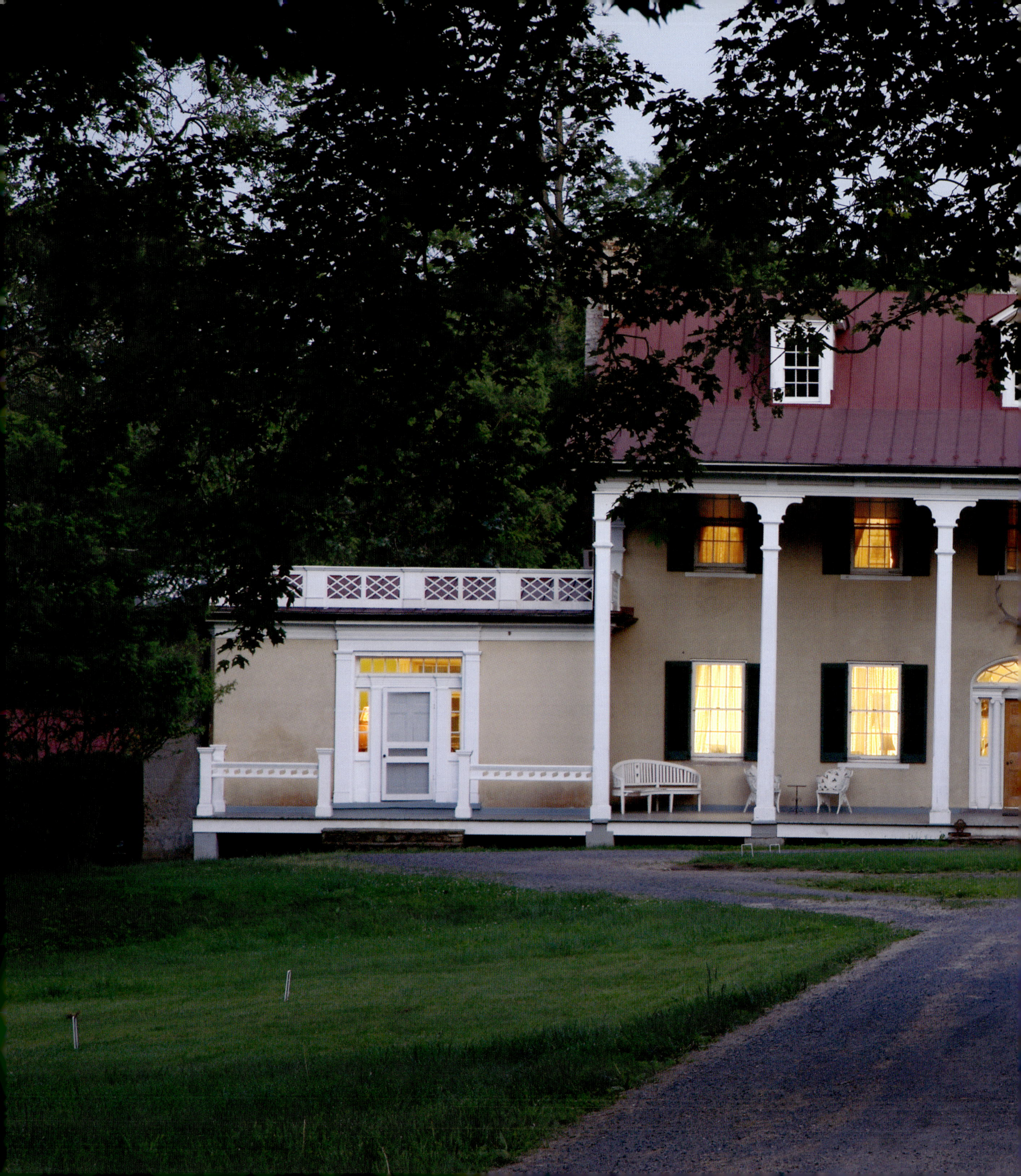

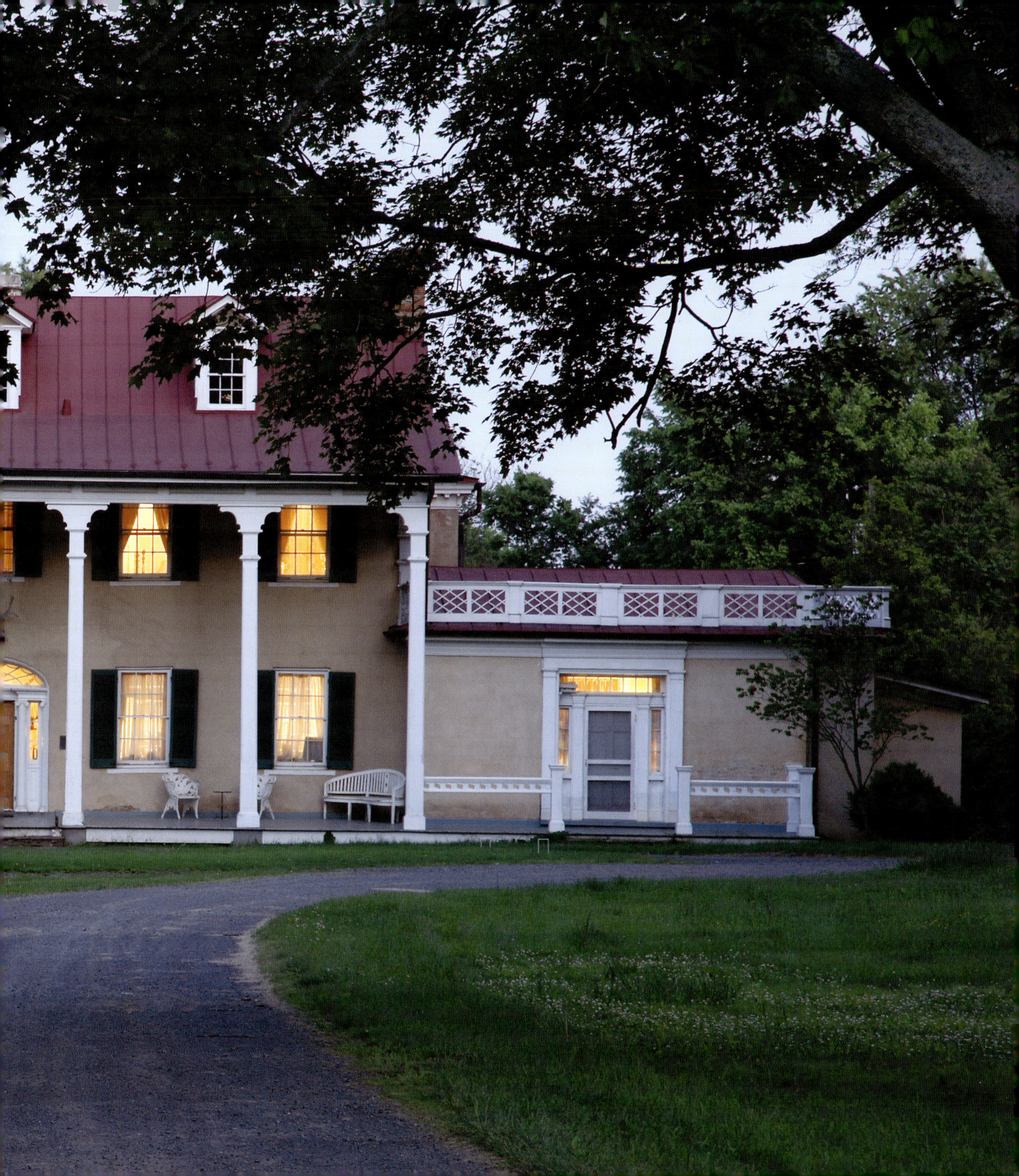

THE TANNERY

Log house, possibly 1790–1831
First stone addition, 1831 or 1850
Second stone portion with second story
of weatherboard over stone units, 1850
1818 log house addition, 1955
Additions, 1985, 2005

The Tannery is an equestrian farm of nearly a hundred acres of pasture and woodlands surrounding a pristine fieldstone stable and barn complex and a rambling, cozy house that has evolved through the centuries into one of the most picturesque homesteads in Virginia. The complex consists of a series of small connected houses that terminate at an intimate walled courtyard. The rusticity of natural building materials, hand-hewn logs, fieldstone, and weathered lumber, create a strong sense of permanence and rich textural beauty. Because of its particularly evocative architecture, The Tannery has often been photographed as emblematic of this region of Virginia's hunt country. Many of these images are of the famous Orange County Hunt, of which the owner of The Tannery is a joint master of foxhounds (M.F.H.), and with which Jackie Kennedy (Onassis) often rode. The hunt is named for the county in New York that was the home of its founding members and from which it moved to its present Fauquier County, Virginia, location in 1903.

Although it is believed to be one of the earliest farms in the area, The Tannery's exact dating is unclear. Deed records show that in 1883 the property was known as The Tan Yard Farm, verified by remnants of hides unearthed when the pond was built near the back of the house in the early 1900s. The oldest section, possi-

RIGHT *The Tannery is a horse farm in Fauquier County whose owners have restored the early-nineteenth century farmhouse and stables to perfection. From a log portion the farm has evolved over the centuries with construction of fieldstone, weatherboard, and, again, log structures. The natural materials, sturdy construction, and unassuming design of the buildings make the farm one of the most charming and beautiful in Virginia.*

FOLLOWING PAGES *The red parlor is the original sitting room, located in the earliest fieldstone portion of the house. The parlor's deep bold color palette sets off original art, such as the small still life by Robert White over the side chair, and antique furnishings, such as the late-eighteenth-century desk and the delicate painted nineteenth-century tole tray-on-stand.*

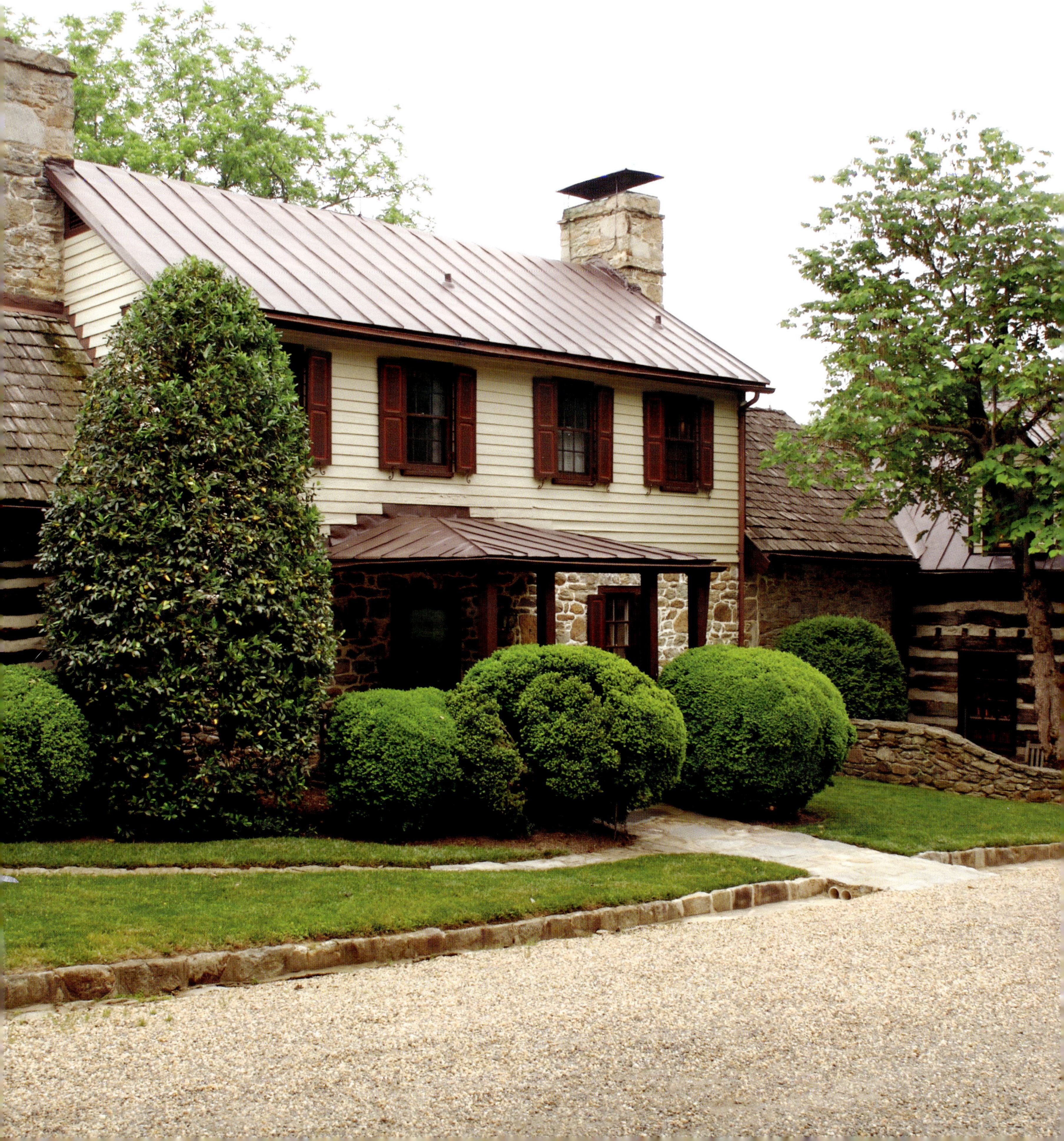

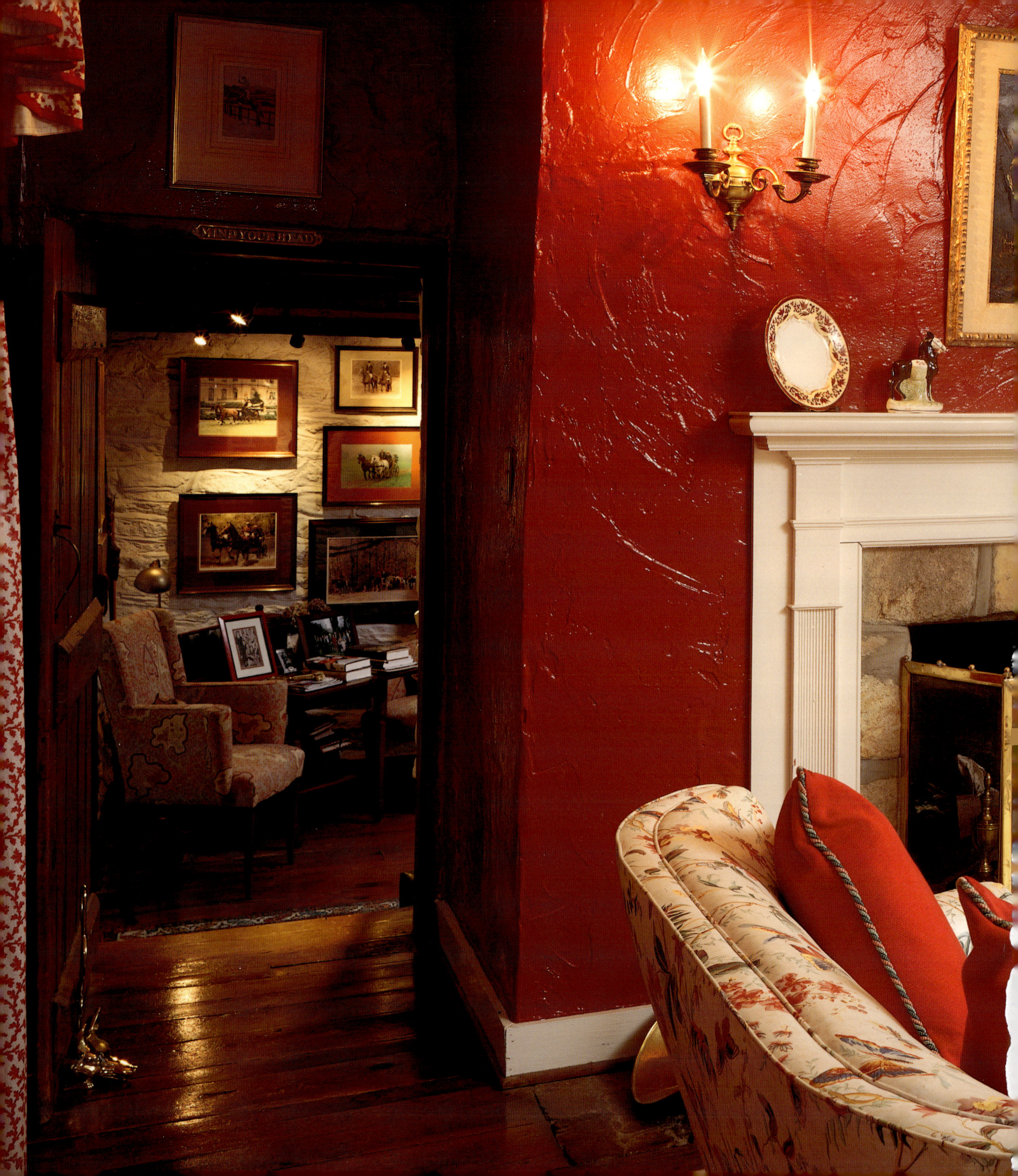
MIND YOUR HEAD

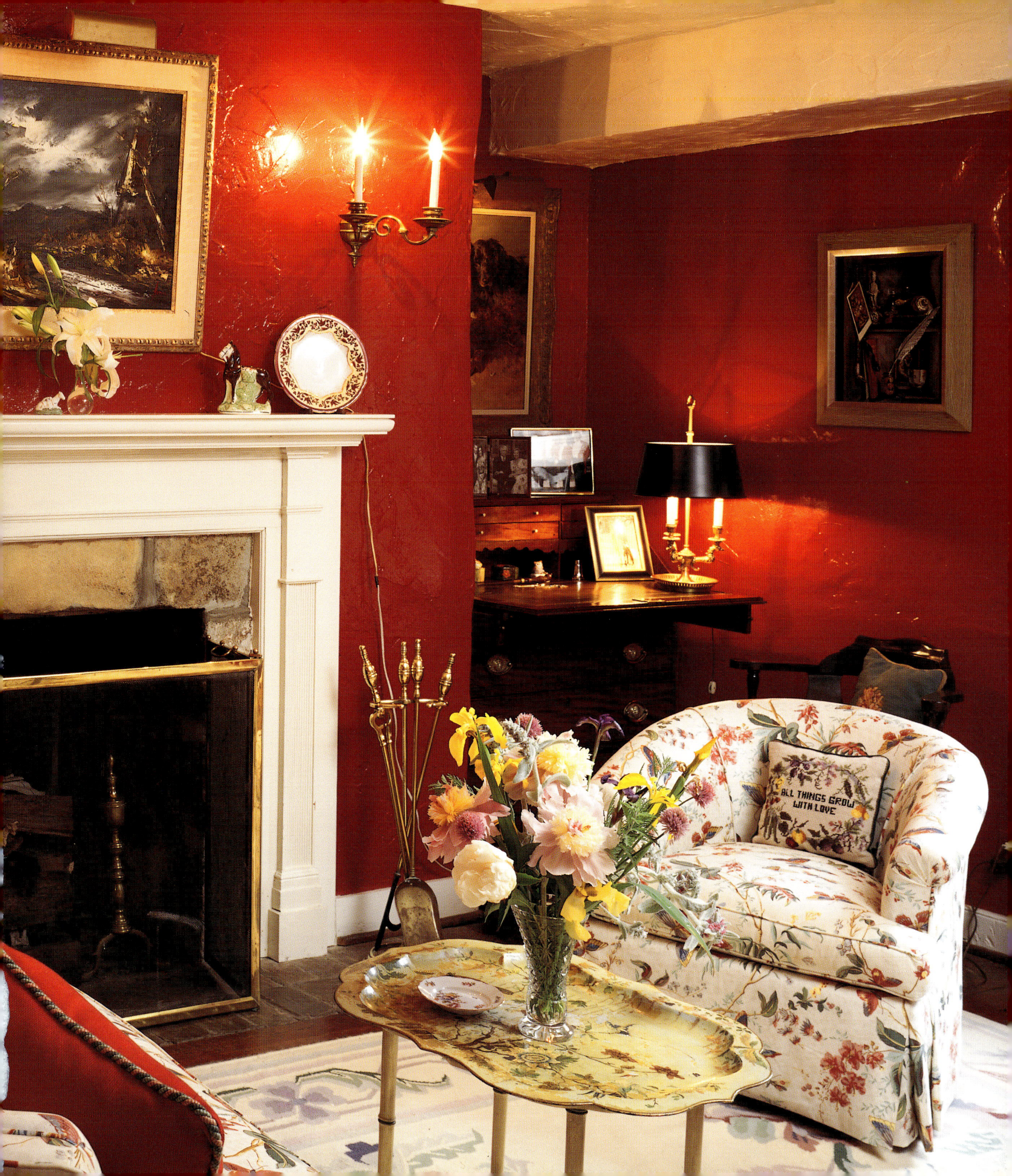
ALL THINGS GROW
WITH LOVE

ABOVE *The living room is part of a large addition that the current owners made in the 1980s to the back of the historic house. Above the heart pine mantel is an original Wally Nall portrait of the owner, a joint master of foxhounds of the Orange County Hunt, and on the far wall is a portrait of his wife by Molly Bishop.*

RIGHT *A wall of windows in the dining room affords magnificent views of a nearby pond, the wooded countryside, and the Bull Run Mountains beyond. On one side of the room a Roselin Moore painting hangs above the faux tortoise buffet with the family silver tea service while on the other side an early-nineteenth-century walnut chest of drawers holds an antique oak tea caddy. The large dining room table and chairs are of mahogany.*

bly dating to the late 1700s, but certainly on the property by 1831, is a log house with an end chimney built of fieldstone. Two stone structures were added to the original house in 1831 and 1850, with a second story of frame construction faced in weatherboard over the stone portions. In 1955 an 1818 log house was brought from nearby Paris, Virginia, and attached at a right angle to the farthest stone structure, completing the early American ensemble.

Extensive restoration and remodeling by the current owners has expanded the farmhouse substantially. Because of skillful integration with the rest of the structure these additions have not compromised the integrity of the early design, and have preserved the historic front facade. Inside, authentic materials such as hand-wrought iron hinges and door hardware, heart pine flooring with a fine patina, and the rubble fieldstone and hand-hewn log walls add unsurpassed warmth.

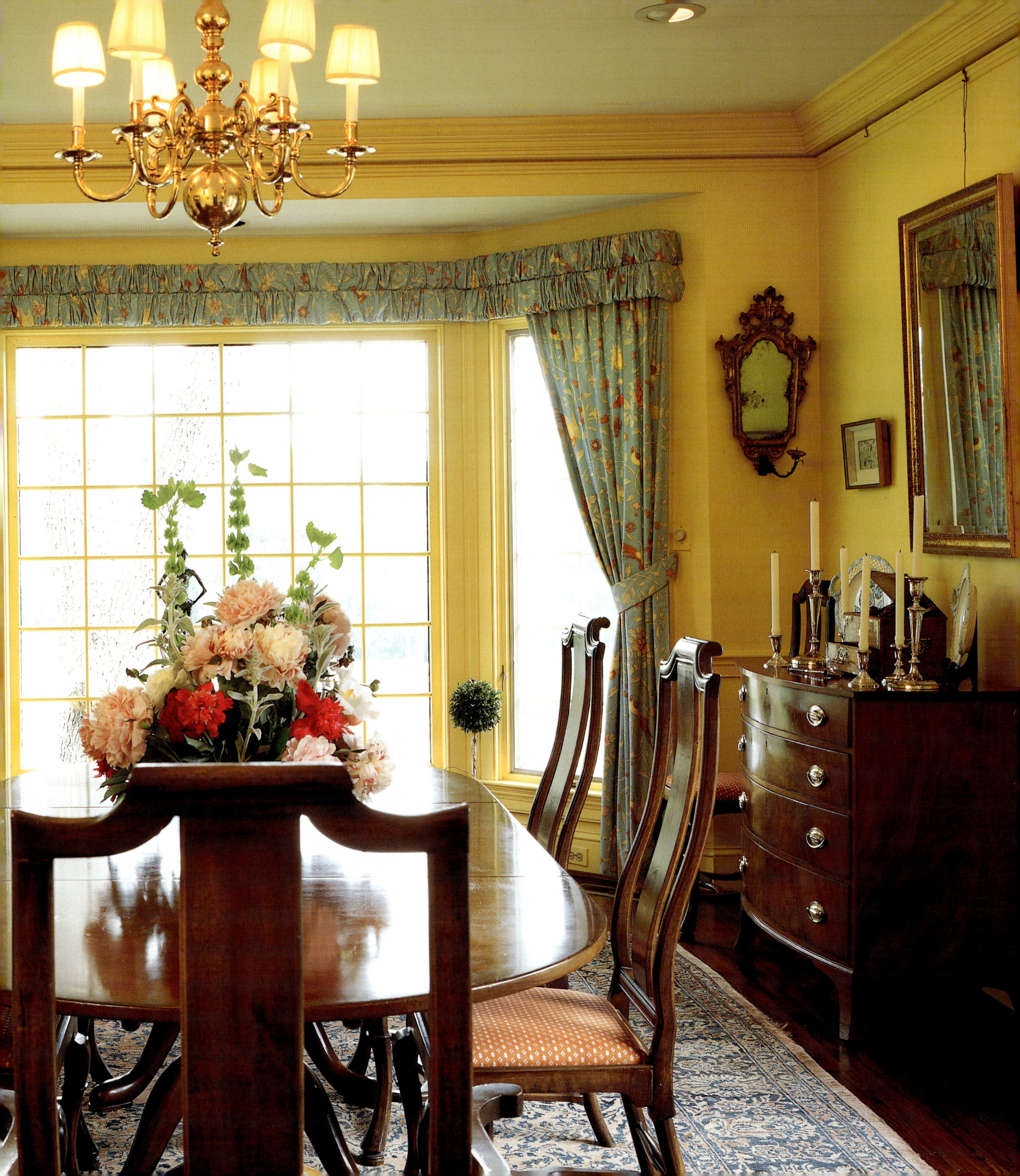

LEFT *A new breakfast room at the southern end of the house was added in 2005 when the adjacent kitchen was remodeled. A wall of windows faces a colorful view of a flower garden and the stone springhouse.*

BOTTOM LEFT *The cozy family room is in the 1818 log structure that was moved in 1955 from Paris, Virginia, a few miles away, and attached to the existing house. Antiques include hand-wrought iron andirons that were the owner's great-grandfather's, an unusual set of antique English copper "measures" that line the mantel, and a copper coaching horn.*

OPPOSITE *Adjacent to the red parlor (p. 72–73) is the den, another room in the early-nineteenth-century stone structure. The rusticity of its painted fieldstone walls, original wood mantel, and hand-adzed ceiling beams creates an enveloping, casual atmosphere.*

Illegitimi non Carborundum

ABOVE *The fieldstone and weatherboard stable is set down and across the drive from the farmhouse. The natural material and matching russet paint trim of both structures give the complex a visually pleasing cohesiveness. Fieldstone walls line pastures and paths throughout the almost hundred acre grounds.*

RIGHT *The late-eighteenth-century or early-nineteenth-century stone springhouse protects the natural water supply and provides a picturesque focal point when enjoying a view of the backyard pond (not shown) and one of the abundant manicured flower gardens.*

The owners had a vision for the farmhouse's renewal when they first saw it, deserted and dilapidated. And though they contracted to purchase the farm in the mid-1970s with the intent of making it their second home, work began in earnest in 1982 when the husband moved there from Washington D.c.to oversee its restoration and remodeling. Over the past two decades the couple's determination and style have revived the historic property, transforming it into a comfortable country place and their permanent home.

The energetic couple thrives in the atmosphere of the hunt country. Though often at her Washington DC office, the wife maintains a full schedule of social events and finds time for the lovely gardens. And with effervescence and boundless enthusiasm the husband pursues the equine sport of foxhunting and is the head of his Scottish clan in the United States.

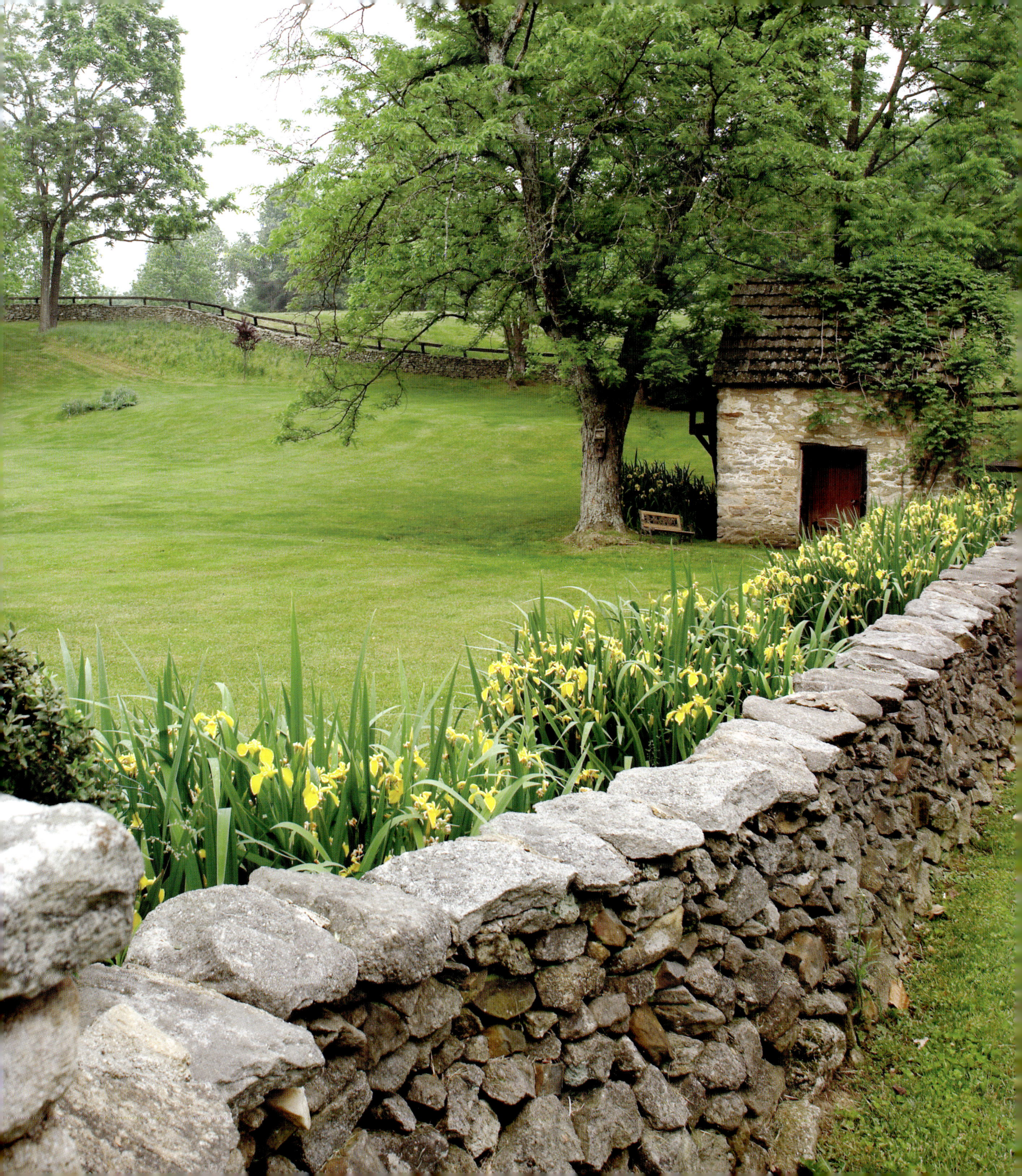

SEVEN SPRINGS FARM

Smoke house, springhouse, possibly c.1790
Stone section of main house, possibly c.1790; stone and stucco addition, c.1818
Restoration, remodel, additions, 1955
Barn complex, c.1890; restoration, 1955, 1970s

Seven Springs Farm is an agrarian complex of late-eighteenth- and early-nineteenth-century buildings and 160 acres of farmland found at the end of a country road in hunt country's Loudoun County. The farm's black barn and bright white house create a striking graphic effect against the deep green pastures edged with weathered fieldstone walls. Cattle graze the land, the buildings are pristinely restored, and lush gardens grace the immediate grounds. It is an idyllic setting for the country life.

The documented provenance of Seven Springs Farm leads from the pre-Colonial era through the Civil War era, the Depression years, and early restoration in the 1950s, to its current stature as a fully restored historic property and a working cattle farm. Beginning with a 1740 grant by Thomas, Sixth Lord Fairfax, 130 acres was eventually conveyed to William R. McCarty. It is presumed that a dwelling, which may have included the current dining room, was built before the sale in 1817 when construction of the main farmhouse and outbuildings most probably began. During the Civil War the farm was owned by John W. Dodd, whose son served in the 43rd Virginia Battalion under Col. John Singleton Mosby. The farm may have been a boarding house for other young Mosby Rangers, and a trap door in the main parlor's floor signifies the need for concealment from enemy forces. The farm saw military activity, as cavalry of both forces used the nearby road as a thoroughfare. In 1862 the house was damaged by cannon fire. In the following years the farm became a cattle operation, and later tenant farmers worked the land through the Depression. Restoration began in 1955, at which time electricity and plumbing were installed.

RIGHT *Seven Springs Farm was purchased in the mid-1970s by its current owners, who then began a restoration of the historic farm and conservation of its land. Seven Springs Farm is now a thriving 160-acre cattle farm and the eighteenth- and nineteenth-century stone-and-stucco main house is surrounded by lush manicured gardens that are based on a historic plan.*

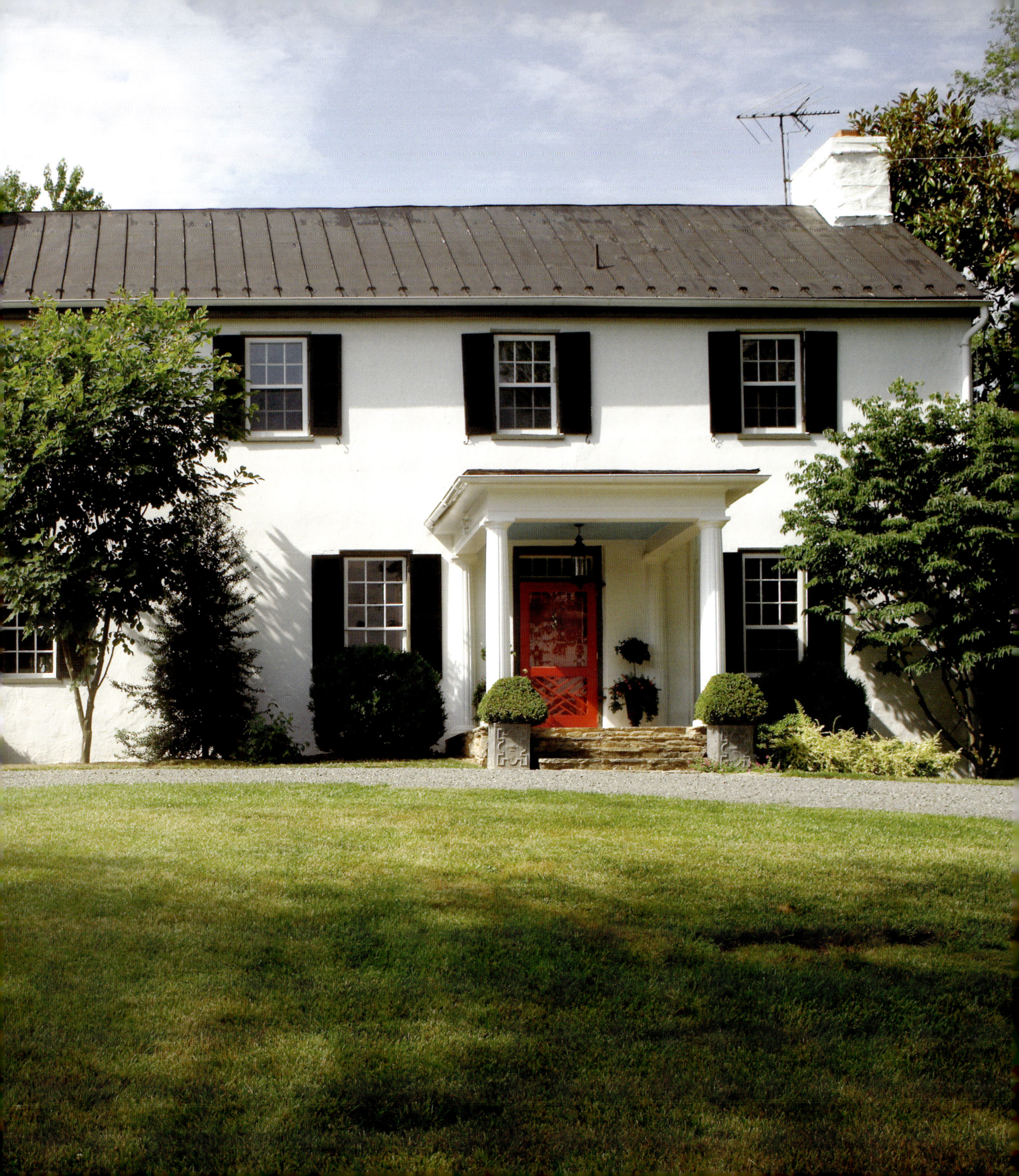

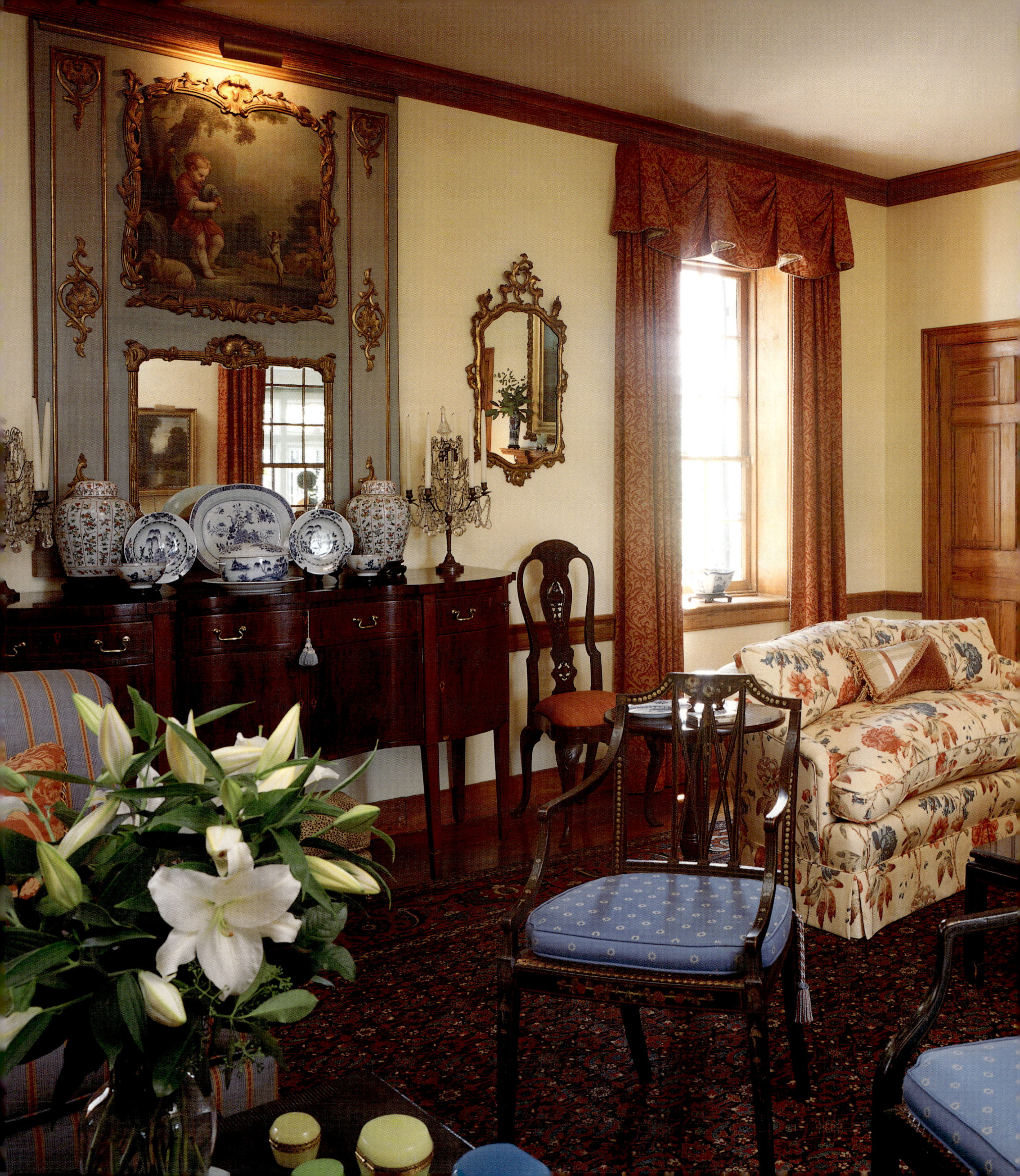

LEFT *A relaxing palette of butter cream, pale creamy coral, teal, and blue in the living room enhances the rich tones of the antique furnishings that include a late-eighteenth-century English mahogany sideboard. Chinese export ware includes a collection of ginger jars that are reflected in the eighteenth-century French Trameau mirror. Facing a collection of French opaline boxes are a pair of painted, cane-seated English Regency chairs. Over the mantel is a work by Gunther Hardwick, an American painter of the Hudson River School. The small coffee table is eighteenth-century Chinese black lacquer.*

ABOVE *The entry hall shows the owner's flair for design.*

The current owners moved to Seven Springs Farm in 1975 while searching for a small farm with an old stone house. They have immersed themselves in Virginia history and contribute much of their time and expertise to a number of non-profit organizations. The husband's interest in and knowledge of the region's history, particularly the Civil War era, has led him to serve as president of the Loudoun County Historical Society. He is also president emeritus of The Mosby Heritage Area Association, an organization dedicated to increasing the knowledge and appreciation of the area's rich historical qualities. The wife's passion is gardening, but it was not always so. The gardens at Seven Springs Farm were in such decline when the couple moved in that nothing was done for nearly a decade. Then, after attending a

ABOVE *The dining room is the original eighteenth-century part of the house. Its rich wood paneling sets off the family's silver collection and unusual, fine porcelain pieces. The Hudson River School painting is of a Civil War soldier on a riverbank by Clinton Loveridge, who served in the Berdan Sharpshooters.*

RIGHT *The well-appointed library is in the stucco-over-stone portion of the main house. Its wood paneling, muted color scheme, comfortable seating of down cushions, and family pictures make it amiable as well as chic. A Robin Hill gouache of cranes is displayed over the mantel, while a hand-painted fan screen by Marcia Ray guards the hearth. The ten delicate turquoise Chinese porcelain figures, representing ten of the twelve Chinese New Year's figures, were a wedding present to the husband's parents.*

FOLLOWING PAGES *The much-used sunroom is ethereal and bright. The conservatory-like, fully fenestrated space creates an easy transition from the spacious kitchen at the back of the house to the patio and gardens. Its fresh white wicker furniture and peach, leaf-motif decorated upholstery only enhance its charm.*

horticultural symposium, the wife enthusiastically undertook the immense task of renewing these gardens. Renewal grew into creation, and now a series of magnificent gardens are highly sought after for study and enjoyment by such groups as the Garden Club of Virginia, for which the owner is currently vice chairman of the Visiting Gardens Committee. With transformation of the grounds into lush gardens, preservation of the architecture, and conservation of the farmland, the owners of Seven Springs Farm have preserved the integrity and beauty of an important part of Piedmont Virginia's heritage.

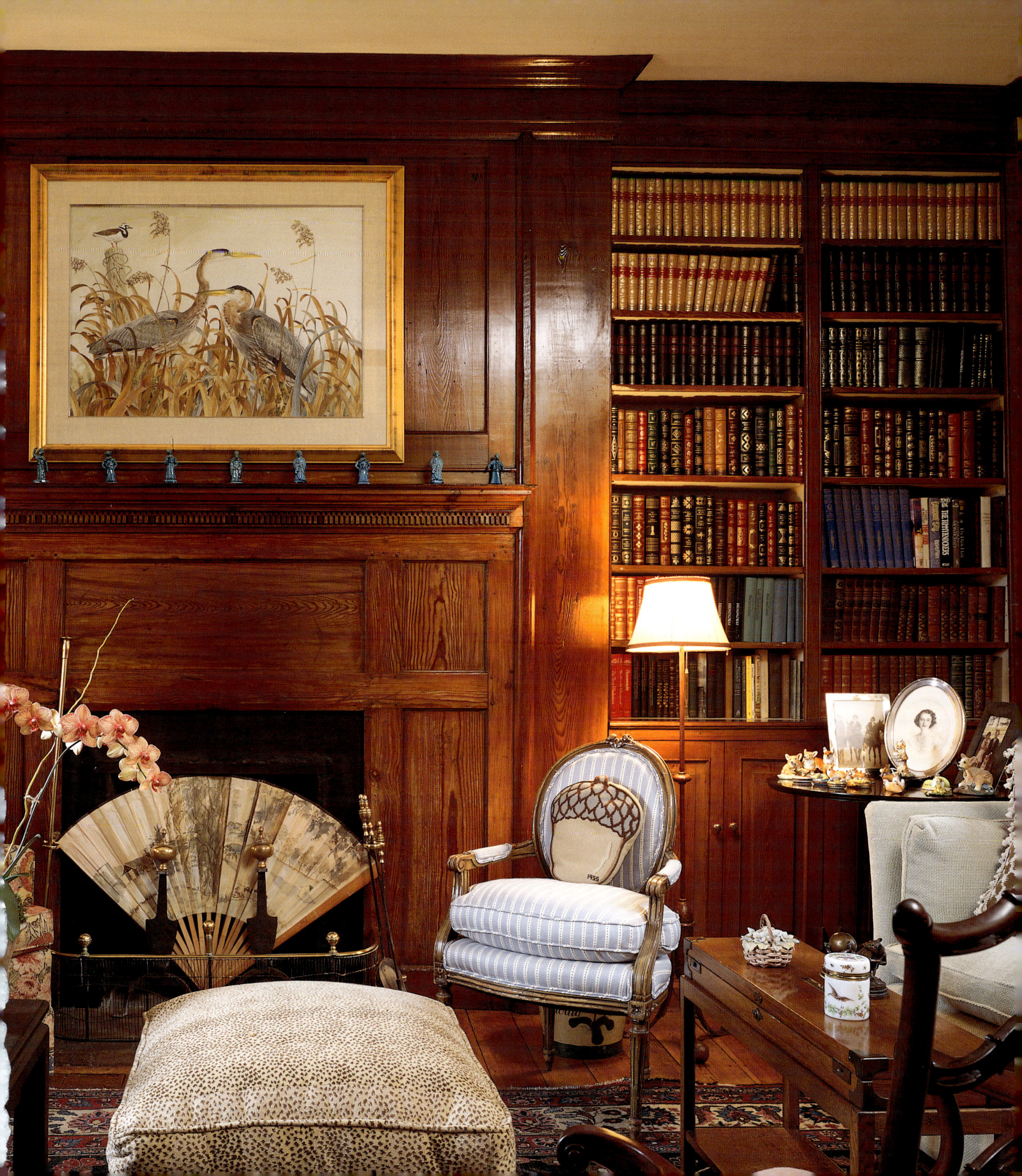

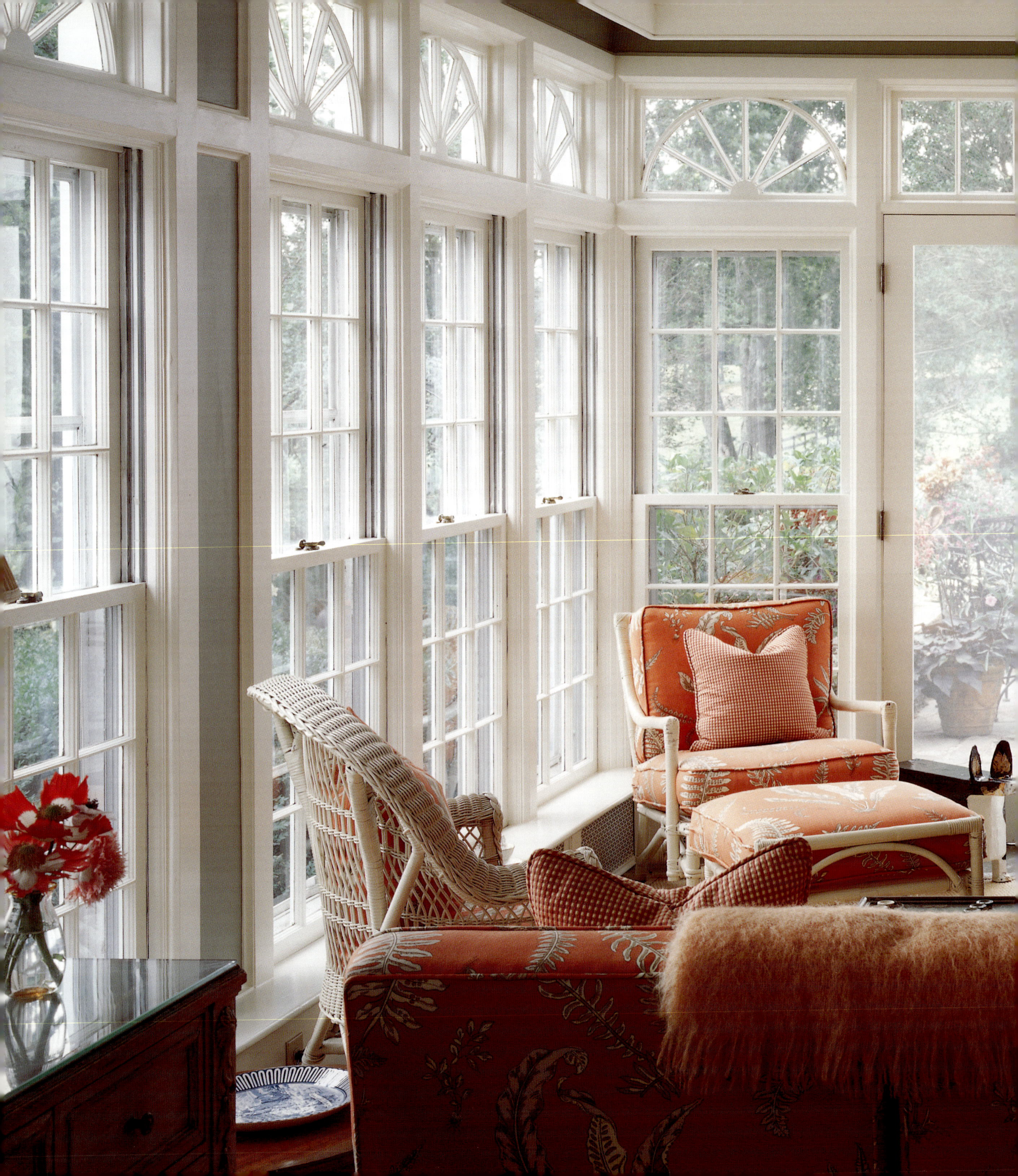

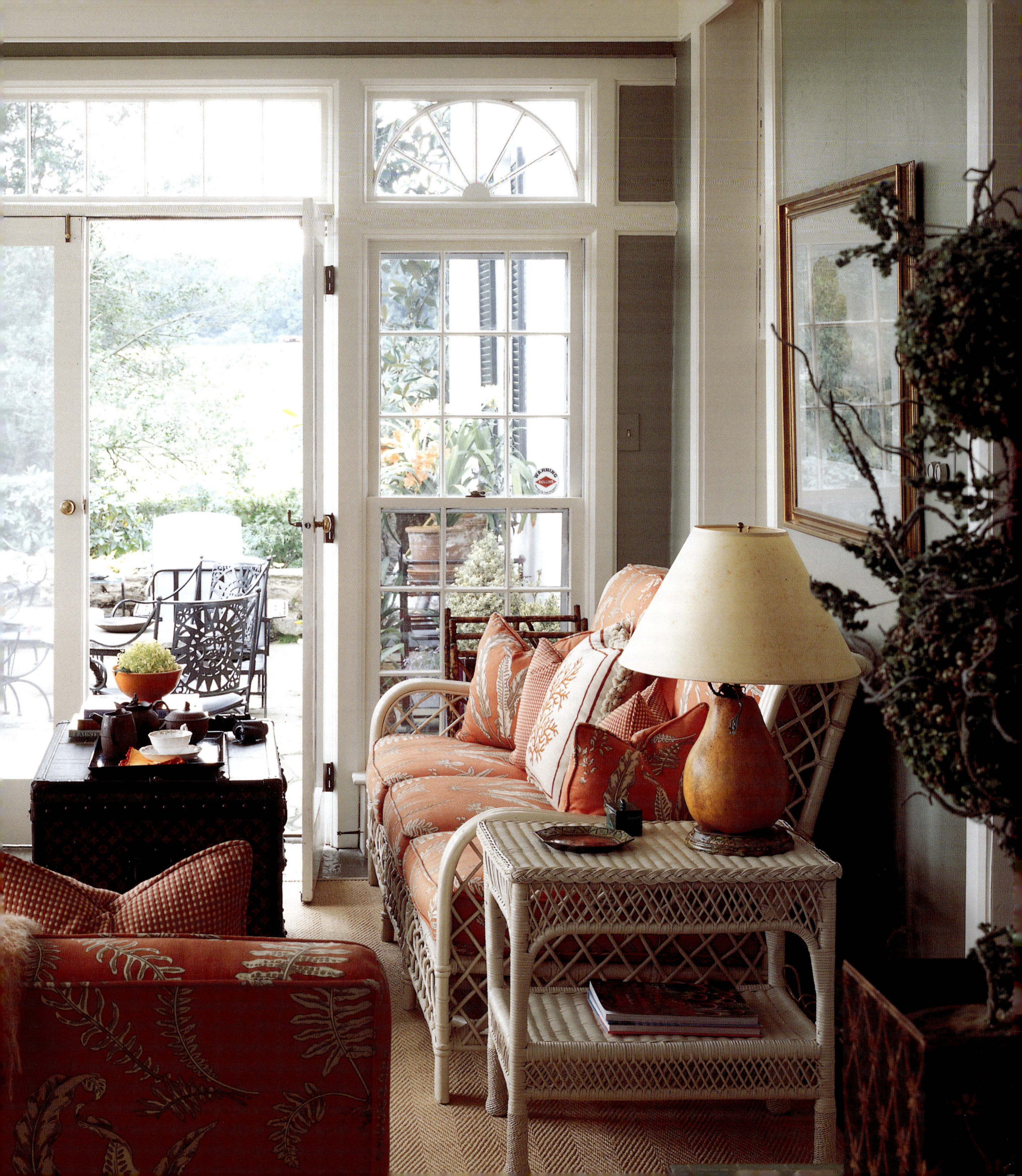

LEFT *The gardens at Seven Springs Farm are lush, imaginative, and thoroughly delightful. Of particular interest to the myriad garden clubs that visit annually are the English boxwood parterres of the side garden. Pastures and woodlands, transversed by weathered stone walls, serve as an exquisite backdrop for the masterful composition of the many specialty gardens that immediately surround the house.*

OPPOSITE *The centerpiece of the Seven Springs is the hilltop stone and stucco farmhouse, but the barn, painted a dramatic black with stark white trim, stone auxiliary buildings that include the small springhouse, and the miles of bright white fencing and weathered fieldstone walls set in the clear green pastures, help create the irresistible charm of this historic farm.*

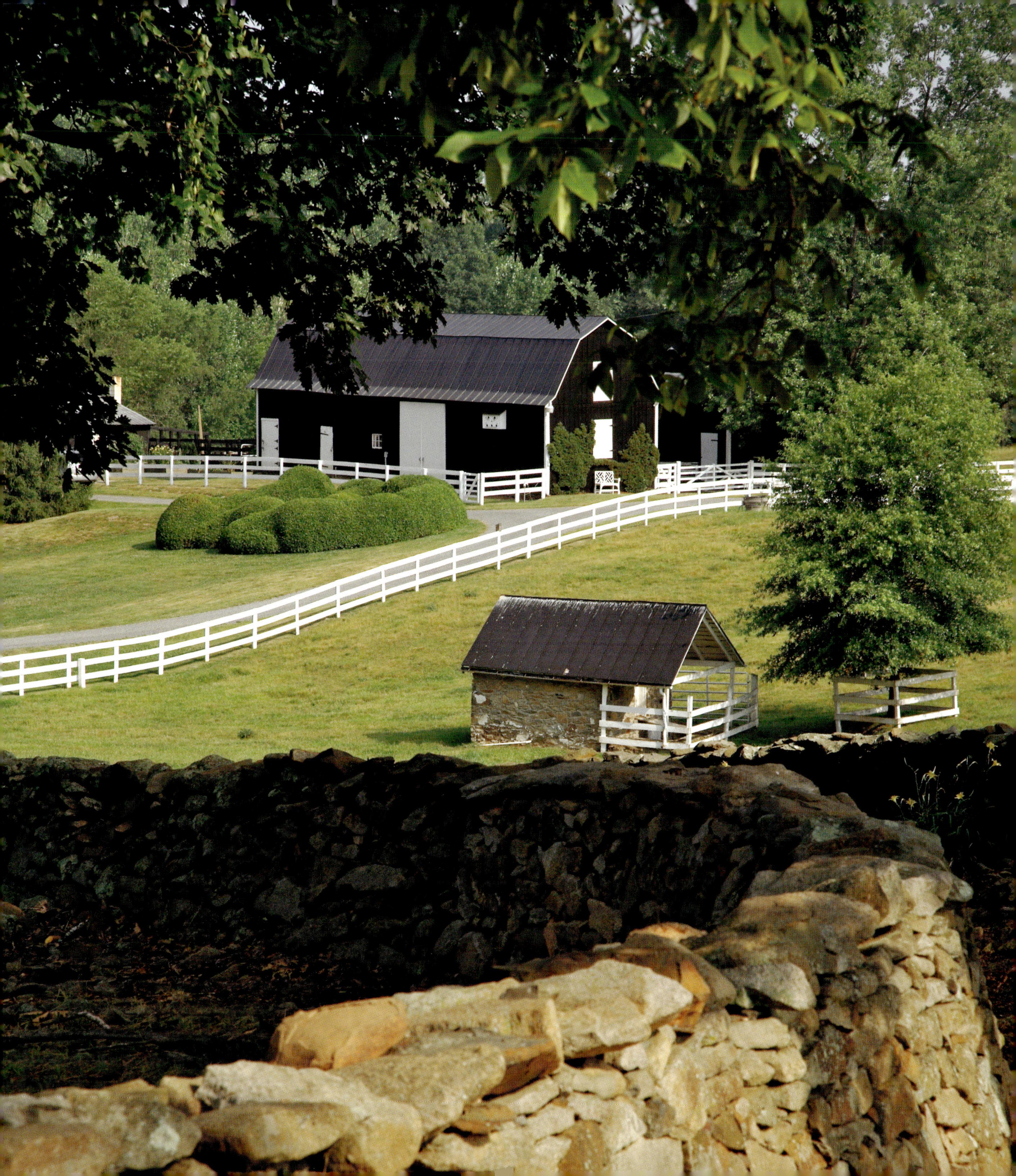

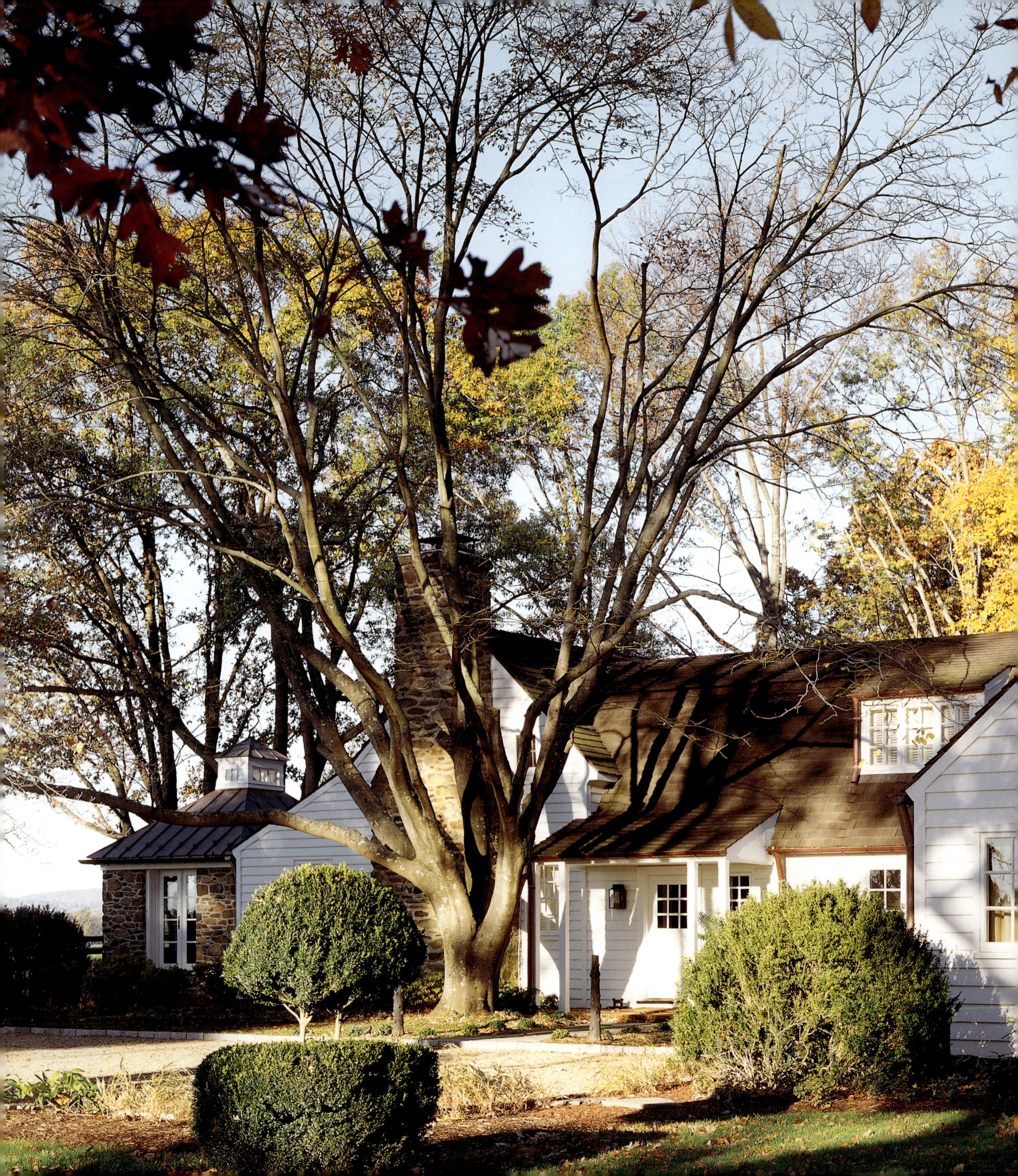

EDGEWOOD

Log houses, c.1790; additions, 1938,
Palmer and Lamoin, architects
Remodel, 1955, Cross & Sons, architects
Remodel and additions, 2005, Tommy Beach, architect,
Jean Perin, architectural designer

Edgewood, a rambling country cottage with centuries-old fieldstone chimneys and freshly painted white weatherboard siding, was skillfully designed with a low-key profile and natural materials to perfectly blend with its woodland setting. A surprise of the interior is its spaciousness and light. Edgewood was set back from a country road and nestled in a grove of trees for aesthetics as much as privacy when it was moved to its present site from another location nearby by then-owners Mr. and Mrs. Paul Mellon. A pair of interconnected c.1790 log houses serves as the core of the residence, which had been enlarged in 1938 and moved in 1955. In 2004 current owner interior designer Jean Perin began a collaboration on the present design with distinguished local architect Tommy Beach. At the completion of the nearly two-year restoration and extensive remodeling Perin's vision for the property had become a reality.

Perin's design maintains the integrity and rusticity of the eighteenth-century log structures and other earlier stylistic elements while creating spaces functional for a twenty-first-century lifestyle. Significant changes included conversion of the existing garage to a spacious office with a sitting room, mudroom, and laundry facilities, and creation of a new light-filled, state-of-the-art kitchen that takes advantage of a formerly dark space and opens to an adjacent cheery blue conservatory with views of the English gardens. A master suite added at the back of the house captures unsurpassed views of the Blue Ridge and Cobbler Mountains. Toward the south a sunroom that extends the living space beyond the log walls opens the house with a fully fenestrated facade that also takes full advantage of the magnificent mountain view.

LEFT *Edgewood is a rambling country house that began as two connected eighteenth-century log structures but is now a spacious, open country place with twenty-first-century amenities and sophisticated casual interiors. Its log, stone, and weatherboard construction, wooded setting, and fine, English-garden-style landscaping make it one of the most beautiful estates in Fauquier County.*

LEFT *The homeowner, interior and architectural designer Jean Perin, worked with architect Tommy Beach to create spaces that would reflect the integrity of the historical property in their materials, surface detailing, and scale. The cupola room at the far end of the new sunroom was designed with a funnel ceiling and skylight to define the space and give it volume. An English handwrought iron pendant lantern is hung over an eighteenth-century French pine circular dining table with a highly carved pedestal. The floors are of French limestone.*

OPPOSITE *A new breezeway connects the public rooms to the master suite. Its warm caramel color and the double windows and French doors illuminate the gallery-like space. The nineteenth-century bronze equestrian sculpture is by I. Bonheur. A seventeenth-century Italian landscape hangs above one of a pair of nineteenth-century English walnut gothic-style side chairs. Centered on the far wall of upholstered linen damask is a portrait of a lady with hound in a gilt late-sixteenth-century frame.*

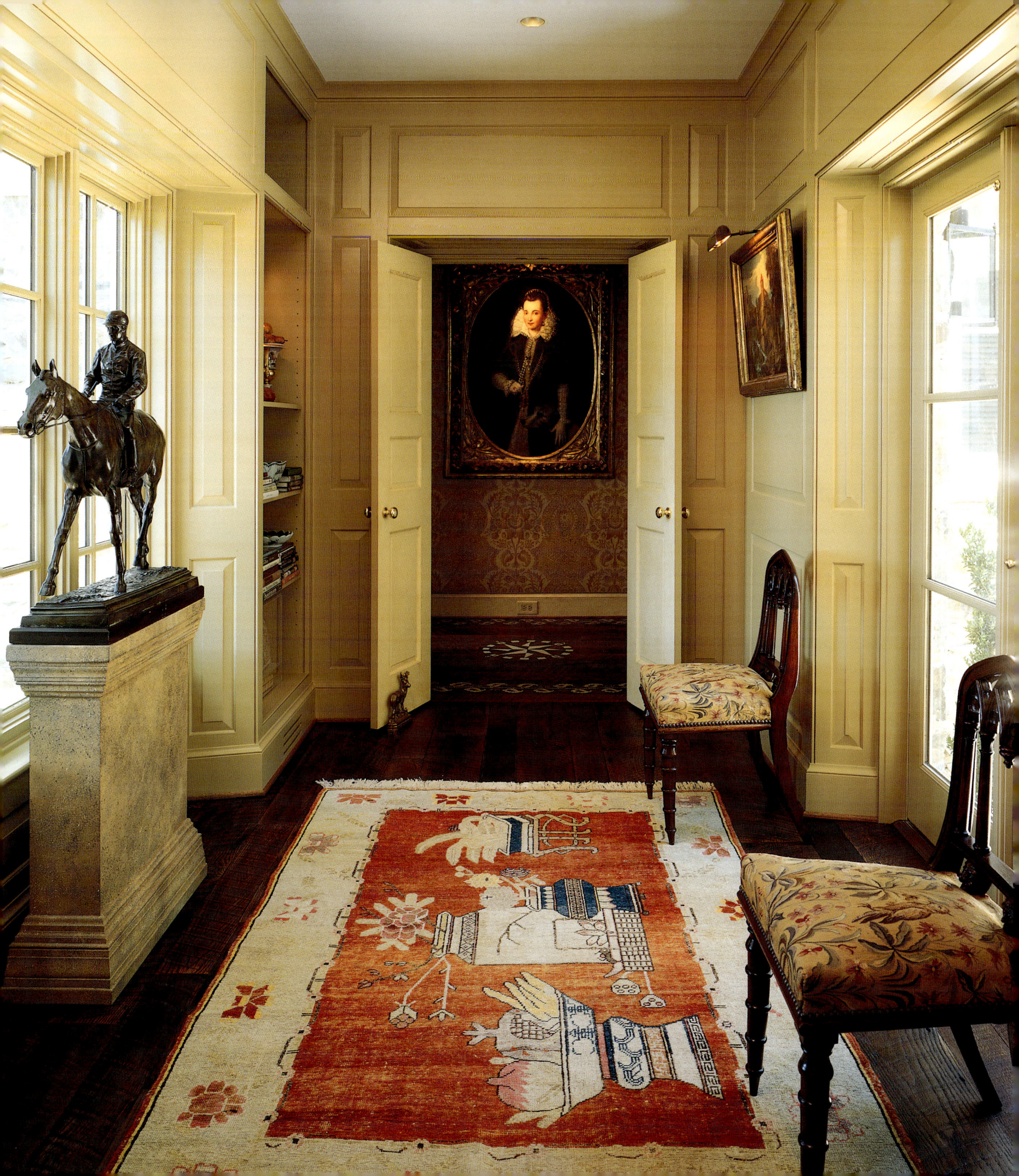

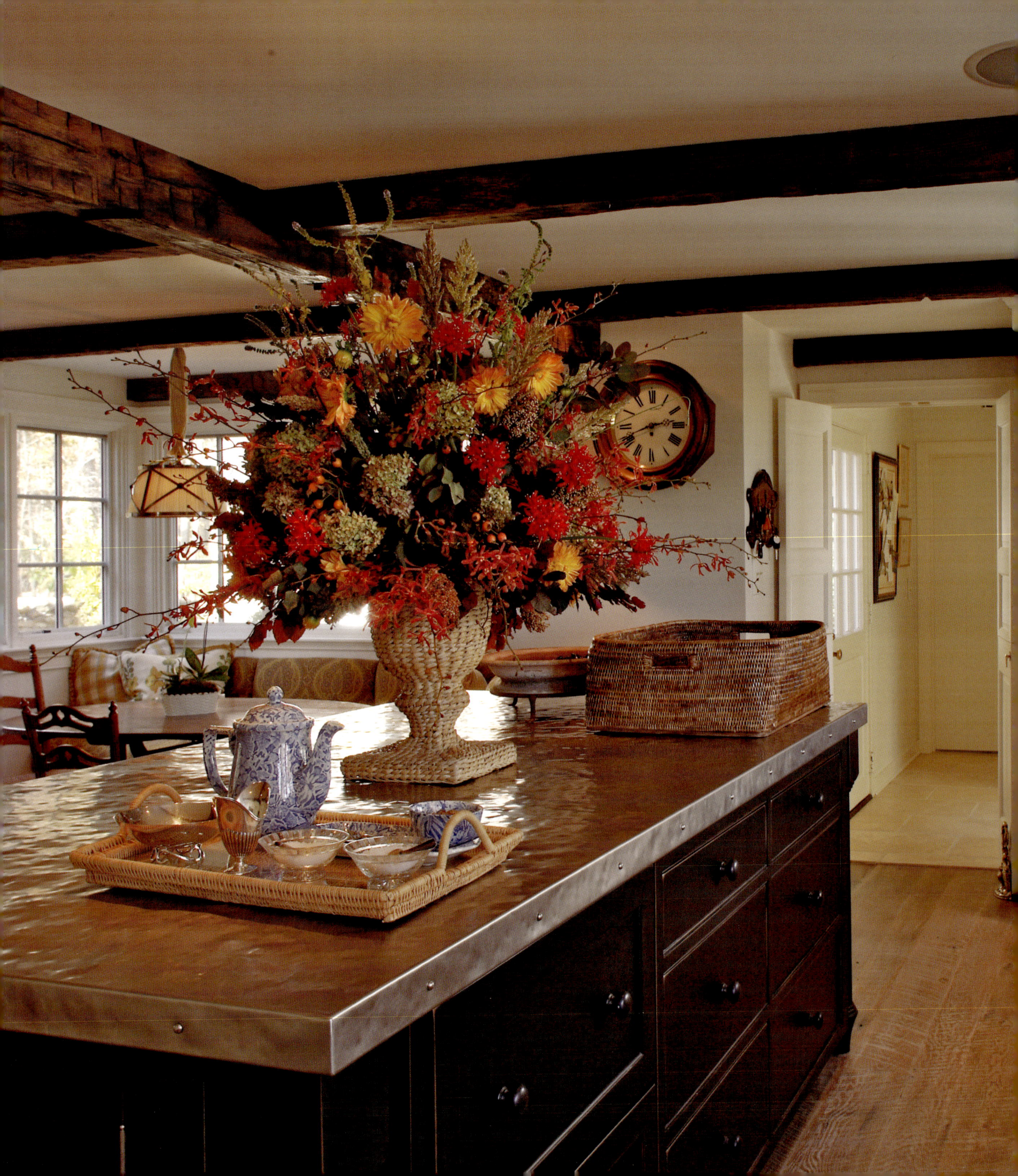

LEFT *The kitchen is a state-of-the-art facility. Its spaciousness, with room for a large center counter and adjacent breakfast area, was created by opening up two smaller dark rooms. Slate countertops complement the unusual random-width, mill-sawn, whitewashed oak flooring. A new hallway at the far side of the kitchen connects the new office, mudroom, and laundry room, spaces that were once part of the garage.*

ABOVE *Perin entertains with extravagant perfection in the formal dining room, providing the best food and wine, often accompanied by a spectacular floral arrangement by Perin's favorite florist, Stephanie Fassold of Lavender Green in nearby Paris. Perin custom-designed the painted wood and upholstered highback chairs to have a theatrical Venetian flair. The painted tole chandelier, also a Perin design, illuminates the intimate space and reflects the shine of the Sheraton mahogany dining table.*

Chief among the reasons for the transformation of the cottage into a gracious, completely livable country home is the successful design collaboration of Perin and Beach. Their combined expertise and up-to-the-moment sensibilities resulted in a creative solution that brought a modest 1930s design into the twenty-first century. Edgewood remains an authentic piece of the earliest history of settlement in the Piedmont while giving a fresh take on traditional style in a contemporary architectural design.

Having owned a home in the Middleburg area since 1980, while still residing in Washington D.C., Perin often came to the country to foxhunt. In 1989, however, because of her love of horses, the camaraderie of like-minded horse sports enthusiasts, and her growing commitments in various conservation organizations, Perin decided to live in the Piedmont full-time. Since her move the majority of her clients are now in the area.

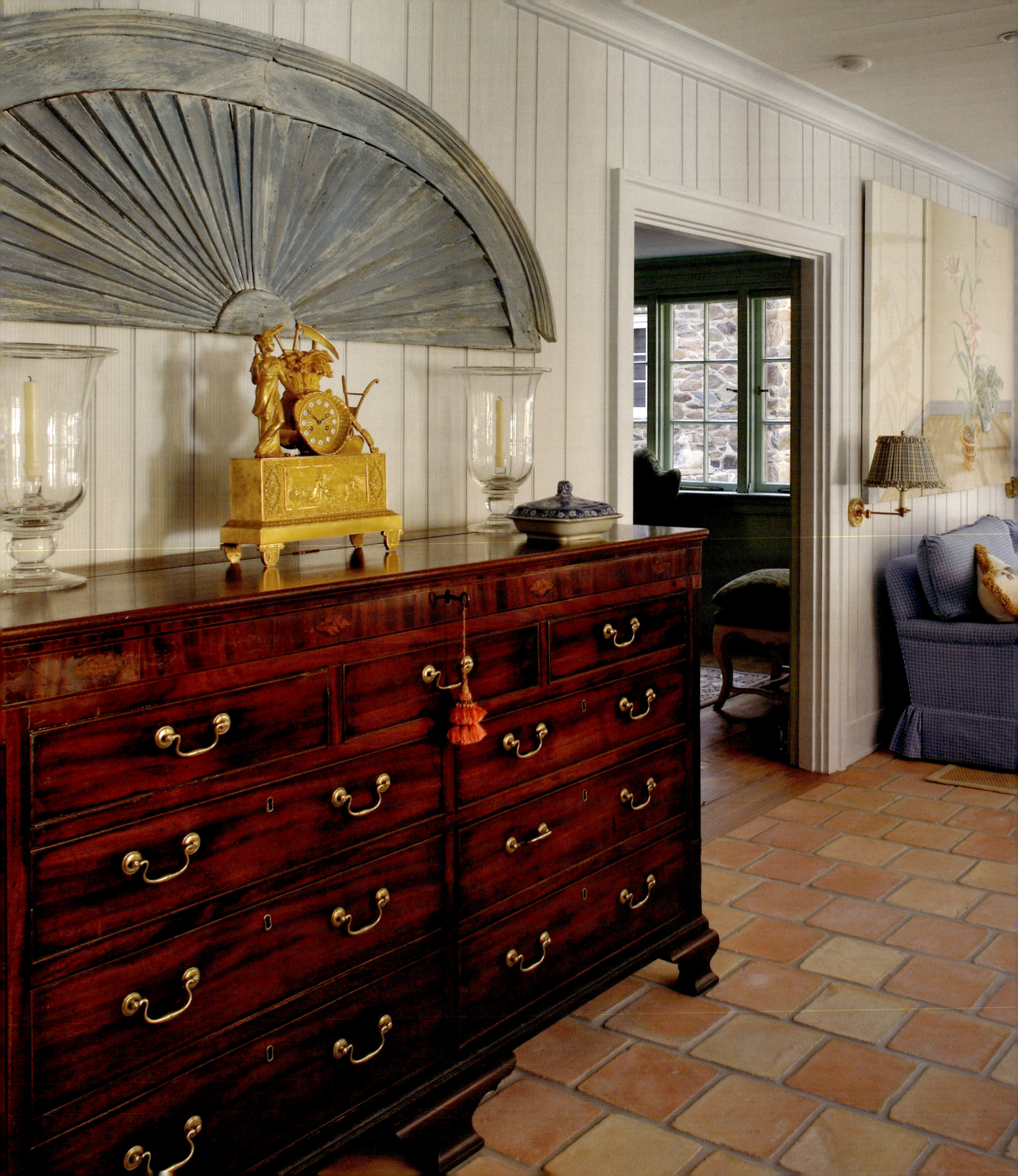

Perin's command of color is most evident in the intense cheery blue of the conservatory. The room is centrally located between the kitchen and the dining room and provides a casual space for relaxing. One set of French doors leads to the swimming pool, lawn, and woodlands while another set opens to the manicured gardens and English-style thatched shed.

ABOVE *The eighteenth-century log section of the original house forms a common wall between the formal sitting room and the new addition's dining space and sunroom. Wood is used in a variety of surfaces throughout the house. Log walls are left exposed, historic carved pieces, such as the mantels, have been restored, and finely detailed paneling melds gentility with historic rusticity.*

RIGHT *The sunroom extension has a southern exposure that floods the entire house with light. Dark furnishings are bold against a subtle, natural-tone color palette. A Chinese Chippendale frame with painting-over-mirror, the nineteenth-century tufted wing chair of deep-toned leather, and the black painted arm chairs create depth, while natural materials, such as the sisal rug, the unbleached linen upholstery, and the woven rush seating are viscerally relaxing.*

THE WORLD OF SHOOTING
DECORATING WITH PICTURES
NTRY MANORS OF PORTUGAL

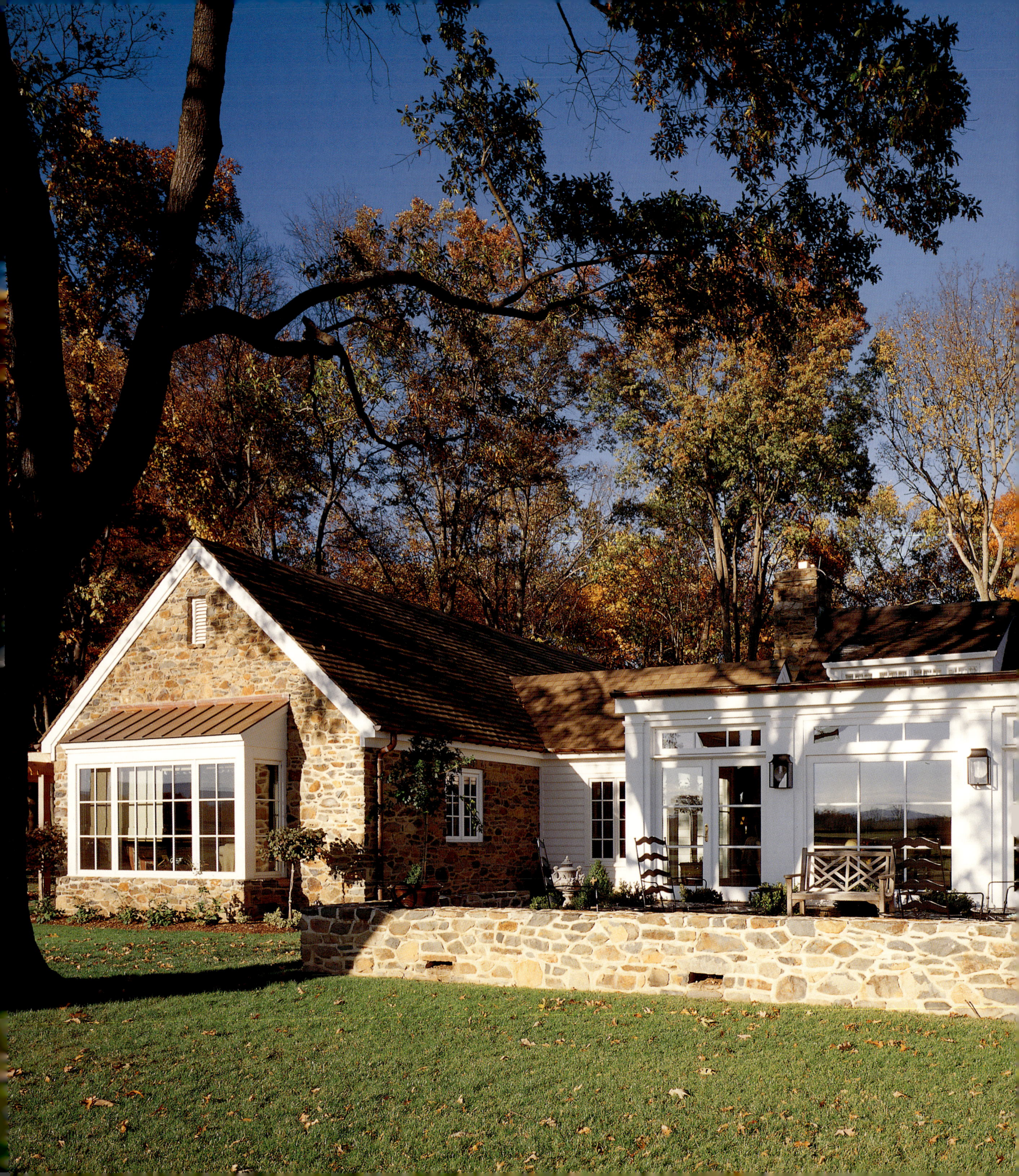

LEFT *The 2005 addition to the south end of the house created a beautiful facade filled with windows. The design includes an enclosed porch that flows into an extended sunroom, a well-lit breezeway, a spacious master suite, and an outdoor patio defined by a low fieldstone wall.*

ABOVE *Perin's skill as a designer is evident in the various specialty gardens throughout the property. Outside the kitchen, an elevated bed with the hybrid nepeda (cat mint) "Six Hill Giant" is contained within traditional English hurdles, woven willow panels that form small sturdy walls. A charming fieldstone shed with a thatched roof is both whimsical and functional.*

And while her sought-after design work shows an understanding of the hunt country aesthetic, it incorporates the urbane sensitivity she perfected in designs for her former city clients. Perin blends sophistication with comfort, discrimination and restraint with a sense of fun, and a keen sense of color with a refreshing clear rich palate. Her interpretation of traditional design elements makes them appropriate for the historical settings as well as the busy lives of her clients. She is also a professional with a conscience. Her land is in a scenic conservation easement and she works tirelessly to protect the area's open spaces as a long-standing board member of the Piedmont Environmental Council and of the Virginia League of Conservation Voters.

HICKORY HOUSE

House, c.1795; remodel and additions, 1970s, 1980s,
Barbara Robinson, architectural designer
Barn, c.1790; remodel into guest house, 1980s
Training barns, racetrack, c.1920; renovation, ongoing
Pool house and pool, 1980s; Susan Shipp, architectural designer

The owners of Hickory House are a couple whose wide circle of friends both here and abroad and a variety of interests that include the love of horses, fox hunting, and the open countryside, keep their schedules full throughout the year. Their long-standing dedication to land conservation in the Piedmont of Virginia has been particularly instrumental in saving and preserving some of America's most valuable historic sites and open spaces.

The wife moved from New York to Virginia as a child in the mid-1940s. She had acquired a love of the countryside on vacations at her grandmother's farm in the Bull Run Mountains. When her family decided to move, it was to the familiar northern Piedmont in Virginia. They acquired land in the Middleburg area of Fauquier County and began a purebred Hereford operation. Over the decades the property would increase to over 1,400 acres, enlarged by the family's acquisition of three adjacent farms. The most well-known of the farms was Burrland, renamed Hickory Tree Farm to honor a legend that said a large hickory tree that once stood on the edge of the property had been the rendezvous site for the local Confederate hero, Colonel John Singleton Mosby, and his cavalry unit known as Mosby's Rangers. This area is now designated as the Burrland Historic District. Hickory Tree Farm, with farmlands, barn, and racetrack, was sold to new owners in 2007.

Hickory House has been an integral part of the history of Hickory Tree Farm since the house and its lands were purchased by the owner's mother for offices of the Thoroughbred operation she would begin. Hickory House's original section is a c.1795 early settlers' house constructed of local limestone. Additions to the sides and back of this stately Virginia structure have made it larger but maintained its innate charm.

RIGHT *Hickory House's original c.1795 fieldstone house was restored and enlarged during the 1970s and 1980s with extensions to the sides and back that make the house more functional for modern life. The design of the front facade's cascading architectural forms mitigate the visual impact of the additional masses and maintain the integrity of the historic Virginia farmhouse.*

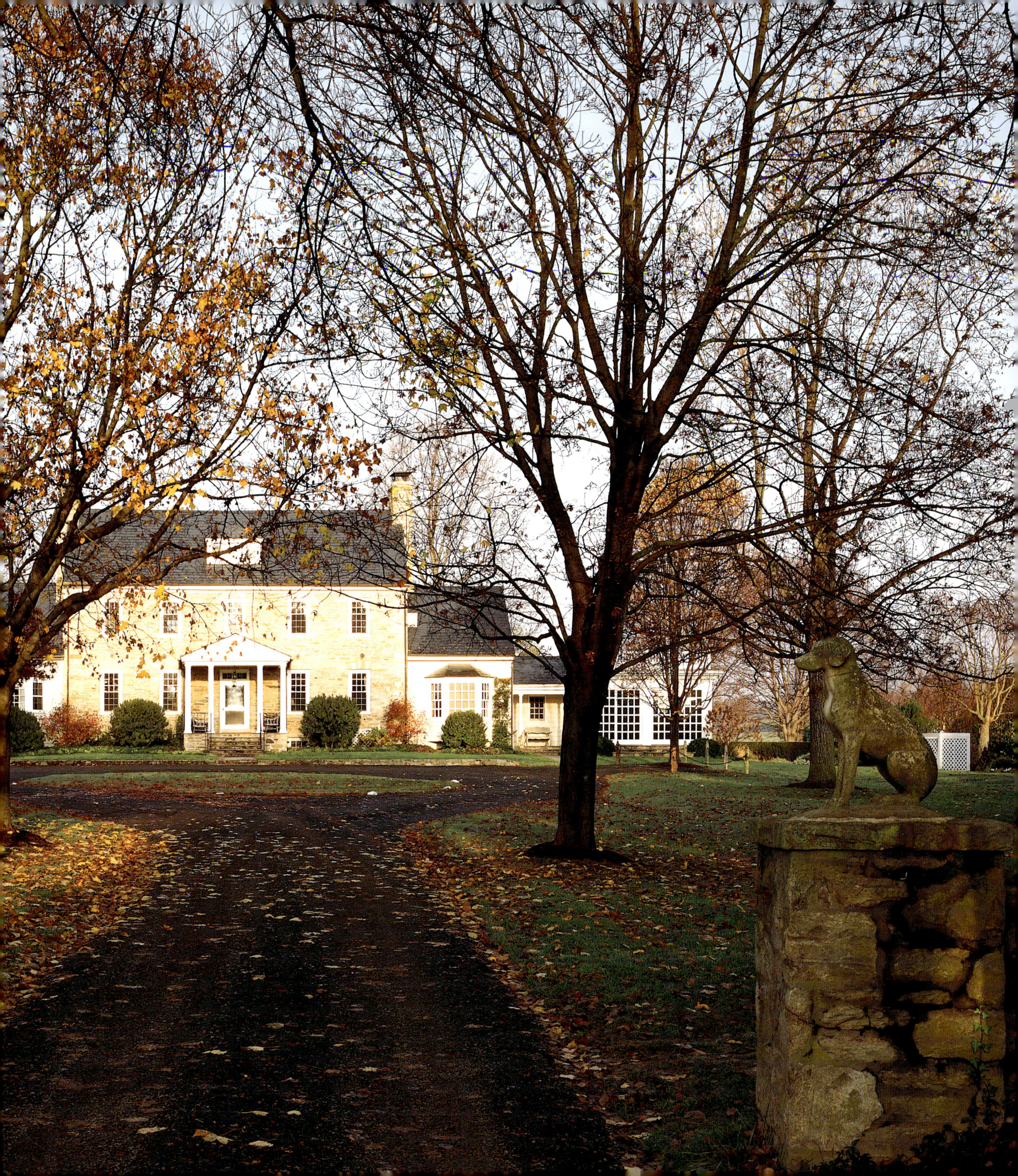

LEFT *The large drawing room was added to the back of the house with a large bow window, inspired by one in the White House, that allows a wide view of the nearby garden, pond, fields, and Blue Ridge Mountains. New York interior designer Mario Buatta created the elegant and graceful room with references to the English country house. Its antique furnishings include a pair of eighteenth-century Georgian chairs, a nineteenth-century black lacquer tray table and gilt-framed portraits.*

BELOW LEFT *The library is one of the rooms in the eighteenth-century portion of the house. Its interior reflects the traditional English lifestyle of its owners, with an array of memorabilia, photographs, rare books, bronze sculpture, French and English traditional seating that includes a Louis XVI fauteuil with original paint, and sporting and animal art such as* Japanese Spaniels at Play with Oranges on Tabletop *(1920) by English painter Maude Earle.*

OPPOSITE *The India Room is part of the latest remodel. It provides substantial space as a conservatory, sunroom, and office. The magnificent ceiling mural painted by trompe l'oeil artist Dana Westring of Marshall, Virginia, opens the room to the sky. Daphne Cheatham created needlework seats with a design based on the family coat of arms for a pair of inlaid mother of pearl and ebony side chairs; the design of the chairs, commissioned by the owners while they were visiting Udipoor, is based on chairs in the maharaja's palace. A ceramic lamp glazed with a peacock design sits on the walnut desk.*

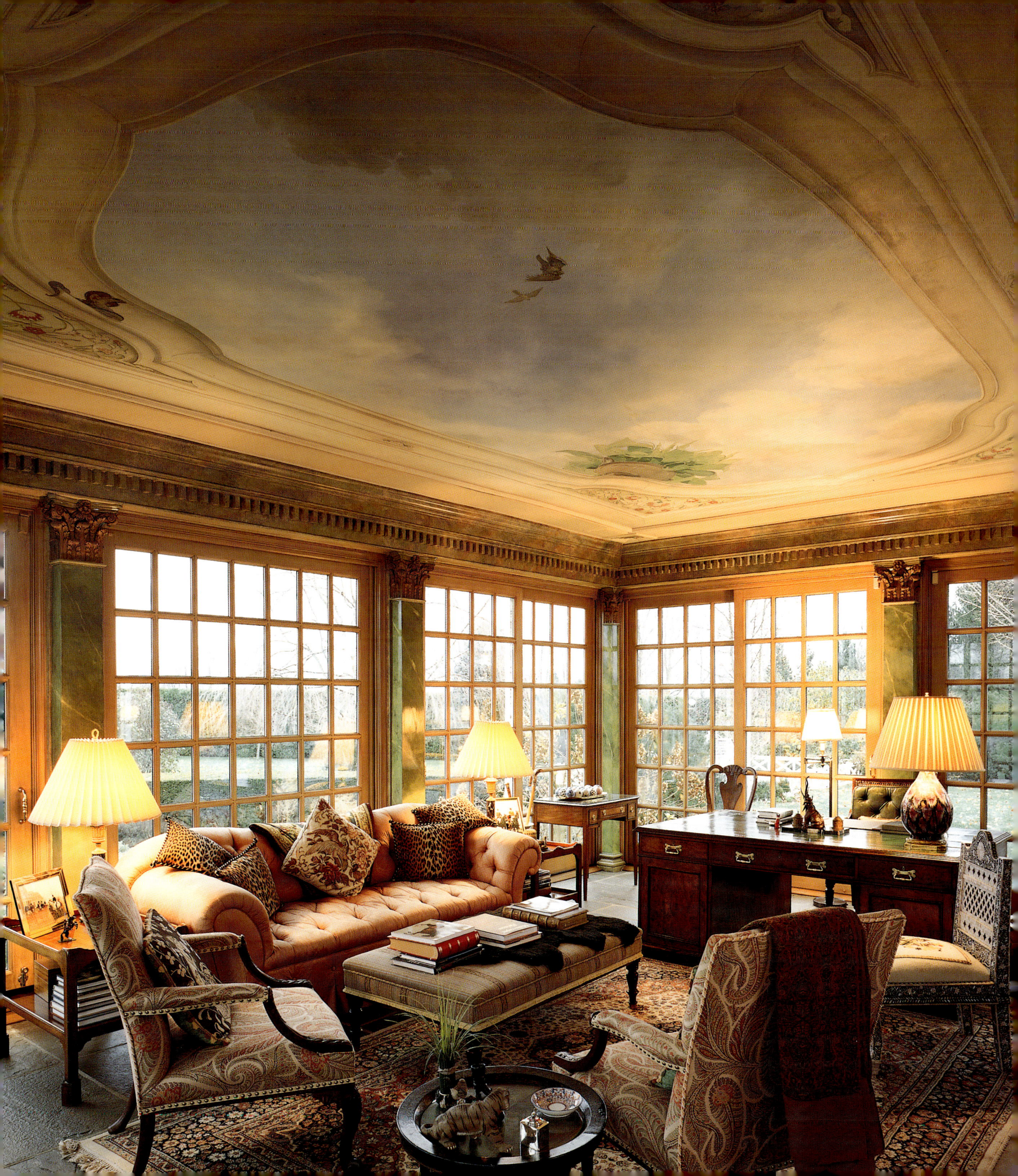

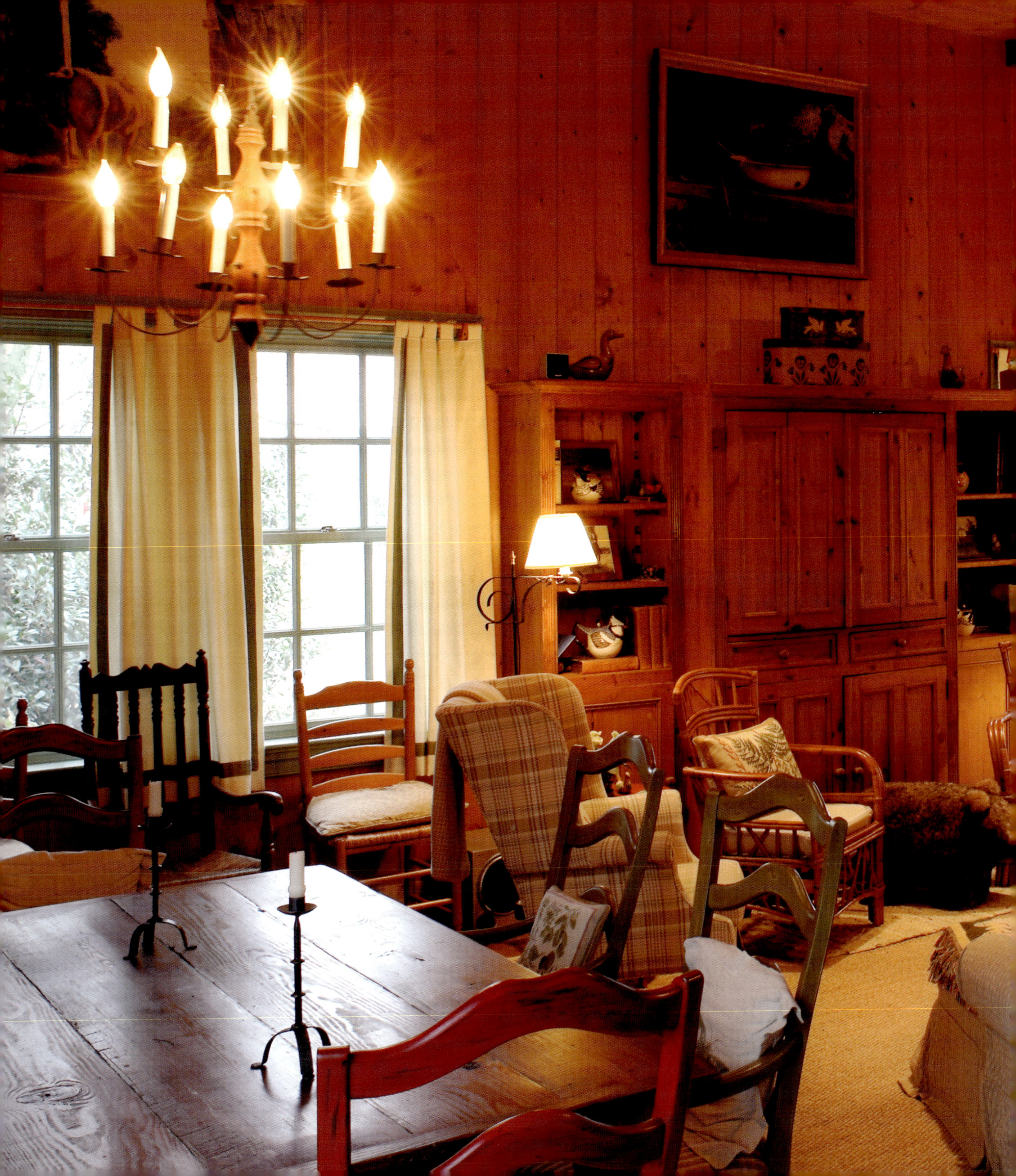

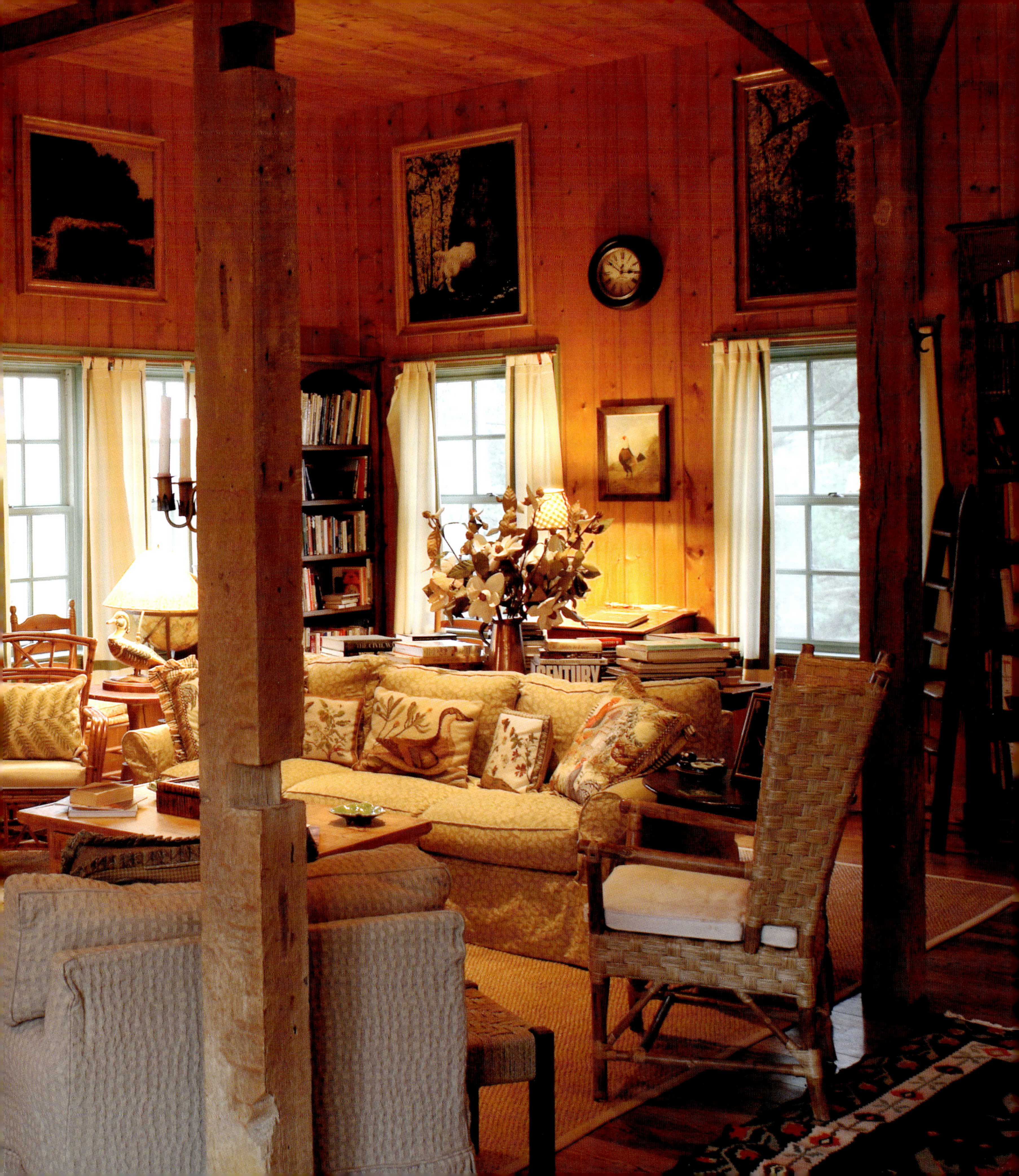
CENTURY

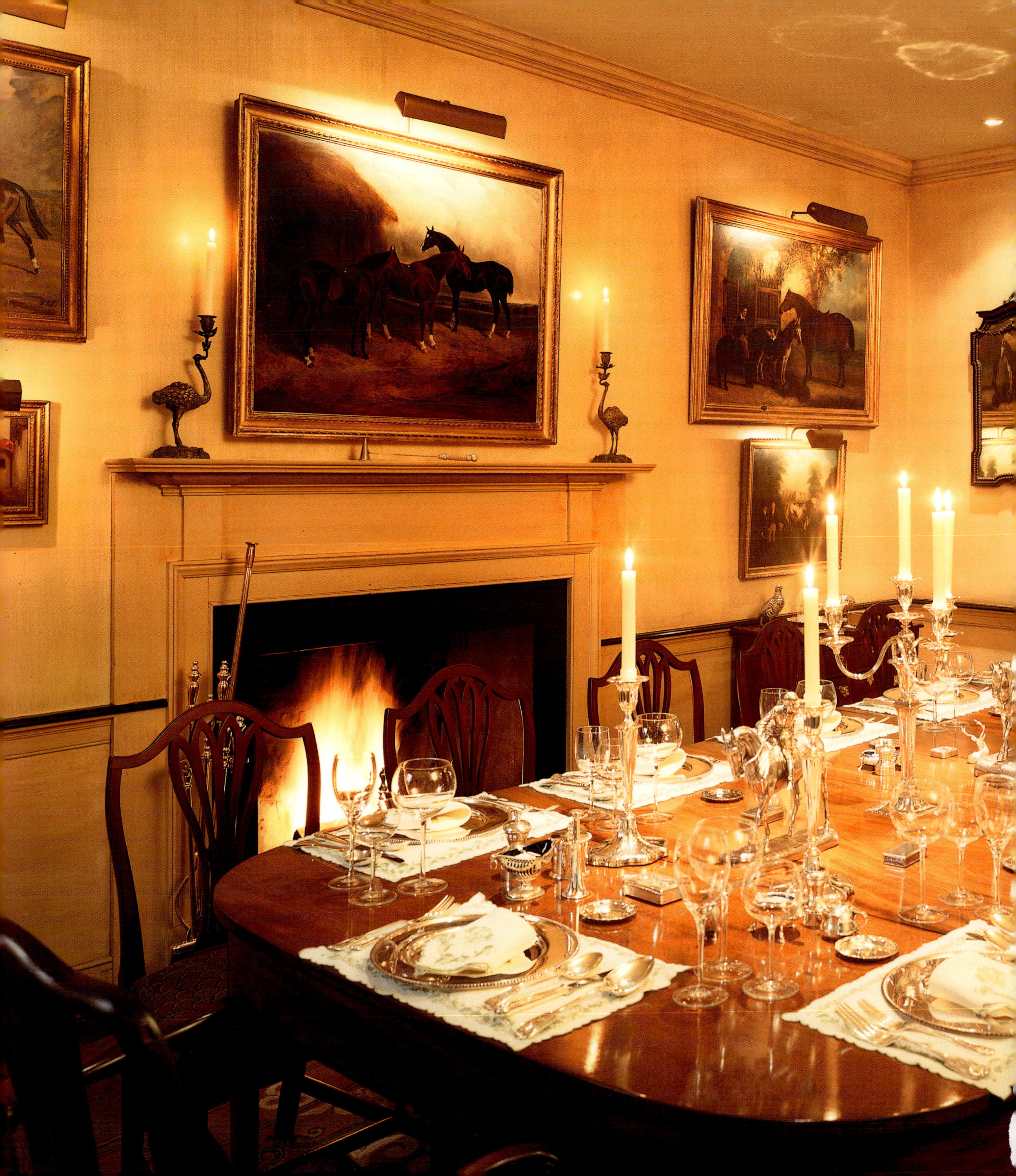

PRECEDING PAGES *A historic barn located a few hundred feet from the main house has been remodeled into an accommodating two-story guesthouse. With interiors altogether more casual than the main manor house, the large first-floor room (shown here) of the guesthouse is made intimate with mellow pine paneling and the exposed structural beams of the barn. The room is used as a family room with a dining area, a living room, and as a meeting room when the owner holds business engagements. The room features the rural art of Jamie Wyeth.*

LEFT AND ABOVE *Equestrian art adorns the walls of the formal dining room. The magnificent silver sparkles, adding extra festivity to any dinner party. Large silver equestrian sculptures as well as a collection of small silver engraved boxes are often placed decoratively on the table. The dining table and sideboard are both eighteenth-century Maryland pieces. Gone Away by Henry Alken (1785–1851) hangs above the silver tureen, a trophy for a win at Belmont.*

109

LEFT *The husband's study contains his library, many equestrian photos, and his many certificates of government appointment for land conservation.*

OPPOSITE *The master suite upstairs has furnishings that include a Georgian-style mahogany canopy bed with a hand-painted cornice, a French "bureau plat" of inlaid satinwood, and an eighteenth-century English inlaid walnut three-drawer dresser with an early-nineteenth-century gilt mirror above it. Delicate eighteenth-century English hand-painted porcelain vases complement the collection of figurines, also fine hand-painted English porcelain.*

FOLLOWING PAGES *The twenty-eight-stall training arn on the historic farm was built in the 1920s by then-owner William Ziegler, who was among those who moved from New York to foxhunt in Virginia. When the current owner's parents moved here in the 1970s they purchased three adjacent farms to increase the acreage for their extensive Thoroughbred breeding and training operation, which became one of the most successful in the country during that time. A three-quarter-mile racetrack is located immediately in front of the barn complex. A large portion of the farm that includes the barn and racetrack were sold to new owners in 2007.*

Later additions of a Palladian-style pavilion and outdoor pool and the evocative landscaping of the immediate backyard and pond have created a quiet southern ambiance for the historic estate. Famed New York designer Mario Buatta designed the interior of the magnificent drawing room in a decidedly "undecorated" elegant country style that complemented the rest of the house. The historic Virginia farmhouse has been transformed into a pleasant and elegant English country home. The wife, an Anglophile from her first visit to England in her teenage years and her husband, a born and bred Englishman, respect the traditions and rhythms of an English way of life at their Virginia estate, from fox hunting with the Orange County and Piedmont hunts, to elegant intimate dinners with friends, to gracious involvement in land conservation issues of the area.

Hickory Tree Farm, now a separate farm, was renowned throughout the 1970s and 1980s as one of the leading Thoroughbred farms in America. During those years the farm had an outstanding reputation for breeding and training home breds to become champion Thoroughbred race horses and field hunters and was a stable of stakes winners, champion studs, and pure bred foals. And now, since the sale of Hickory Tree Farm, the high pitch of the Thoroughbred operation is no longer part of their lives, but the social milieu of the owners, their love of open countryside and horse sports, and their philanthropic and environmental work continues unabated.

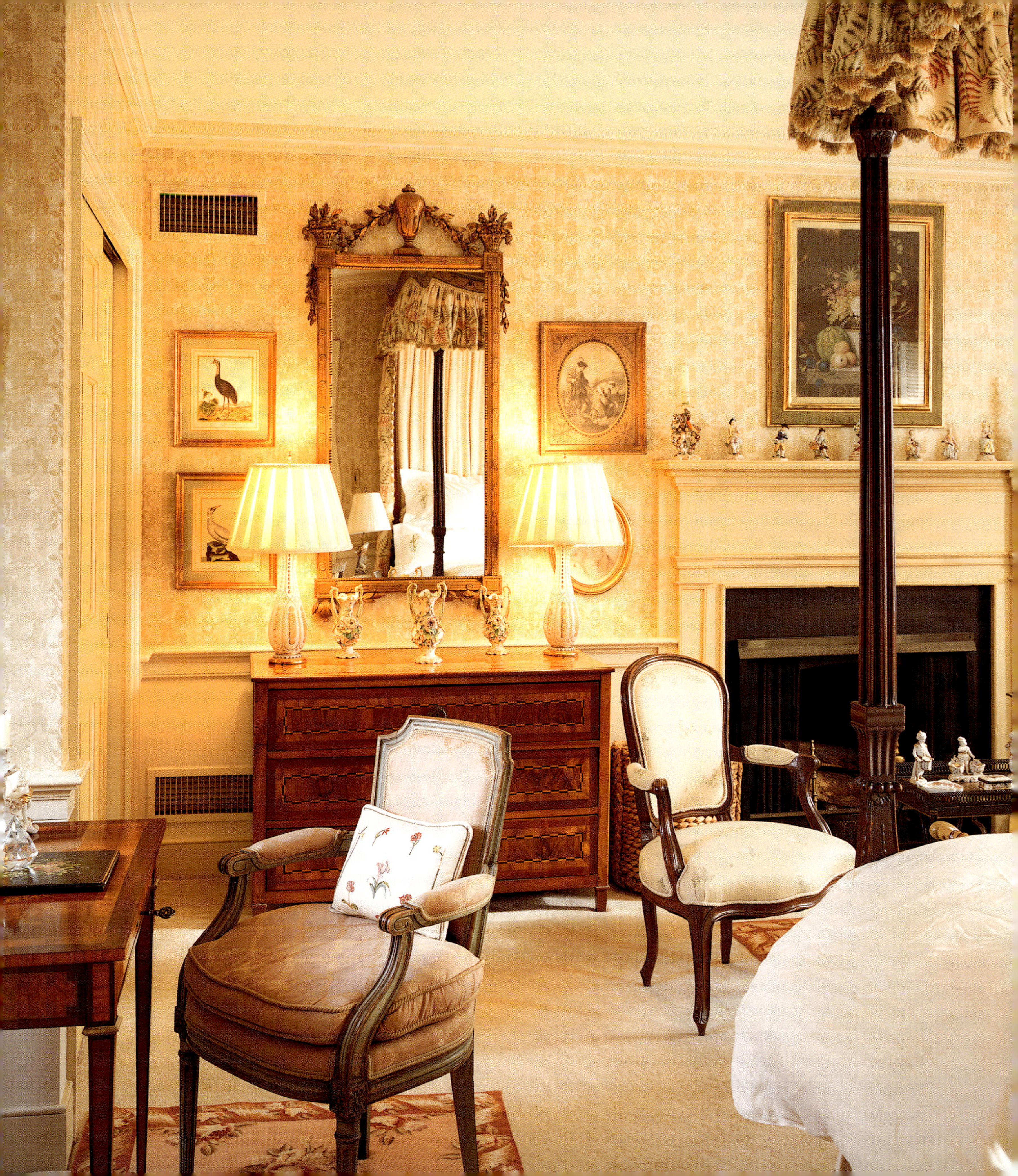

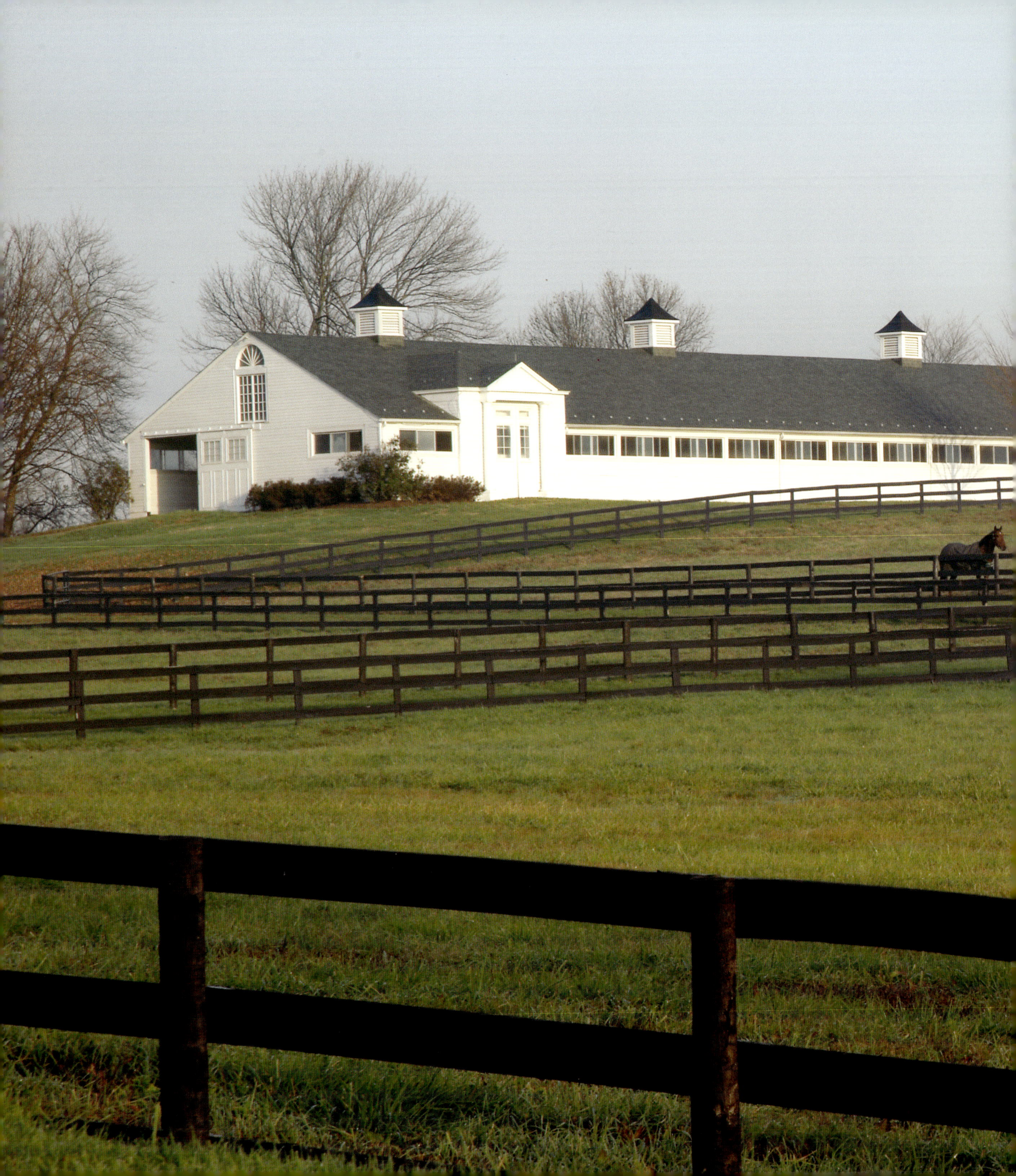

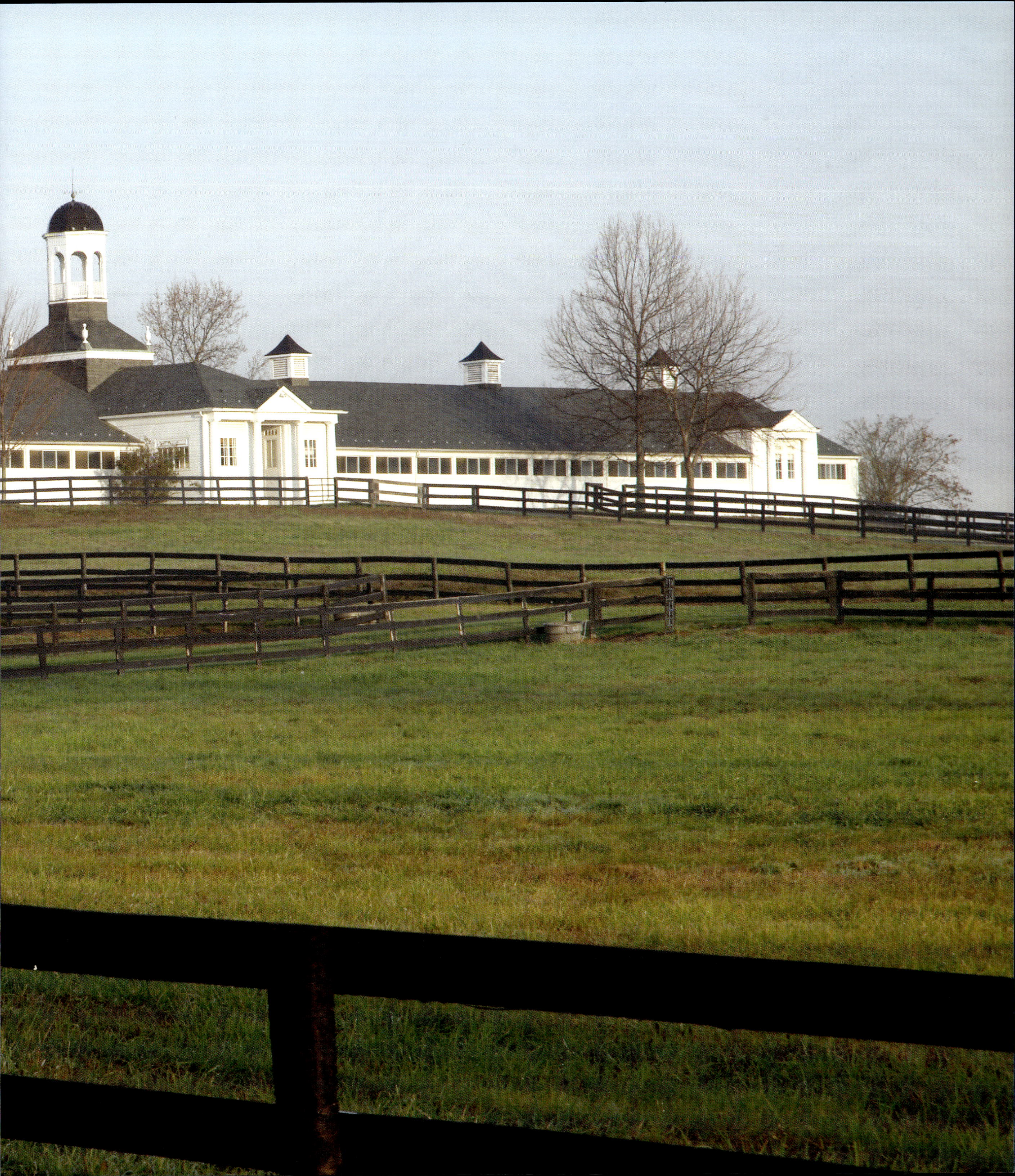

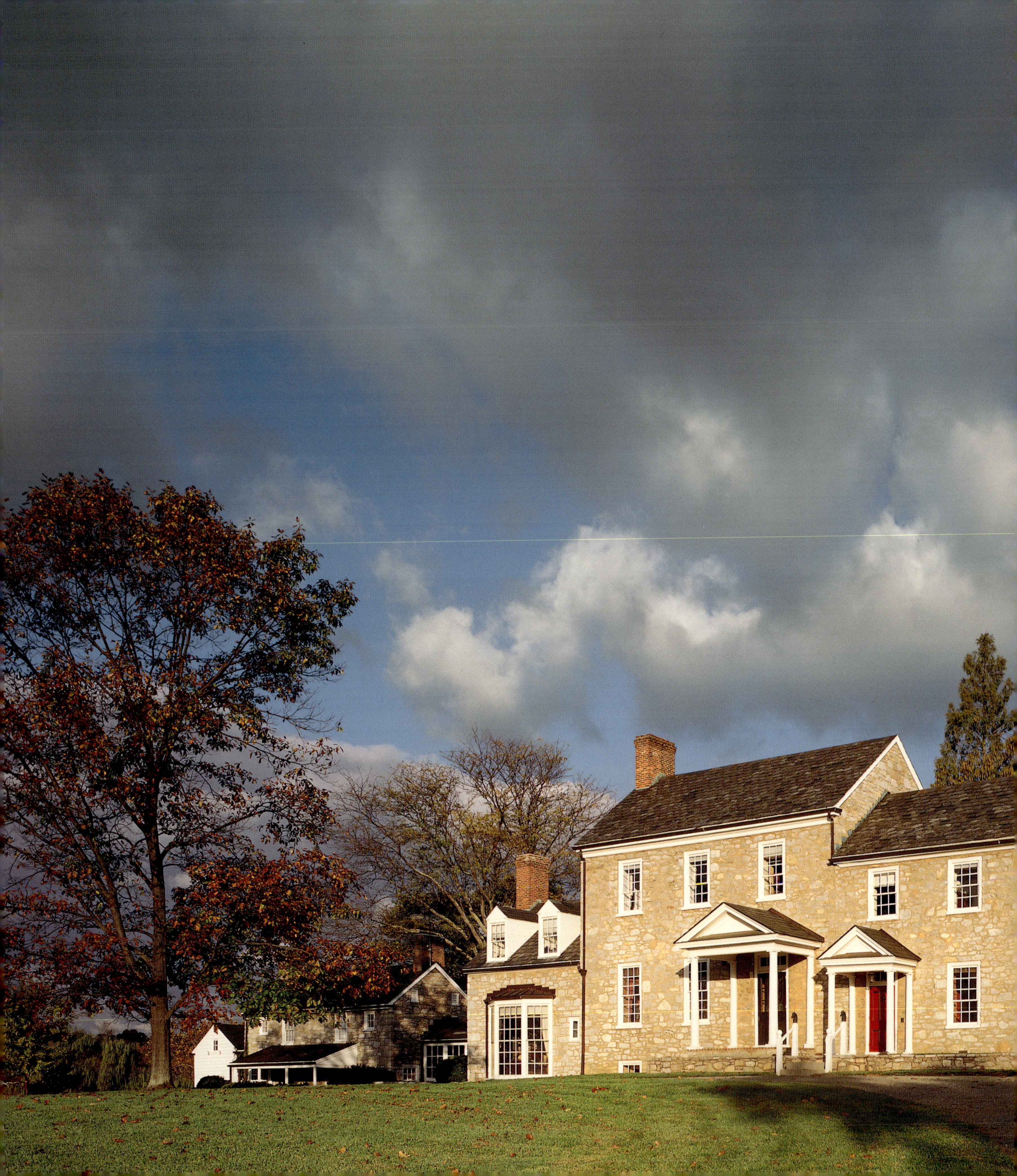

CHAPEL HILL FARM

Listed on the National and Virginia registers of historic places
Original dwelling, possibly c.1790
Main stone structure, 1826
Restoration, remodel, additions, 1941; George L. Howe, architect
Restoration, remodel, additions, 2002; Jack McCartney, architect

A passion for country life and dedication to conservation led the owners of Chapel Hill Farm to leave their home in Washington D.C. seven years ago to become full-time residents of Virginia. They now find themselves stewards of one of the most historically significant properties in Clarke County, whose house, outbuildings, and land are listed on the

LEFT *Chapel Hill, listed on the National and Virginia registers of historic places, is a historic house constructed of local limestone and a farm of nearly 500 acres. The property has been owned by members of many of the first families of Virginia, including the Fairfaxes, Carters, Lewises (Washington relatives), Byrds, and Burwells.*

ABOVE *An early-nineteenth-century pine door with an unusually fine fanlight and sidelight door-surrounds and original hardware was added during the 1941 remodel by then-owner William "Wild Bill" Donovan, who started the O.S.S., the precursor to the C.I.A.*

115

RIGHT *In the living room, interior designer Sarah Smith of New York has displayed export Chinese ginger jars and a bronze* Victory *on the early-twentieth-century Steinway with a glazed ceramic pot by Mark Hewitt of North Carolina below it. Various bronze sculptures throughout the room, an earthy palette, and historical references such as the heirloom family portrait give the large space warmth and vitality.*

FOLLOWING PAGES *The intimate dining room, with rich-toned terra-cotta color walls, is designed with country flair. Porcelain animals on the cherry dining table are Chinese export, while a collection of early nineteenth-century colored glass candlesticks line shelves, and clambroth dolphin-shaped candlesticks are displayed on the rare c.1820s Shenandoah Valley walnut sideboard. Mid-nineteenth-century family portraits include those of Mr. and Mrs. Ross of McVeightown, New York.*

National and Virginia registers of historic places. Their nearly 500 acres is managed for conservation of wildlife habitat and preservation of an endangered heritage breed of cattle.

Both of the owners continue their involvement in the Washington D.C. area. The wife is a vice regent and treasurer of the Mount Vernon Ladies' Association, America's oldest national preservation organization. Much of her time is spent supporting the preservation of Mount Vernon, its various outreach programs, and its new, state-of-the-art Ford Orientation Center and the Donald W. Reynolds Museum and Education Center. The husband has continuing business interests in D.C. that support his passion, stewardship of his land and the rescue of the rarest colonial American breed of cattle, the Randall Lineback. Through his reintroduction of prairie grasses and prescribed burns, he has created habitat for native wildlife that includes northern bobwhite, wild turkey, and songbirds. To restore and protect the watershed, the spring-fed stream of Chapel Run has been fenced off from cattle. A spring creek has been created for the introduction and support of the only population of wild brook trout in the Shenandoah Valley.

The house at Chapel Hill Farm is an elegant limestone structure, located in what was the frontier of European settlement in the early eighteenth century, the farthest reaches of the five-million-acre Proprietary of the Northern Neck. By 1781 ownership of 1,000 acres that would include Chapel Hill had been transferred to a nephew of George Washington, Fielding Lewis, Jr.,

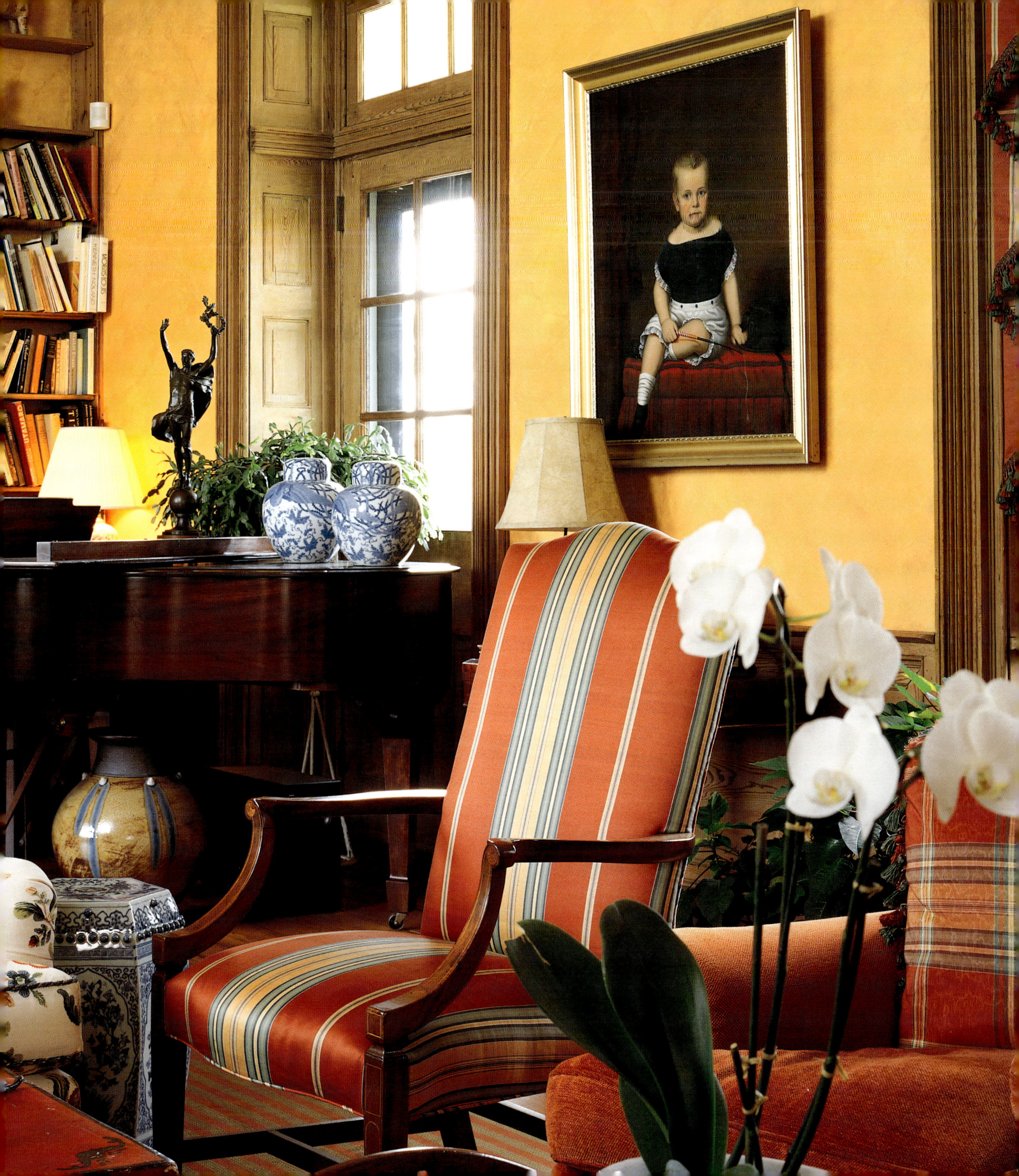

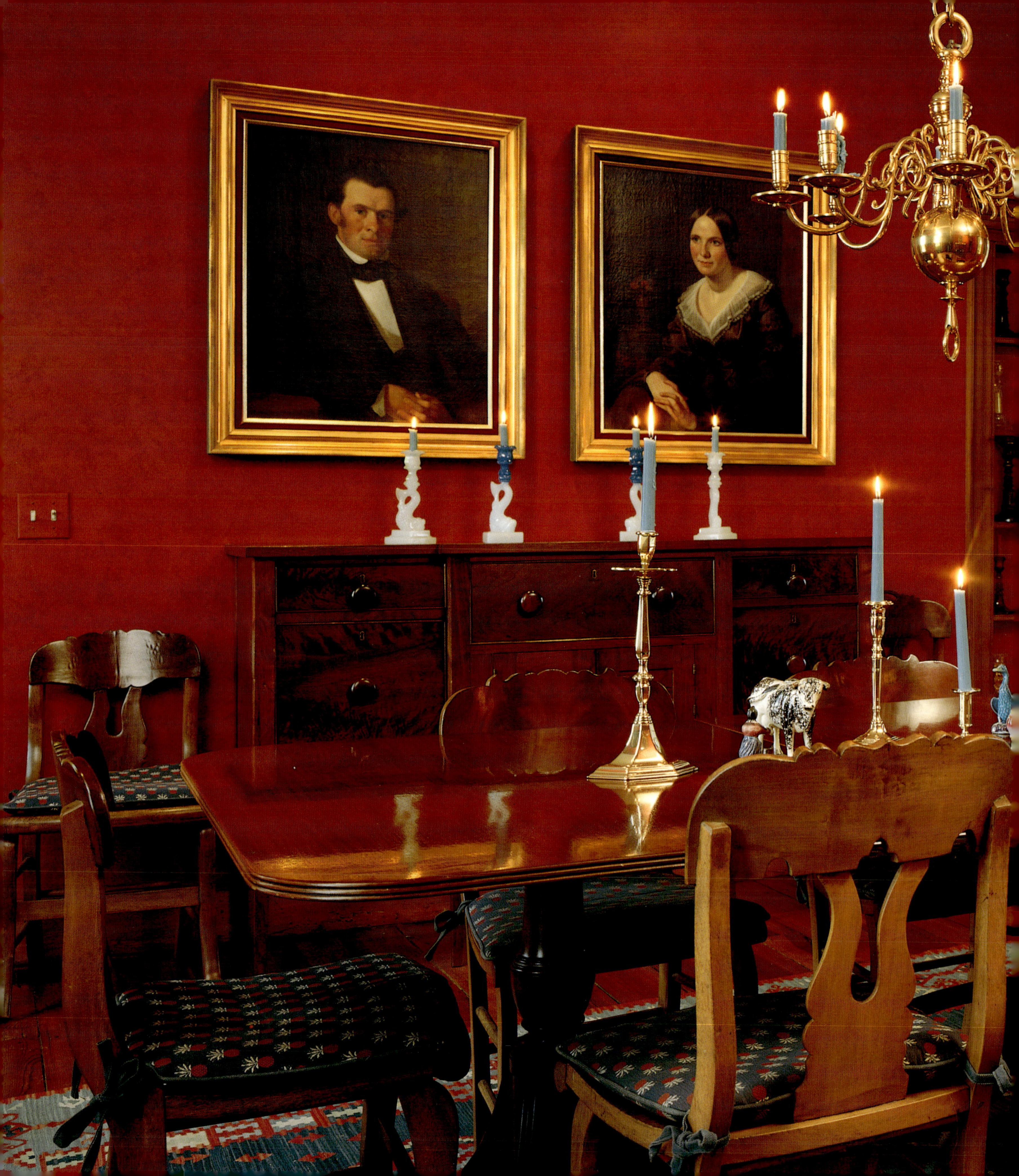

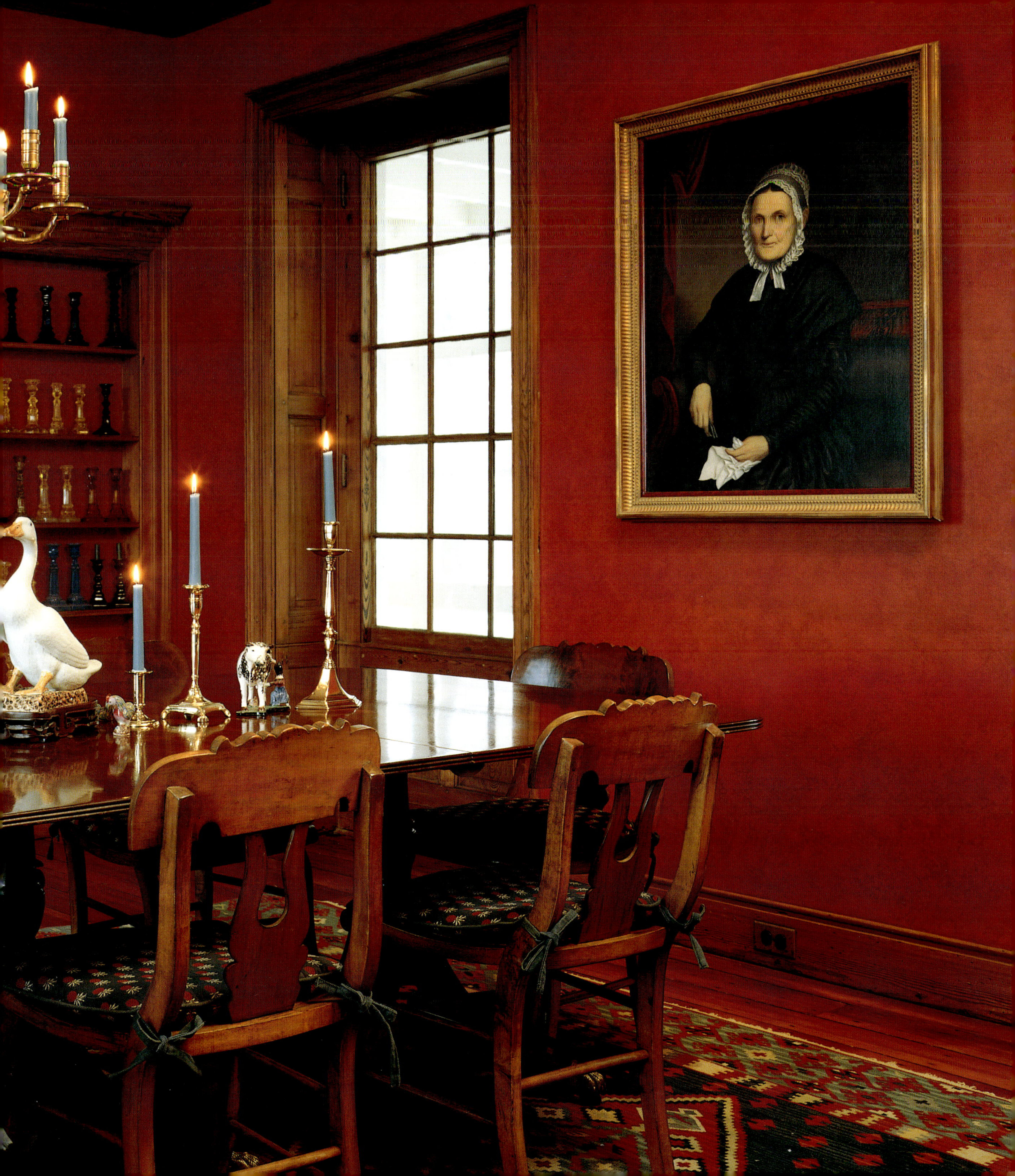

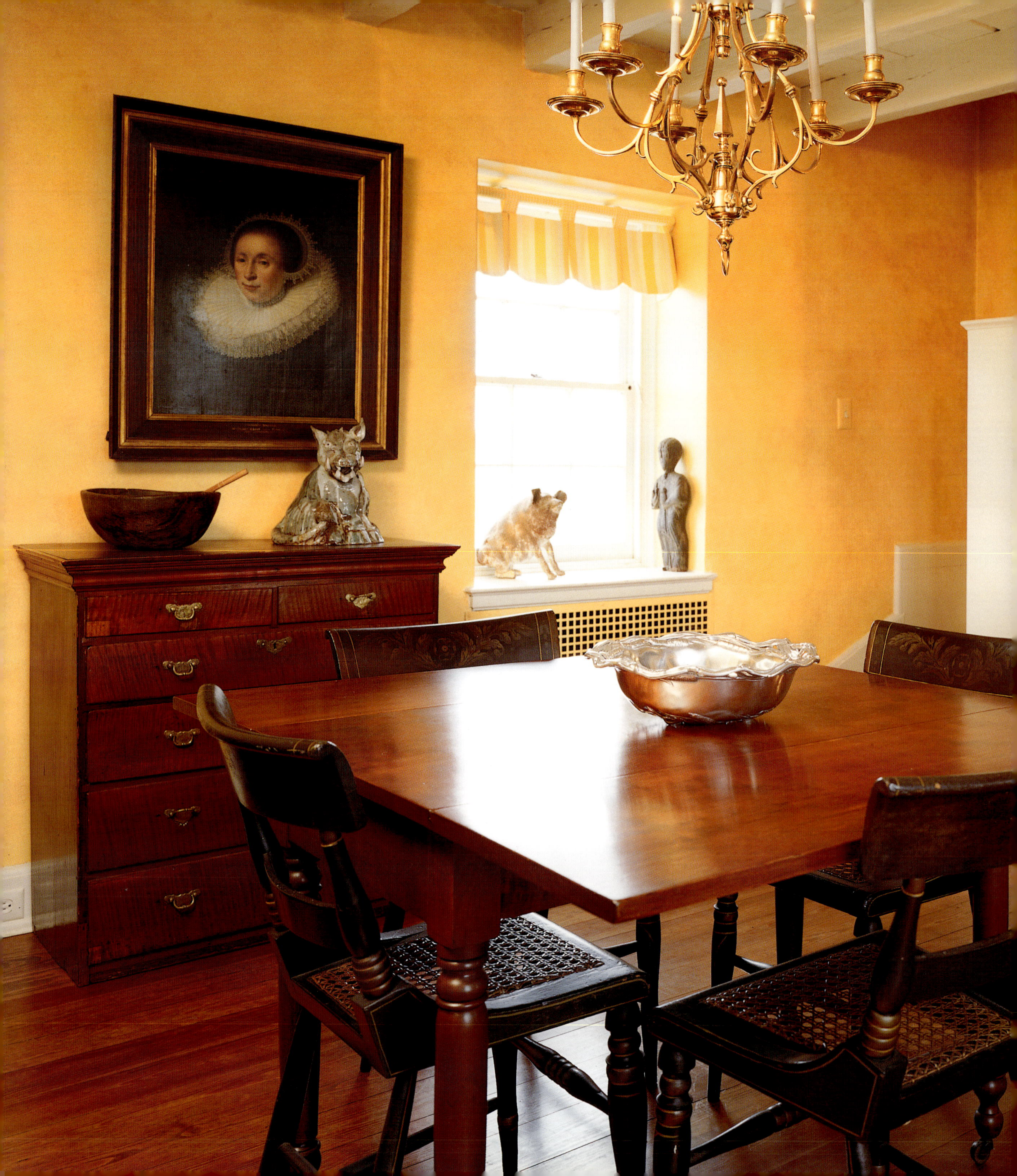

LEFT The oldest portion of the extended stone farmhouse was possibly once a late-eighteenth-century cottage. It is used today as a guest suite with its dining room on the first floor. Furnishings include a seventeenth-century Dutch portrait and Dutch brass chandelier, a set of nineteenth-century hand-painted and stenciled Hitchcock chairs, and a Connecticut cherry drop-leaf table.

ABOVE The single-story limestone breezeway that connects the original stone cottage to the larger fieldstone house also serves as a conservatory in the winter. The useful space contains iron lanterns hung from the open-beam wood ceiling, a slate floor, and a school-of-Tiffany stained glass window from Essex, Massachusetts.

On the northwest side of the house a large raised terrace patio that is paved with slate serves as the main outdoor entertaining area, used for barbecues, family gatherings, and hunt breakfasts. From the large patio a series of gardens, smaller private patio areas, and a reflecting pool cascade along the back of the farmhouse. A 1918 bronze sculpture by Harriet Frishmuth entitled Play Days *is featured in the pond.*

who is believed to have lived on the land. By 1826 Dr. Charles Byrd had constructed a small cottage and two attached impressive two-story limestone houses. In that year these structures and 168 acres were sold to Philip Burwell, son of Col. Nathaniel Burwell of Carter Hall. Many of these early settlers, including Carters, Lewises, Byrds, Randolphs, and Burwells, lie in the cemetery at Old Chapel, for which Chapel Hill is named.

In 1938 General William "Wild Bill" Donovan, founder of the Office of Strategic Services, precursor of the C.I.A., purchased Chapel Hill and hired Washington D.C. architect George L. Howe for an extensive remodeling that included integration of the historic houses and additions in the Colonial Revival style. The farm was also increased to nearly 500 acres.

In 2000 the current owners undertook a complete restoration of the historic house and outbuildings that maintained the integrity of the original Federal style and Howe's Colonial Revival remodel. They share their historic property with the community and neighbors, seasonally hosting the Blue Ridge Hunt and the Nantucket-Treweryn Beagles.

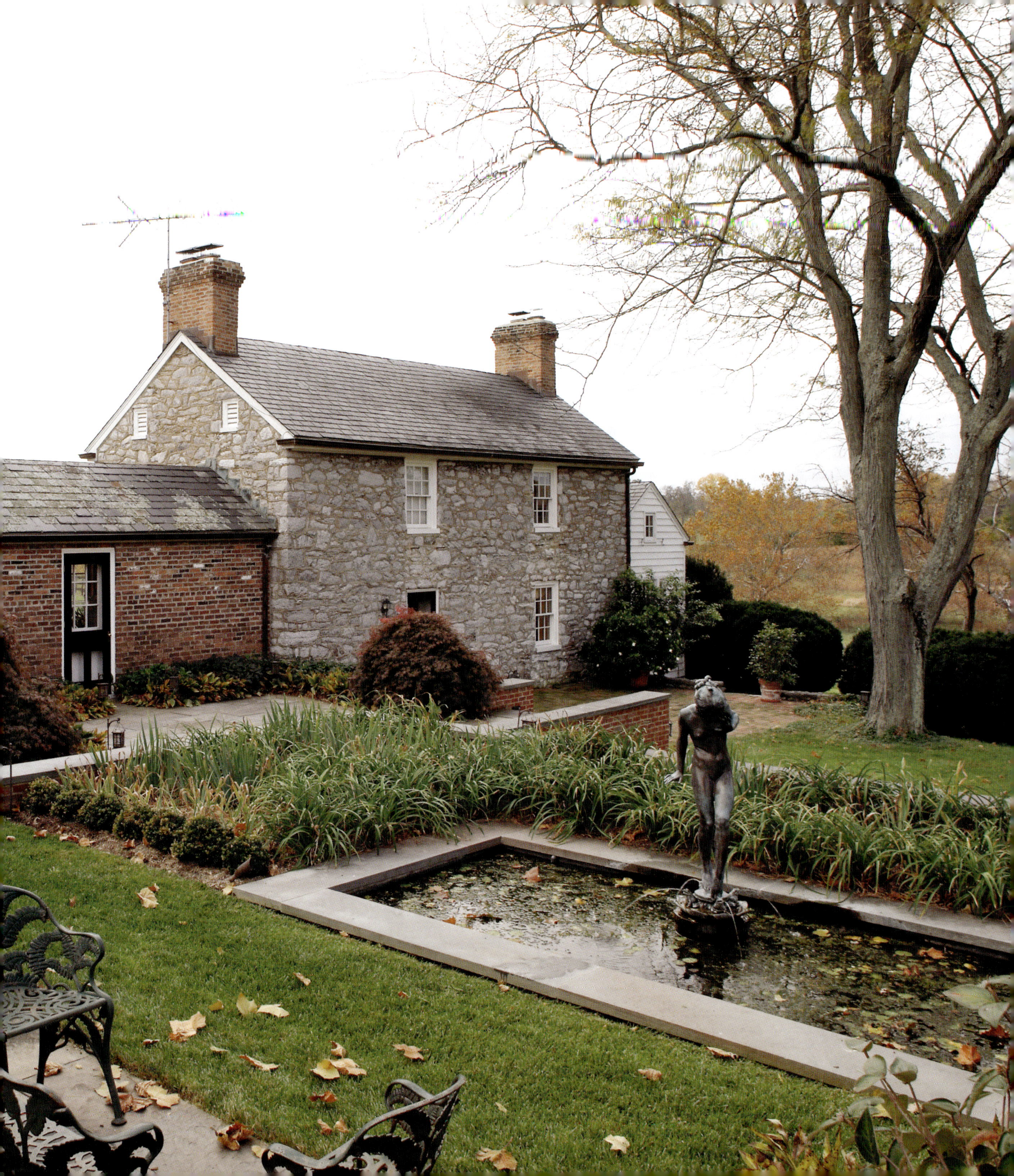

LLEWELLYN

Residence of Dr. Frank H. Reuling, Jr., and Tressa Borland Reuling
House, c.1825; remodel and north wing & west porch additions, 1930s
South wing addition, 1975; Dr. Frank H. Reuling, owner
South wing remodel, 2003; Erroll Abel, architect
Spring house, pre-1829
Summer kitchen, pre-1829; remodeled into guest house, 1930s
Equipment barn, 1986

In the early nineteenth century Llewellyn faced one of Clarke County's well-traveled country roads that has long-since been abandoned and integrated into the landscape, leaving the farm to rest in the tranquil midst of pastures and gentle hills that overlook a small valley and afford a superb view of the Blue Ridge Mountains. The rural atmosphere that still prevails in Clarke County is strongly felt on this 315-acre working cattle farm. The owners, Dr. Frank H. Reuling, Jr., and his wife Tressa Borland Reuling, who moved to the area over thirty years ago for a life in the country and Frank's passion for polo and foxhunting, have since given up these sports and now ride more leisurely. Another worthwhile pursuit for the Reulings has been the gardens at Llewellyn, which have been opened for tours during Virginia Garden Week. The gardens surrounding the house combine a plethora of flowering plants, a sweeping lawn that complements the east facade of the house, and majestic trees throughout the grounds that have matured through the decades. Far off and up a hill a stone was placed by The Descendants of George Washington in dedication to the memory of Warner Washington.

The large manor house was built of local fieldstone, with a plan similar to the plantation houses of Virginia's Tidewater region. Members of the dynastic first families of Virginia such as the Byrds, Washingtons, and Burwells settled in Clarke County in the latter part of the eighteenth century. The stately houses built by these families contained wide central hallways flanked by two-over-two rooms. One of the most beautiful of

RIGHT *The west facade. The original central portion of the large fieldstone manor house of Llewellyn, in Clarke County, is believed to have been built between 1825 and 1829 by Warner Washington II, the grandson of George Washington's uncle John. In the 1930s and 1970s, the historic house was extended with additions to the north and south.*

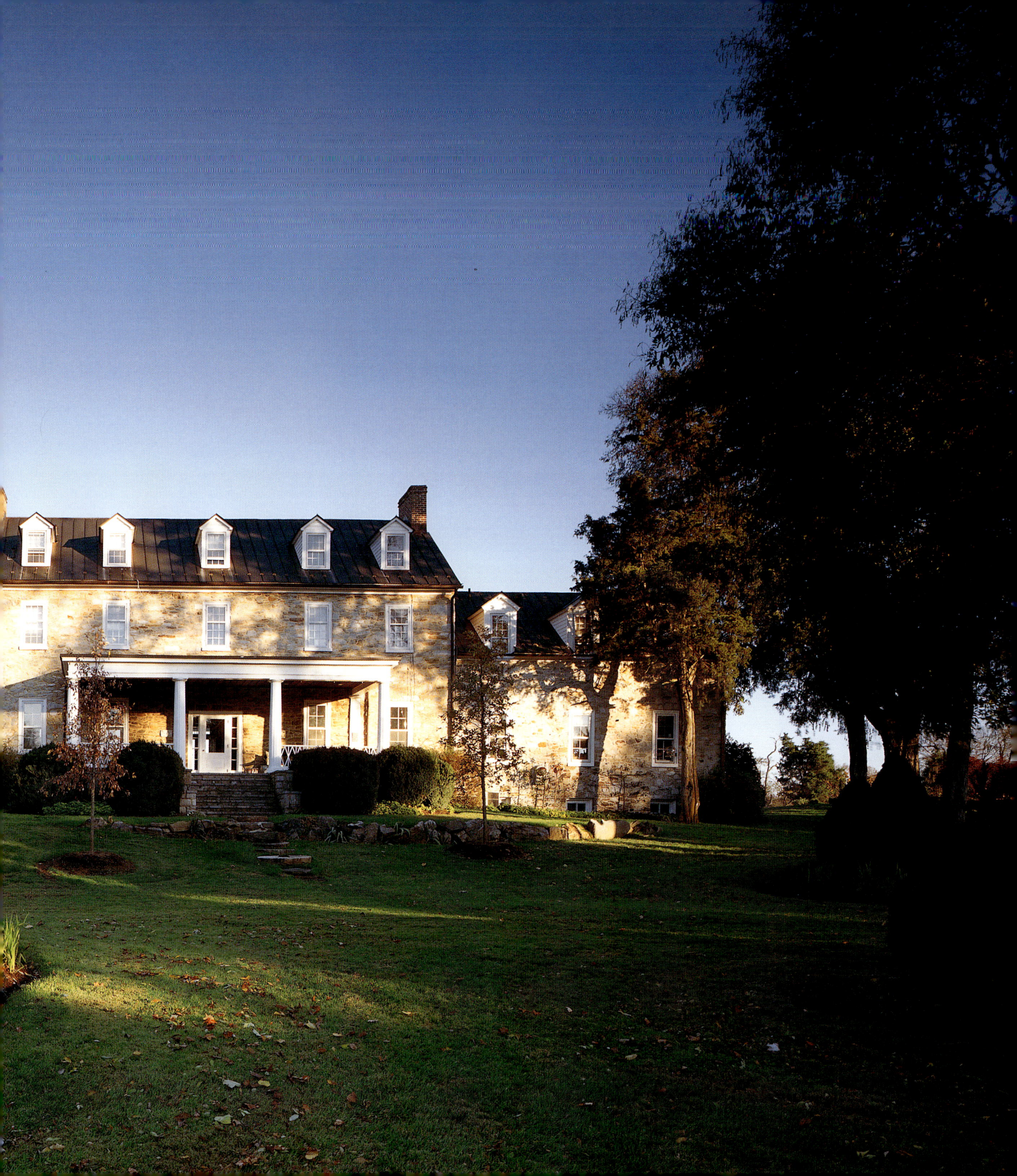

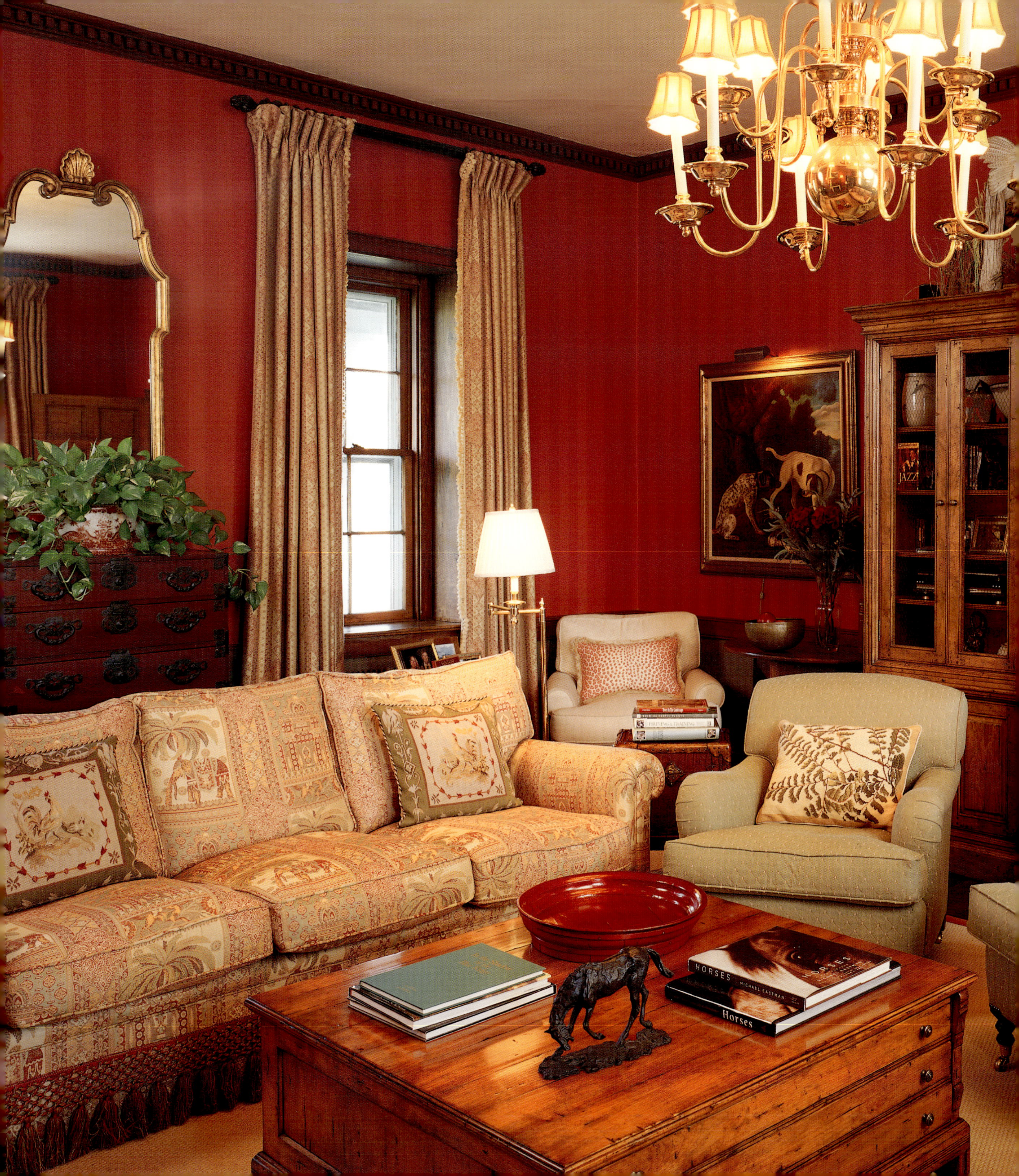

HORSES
MICHAEL EASTMAN
Horses
JAZZ

LEFT AND ABOVE *The plan of the c.1825 house is similar to that of a Tidewater area plantation house, with a wide central hallway and two-over-two rooms on either side. Large doors at either end of Llewellyn's spacious hall provide ventilation and light. The large rooms of the first floor of the original house are now the family room (left) and the formal dining room (next page). The family room's design is that of an elegant country house, with yew wood furnishings that include a large breakfront and coffee table.*

FOLLOWING PAGES *A set of carved Georgian-style chairs in the formal dining room seat fourteen at the three-leaf mahogany table. Reuling family pieces include the silver from Winchester displayed on the Midwestern hutch. The grandfather clock from Georgia is also a family piece. The yellow pine woodwork and mantel that have been oiled and waxed to a fine patina are original to the house. The mantel's design, which possibly originated in the Shenandoah Valley, is that found in numerous early nineteenth-century houses of well-to-do northern Virginia Piedmont farmers. Sporting art includes the nineteenth-century English painting over the mantel.*

these stone manor houses is Llewellyn, which is believed to have been built between 1825 and 1829 by Warner Washington II, the son of George's first cousin Warner Washginton I. The stone springhouse not far from the front door and the summer kitchen building are probably from an earlier period.

In 1818 Warner Washington II purchased the property of Llewellyn from Lawrence Lewis, who had inherited the farm from his father Col. Fielding Lewis. At that time Washington resided at Clifton, a nearby farm, and had previously lived at Audley, also close by, which he had built. Audley was traded to Lewis in exchange for Llewellyn and $50,000 cash. Washington and his family lived at Llewellyn from 1825 to 1829.

127

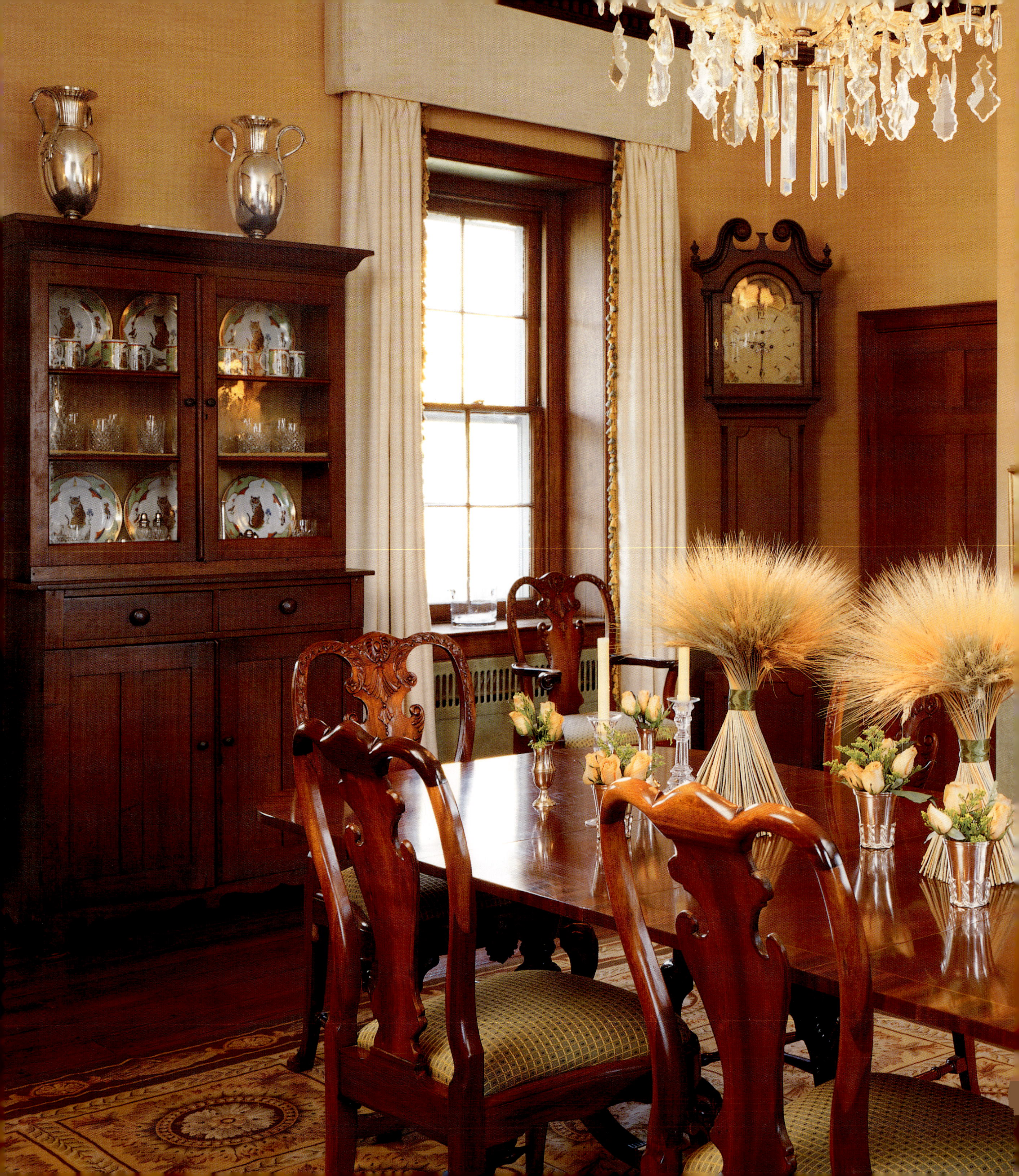

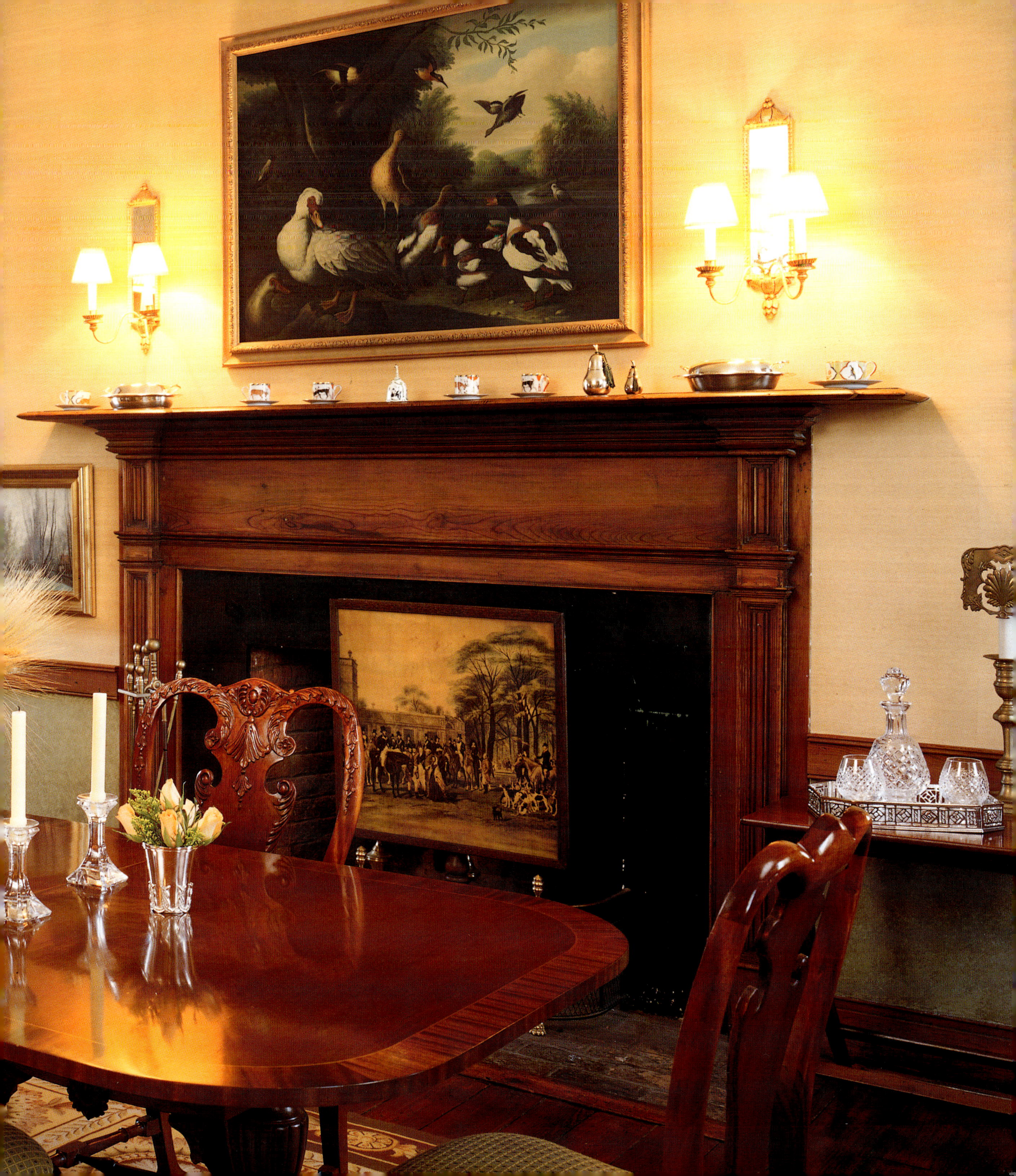

ABOVE AND RIGHT *The 2003 remodel of the south wing created a large country kitchen that opens to an inviting family room space with fieldstone fireplace. The addition has "found" pine flooring from an early-nineteenth-century barn.*

FOLLOWING PAGES *A view from the spacious porch on the west facade is of a lush green landscape and nearby countryside. Manicured gardens share lawn space with mature towering trees amidst the hills' natural fieldstone outcroppings. The stone springhouse faces what was once a busy country road (road is not visible).*

The manor house and farm have evolved and changed through the past two centuries yet have remained representative of the exquisite rural beauty of Clarke County. In 1833 the Washington family sold Llewellyn to John Kerfoot, whose family owned the farm until the 1970s. Llewellyn withstood the devastation that the Civil War brought to the area and was unharmed while other farms in the area were destroyed. In the 1930s Alfred M. Kerfoot modified the house with the addition of a two-story stone wing to the north of the original section. Dr. Frank H. Reuling purchased Llewellyn in 1975. He later consulted with William Kerfoot, an architect who had grown up at the farm and loved the house, about a new south wing. Following Kerfoot's advice, Reuling built the south wing to match the north wing. In 2003 the Reulings hired architect and interior designer Erroll Adels of Middleburg to remodel the south wing into a kitchen and family room space that is accommodating and accessible. Once again Llewellyn has changed yet its architectural integrity remains.

130 LLEWELLYN

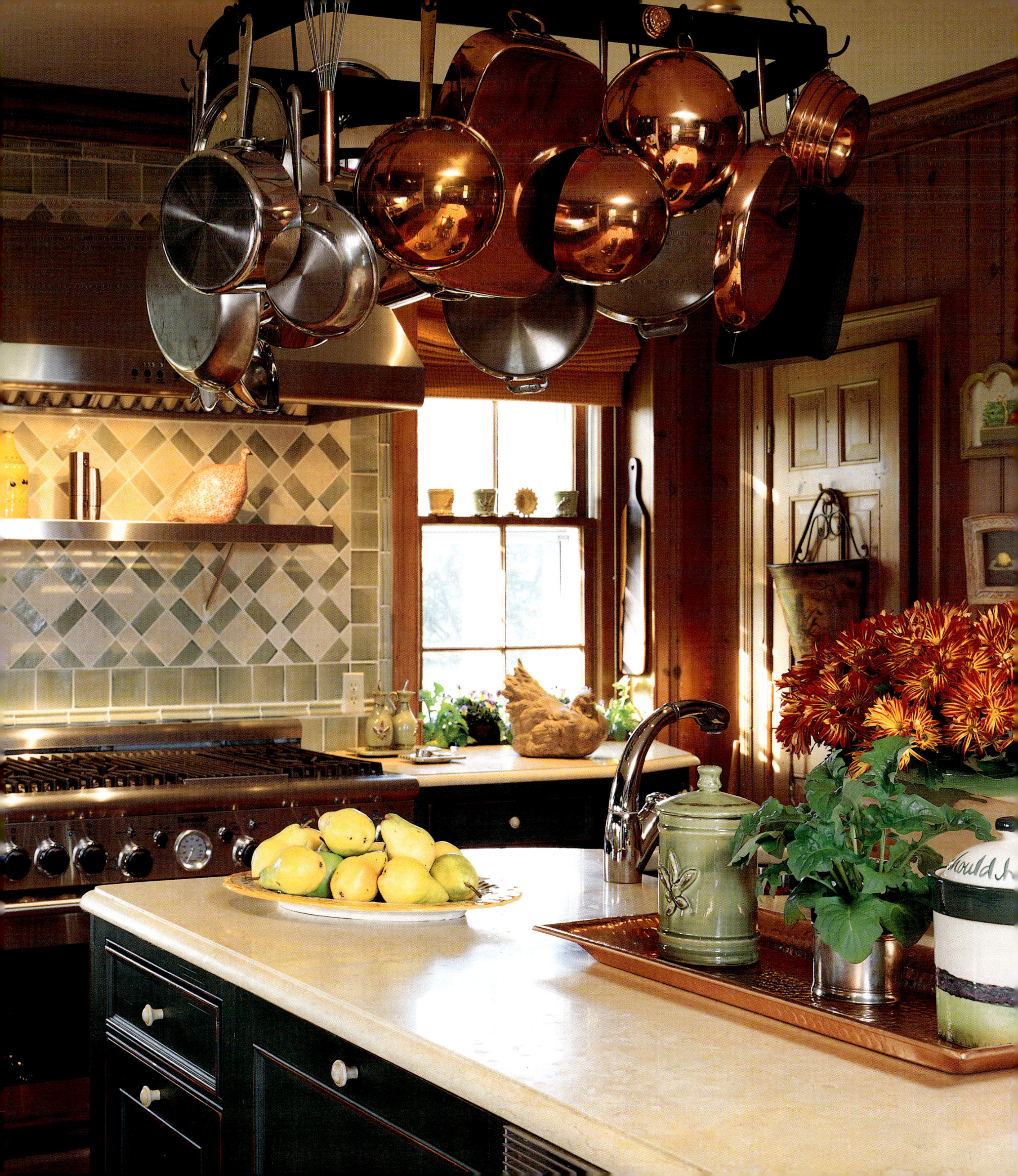

132   LLEWELLYN

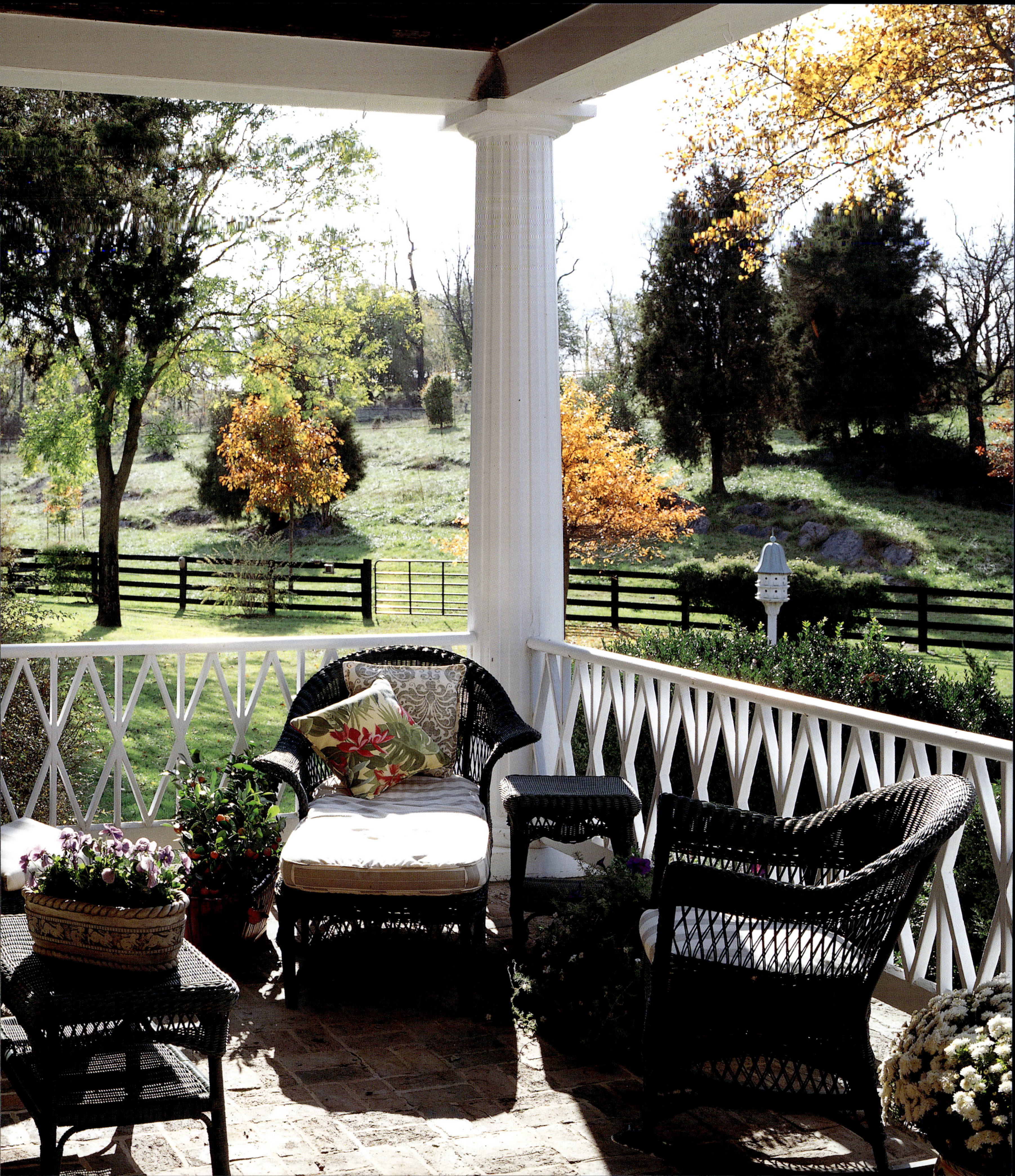

OVOKA FARM

Probable home site prior to 1768
Log house foundation under current kitchen, possibly late 1700s
Main house, c.1830s; additions, c.1860s; remodel, 1930s and 1950s; restoration and remodel, 2004
Two-room stone building in backyard, smoke house (now used as garden tool house), possibly late 1700s or c.1820–1840
Carriage house, barn and silos, c1820–1840
Log house/mill house, possibly pre-1830
Barn remodel and new stable, 2006

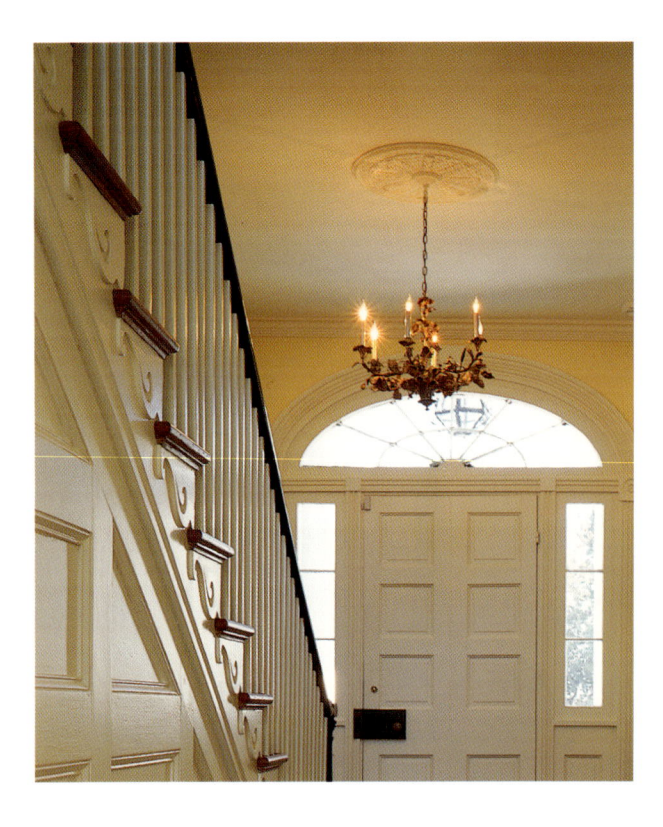

Ovoka is an elegant Virginia farm nestled against a hillside in the Valley of the Crooked Run. Its white stuccoed main house, with two-story painted wood columns that grace the front portico, is surrounded by a mannered array of auxiliary farm buildings that includes the original white weatherboard carriage house, a stable and barn complex that rests on a hill above the house, and a two-room stone building

The main manor house and the ancillary buildings at Ovoka Farm have undergone an extensive restoration and renovation that was completed in 2006. The historic house features a c.1830 double front door with fanlight overhead and a portico with two-story columns added in the 1840s. Much of the interior has finely crafted Federal-style details in the original woodwork, doors, windows, and pine floors that have been restored to a beautiful condition.

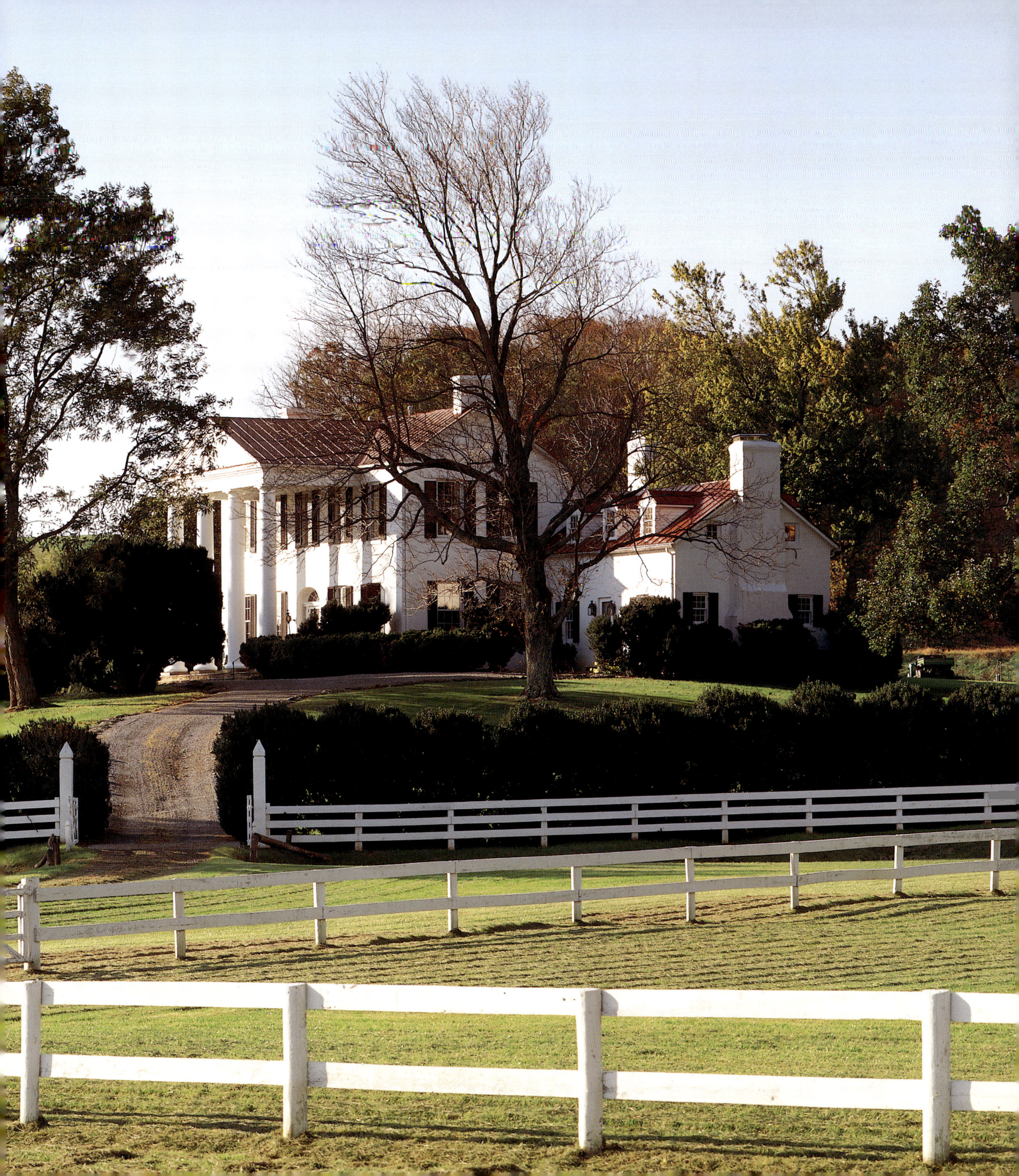

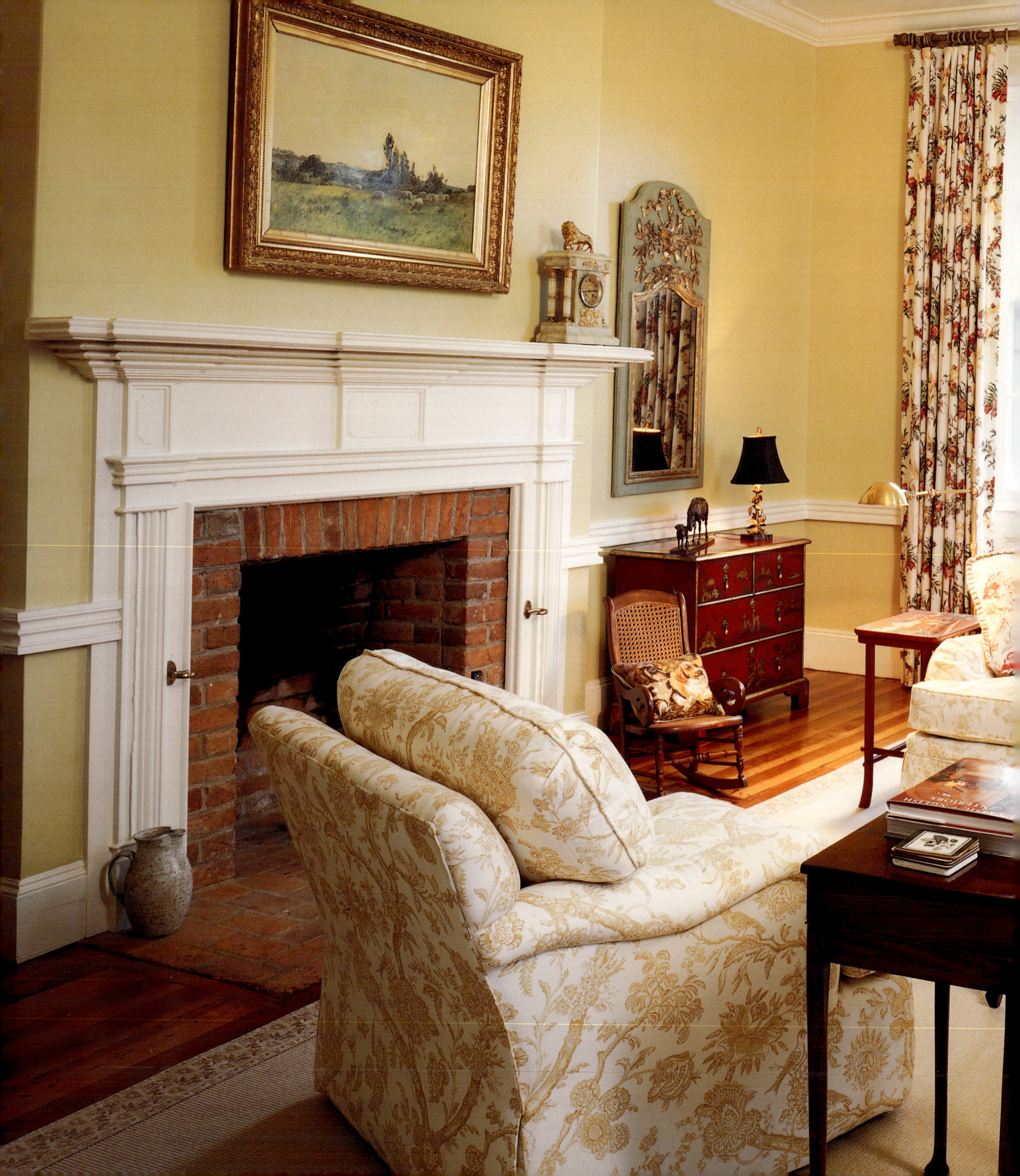

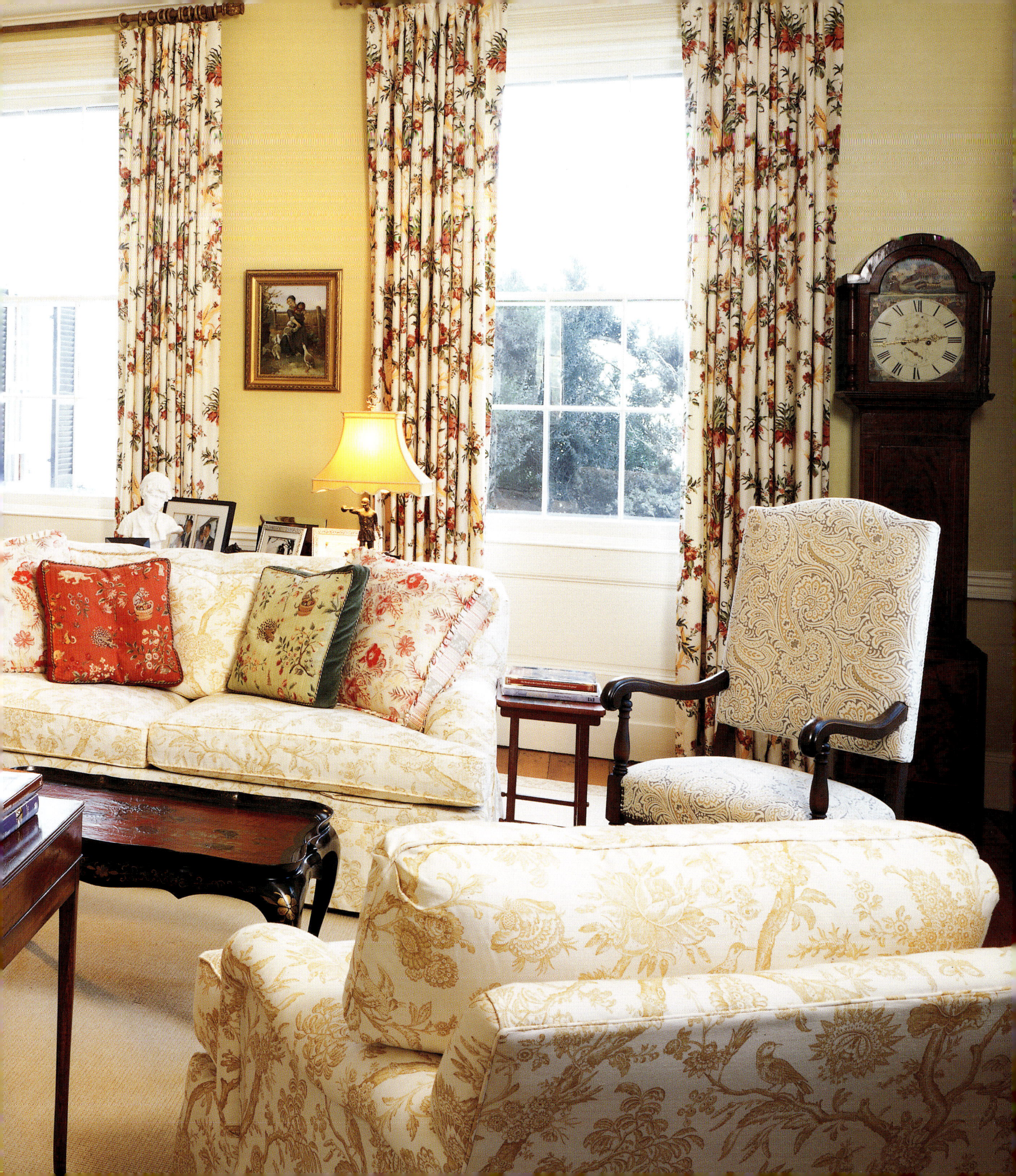

PRECEDING PAGES *The living room has a light feeling, enhanced by its eleven-foot-high ceiling and the subtle color of custom-blended paint used on the walls. Fine antiques fill the welcoming space, including: a nineteenth-century French marble and bronze clock on the original mantel, over which hangs an early twentieth-century French landscape; an eighteenth-century French Trameau mirror over an eighteenth-century English Chinoiserie walnut dresser; a late eighteenth-century lacquered coffee table; and a late eighteenth-century English grandfather clock of mahogany with walnut inlay.*

LEFT *The library walls are covered with a custom-blended paint color that the owner likens to burnt tobacco. Its warm tone complements the original oiled and waxed pine woodwork of the over-mantel and mantel. The mantel's identifiable Virginia design is most likely that of a nineteenth-century carver in the Shenandoah Valley and found in nineteenth-century rooms throughout northern Virginia's Piedmont.*

OPPOSITE *The kitchen was built over the oldest portion of the house, which possibly dates to the late eighteenth century. The existing kitchen was a c.1930s two-story room that was opened up by the new owners, who removed the second story but kept the original windows, added hand-adzed oak beams for structural soundness, and kept the brick load-bearing walls in back of the AGA range. The country kitchen has an English farm sink, a countertop of tiled soapstone, slate flooring, and a French farm table.*

in the backyard. The idyllic farm also includes five spring-fed ponds, riding trails, a historic family cemetery, and the site of the first trotting track in America.

The current owners, who purchased the farm in 2003 and completed a restoration and remodel of the property in 2006, came to Virginia from New England attracted by a climate that was milder and more conducive to year-round enjoyment of outdoor sports. The mountains and hills surrounding the farm provide the husband with many contemplative hikes and a stable of fit horses keeps the wife, an avid equestrian, active on the farm's trails and riding ring as well as foxhunting with local hunt clubs. The couple's personal interest is not only in their historic farm but extends to the natural beauty and cultural heritage of western Fauquier County and northern Virginia. They have put their farm into a conservation easement, have further helped to protect another 2,000 acres in easement surrounding it, and promote the preservation of land and historic resources in the area through their affiliation with the Piedmont Environmental Council.

Ovoka is not only one of the most picturesque and complete farms in Fauquier County, but has great historic significance. It was part of the large George Carter land patent of 1731 that George Washington surveyed in 1769. Washington's familiarity with this area of northern Virginia and his eye for good land led him to purchase 2,712 acres of the Carter land that lay directly across the valley from Ovoka, that he held throughout his lifetime and leased to tenant farmers. Washington

138 OVOKA FARM

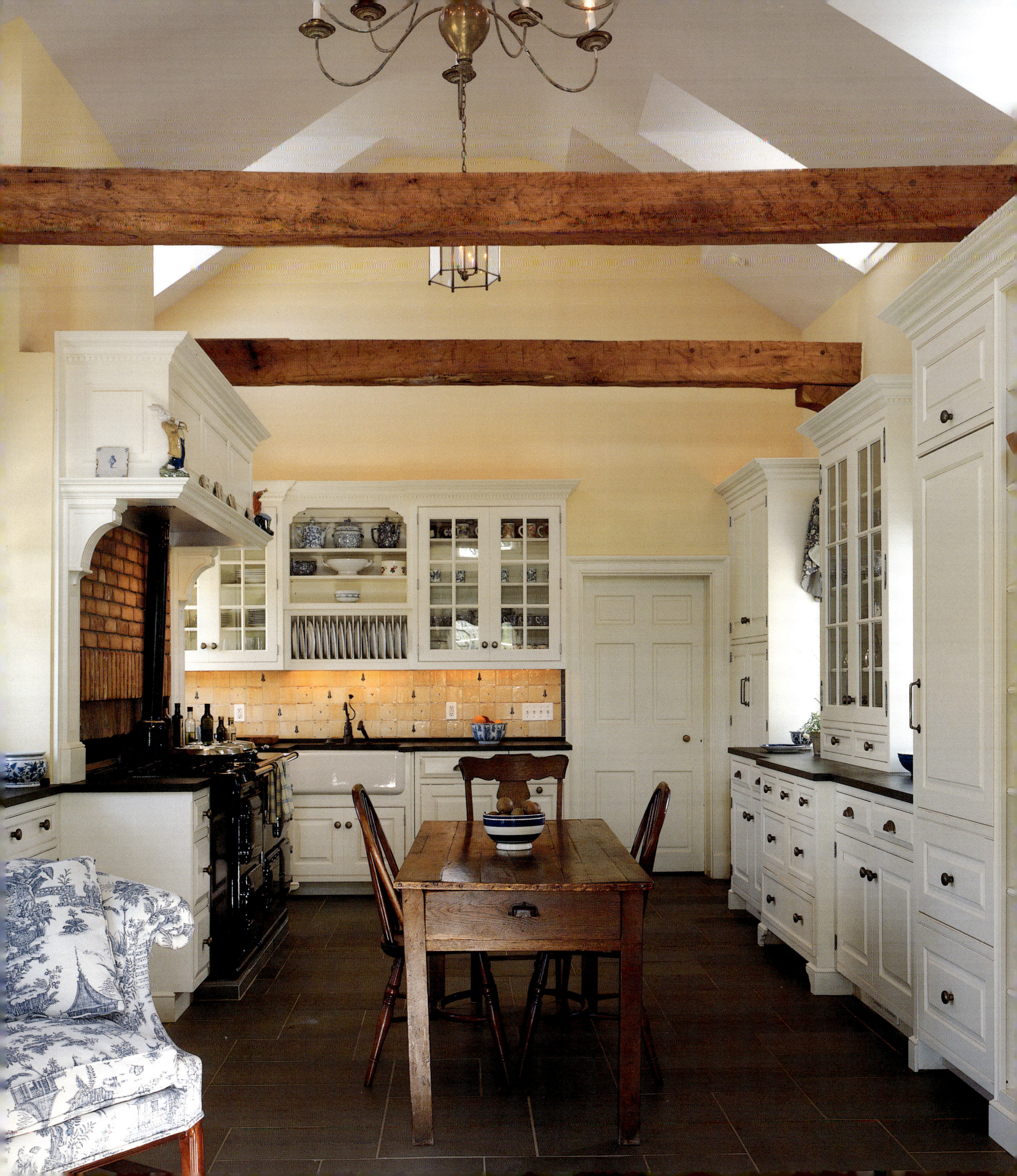

TOP *The early-nineteenth-century weatherboard carriage house has a metal roof and is painted bright white. Its hand-wrought iron hinges and hardware are original.*

ABOVE *A two-room building in the immediate backyard was constructed of fieldstone with a slate roof. Its center chimney serves both rooms. The structure, with its timeworn materials, its human scale, and its mystery, may have been an early-nineteenth-century dwelling or an office.*

RIGHT *A barn complex on a hillside overlooking the house and ponds is picturesque as well as functional. In 2006 the original post and beam barn beside the original silos was remodeled and a new stable was built. The stable's design has an unusually wide center aisle that allows for better air circulation.*

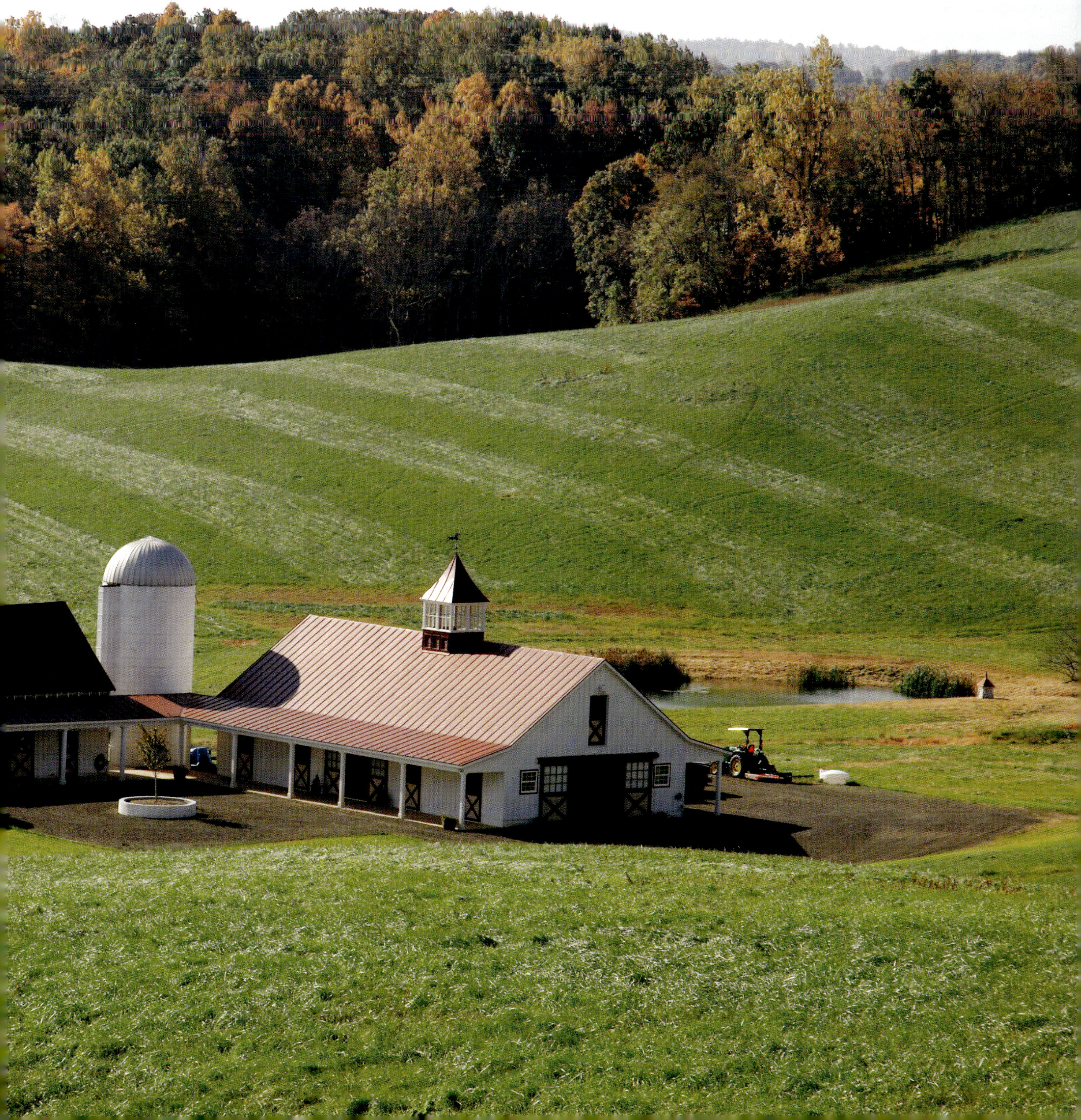

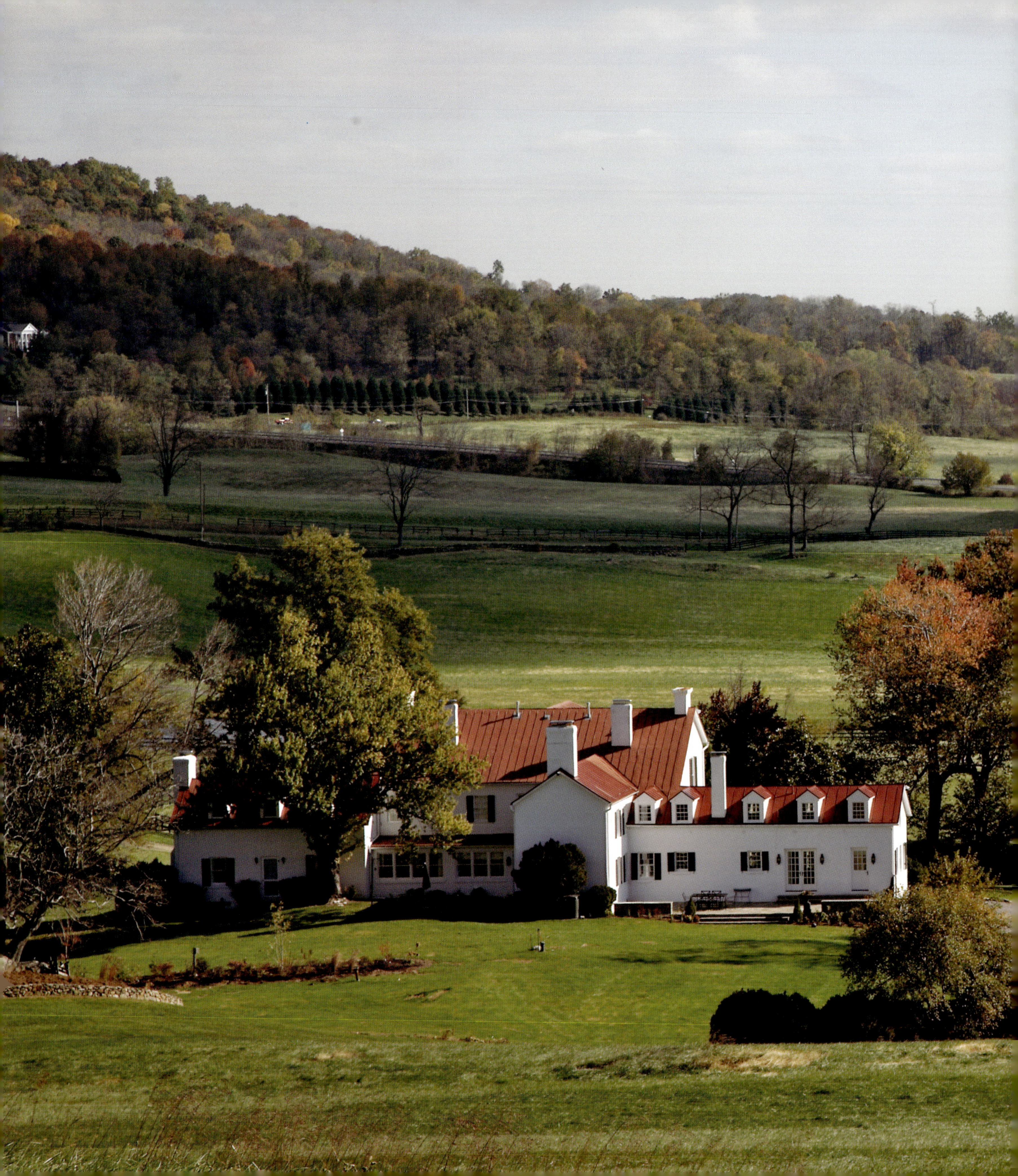

LEFT *In the Valley of the Crooked Run, a Rural Historic District in Fauquier County, Ovoka Farm presents a picture of one of the area's most beautiful and important natural, historic, and architectural resources. The valley and distant countryside will remain as they are thanks to the conservation efforts of many Fauquier County landowners. The previous owner of Ovoka put a large amount of the surrounding land into a conservation easement. The current owners have worked with neighbors to protect the Valley of the Crooked Run and 2,000 acres that surround Ovoka.*

FOLLOWING PAGES *At Ovoka the ponds thrive, the land is protected, and its walking trails, outdoor arena, dressage and jumping ring, and historic house are filled with activity and excitement ushering in a vibrant, new life for the historic estate.*

family descendants settled in Fauquier and Loudoun Counties as well as what would become Clarke County, Virginia, and parts of West Virginia.

Beginning with purchase of 630 acres of the George Carter lands by Thomas Middleton in 1768, there have been a succession of owners and with them a fluctuation of the acreage belonging to Ovoka. Prior to that date Ovoka is believed to have been a home site for John and Margaret Young, who may have settled on 200 of the 630 acres earlier than their purchase date of 1770. The Youngs are listed in the Fauquier County Deeds books as selling the same tract with all of its houses, buildings, and other improvements in June of 1771.

The grand house and farm buildings seen today date from the 1830s and 1860s and were built by then-owner Charles J. Stovin after he bought the 394-acre farm in 1830. For much of the last century, the home was owned by C. Reed Thomas, a Master of Foxhounds and founder of the Hunt Country Stable Tour. Modifications were made to the main house during the 1930s and 1950s, including the addition of the den, whose cherry-paneled walls and black walnut flooring were harvested from the farm's orchards, and a second story (now removed) built over and a garage built under the kitchen, which may have been an original building. In 2004 the current owners beautifully restored the entire house, remodeled the kitchen with hand-adzed beams and a ceiling opened to the full two-story height, and remodeled the original barn and silos. A generously proportioned stable was added to the complex in 2006.

Altogether, Ovoka Farm is a compound that is not only fully functional but one most worthy of accolades for its architectural preservation and land conservation.

143

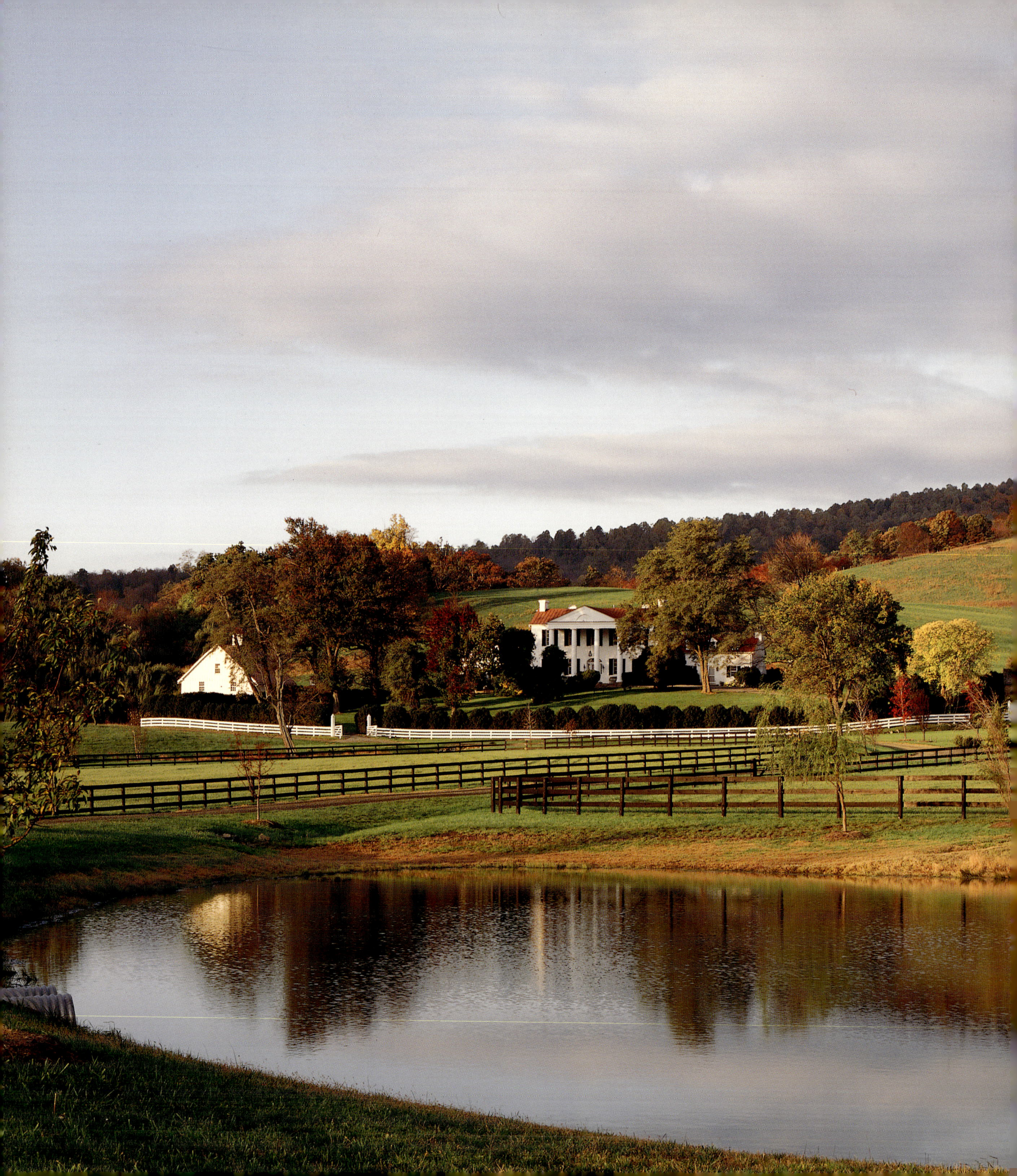

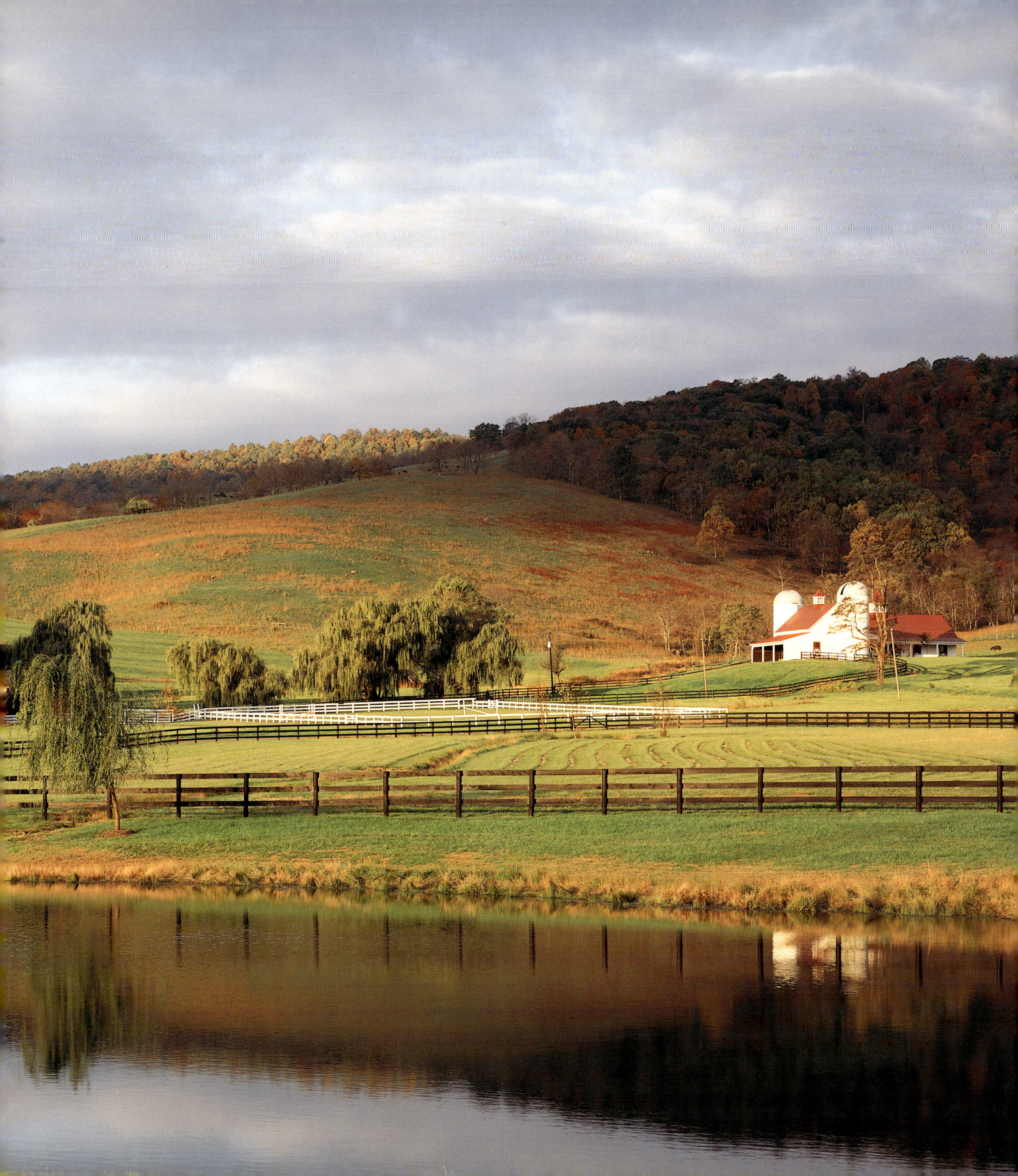

KINROSS FARM

Brick house, c. 1830; restoration and remodel, 1996
Stone garage, 1996
Hunter barn, equipment buildings, c. 1960; renovation, 1999
Maintenance facility, outdoor area, 1999
Training barn, indoor arena, all weather gallop, office, 2002
Stables, c. 1960; remodeled into guest house, 2000

Kinross Farm is a 650-acre estate that is home to the renowned Kinross Training Stables, including the hunter and training barns, indoor and outdoor arenas, and an all-weather training track laid out among pastures for prize-winning Thoroughbreds and fine hunters. Kinross Farm was the leading owner in America for Steeplechase Racing in 2004, second in 2005, and again leading owner in 2006. It is famous for wins at Belmont, Keeneland, and multiple times at the Virginia Gold Cup. At dawn on any given morning Englishman Neil Morris, the trainer at Kinross, and Chris Read, the 2005 Leading Amateur Jockey in America, who rides for Kinross Farm, may be found

ABOVE AND RIGHT *Since moving from New York over twenty years ago the owners of Kinross Farm have rejuvenated the c.1830 Federal brick house, created landscaping with gardens and over 800 new trees, and have turned the 650-acre farm into the prize-winning Kinross steeplechase and hunting training stables.*

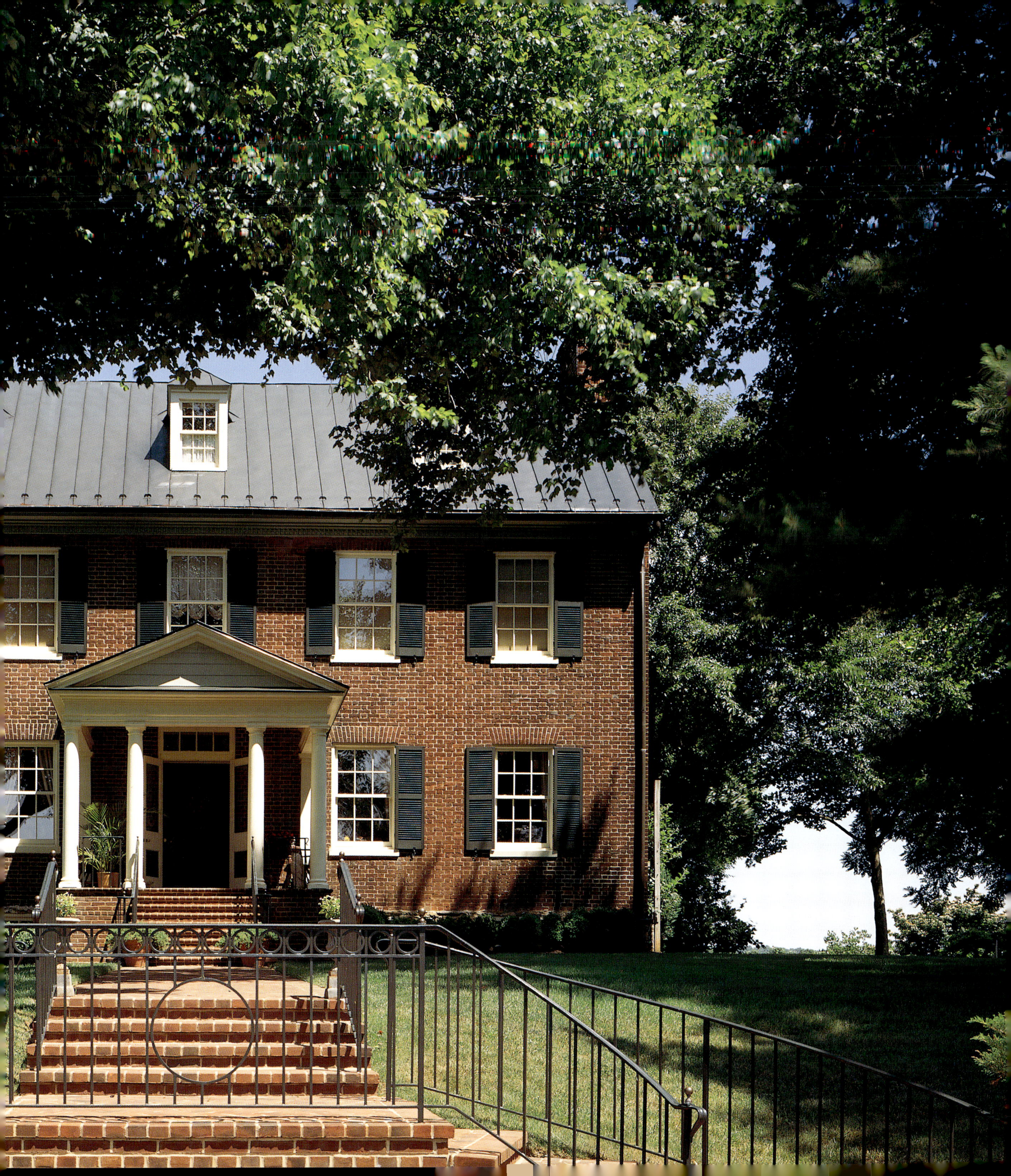

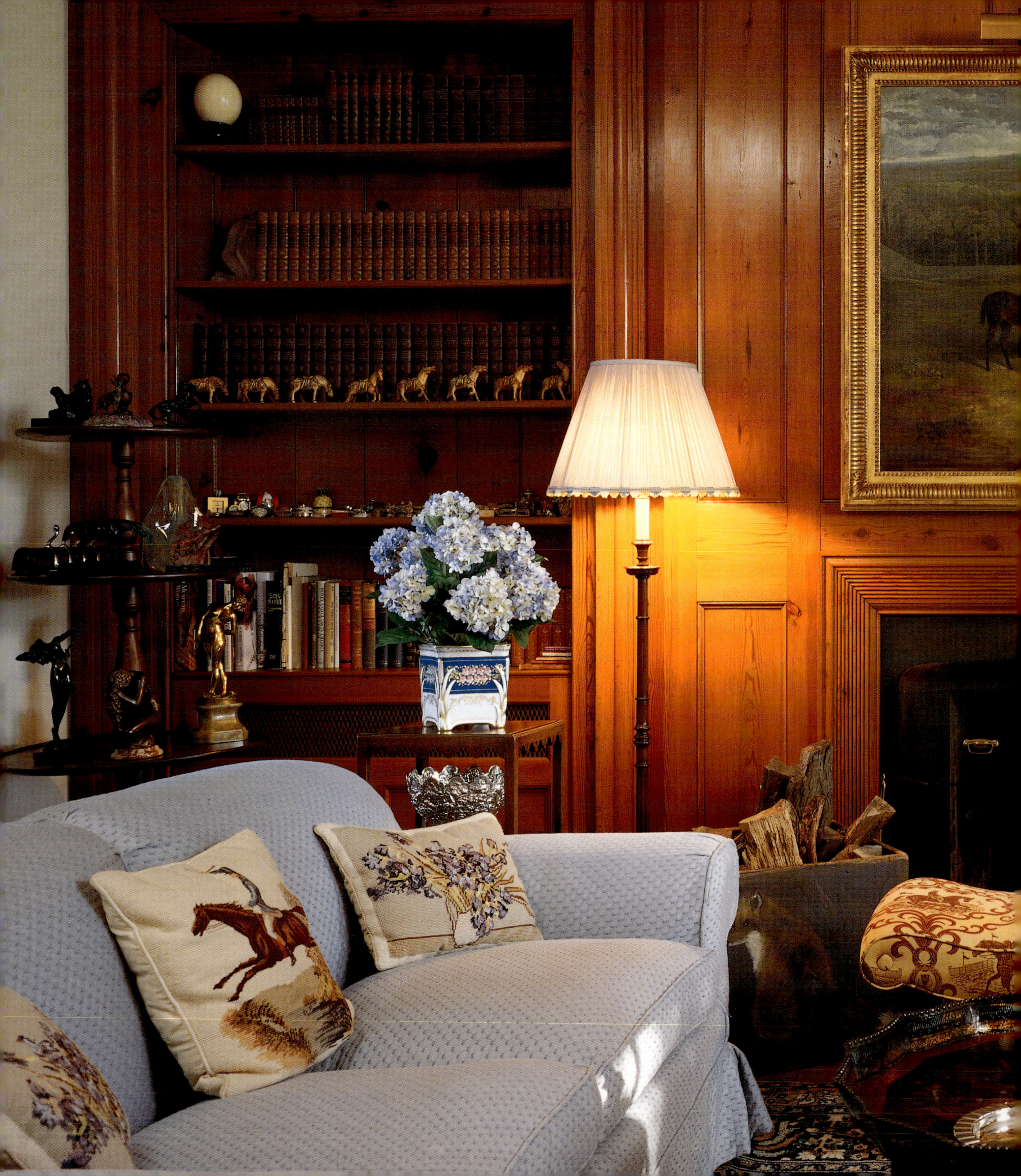

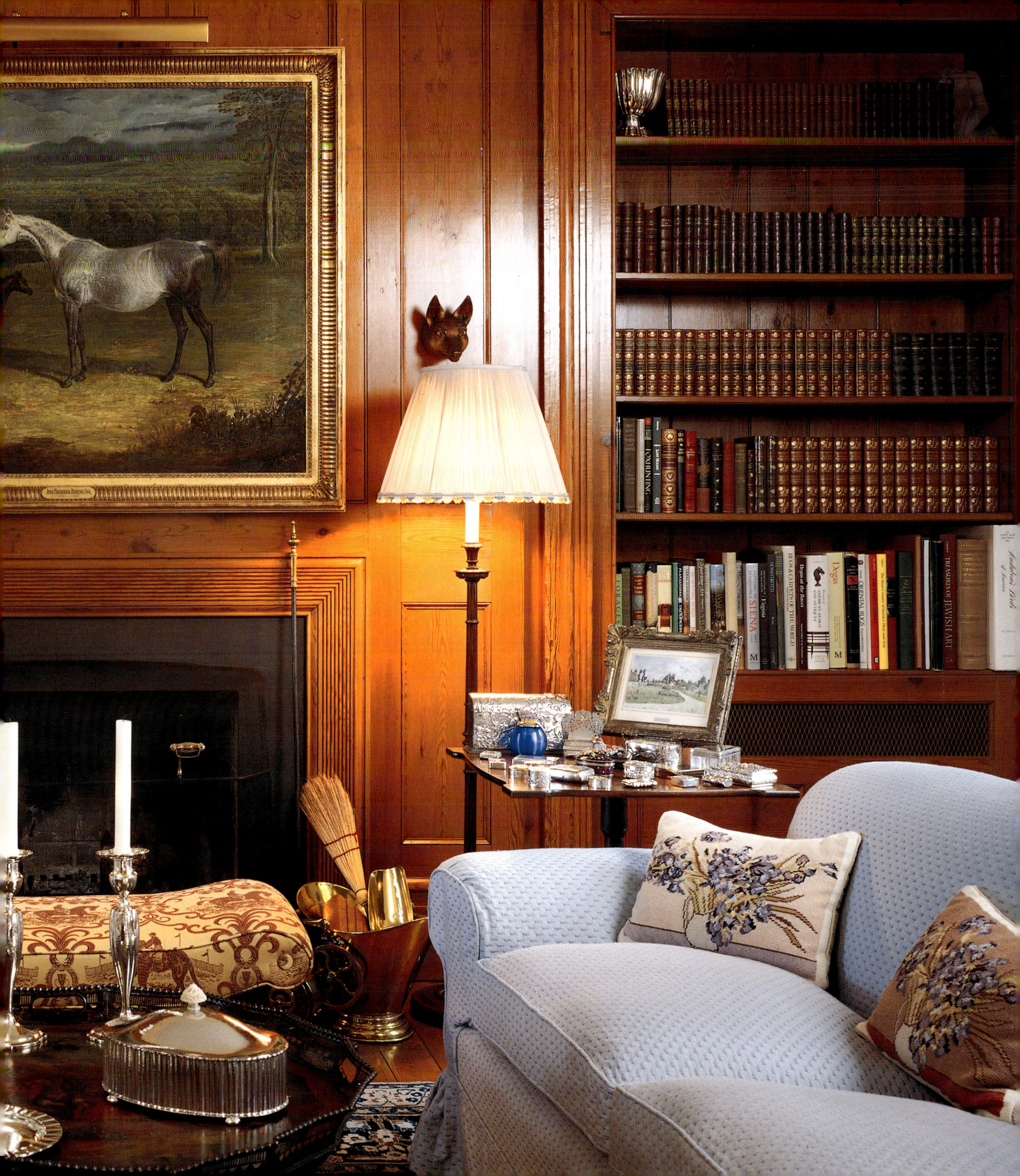

PRECEDING PAGES *The main parlor in the oldest part of the house has original heart pine paneling, trim work, and flooring. On the paneled chimney breast is* Jack Spigot (1818) *by John Frederick Herring, Sr. (1795–1865). A pair of mid-twentieth-century American silver candlesticks with quatrefoil dome bases sits on a late Georgian tole tea tray with a beaded, scalloped, and pierced galleried rim and cut through handles with a painted landscape scene of a falcon hunt resting on an ebonized and partially gilt wood faux-bamboo stand.*

ABOVE *The sunroom holds a selection of Kinross Farm's racing trophies. The trophy for The Temple Gwathmey Memorial Steeplechase Handicap has a special place on a circular side table. The original oil over the carved oak court cupboard is Kinross Farm's* Lord Kenneth, Winner of the 2003 Virginia International Gold Cup, *by Sandra M. Forbush. The bronze of horse and jockey is by Jean Clagett.*

RIGHT *Over the pine mantel that is original to the house hangs the remarkable* Mr. Ogilvy's "Trentham" at New Market (1771) *by George Stubbs. To its left is another museum-worthy painting,* Lady Munnings *by Sir Alfred Munnings, K.C.V.O., P.P.R.A. (1878–1959). The pair of c.1830 silver three-light candelabra is by William Bateman of London.*

150 KINROSS FARM

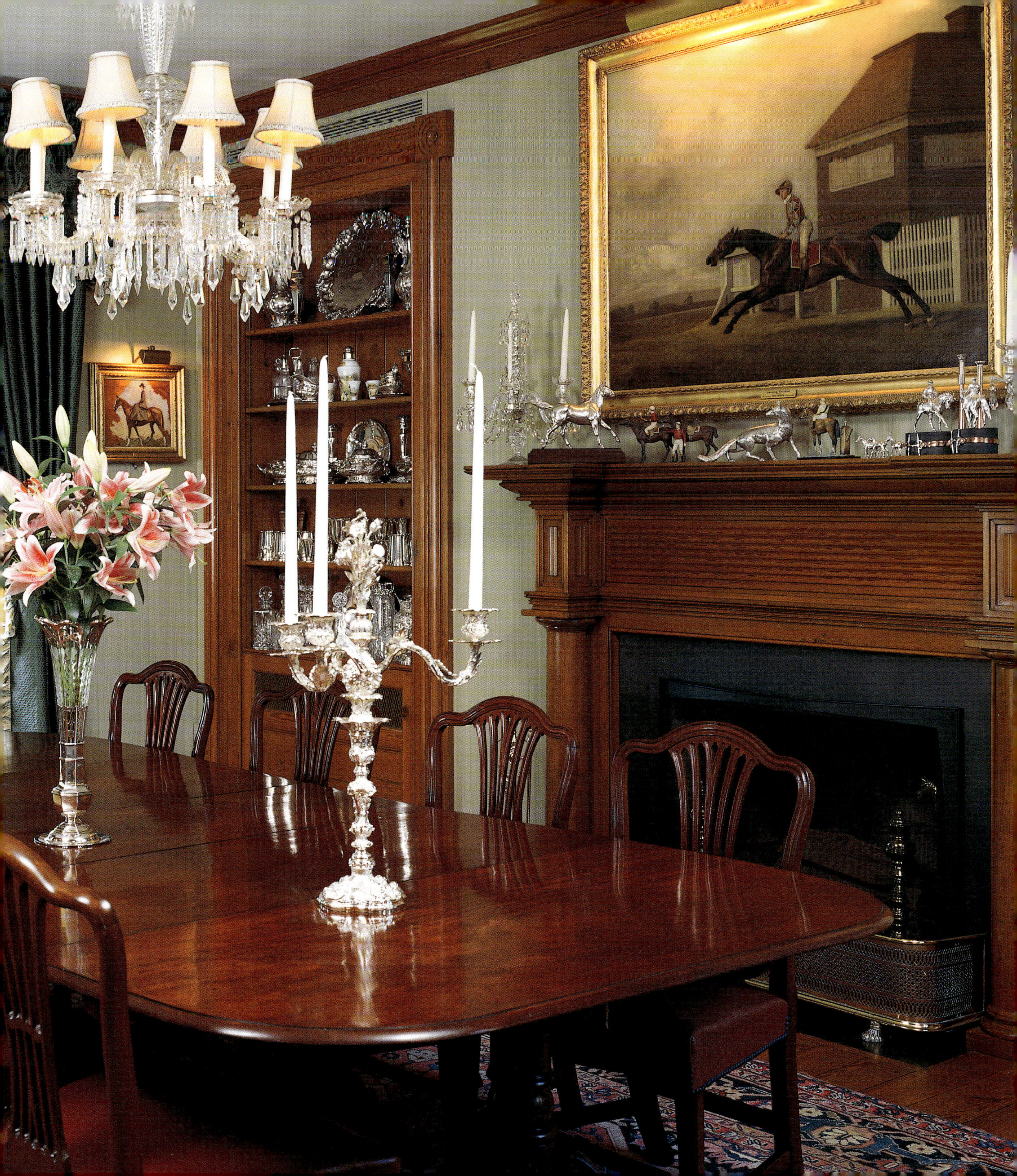

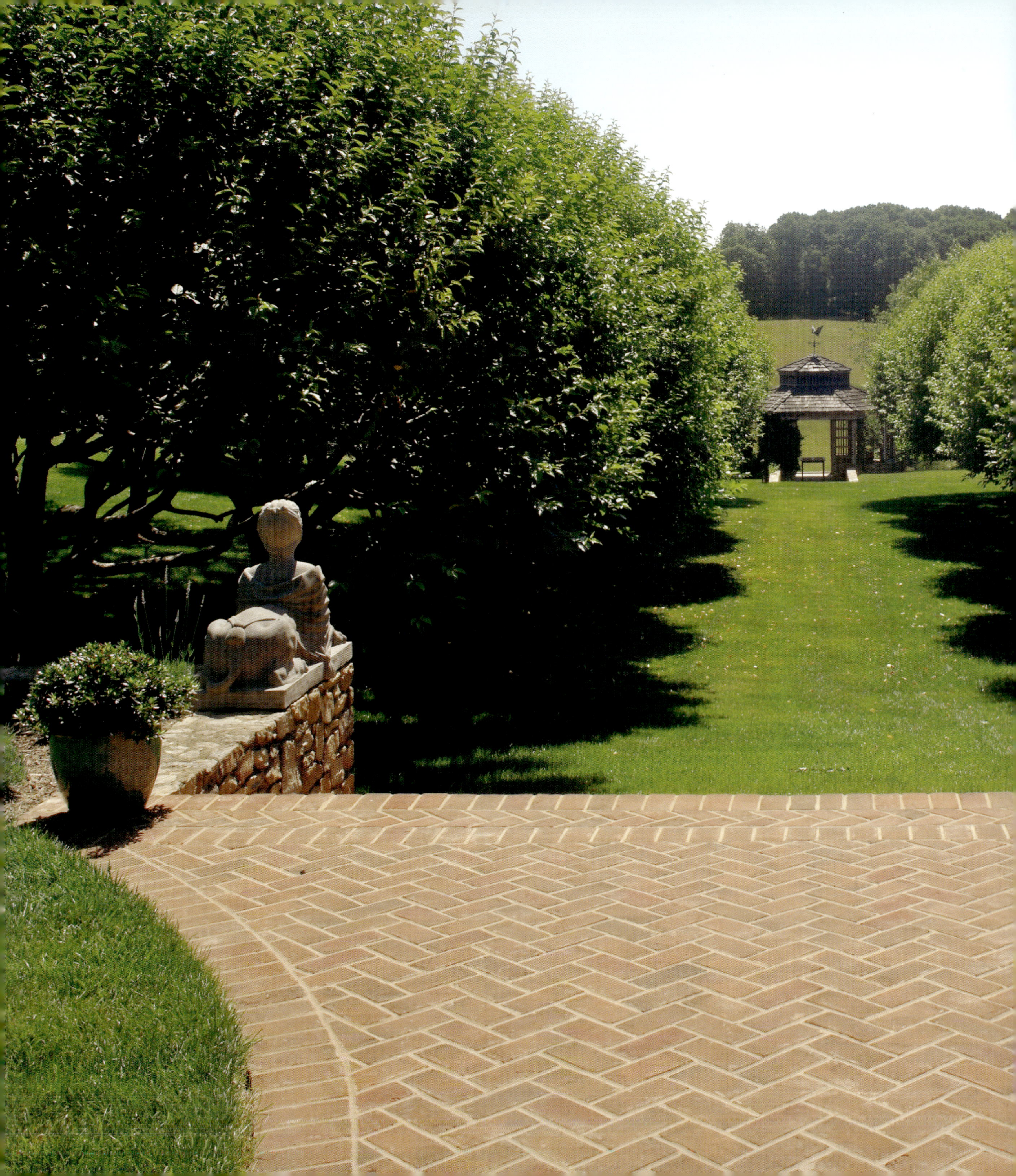

An allée of crab apple trees that reaches from the back patio to the gazebo built among limestone outcroppings guides one's view toward the farm's nearby hills.

training the steeplechase horses for speed on the gallops or agility over hurdles. Champions at the farm include Lord Kenneth, winner of the 2003 Virginia International Gold Cup; Sur la Tête, Leading Hurdle Horse in USA 2006; and Miles Ahead, winner of 2005 and 2006 Virginia Gold Cup, ridden by Chris Read. Other champions include home breds Segregation Lane and Gold Mitten. The immense Temple Gwathmey Memorial Steeplechase Handicap trophy for the hurdle race won by South of Fifty in 2006 has a place of honor in the den.

Ironically, the owners of this thriving Thoroughbred farm did not come to Virginia to train steeplechasers as their primary focus, but rather to fox hunt. While living in Manhattan, they began to increasingly enjoy the sport of riding to hounds, as their schedules allowed. As the husband became more passionate about the sport, the weekends in the hunt country of Virginia grew into a resolve to live there full-time. Over twenty years ago they moved to Virginia and the husband has since been fox hunting seven days a week from October through March, when the hunt season is in full swing. The owner of Kinross Farm is as focused with this rigorous sport as he is with his Thoroughbred operation. The wife, a partner in every sense at Kinross, oversees their full social schedule while being fully involved and passionately committed to animal preservation and protection. Her commitments range from local organizations such as the Middleburg Humane Foundation, to the

153

ABOVE *Among other state-of-the-art facilities is the training barn at Kinross Training Stables.*

RIGHT *Neil Morris on Sur la Tête, Leading Hurdle Horse in the U.S.A. 2006, and Chris Read on Noblest train the steeplechase horses for speed on the gallops in the early morning on the all-weather track.*

FOLLOWING PAGES *Besides indoor and outdoor arenas, an all-weather training track, a new office complex, a hunter barn and various other buildings, Kinross Farm's large training barn is not only picturesque in its country setting, but an efficient facility for the stakes-winning Thoroughbred steeplechasers.*

African Wildlife Foundation and the international Flora and Fauna, in Washington D.C.

The couple chose the Middleburg-Upperville neighborhood of the Piedmont region of Virginia's hunt country for its beauty and openness, the proliferation of hunt clubs, and the opportunity to begin the Thoroughbred operation. Their estate was once a part of the historic Phipps tract and features as its centerpiece a c.1830 brick manor house.

When a fire destroyed the kitchen in 1995, a restoration and remodel were completed by 1996 that appeared as a natural extension to the house, using similar materials and craftsmanship. Lively interiors, particularly bountiful in equestrian art and fine antique furnishings, are made more dramatic with the choice of vibrant colors for fabrics and paint. The centuries-old house, transformed into a beautiful and warm home, is set atop a hill at the end of a long allée of trees and surrounded by rolling green hills. It stands proudly in the landscape, a beautiful representation of Virginia's architectural heritage.

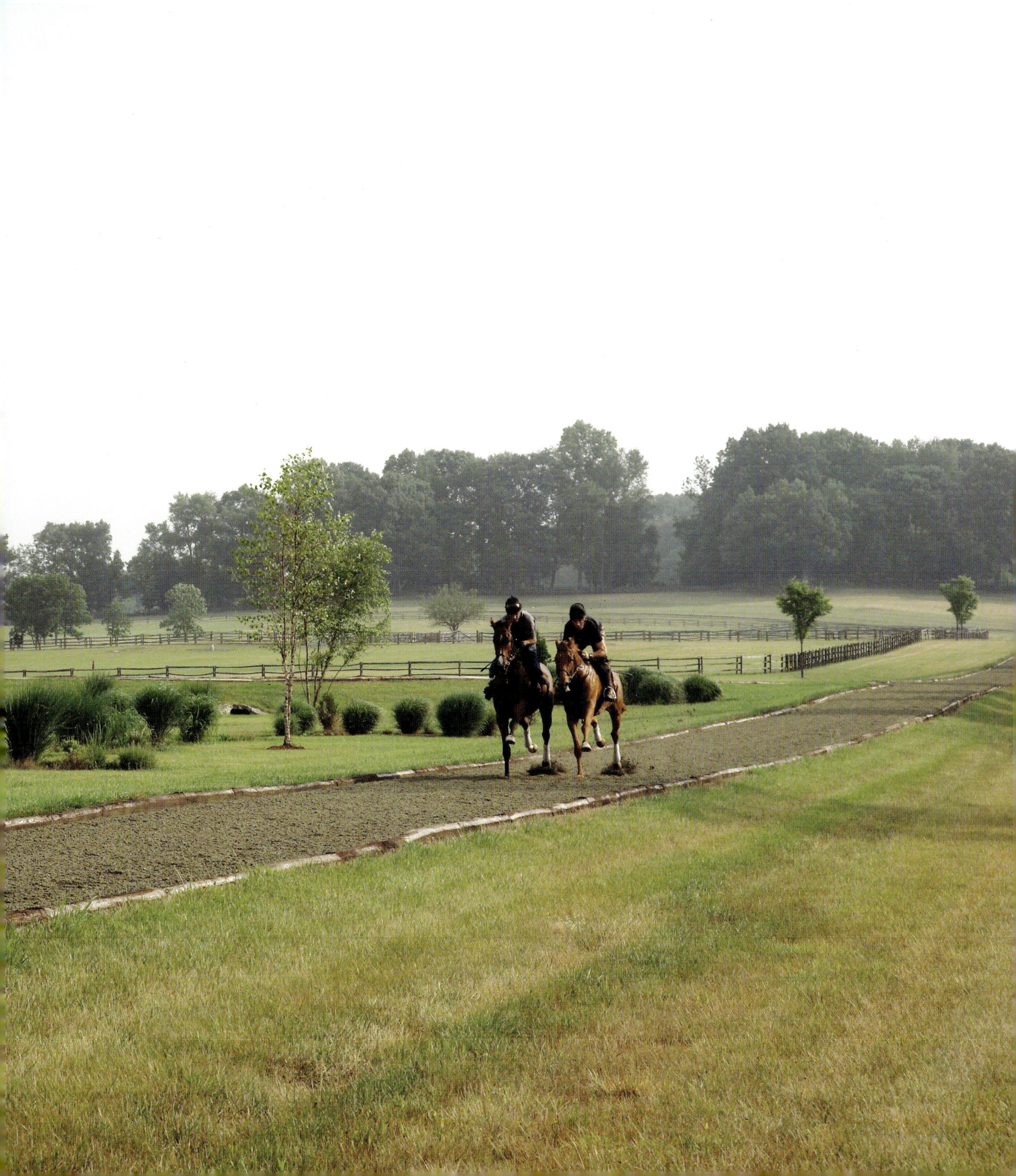

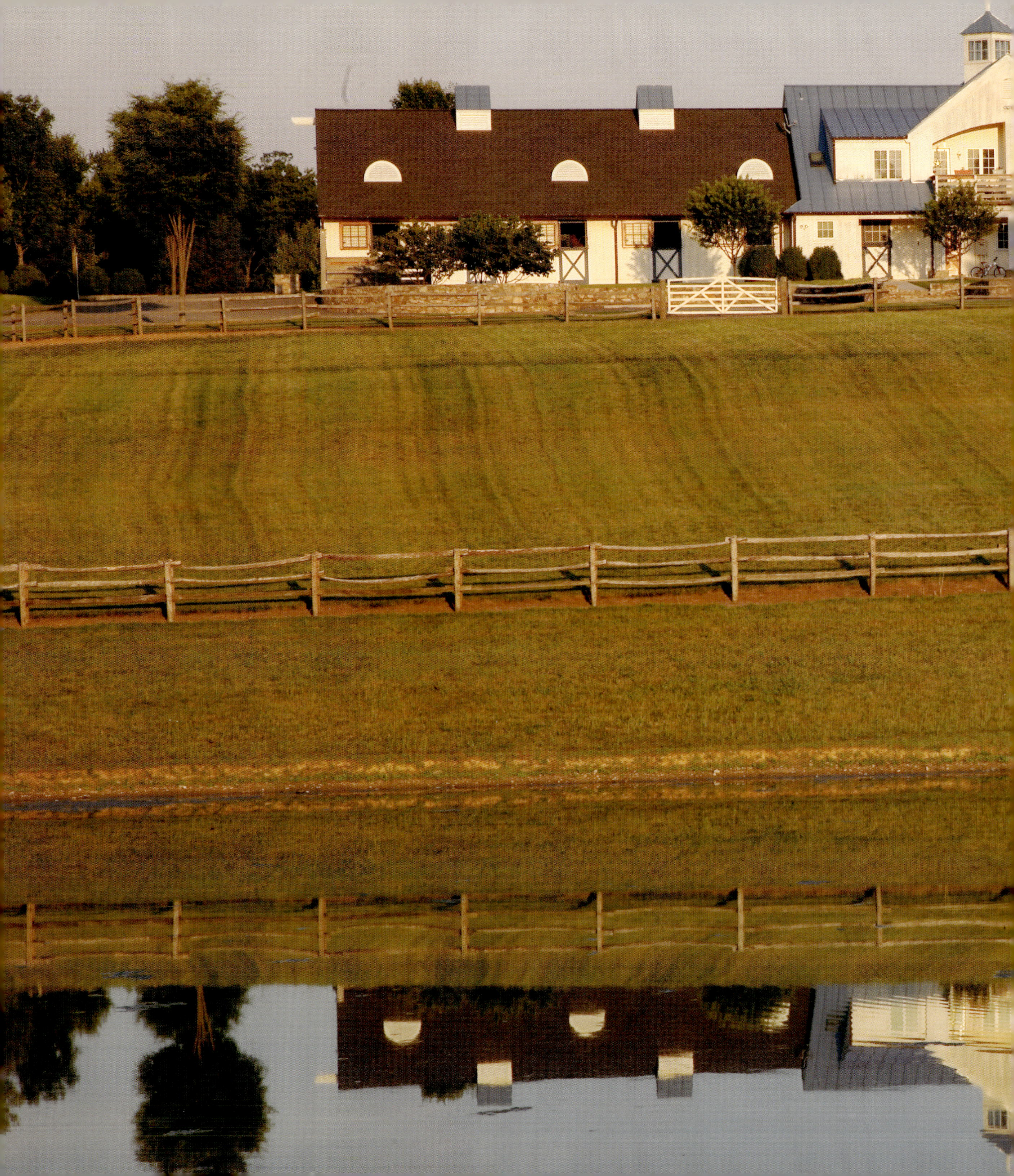

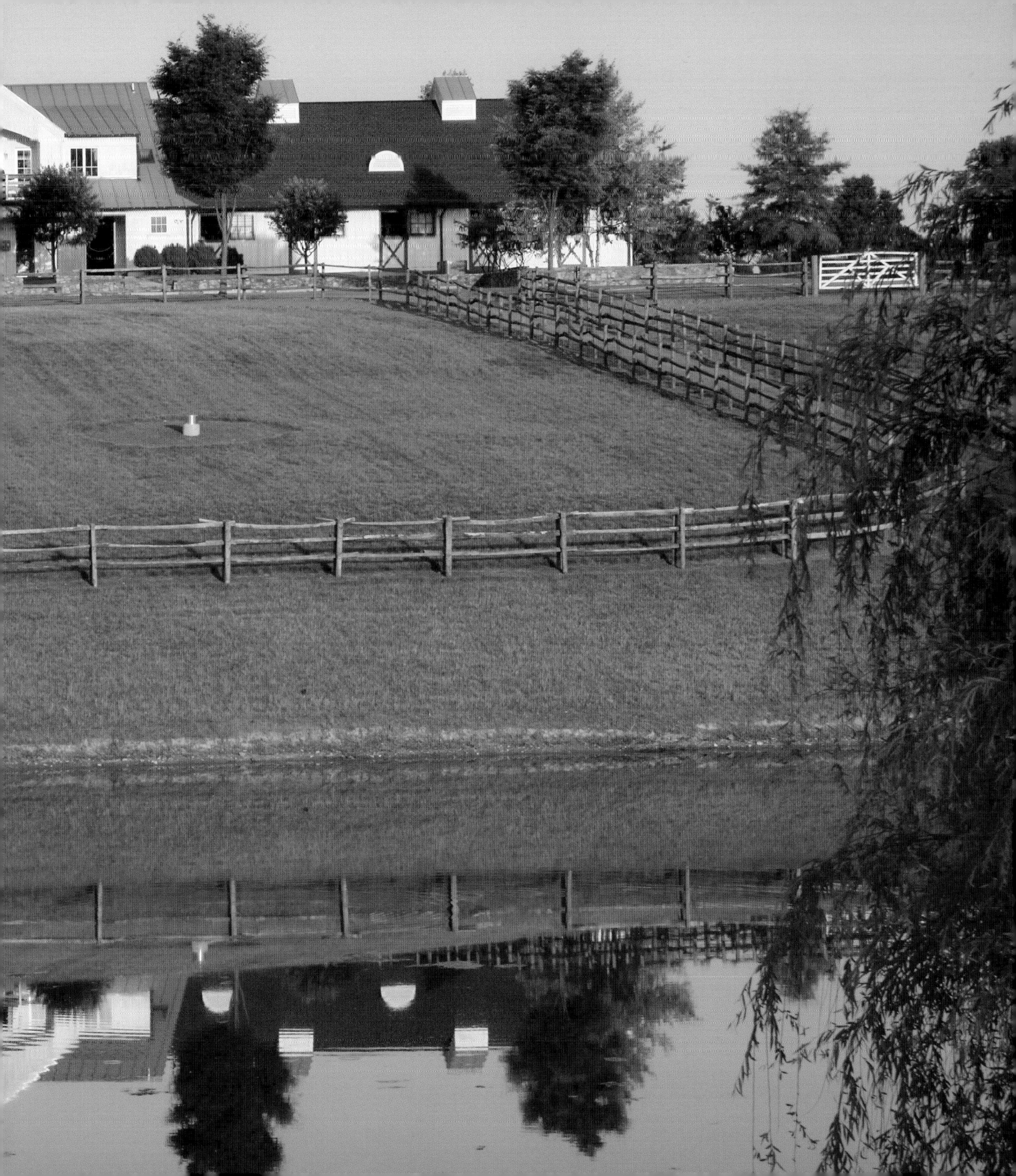

WEST VIEW

Residence of Mr. and Mrs. George N. Slater
Stone and stucco house, 1831
South porch addition, 1910

In the early eighteenth century, the land of West View farm was part of the western portion of the immense Northern Neck Proprietary, in what is now Fauquier County. It lies not far from the Alexandria-Winchester Turnpike, America's first toll road, surveyed and laid out by a young George Washington in the mid-eighteenth century. The house was built in 1831 from the fieldstones gathered from the farmland.

West View has a particular provenance with two venerable Virginia families, the Robert Fletchers and the George Slaters. One of the connecting links between the intertwining families is the famous and elusive Confederate Colonel John Singleton Mosby, known as "The Grey Ghost," leader of a closely knit cavalry unit

ABOVE AND RIGHT *The south porch at West View, an 1831 Greek Revival–style manor house in Fauquier County, has two-story columns, which were added in 1910 by the current owner George N. Slater's grandmother, Tacie Fletcher Slater.*

158

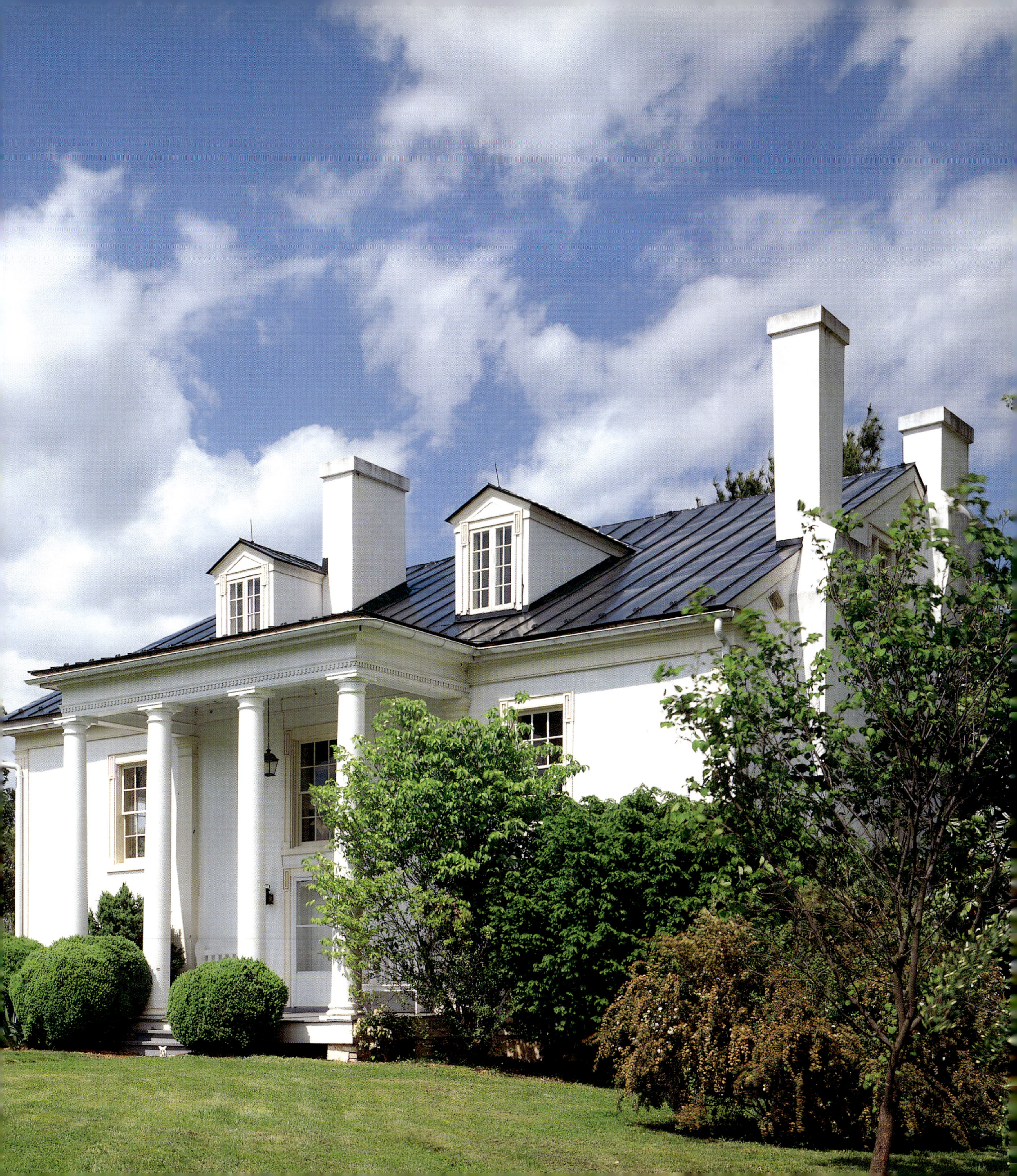

ABOVE *In the main parlor, several masters of the Piedmont Fox Hounds have been elected, including Paul Mellon, Mrs. A. C. Randolph, and Mildred F. (Bucky) Slater. A pair of upholstered pink Victorian sofas belonged to Bucky's grandmother, who died September 12, 1996, at age 107, and who at the time was the closest living descendant of George Washington. The portrait is of Nick's late father, George Robert Slater (at age 6), who served as the president of the Piedmont Fox Hounds and often served as one of its field masters.*

OPPOSITE *The design of the 1831 Greek Revival–style stucco-overstone house has a central hall with square rooms on either side. The main parlor and dining room are at the front of the house on either side of the central hallway, which features wallpaper copied after the hand-blocked 1799 wallpaper used by Colonial Governor Gore of Massachusetts.*

known as Mosby's Rangers, who raided Yankee camps, often dumbfounding the Northern soldiers. Two of his Rangers had children who married each other. Robert Fletcher's daughter Tacie Glascock Fletcher married George H. Slater, George Meacham Slater's son. Before the Civil War, West View was owned by Robert Fletcher's father Joshua Fletcher and after the war the property descended through the family to Robert. In the years since, West View has been continuously owned and occupied by his descendants, of which George N. (Nick) Slater, the present owner, is the fifth generation. Nick is married to Mildred (Bucky) Fletcher of Thornton Hill, Rappahannock County, Virginia.

160   WEST VIEW

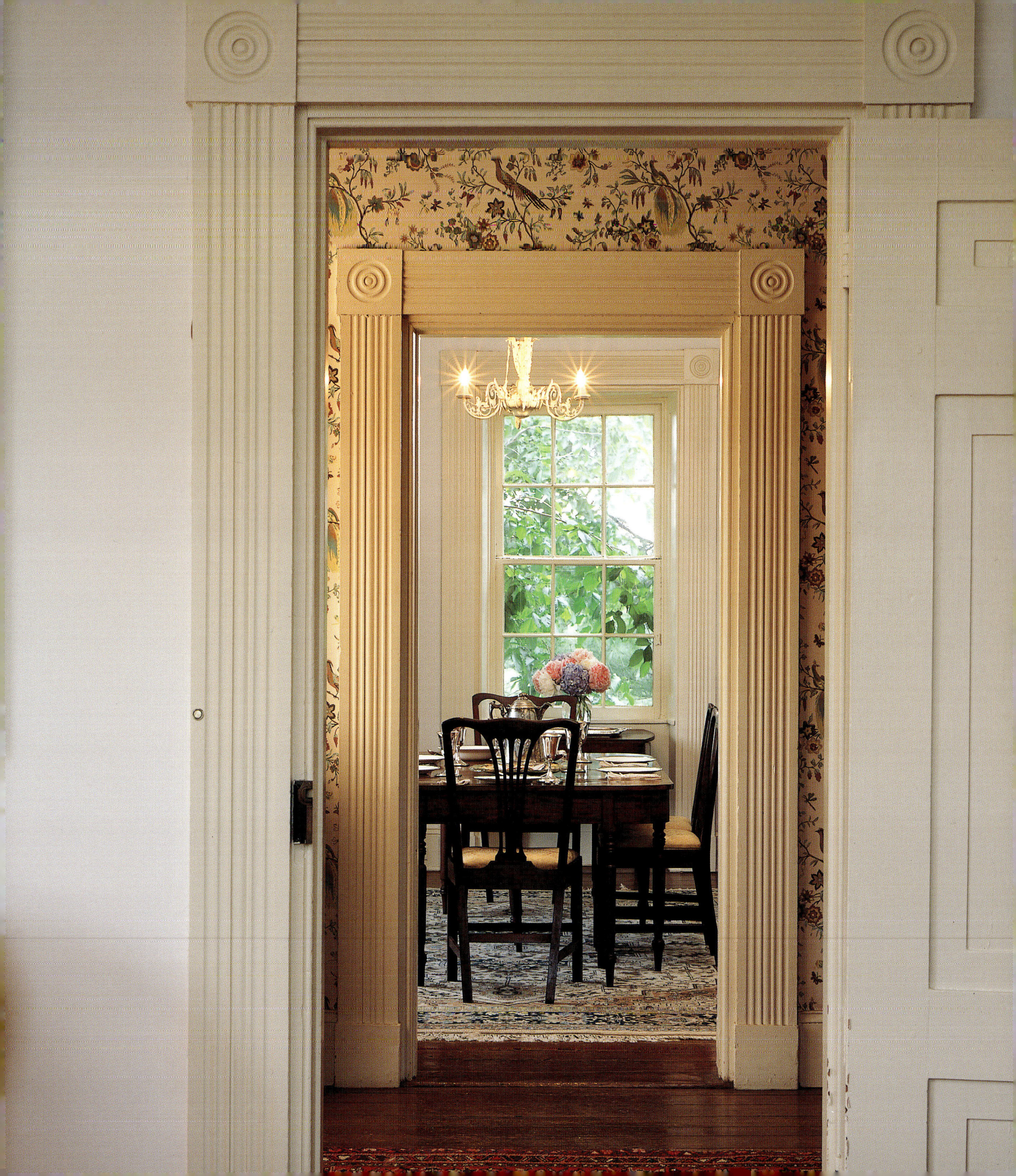

ABOVE *An early nineteenth-century walnut corner cupboard, probably from Virginia, holds a collection of family China. The nineteenth-century gold gilt mirror over the mantel is flanked by a pair of nineteenth-century solid brass candlesticks.*

RIGHT *In the dining room a painting of Mildred Fletcher Slater, a previous master of the Piedmont Fox Hounds, on her horse Mosby's Mistress, hangs near a portrait of the first George Slater, who immigrated to this country from Ireland in 1827. Family silver pieces that include a prized ornate pitcher adorn the mahogany dining table.*

West View and its owners have played significant roles in the history of equine sports, in particular fox hunting and horse shows. A long-running board affiliation with the Piedmont Fox Hounds, established in 1840 and the oldest hunt in Virginia, includes family members who have served as president and master of foxhounds (MFH), most recently past-MFH Bucky Slater.

The owners of West View have also promoted the breeding and showing of horses by their dedication to The Upperville Colt & Horse Show, America's oldest, established in 1853, and one of the most prestigious in the world. Nick, his father, the late George R. Slater, and his grandfather, were each president and served on the board of the horse show for many years. Nick's mother, Kitty Slater, first authored *The Hunt Country of America*, continuously in print since its initial publication in 1967, and a classic among equine sports enthusiasts. The author further recounted the history of the sport through *The Hunt Country of America, Revisited* and *The Hunt Country of America, Then and Now.*

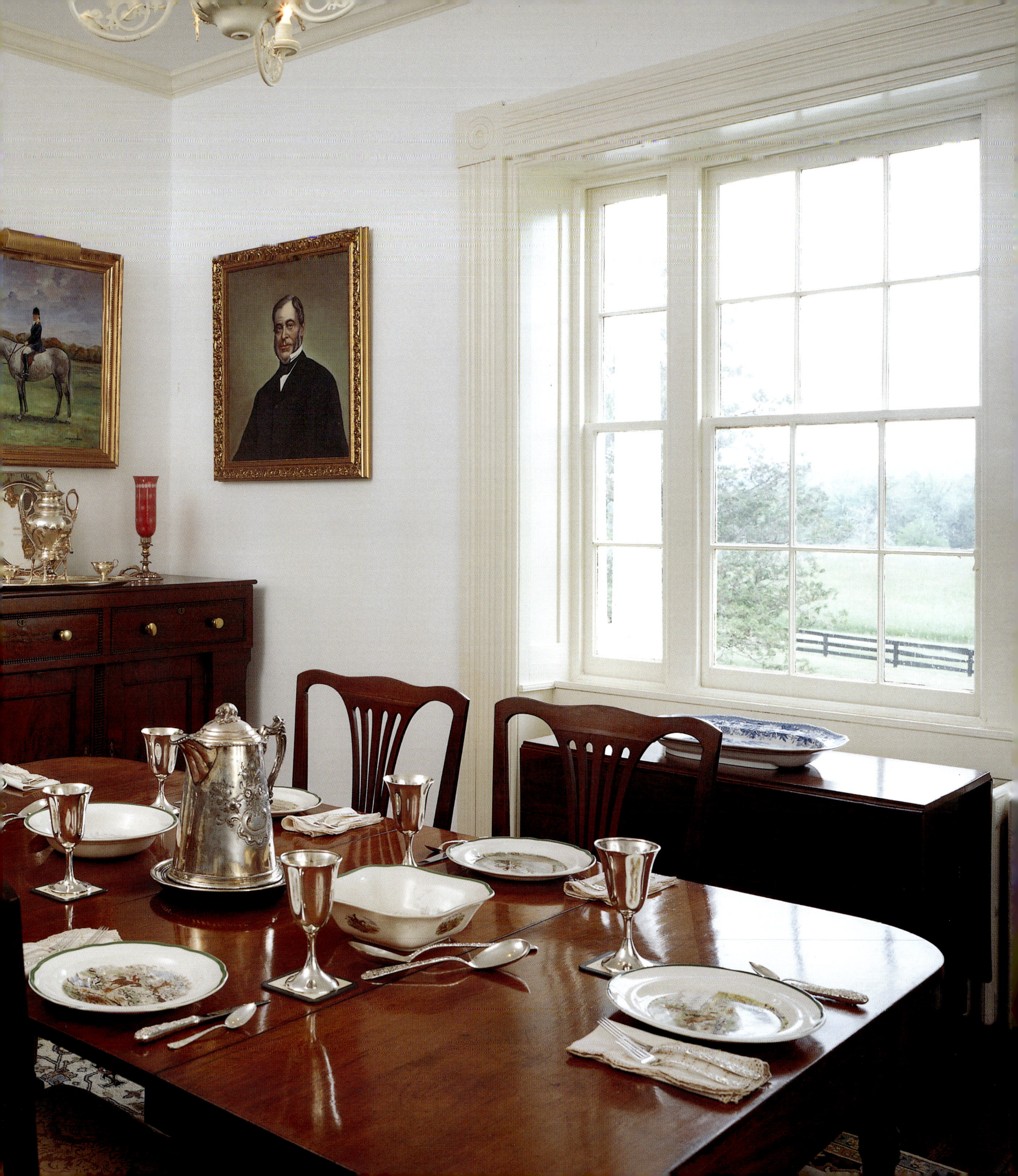

TOP *West View has been owned and/or occupied by members of the Slater family since the Civil War when it was acquired by the current owner George N. Slater's great-grandfather, Robert Fletcher. The original and current entrance is that facing the west, with stairs leading up to a gable-ended covered porch that features two pairs of fluted wooden columns at the far corners and fluted engaged pilasters on the house's facade.*

RIGHT *Two of the Slater's many horses, a dappled gray mare and chestnut colt, stand in the pasture where the Piedmont Fox Hounds (not shown) has met to begin its hunts.*

The house is a Greek Revival-style stone structure that has been replastered over the original sand and horsehair and is now painted white. Standing three stories tall, including the English basement, it is a square, temple-like form whose large south-facing porch with two-story columns was added by Tacie Fletcher Slater in 1910. Today the main entrance remains the original one, which faces west toward the Blue Ridge Mountains, and includes a steep flight of stairs that establishes its importance in the classical and elegant design. The interiors, which feature impressive woodwork, are welcoming and intimate. West View may be an unusual design for the Virginia countryside, but one that flatters the landscape with its scale and perfect form.

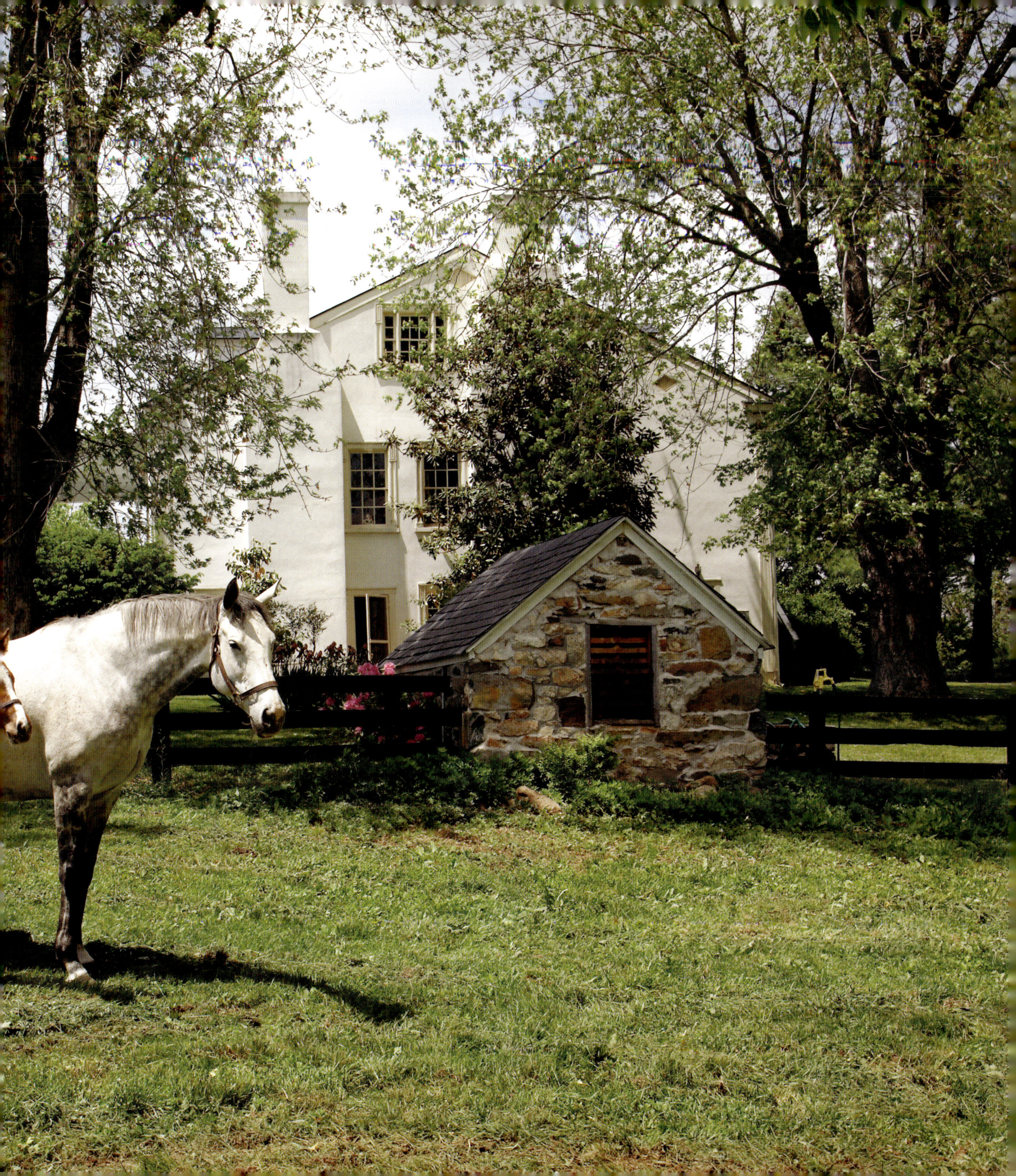

FOXHALL FARM

House and farm buildings, c.1840s
House remodel, 1970s

Gus and Sandra Forbush epitomize the story of Virginia's hunt country, a region where the love of open space and rural life and enthusiasm for horses and horse sports are all intertwined. They live at Foxhall Farm, a mid-nineteenth-century farmhouse and barn complex in Rappahannock County.

Sandra is one of the foremost artists in America specializing in sporting art and portraiture. When young, she studied ballet and drawing, and later worked as a top model. In the late 1970s she began a Thoroughbred breeding operation at Foxhall Farm. She ran this through the 1980s, selling yearlings at Saratoga and Keeneland and at one point boarding 60 horses. In the late 1980s her career path shifted from riding and raising horses to painting them. In her portraits of horses and hounds there is a vigor and reality garnered from her love of the animals and her years of first hand experience with them. Besides her technical skill, Sandra's ability to capture the character and spirit of her subjects in their movements and especially in the expressions of their eyes make her work noteworthy. Her portraits and sports paintings now hang in many homes in Virginia's hunt country, her work has graced the covers of the programs for the prestigious Upperville Colt & Horse Show for seven seasons and the Virginia Gold Cup, and five of her paintings are featured in an exhibit to celebrate the 100th anniversary of the Masters of Foxhounds Association on a 2007 tour of North America.

Gus Forbush is joint master of foxhounds for the Old Dominion Hounds (O.D.H.), an honorary position

RIGHT *Gus and Sandra Forbush's Foxhall Farm is a c.1840s complex with a charming weatherboard farmhouse, barns and stables, and an enclosed lawn and garden set in the bucolic countryside of Rappahannock County. Homeowner Gus is a joint master of foxhounds of the Old Dominion Hounds, who often meet at Foxhall Farm to ride out into its 150-square-mile territory. In the 1970s and 1980s Sandra ran her successful Thoroughbred brood mare and boarding operation at Foxhall Farm.*

FOLLOWING PAGES *Traditional furnishings and a mild color scheme in the music room are punctuated with eye-catching touches of black in the needlepoint rug and pillows, and the piano. The sweeping view out of the front window is of the Blue Ridge Mountains.*

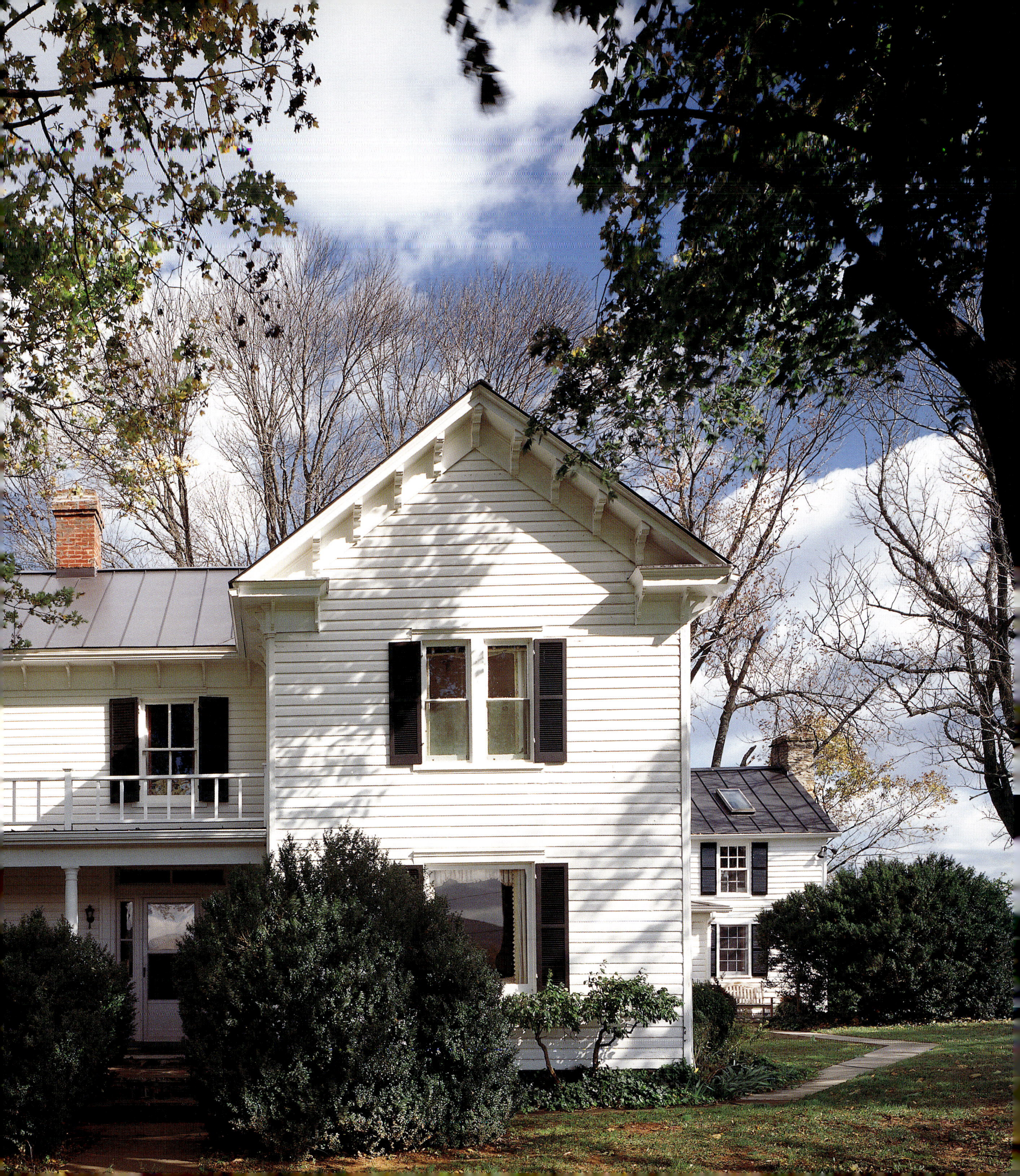

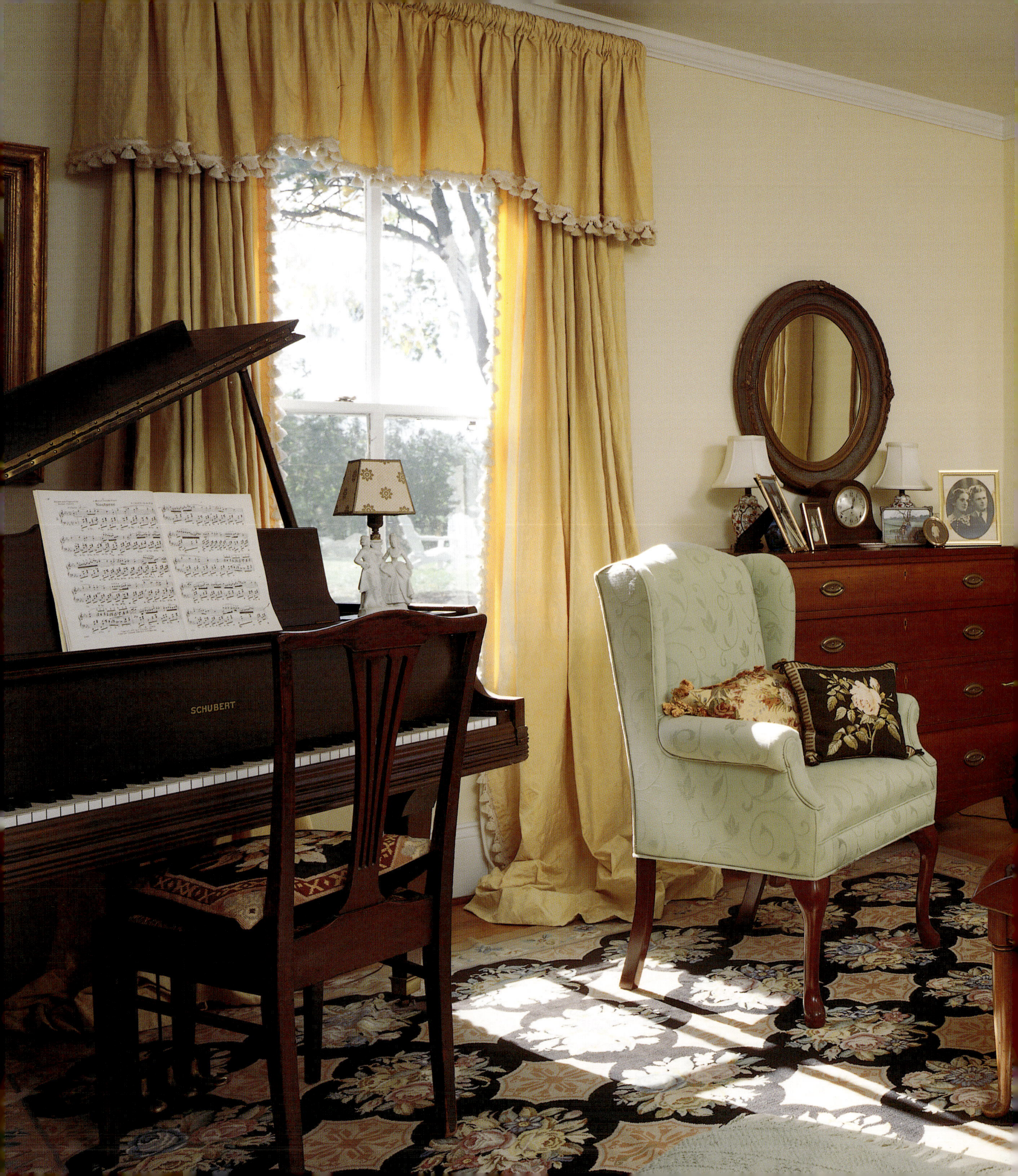
SCHUBERT

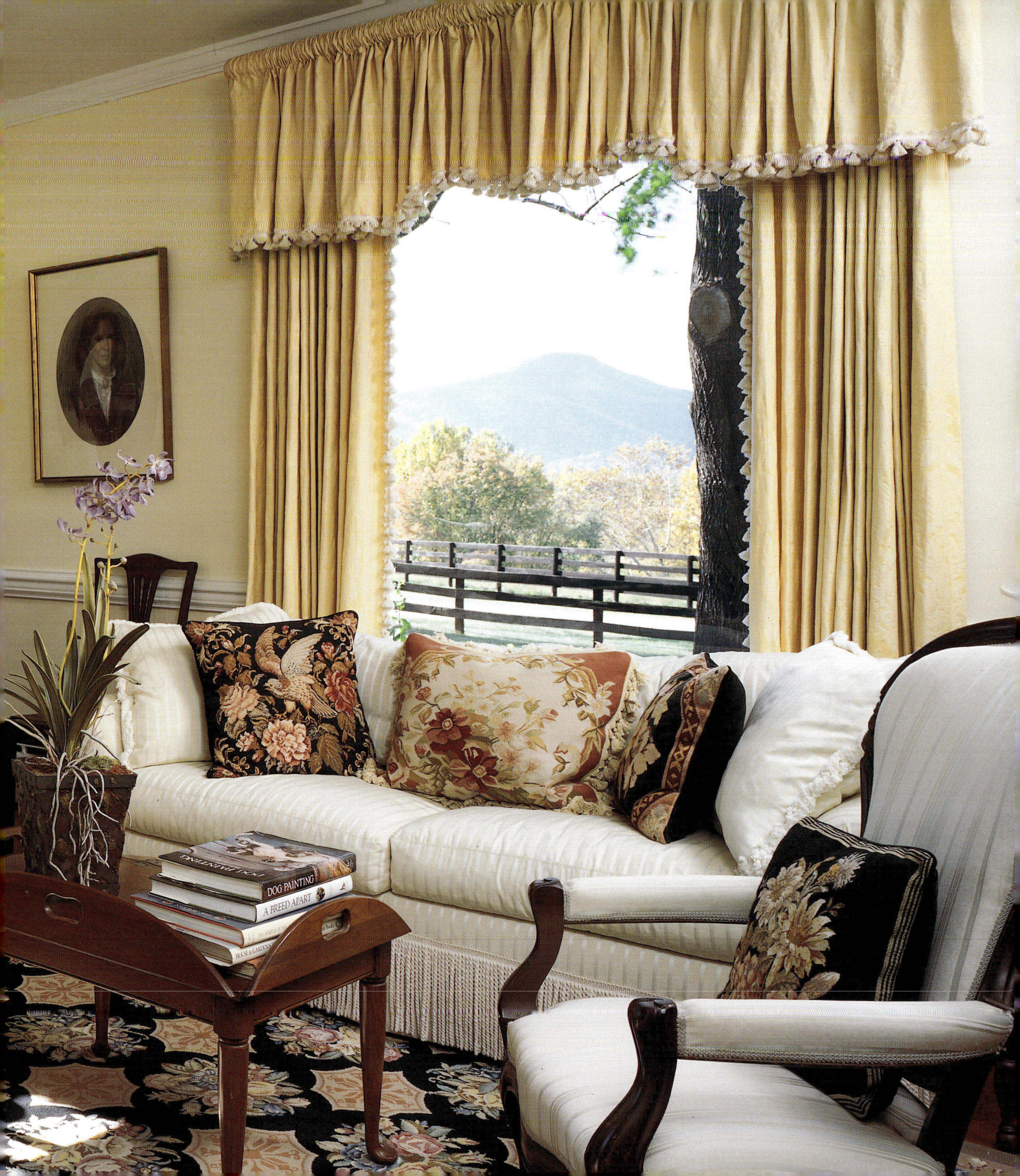
DOG PAINTING
A BREED APART

TOP At the end of the hall, where intricately patterned pillows decorate a painted bench, a skirted wing chair sits beside pairs of Gus's well-worn riding boots. The paintings are The Red Leash above and The Finish below, both by Sandra Forbush.

BOTTOM The dining room is used for special family gatherings. A Sheraton mahogany sideboard holds family China and silver while painted ladderback chairs provide seating at the ample dining room table. The portrait is of Sandra and her sisters.

RIGHT The living room sports a tartan plaid carpet and country pine furniture. Built-in bookcases with sporting books and family photos fill the room with a rustic charm. Seating in the bay window creates another conversation area. The painting over the fireplace is by Larry Wheeler.

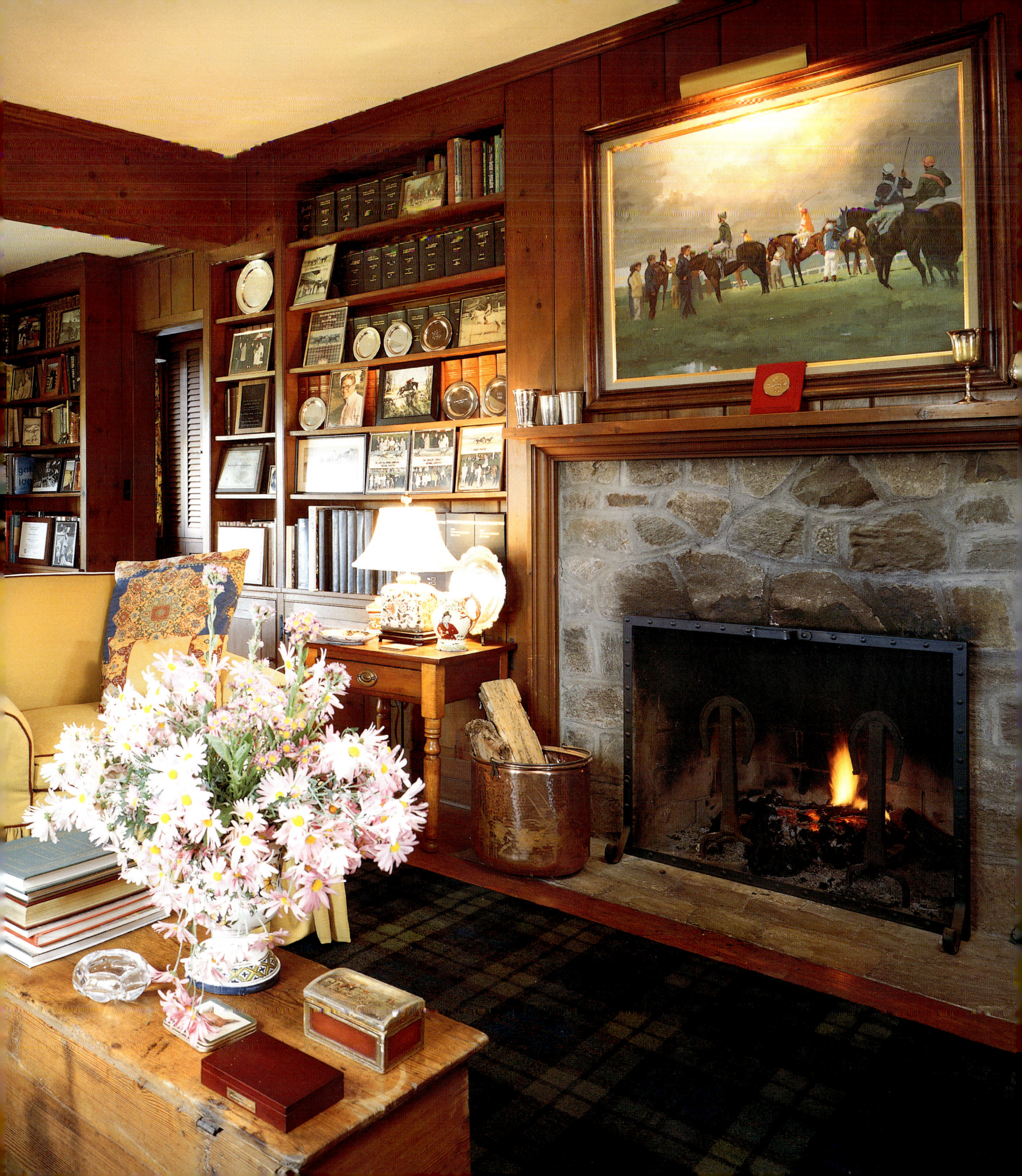

ABOVE *The kitchen (not shown) and a nearby sitting area combine to make one cozy space. At the end of a center island a seating area for casual meals and a comfortable chair and ottoman welcome a good chat and relaxation. A collection of horns lines the mantel, above which hangs a portrait of Gus on Firewall with the Old Dominion Hounds by Sandra Forbush.*

OPPOSITE *A room toward the back of the house is a multi-purpose space, serving as an office, tack room, and den. It holds tack, riding boots, velvet hats, and often a riding coat. The scarlet master's coat is referred to as a "pink," named for the London tailor, Mr. Pinque (or Pink), who fashioned riding apparel using scarlet fabric. On the mantel are a pair of silver julep cups and pitchers, hunting horns, and the master's whip handle. The painting over the mantel is a landscape by Larry Wheeler.*

he has shared with Ms. Douglas Hytla for over ten years. Gus did not grow up riding, but after an exhilarating jump on a runaway horse over thirty years ago, he knew fast horses were for him. He indulged his love of speed as an amateur steeplechase jockey, and still prefers Thoroughbreds as his hunters. Besides leading the hunts at least twice a week, he and Hytla maintain good relations with the 500 landowners in the O.D.H.'s 150-square-mile territory, among other responsibilities. And as far as fox hunting goes, Forbush explains, "The main idea of riding to hounds is to give everyone a safe, lively, enjoyable day of sport. And this includes the fox. In America it is different than in England. We keep the foxes healthy, even feeding them during wintertime, because healthy foxes don't get caught. We don't want to catch them. We want to chase them." Gus, a natural-born raconteur, has endless entertaining stories about the wit and wisdom of foxes. "Foxes have great senses of humor. I've seen a fox run into a herd of cattle to disguise his scent, with the hounds behind him, only to back track, find a good place on a hilltop or a stone wall, and watch the hounds run around in circles." Gus believes fox hunting is all about living in the country and preserving it for future generations.

FOLLOWING PAGES *The mid-nineteenth-century barn complex serves the equestrian farm well. Once the focus of an active foaling and horse training operation, the stables and barns are now the gathering place for the hounds, huntsman, whippers-in, and riders (the field), who meet to hear the greeting and instructions of the master of foxhounds before a hunt.*

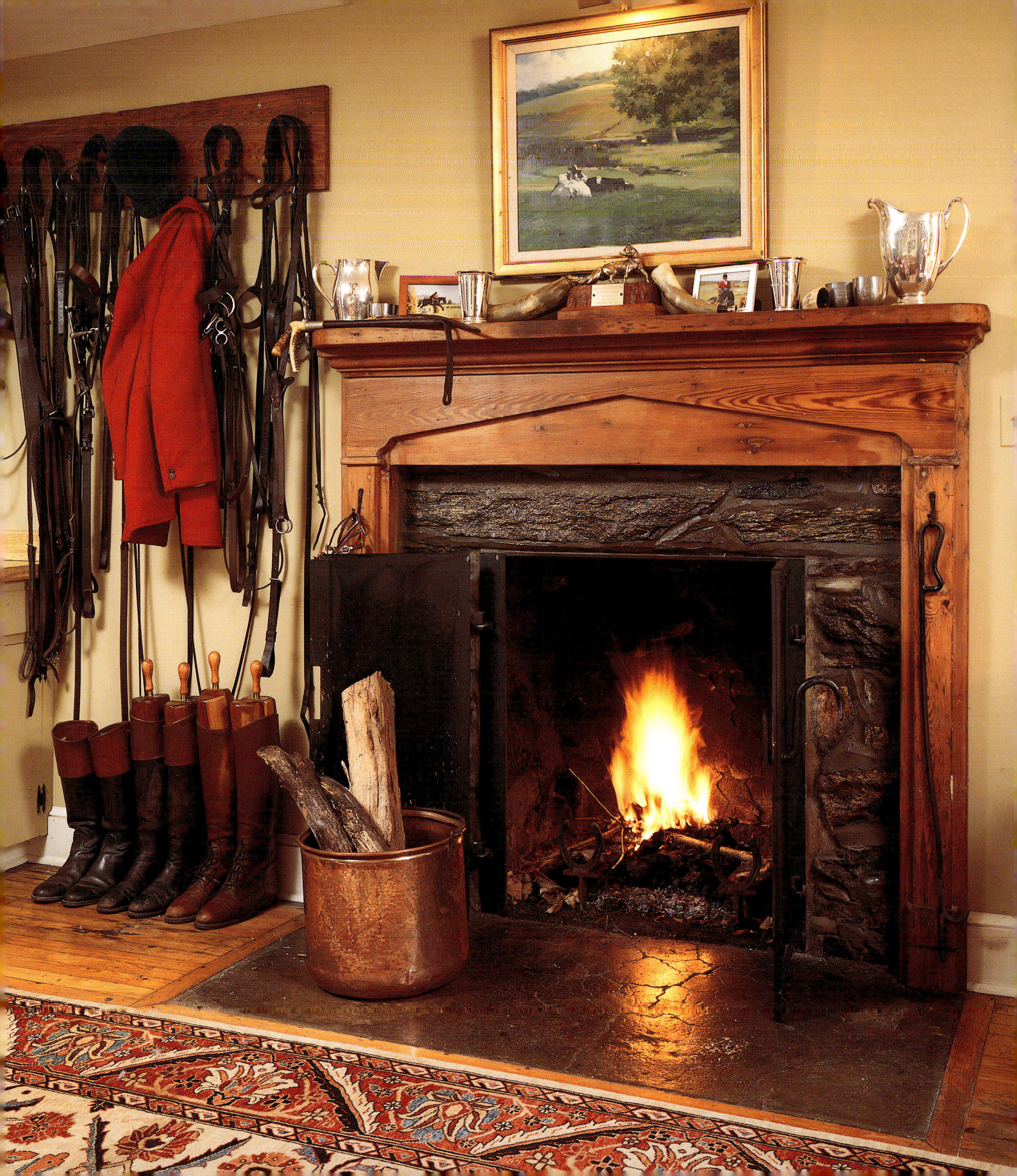

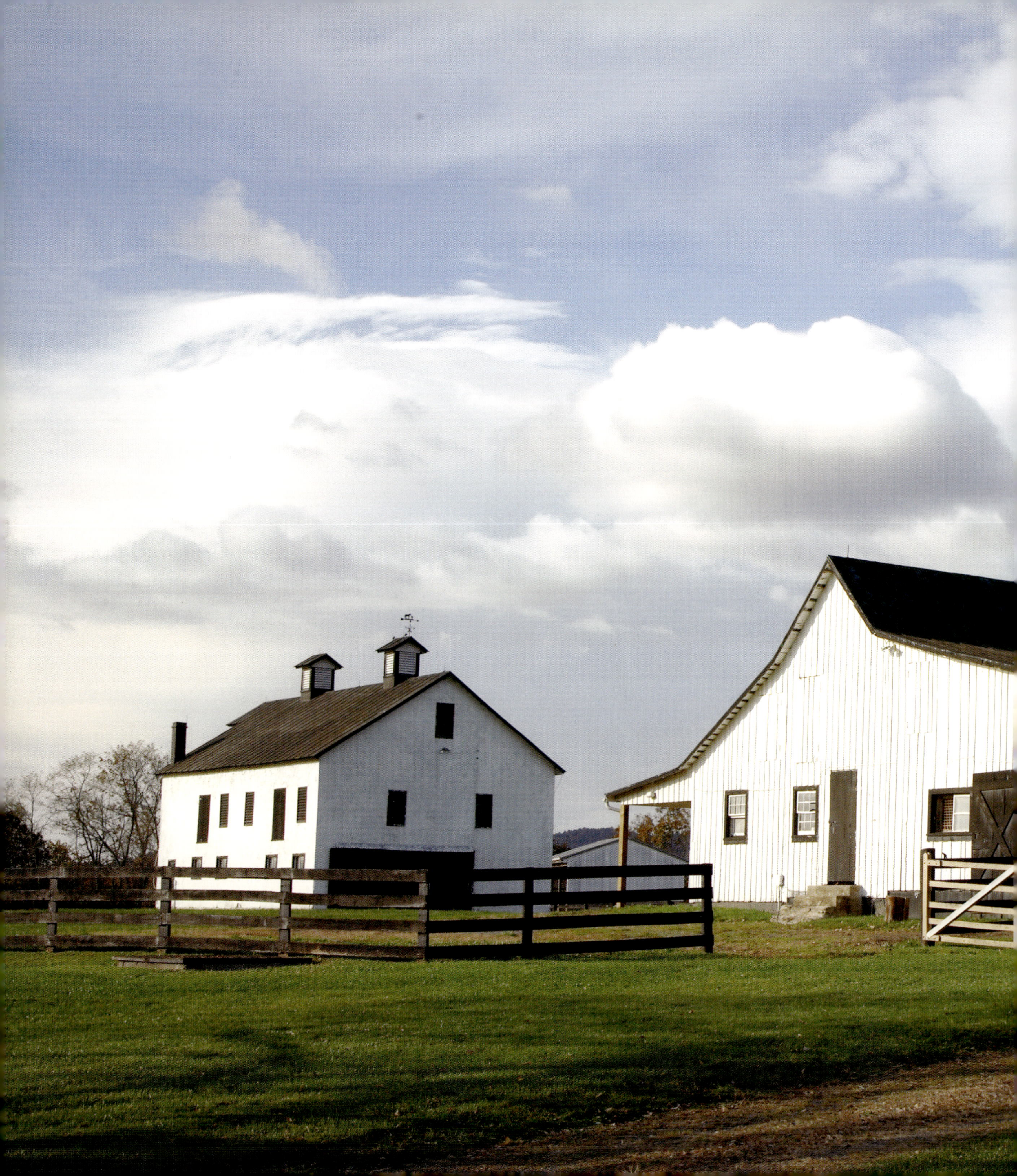

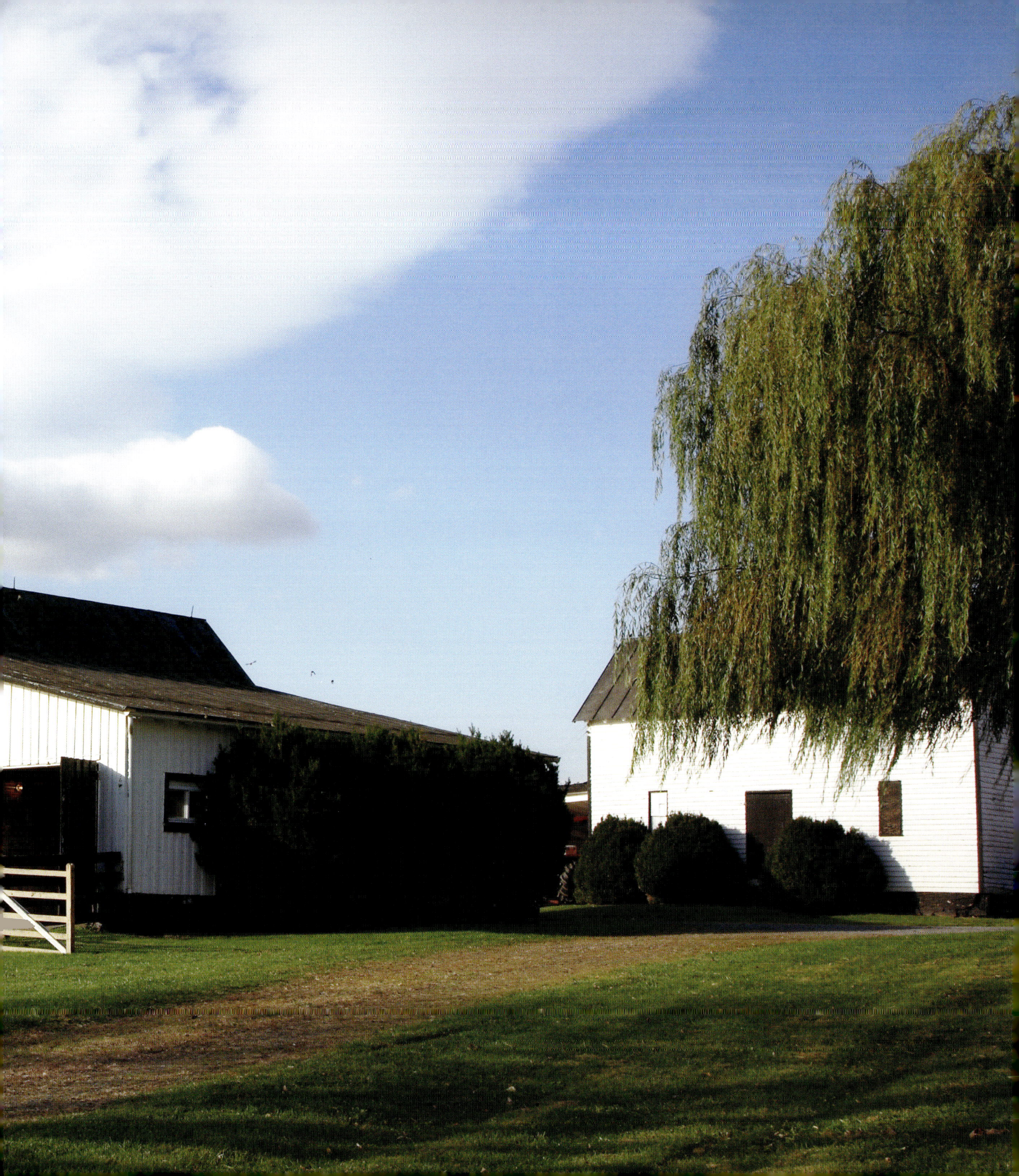

GREENVILLE

Residence of Mr. and Mrs. William W. Foshay, Jr.
Virginia Historic Landmark
Main house, summer kitchen, 1854; Jeremiah Morton, architect
House restoration and remodel, 1998; James Boyd, architect
Barns and stables, c. 1960; renovation, 2003
Pool house, 1999
Garden conservatory, 2002

Greenville is a grand Southern mansion that rests on a vast open plain. It is first visible at a rise along the curvaceous driveway that leads through its farmland from a forested country road. From a distance the stature of the house, a three-story brick square structure silhouetted alone against the horizon, is not yet evident. Upon reaching the entrance, however, the massive scale of the structure, columns, and decorative cornice becomes apparent. Four Doric columns of tremendous girth rise forty-two feet, the full height of the three-story front portico. The over-three-foot-in-diameter columns of handmade curved bricks finished in plaster and painted white define the Neoclassical building. The mansion is unreinforced brick and its ten-foot cornice carved wood. Its effect is awe-inspiring.

ABOVE AND RIGHT *Greenville's back facade that faces south shows the unusual M-shaped roof and the front facade that faces north has three-story, forty-two-foot-tall columns that define the monolithic structure. Corn grew up to the front porch until the current owners unloaded 279 dump trailers of red clay to create the plateau now landscaped with a formal garden and lawn. Greenville's current owners farm the eight hundred acres of producing fields that surround the house.*

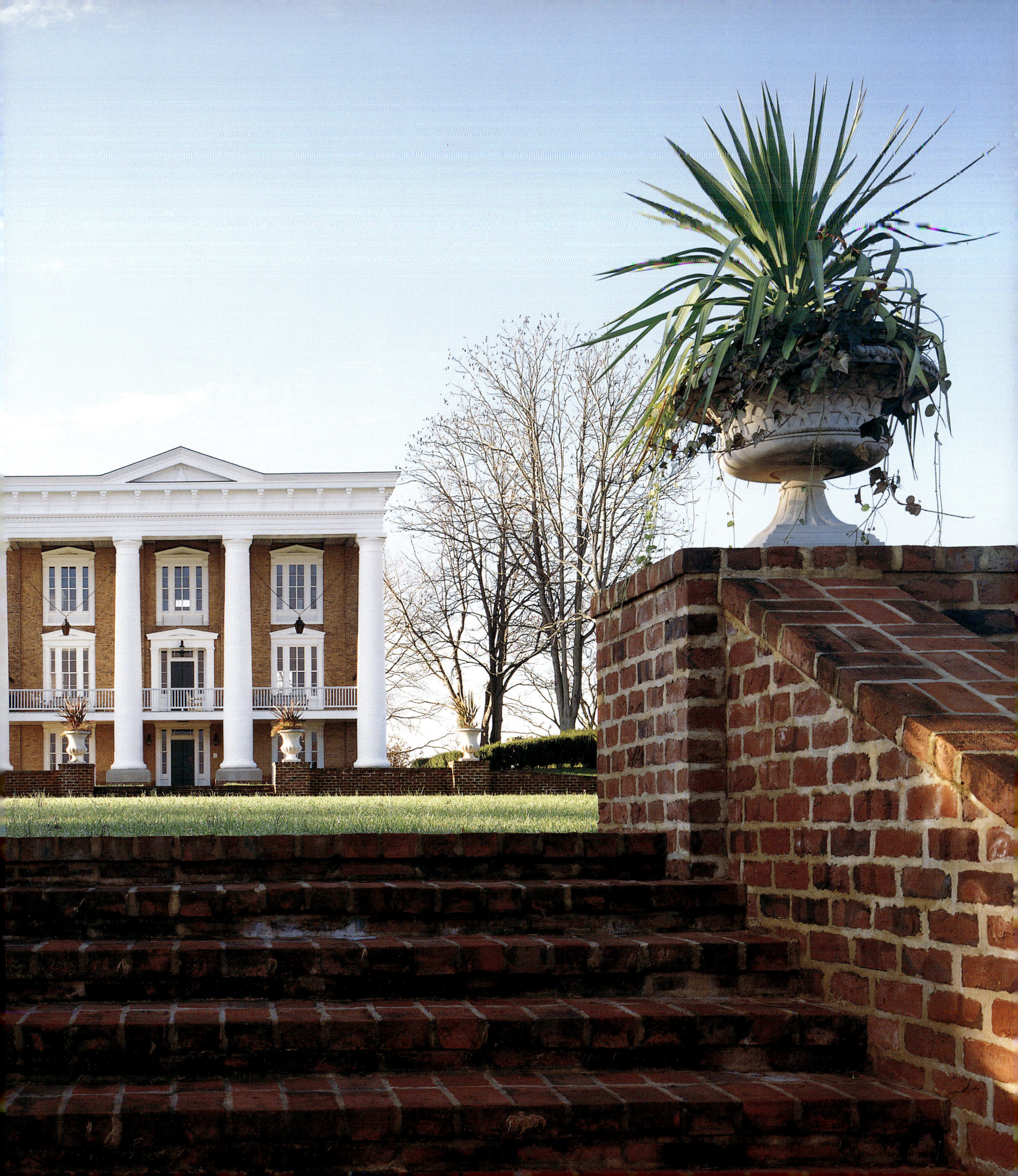

A magnificent circular stairway winds its way up through the middle of the house, rising from the limestone and slate floor of the first level's entry hall to the third floor. The original walnut newel post, mahogany handrail, and pine stairs have been fully restored.

Although bricks had been made in Virginia since 1619, most of the eighteenth century farms in the Piedmont were constructed of hand-hewn logs and later sawn weatherboard. Brick mansions later became statements of wealth and permanence of successful owners who grew tobacco, corn, and beans. By the time Greenville was begun in 1847 corn had replaced tobacco as the main cash crop. When the current owners began work on Greenville, the house had been abandoned for many years and corn grew right up to the front door. Greenville's entrance has since been extensively landscaped into a formal garden and lawn, but corn is still grown in 800 acres, rotated annually with crops of soybeans.

Greenville is one of a handful of classically inspired mansions built by Jeremiah Morton in the mid-nine-

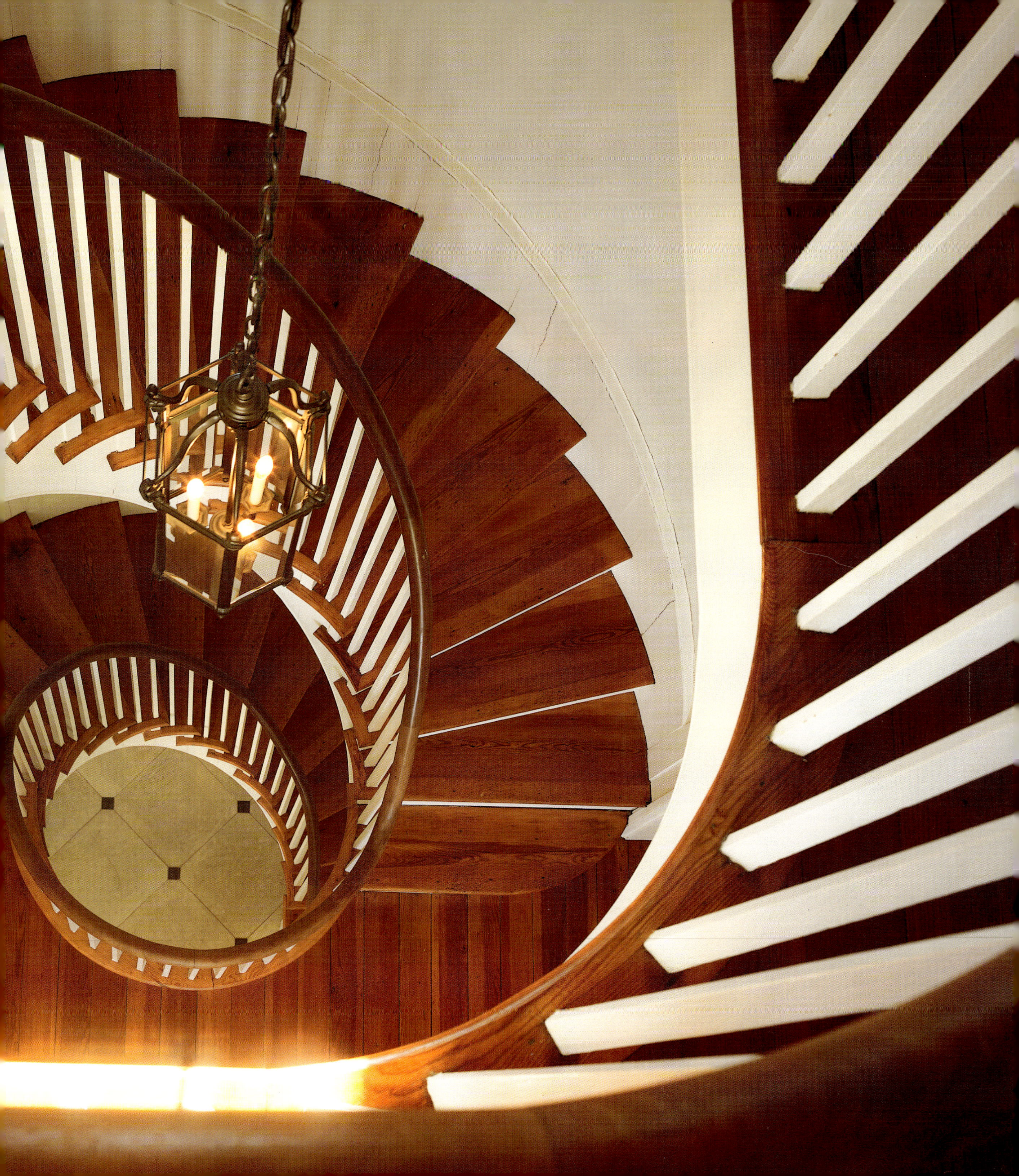

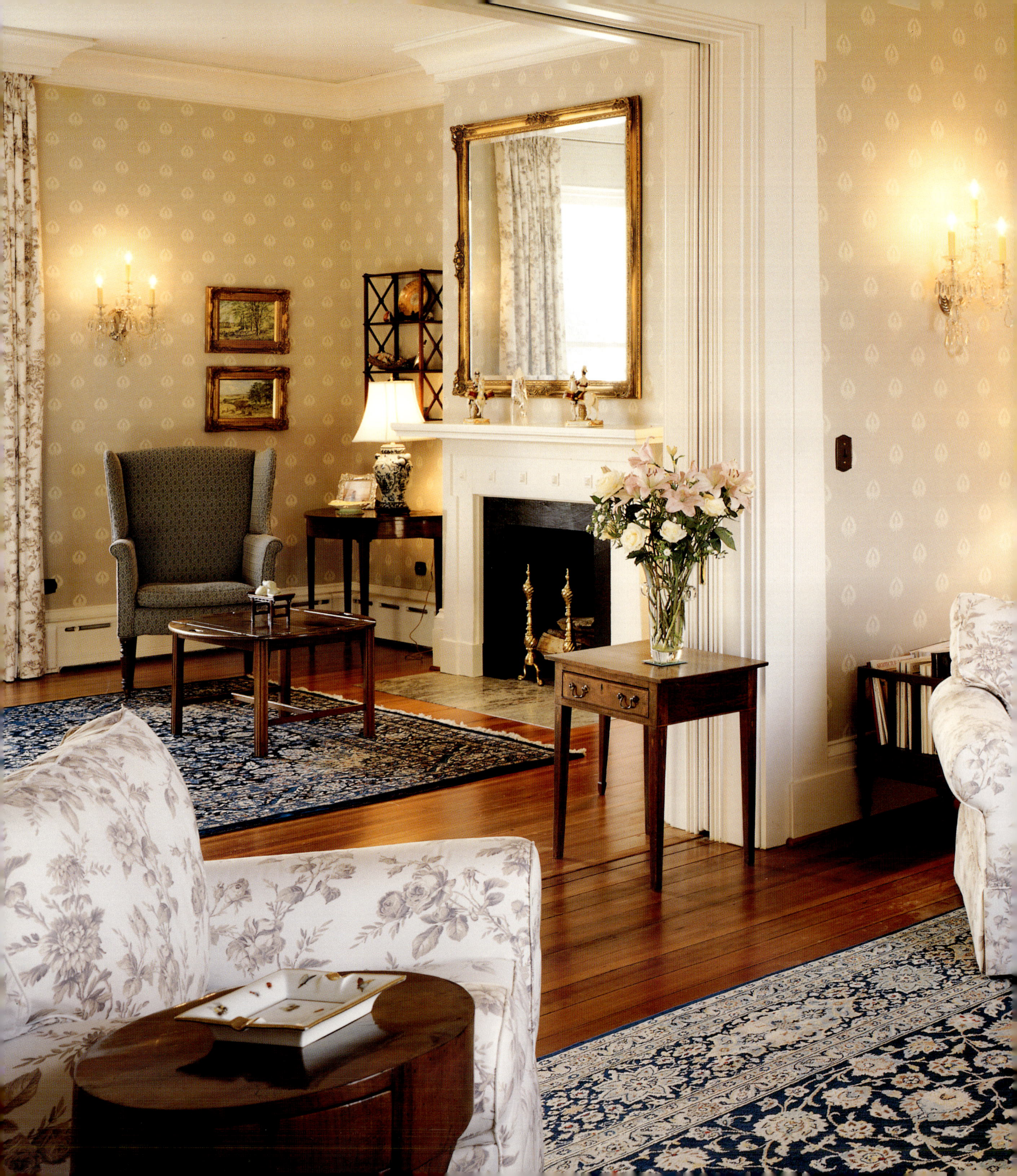

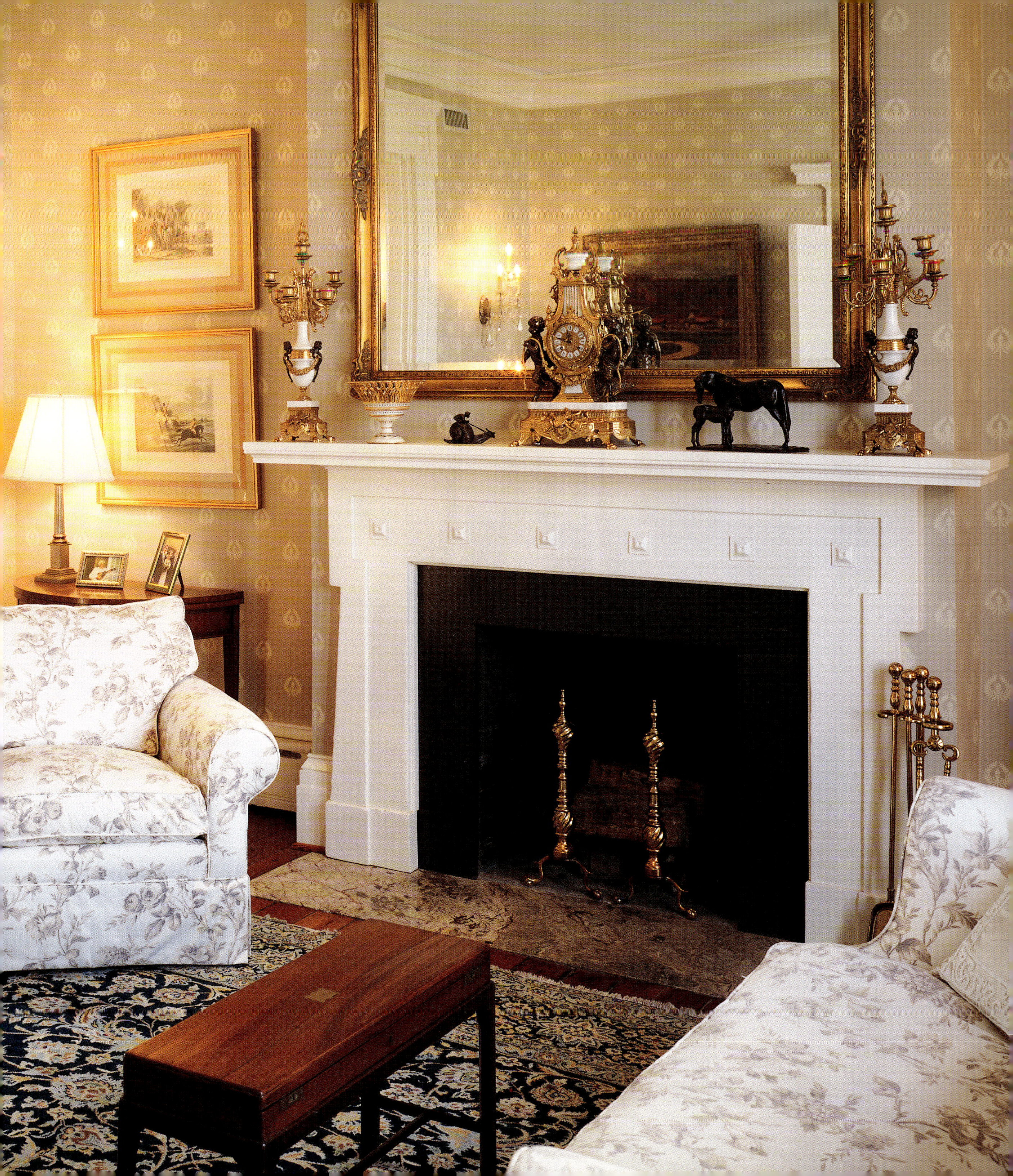

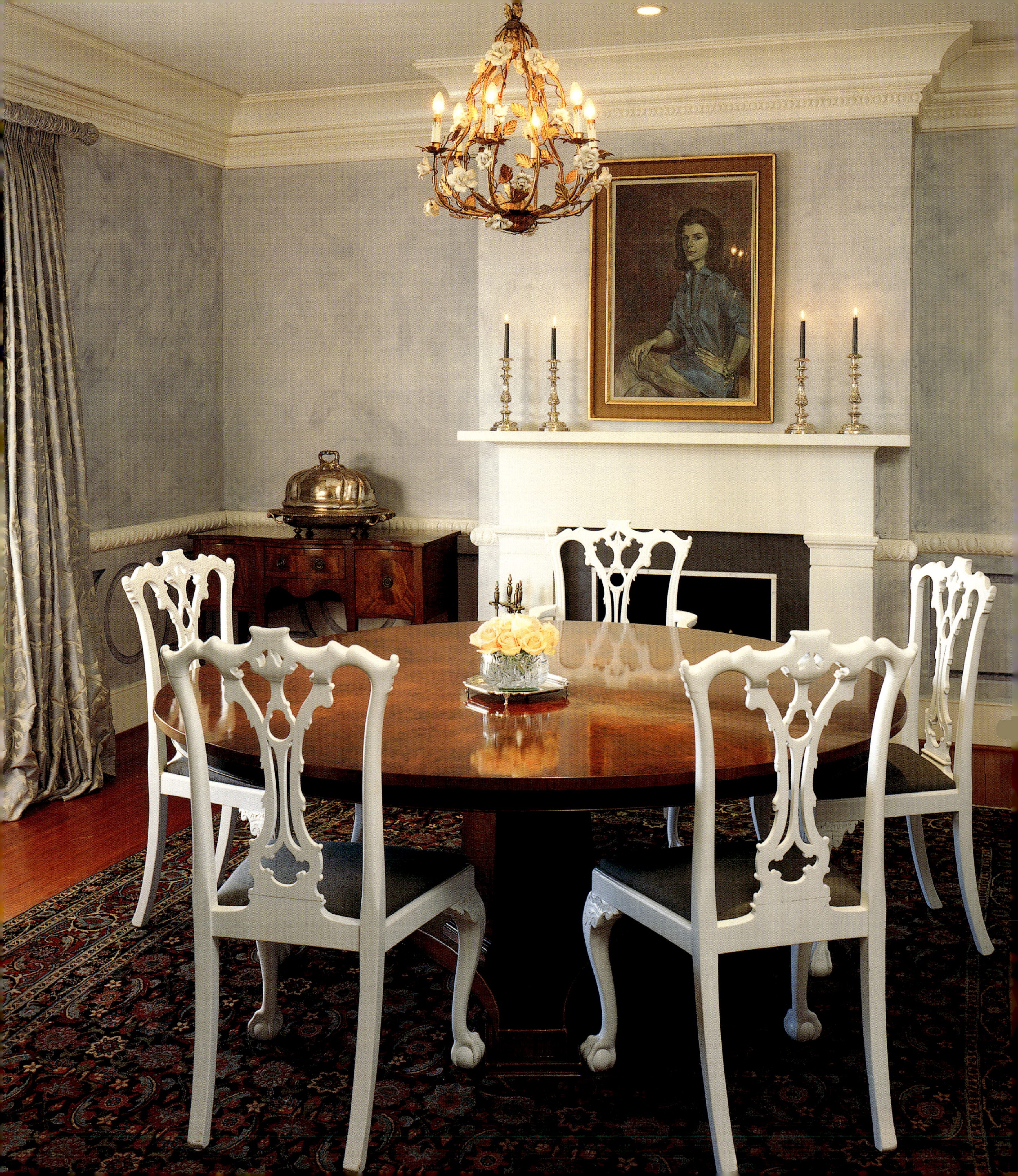

PRECEDING PAGES *The double parlors on the second floor are spacious and well-appointed. Furnishings in the front room include comfortable seating upholstered in cotton, a nineteenth-century wooden gun case that is set on a stand to create a coffee table, a gilt carved mirror over the original mantel, and a pair of marble and brass candelabra and matching clock.*

OPPOSITE *One of the twelve rooms in the house, all with twelve-foot ceilings, this is used as the dining room. Located off the entry foyer, its pale blue glazed faux finish on the walls and bright white paint on the woodwork that includes unusually wide crown molding make it cheery. White paint on the Georgian-style chairs highlights their intricate carving. The arrangement around a circular dining table creates a striking central focus for the room.*

ABOVE *In the kitchen, located in the south portion of the house, a ceramic tile mural designed by Mrs. Foshay features Byland Abbey in Yorkshire and the surrounding countryside. Roli Scassa, an Italian artist, completed the art piece while she was living in Charlottesville. For the custom kitchen cabinetry, the owner specified a finish that resembled one she liked on a weathered wooden shutter. The country farm table was made by a local carpenter of old barn wood.*

teenth century along the Rapidan River in Culpeper County. Morton designed Greenville with generous proportions, as he did with other sizable houses built during this era of prosperity including, among others, Struan, the remodel for the front of Mountain View, and Annandale.

The Foshays, an erudite couple who had left Connecticut to farm in Virginia and had done so in Orange County since 1975, first heard about Greenville in 1984. They bought the property to create a working farm, to breed Fjords and Belgians, and to restore the mansion to its full magnificence. After years of careful reconstruction, they can no longer stand four feet below floor level in the basement and look up through the rafters to the ceiling of the third floor. The entire house has been restored. The exterior has undergone extensive work and continues to be superbly maintained, while the interior that includes freshly plastered walls, has original woodwork, a central staircase, and flooring that have been restored or reconstructed. With their aesthetic sensibilities, love of farming, and commitment to preservation, the Foshays have revived and enhanced this valuable historic estate, now their beautiful family home and a successful working farm.

183

LEFT *The large two-room mid-nineteenth-century brick summer kitchen faces the southern entrance to the house. It has two large brick chimneys and one of the hearths has a large iron crane and three warming closets.*

OPPOSITE *The grandly scaled house looks out on manicured gardens with holly parterres backed with yew, a series of large classical-style urns, and to the northeast a new garden conservatory.*

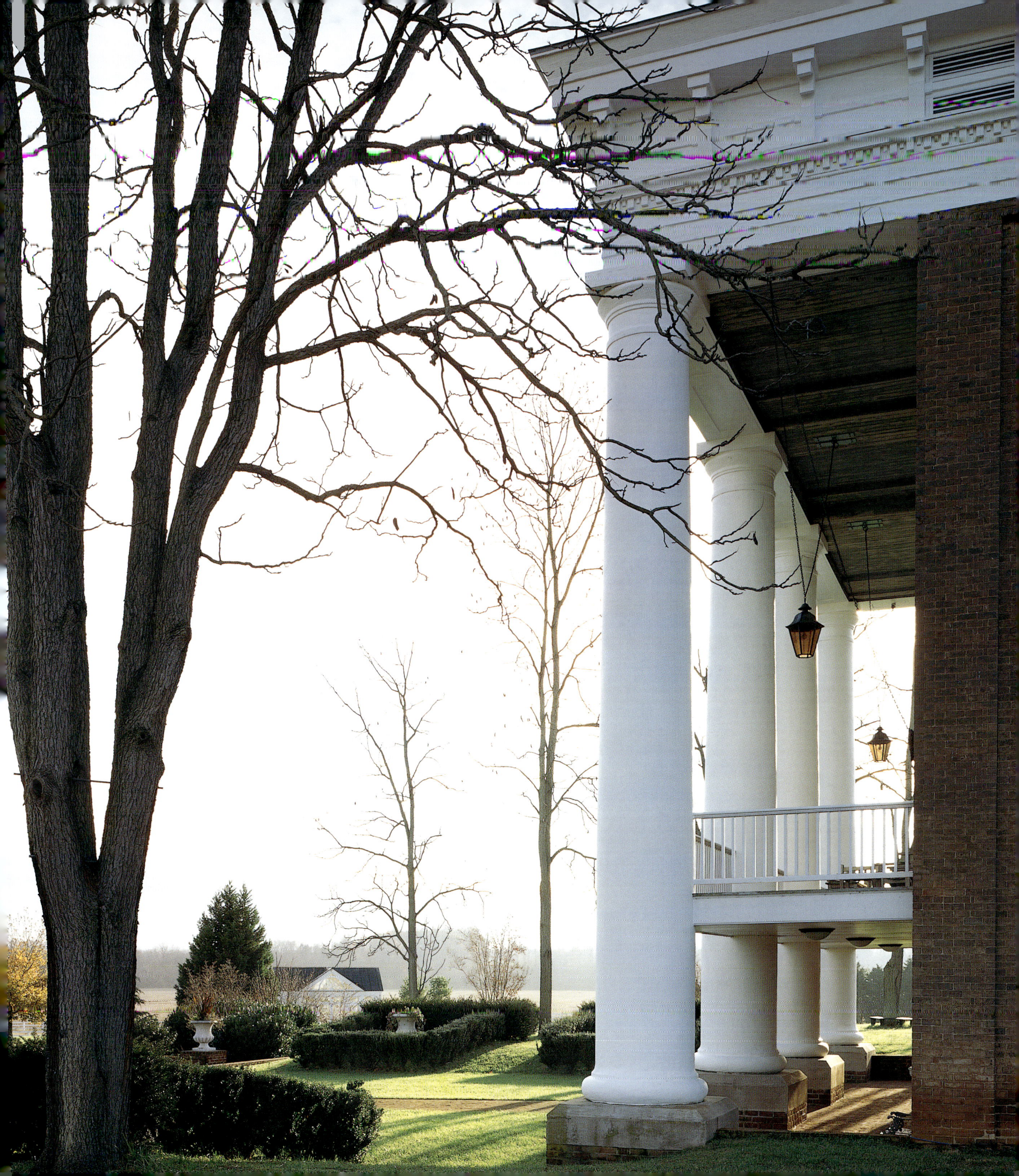

WOODLAWN

Residence of Mr. and Mrs. Justin H. Wiley
Main house, mid-1800s; addition, 1930; remodel and additions, 2005; Dan Frisch, architect
Barn/stable and tobacco barn, c. 1870

The scene at Woodlawn is peaceful and serene. Off the beaten path and oblivious to traffic in Orange County, an unpaved drive bends around a pasture and the front of the cheery yellow Virginia farmhouse comes into view. Its situation among towering centuries-old trees lends to the romance of the setting. In every direction there is an unobstructed view of the countryside, and only the sound of whinnying horses fills the air. From the moment the owner first saw the 50-acre farm he recognized it as a gem and sensed that this could be a place where he and his wife could raise a family. It must have been destiny, because the property fell out of escrow three times before Justin and Nancy Wiley became its owners in 2000.

Fresh paint and some minor restoration were necessary before the couple could move in. Then, in 2004, the Wileys hired New York architect Dan Frisch, who had worked on Justin's mother's house, for an extensive remodel that transformed a modest farmhouse into a Virginia homestead befitting the active twenty-first-century family's lifestyle. By the completion of the project in 2005, Frisch had added two wings, a large master suite on one side and on the other, a formal dining room as well as a space that combines an open plan kitchen and family room, a mud room that serves as an all-purpose foyer with a side entry, and a convenient powder room.

Woodlawn's situation among towering trees, surrounded by pastures and nearby wooded hills, creates an image of idyllic rural beauty that recalls the nineteenth-century Virginia horse farm. In 2005 the owners added wings to either side of the historic farmhouse that complement its straightforward architecture.

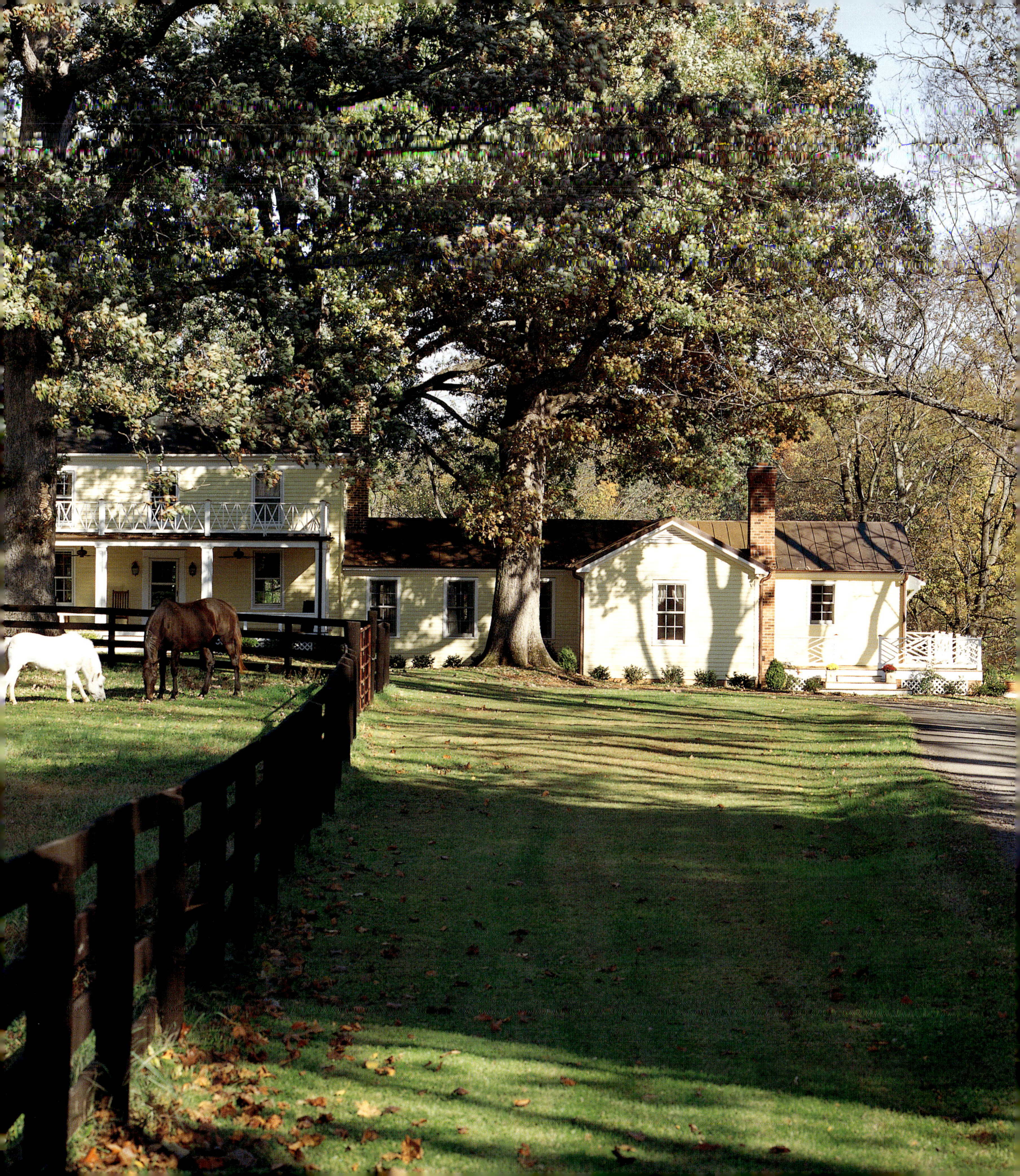

ABOVE *Equestrian art fills the walls in the formal parlor. Above the camelback sofa is a French hunting print.*

RIGHT *A portrait of owner Nancy Wiley by Sandra M. Forbush hangs above the small French three-drawer rosewood cabinet with marble top. A portrait of Justin's father, Hugh Wiley, has a place of honor above the mantel. Hugh won the Individual Gold at the 1959 Pan American Games and was also a silver medalist in the 1960 Olympic games. The child's Windsor chair is a family piece.*

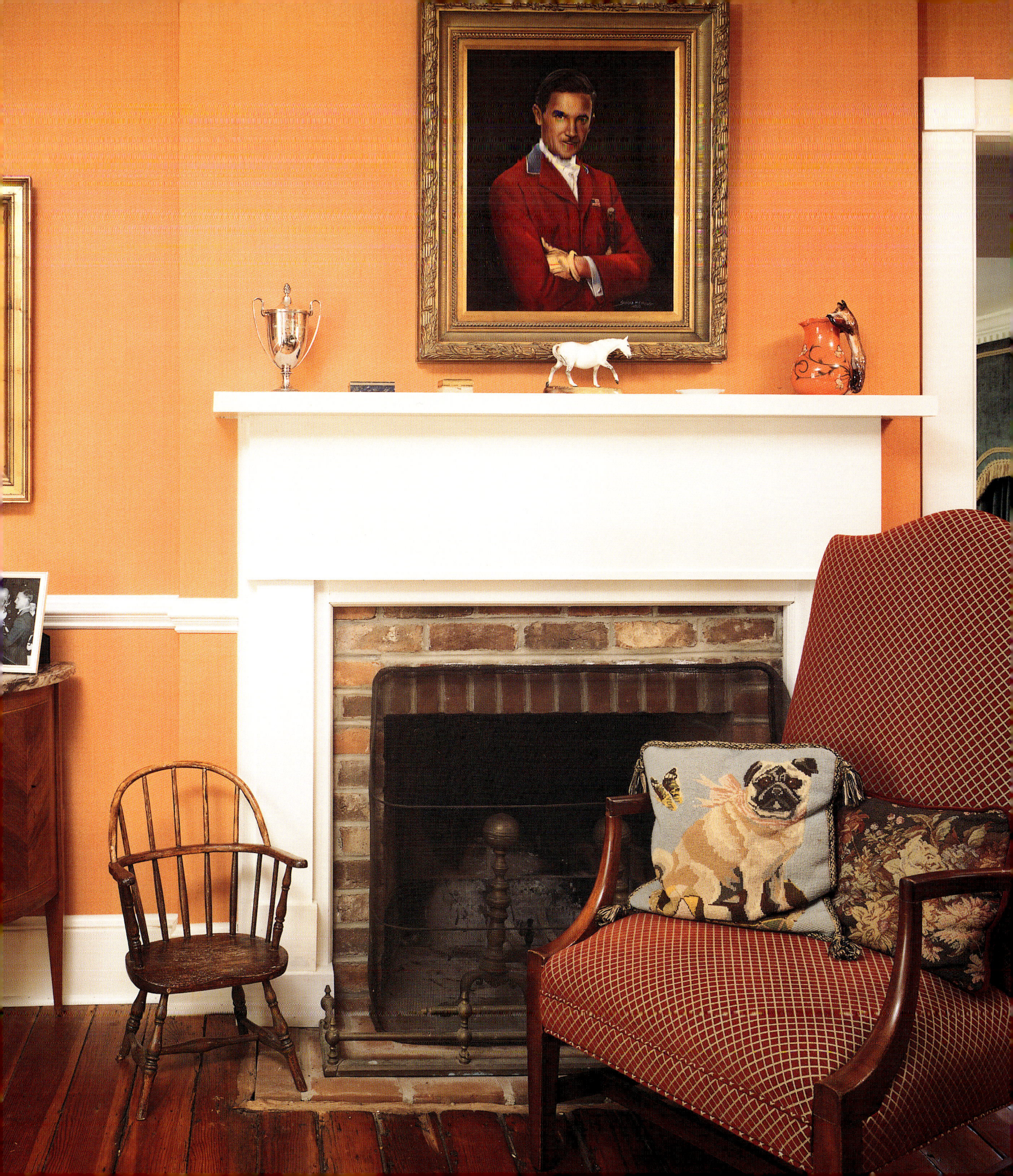

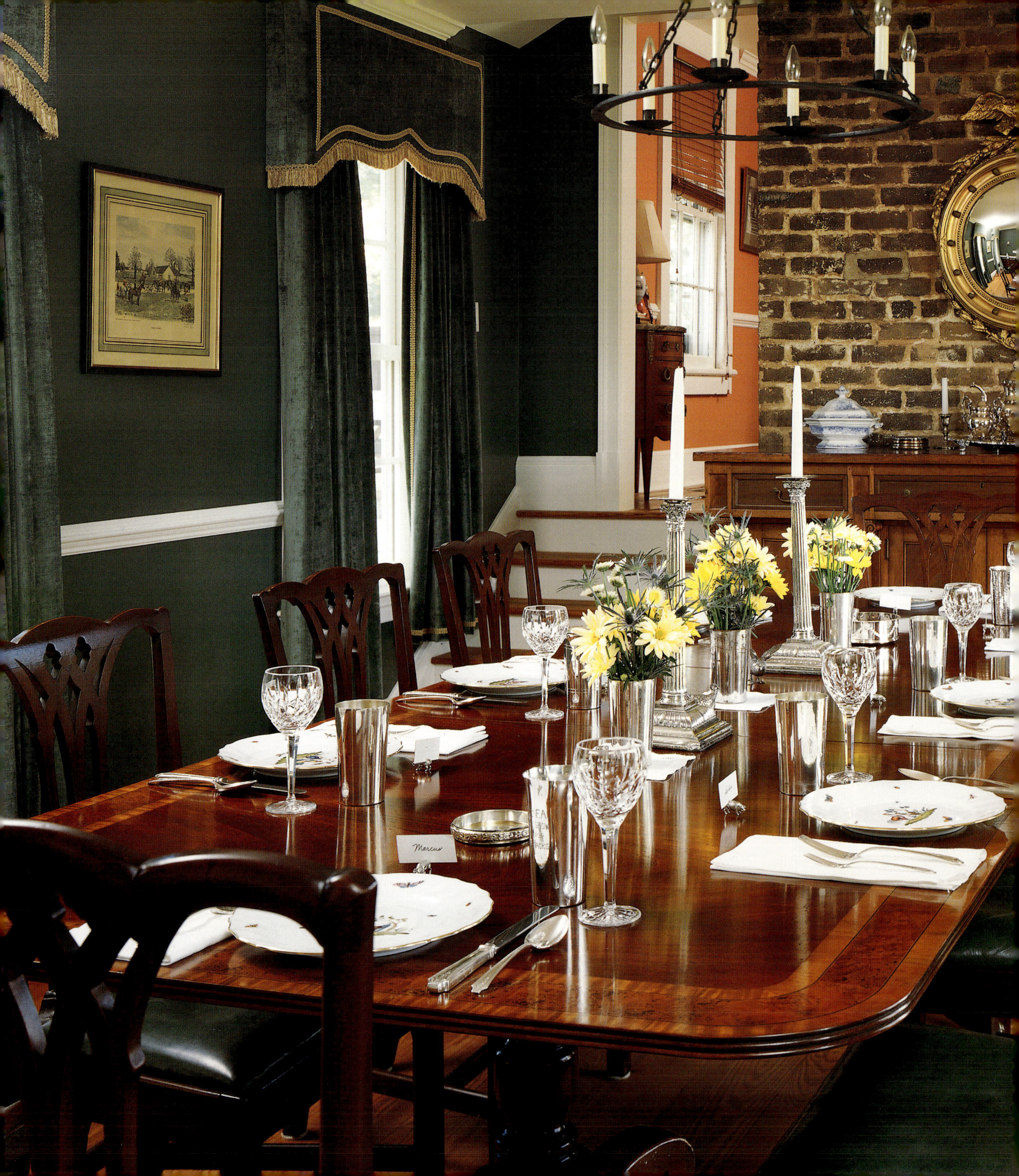
Marcus

LEFT *The dining room's deep hunter green walls and velvet curtains add drama to the intimate space, part of the 2005 addition. A gilt bull's eye mirror above the nineteenth-century walnut sideboard reflects the mahogany dining table and Georgian-style mahogany chairs.*

ABOVE *The library is in the mid-nineteenth-century portion of the farmhouse. Books on equestrian sports fill the bookshelves and silver equestrian trophies are displayed. The drop-front cherry plantation desk provides a quiet workspace.*

The Wileys now have three children, six horses, two ponies, and a dog, and are raising their young family in this historic atmosphere. The farm's proximity to Orange, Culpeper, Charlottesville, and even Middleburg makes it the perfect location for Justin's real estate business. And the Wileys made sure that nothing will damage the bucolic setting by adhering to a multitude of deed restrictions. Justin and Nancy, both members of the Piedmont Environmental Council, are proponents of preserving Virginia's cultural and architectural heritage, and applaud the growing awareness of the need for land conservation in Virginia.

Large double-hung windows with views of the nearby pastures and a fourteen-foot ceiling create spaciousness in the well-lit main room of the master suite that was added to the far north of the historic house. A painting by Sandra M. Forbush hangs to the left of the bed. The dark wood of the major pieces of furniture ties the room together. A whimsical bed designed with intertwined branches and a nineteenth-century spinning wheel add touches of rusticity, while the nineteenth-century mahogany highboy and a nineteenth-century mahogany drop-leaf table anchor the room with refinement.

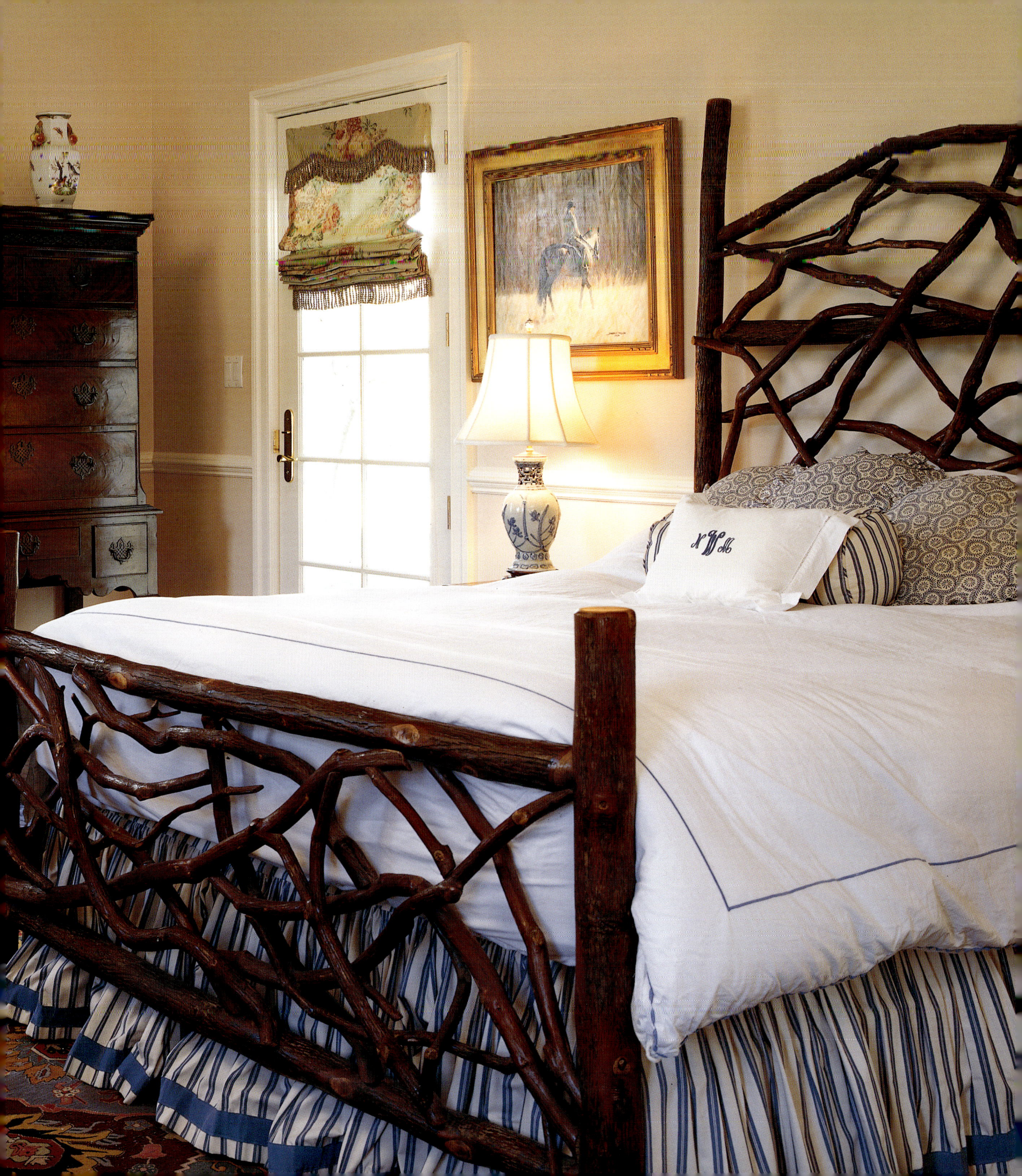

ABOVE *A nineteenth-century tobacco barn beside the lower pasture is left to weather naturally.*

RIGHT *In the backyard, the painted weatherboard barn and stable is large enough for the functioning farm, with eleven stalls for the Wileys' horses and ponies and room for farm equipment and supplies.*

Part of the joy with which they experience their land is a result of its location in the territory of the Keswick Hunt. Horsemanship has deep roots in both families. Justin and Nancy are foxhunters who have ridden their whole lives. Nancy grew up with a master of foxhounds and Justin's father, Hugh Wiley, was on the U.S. Olympic Show Jumping Team in 1956 and in 1960 when the team claimed the Silver, and he won the Individual Gold at the Pan American Games in 1959. So it is no wonder that daughter Lilly at age 3 ½ and son Hugh at age 1 ½ have already ridden ponies on lead lines in the Keswick Hunt. During the season, the whole family may be out on horses and ponies, as getting to a meet is often as effortless as walking from the barn to the front lawn or hacking over the nearby hill. They have made their Virginia dream a reality.

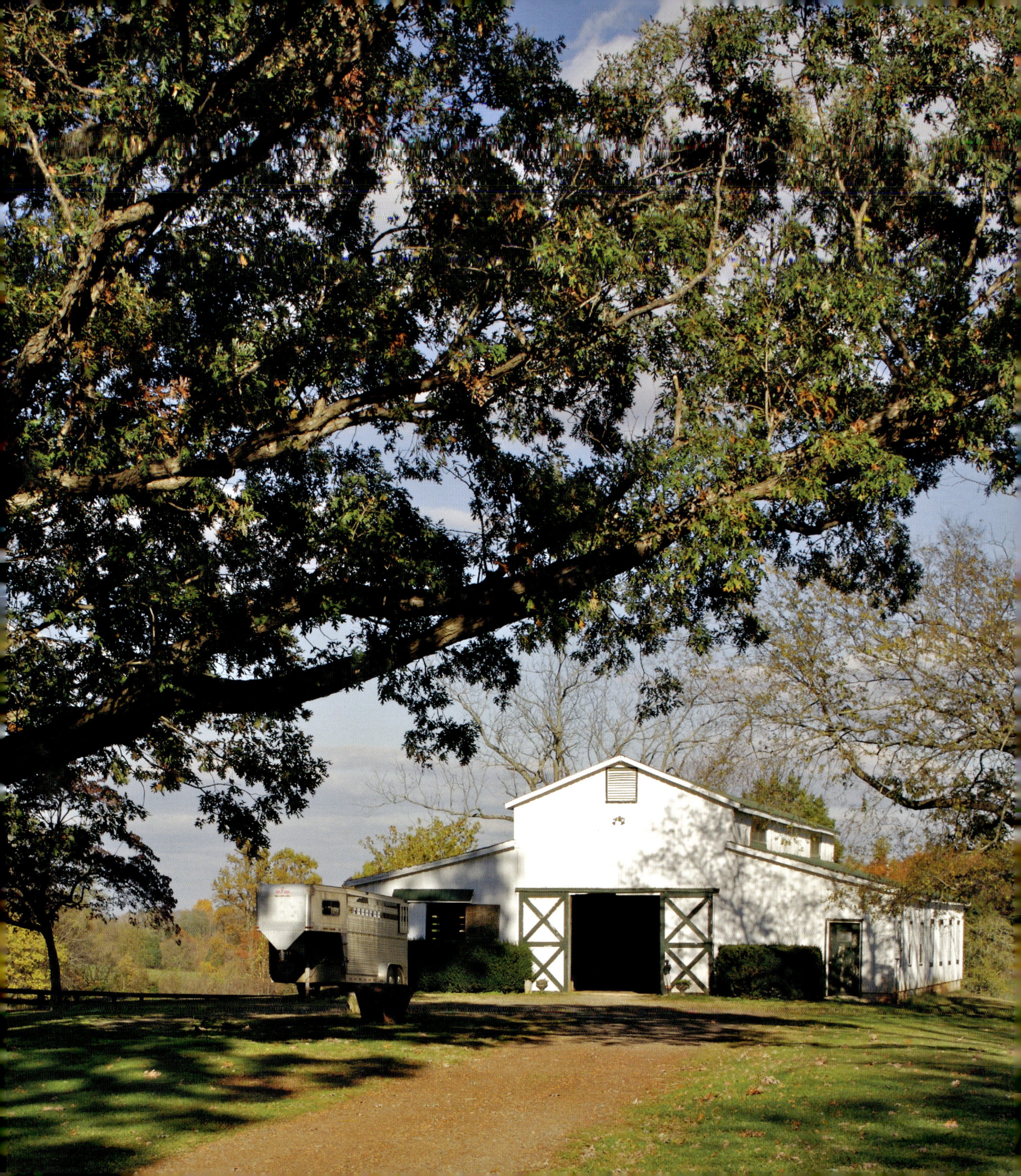

MORROWDALE FARM

Farmhouse, barns and stables, ice house, school houses, 1880s
Farmhouse restoration, school houses remodeled, 1970s
Mid-1800s
Munday family log house from Westover Farm moved to property, 1999

Morrowdale Farm is a quintessential Virginia estate that has maintained its original purpose as a family home and self-sufficient farm for over a hundred years. Its current owners are both Virginians who moved from Charlottesville over thirty years ago to raise their family, run a hay farm, and breed registered polled Hereford cattle and Thoroughbreds on over three hundred acres in Albemarle County at the foot of the Blue Ridge Mountains. The nineteenth-century farm sits amidst white-fenced pastures and far-reaching hay fields, and has an outstanding view of the nearby mountain range.

Morrowdale Farm, formerly called Fair View, was part of the 1748 land grant to Fredricksville Parish in what would become part of Albemarle County. A portion of that tract later became Midway, a plantation of more than 3,500 acres that reached from Whitehall to Ivy. Thomas Layton Rodes was born there in 1829. He grew up riding to hounds and enlisted in a Confederate cavalry unit during the Civil War. After the war he moved to Richmond, where he married and had three children. In 1881, after his wife died and their house in Richmond burned down, Rodes returned to Albemarle to raise his young family there. He built what would become Morrowdale Farm on a western portion of his family's Midway Plantation on the rise that takes advantage of an outstanding vista of the Blue Ridge. He married again in 1887, had another daughter, and died in 1902.

RIGHT *Morrowdale Farm, in Albemarle County, is a working Thoroughbred, beef cattle, and hay farm on over three hundred acres at the base of the Blue Ridge Mountains. The spacious porch and patio at the front of the painted weatherboard manor house provide pleasant gathering spots where the owners can display their warm Virginia hospitality.*

FOLLOWING PAGES *The sunroom/family-room is an addition that the owners made in the 1970s when they purchased Morrowdale Farm. The well-lit space has comfortable seating and antique furnishings that are pieces from the couple's two deeply rooted Virginia families.*

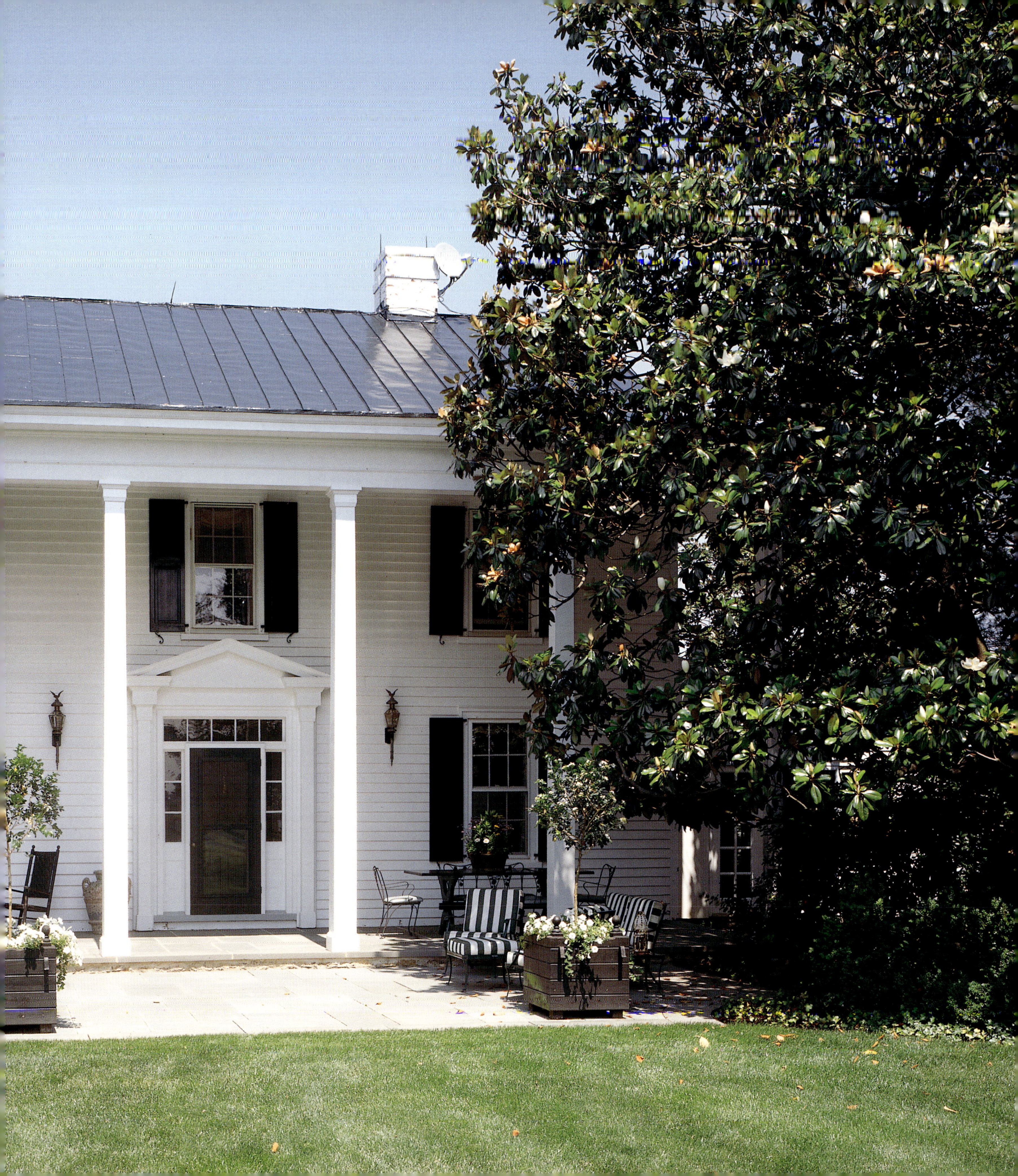

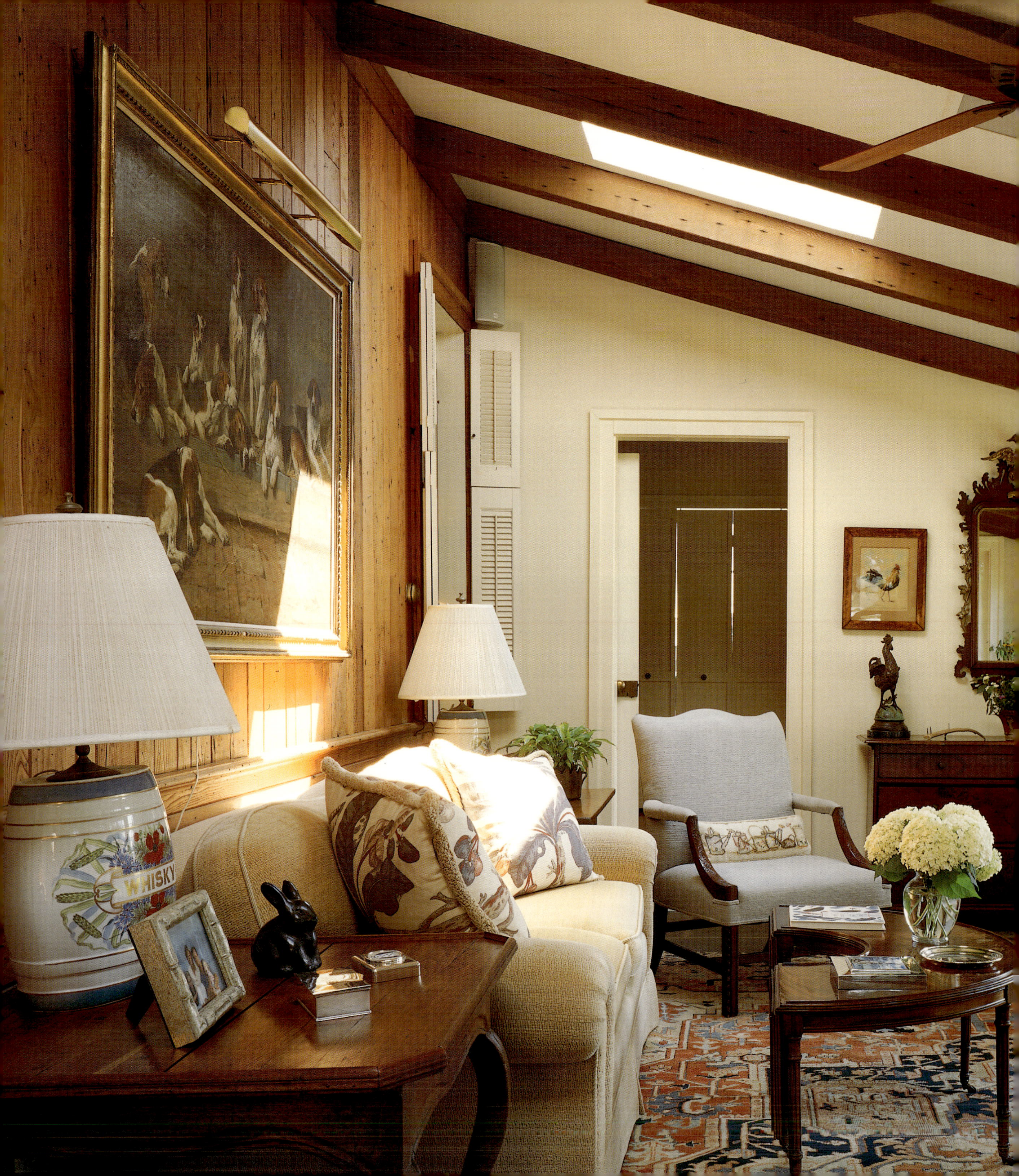
WHISKY

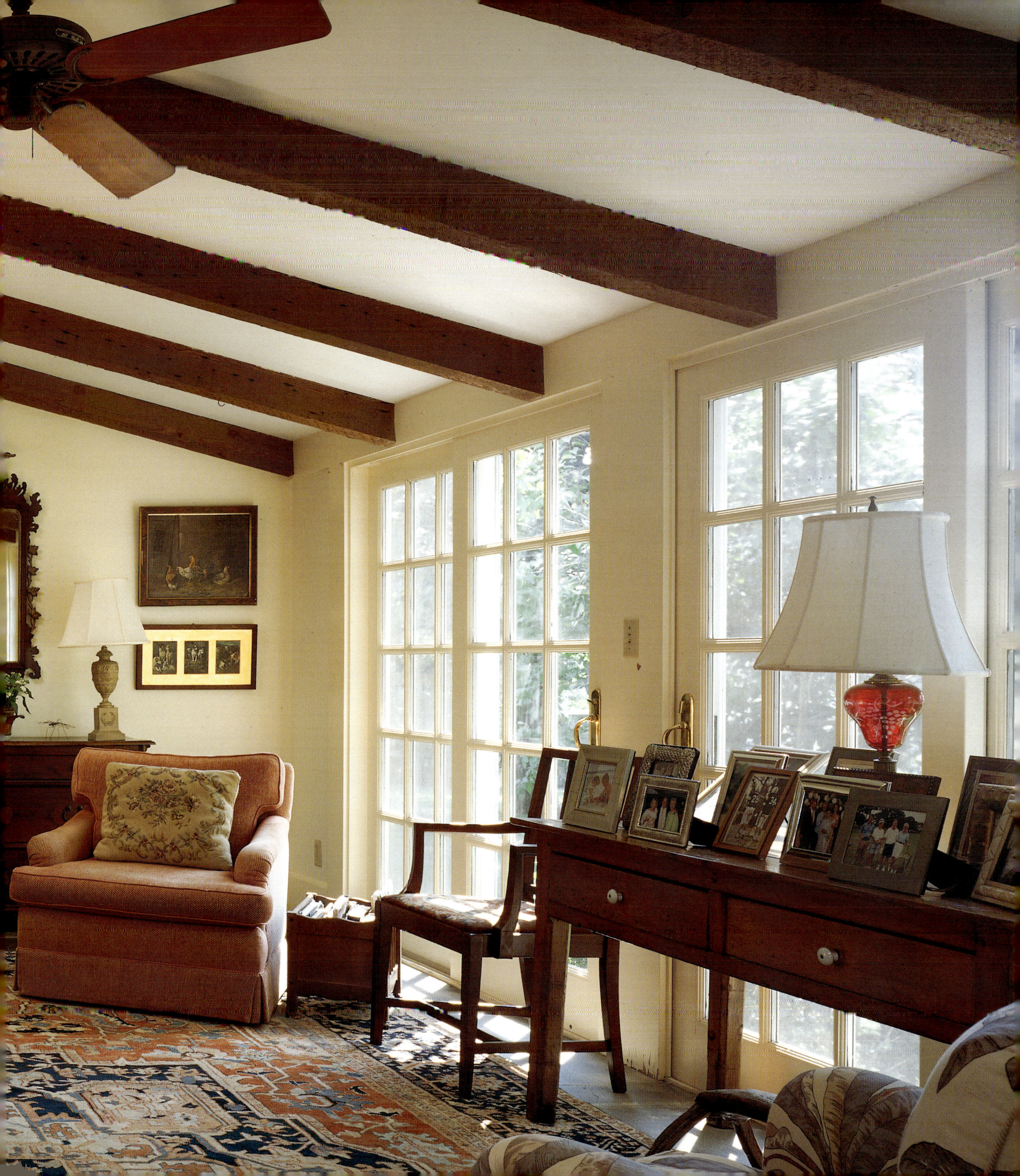

TOP *In the dining room an elaborate gilt wood Chinese Chippendale mirror reflects an eighteenth-century American red walnut corner cupboard that holds family China and silver.*

ABOVE *A late-eighteenth-century blockfront desk holds porcelain and silver pieces. The mirror hung above it is nineteenth-century Chippendale style. A tole tea-tray-on-stand is also nineteenth century. The deep tones of these furnishings anchor the sitting room's decor.*

RIGHT *The bright and spacious country kitchen is easily accessible from the dining room, library, and sunroom/family room.*

FOLLOWING PAGES *A restful, subdued palette was used in the guest bedroom. A painted screen depicting a country scene complements the room's tone with its muted colors. The dark walnut of the nineteenth-century chest of drawers and the mahogany canopy bed looks rich against the pale background.*

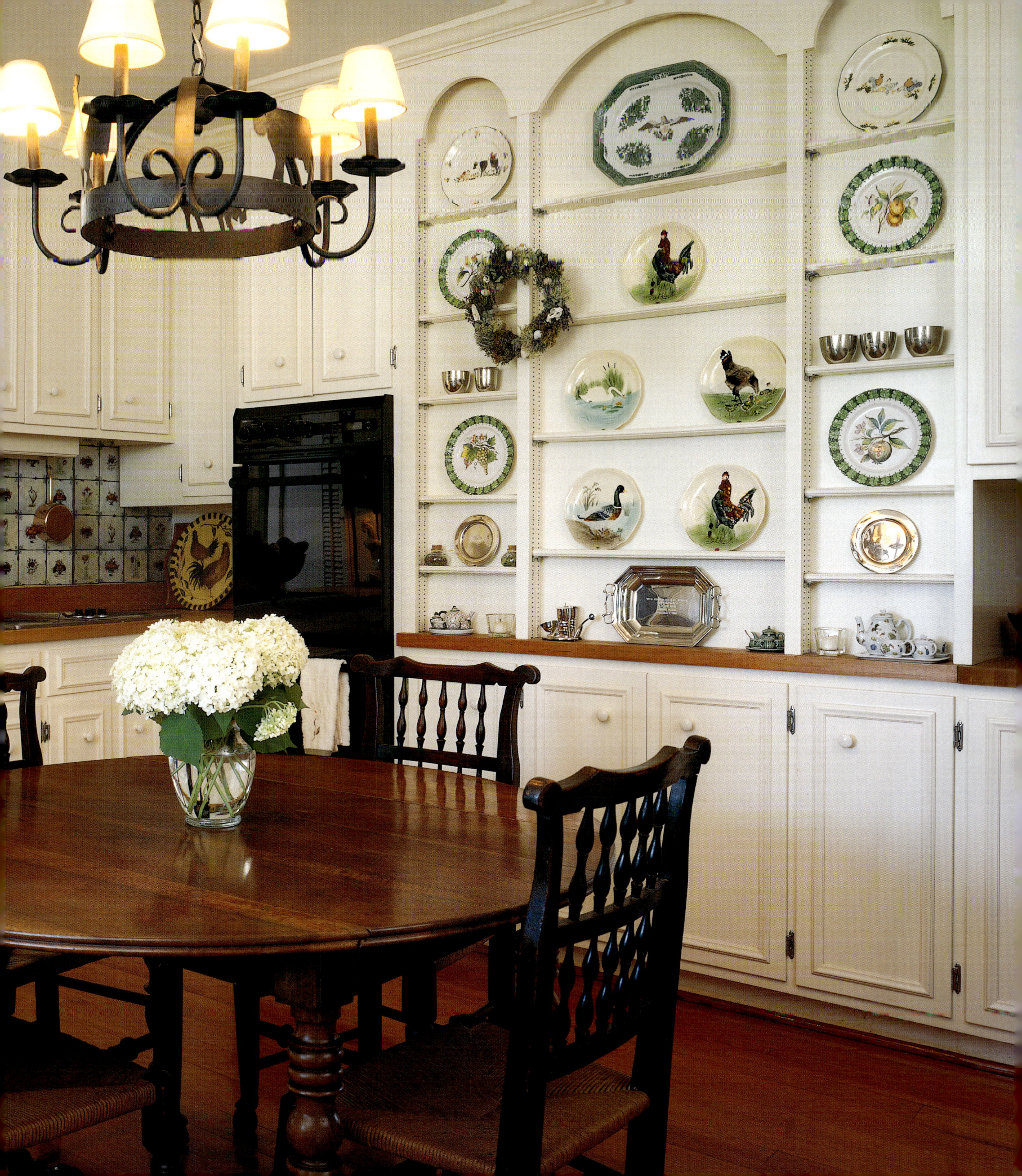

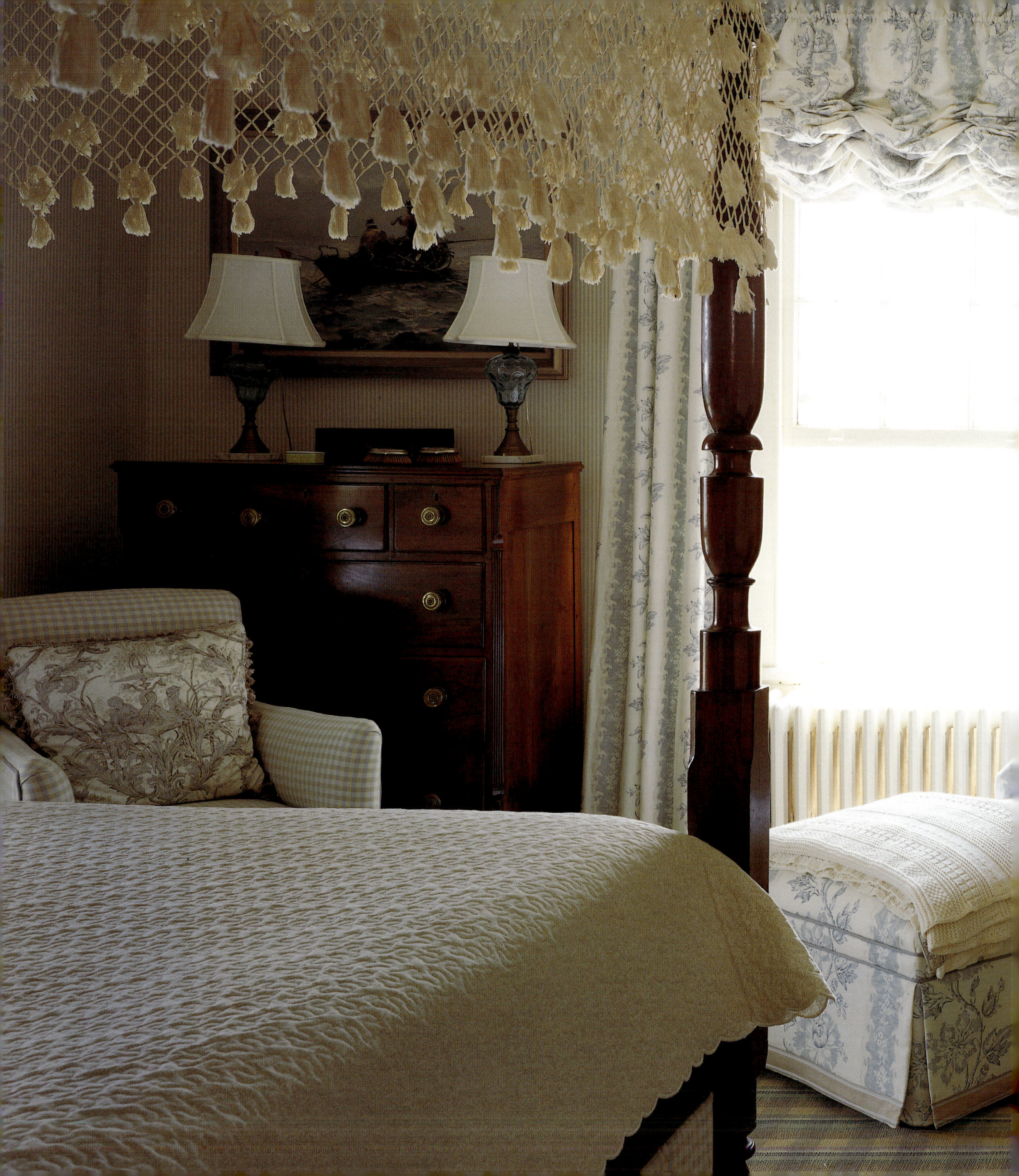

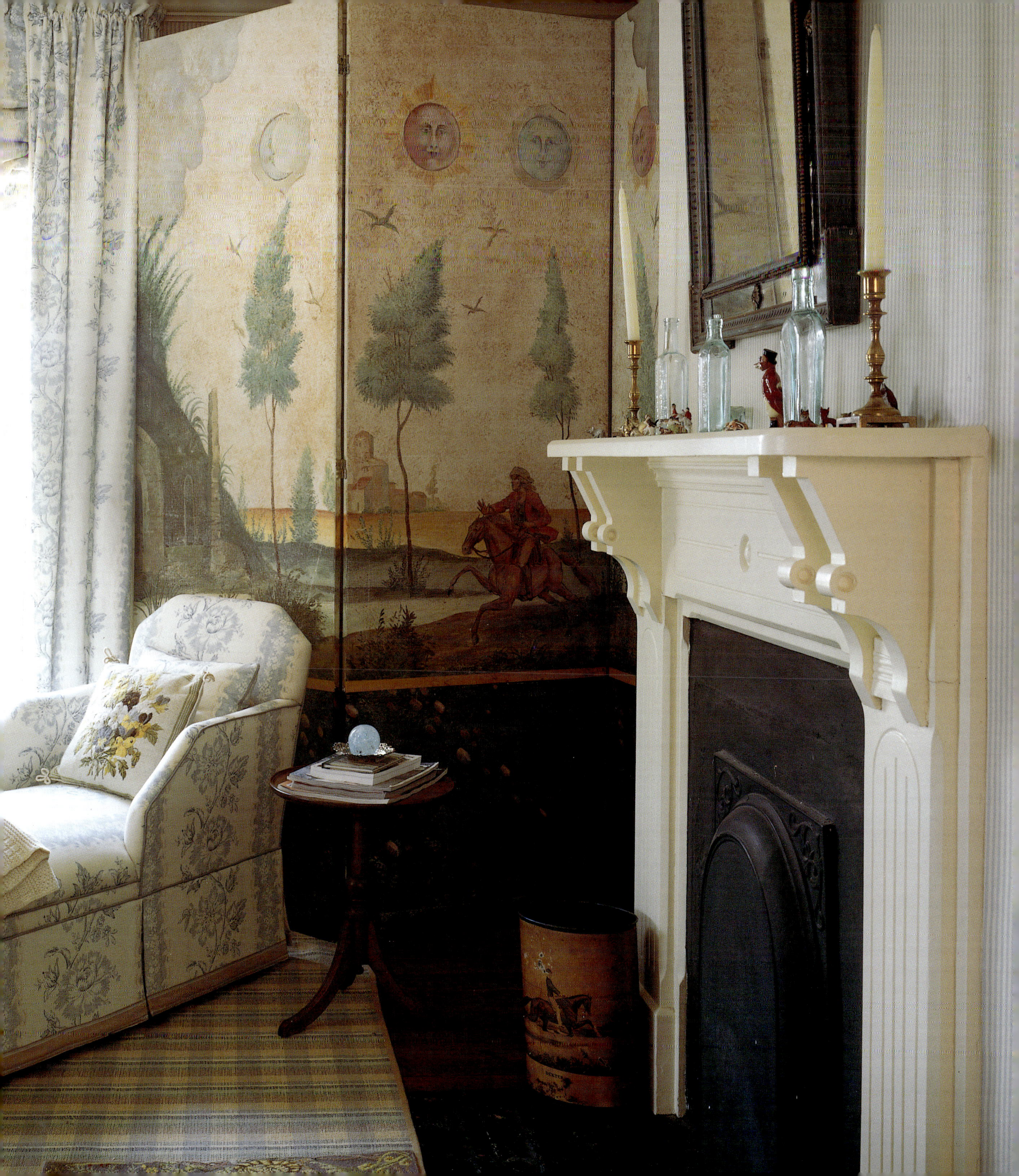

LEFT *The library, which holds the owners' books on Virginia history, is furnished with a French double-door cabinet whose warm fruitwood complements the house's original pine woodwork and mantels.*

OPPOSITE *The central hallway runs the full length of the house. The Aaron Willard tall-case clock is a family piece.*

The picturesque farmhouse is a frame structure sheathed in weatherboard that has been painted white. Though large, it has a traditional design of a central hallway with two rooms on either side with the same configuration repeated on the second floor. The massing of the historic house and its setting among towering trees gives it a Southern gentility and palpable solidity. Its large front and back porches are outstanding features of the late-nineteenth-century architecture. Large white columns at the main entrance lend a formal air to the country place, and at the back of the house, open double porches allow for cool breezes in the summertime. A dependency building that has been remodeled into a pool house, a restored schoolhouse that has become a tenant cottage, cattle and foaling barns and stables, and the original ice house, are all detailed similarly to the main house and present a cohesive and beautiful design for a farm in the lush Virginia landscape. To complement the bright white buildings, paths of rich Virginia clay fired into deep red bricks lead along dark green hedges of English boxwood and wind their way from the pool house and pool to the vegetable and cutting gardens that surround the original well. With the backdrop of an open-wide blue summer sky, pastures of golden hay, and lawns of thick healthy grass, Morrowdale presents one of the most serene and pleasing images of a working farm anywhere in Albemarle County.

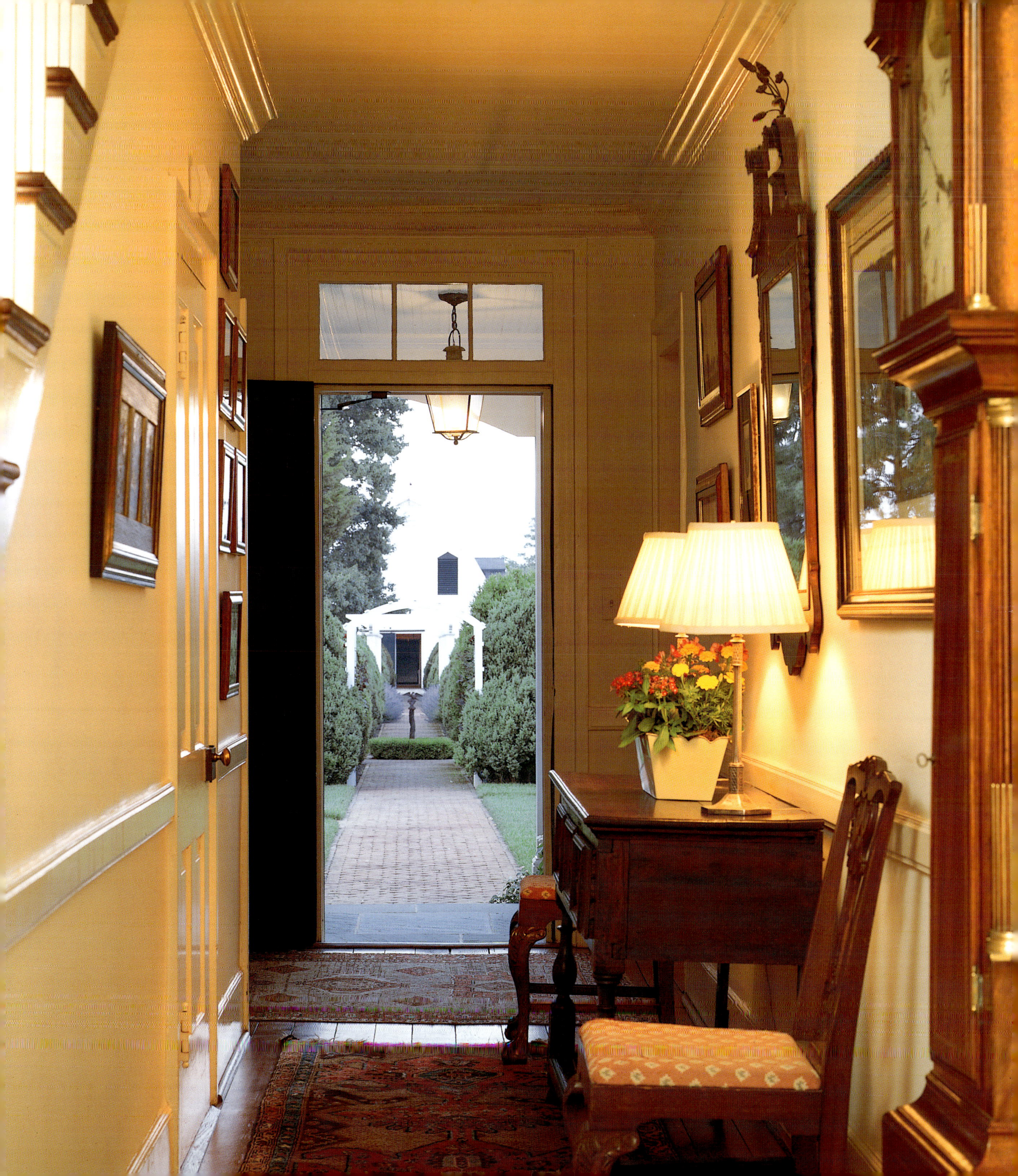

LEFT *A well-proportioned pergola extends from the back of the main house to the horse barn.*

BELOW LEFT *The vegetable and perennial gardens have a formal plan that surrounds the original well. Enclosed within a low white picket fence are English boxwood parterres, American boxwood that has been trimmed into conical shapes, and plantings of seasonal vegetables. A variety of flowering plants add touches of color.*

OPPOSITE *A brick path with lavender and English boxwood is set on a perpendicular axis to the house. The dark metal roof and deep black shutters and doors accentuate the fresh white of the house. The back facade features double-porches that run the length of the house.*

FOLLOWING PAGES *The horse, cattle, and hay farm is over three hundred acres of pastures and farmland situated at the base of the Blue Ridge Mountains.*

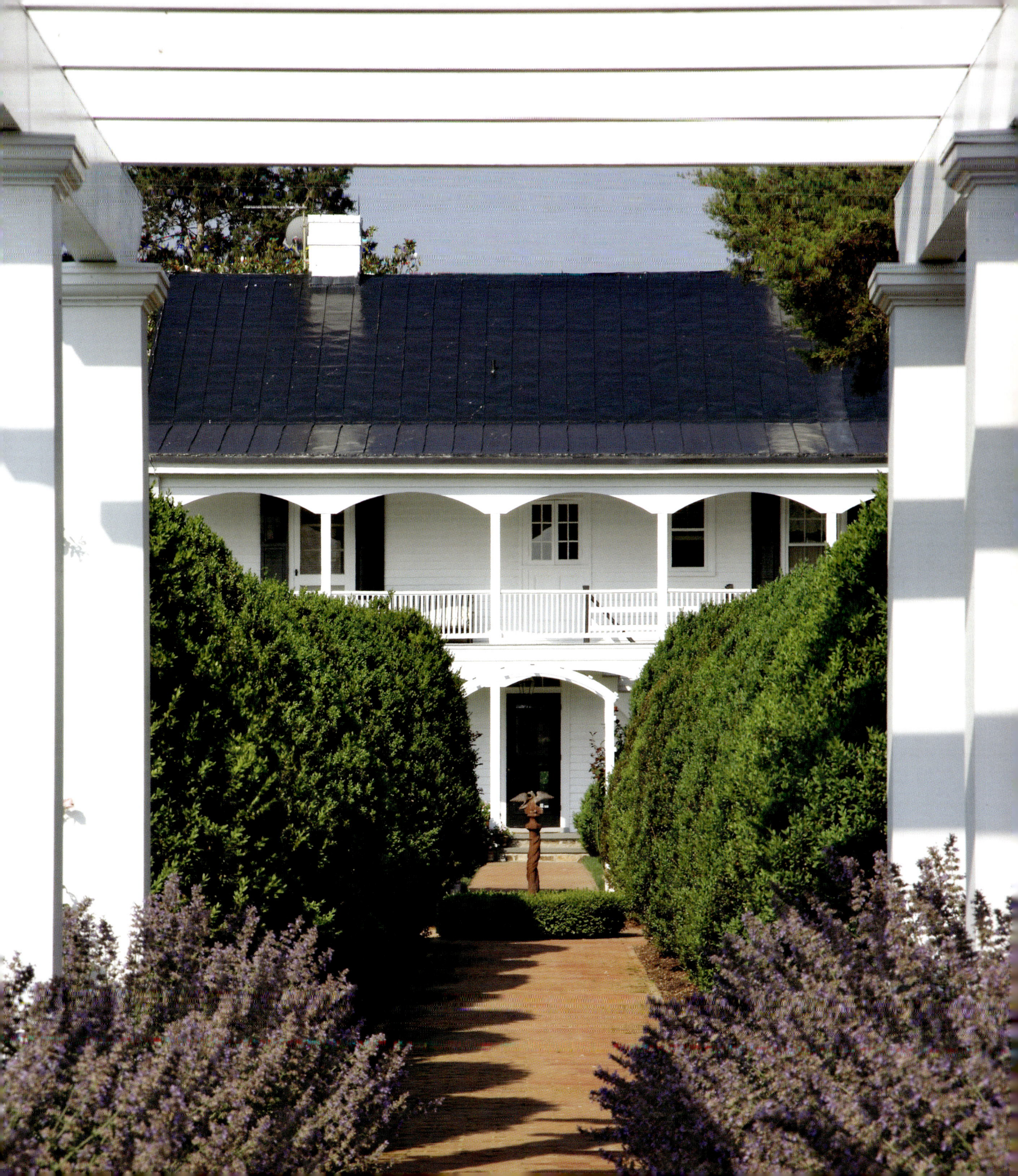

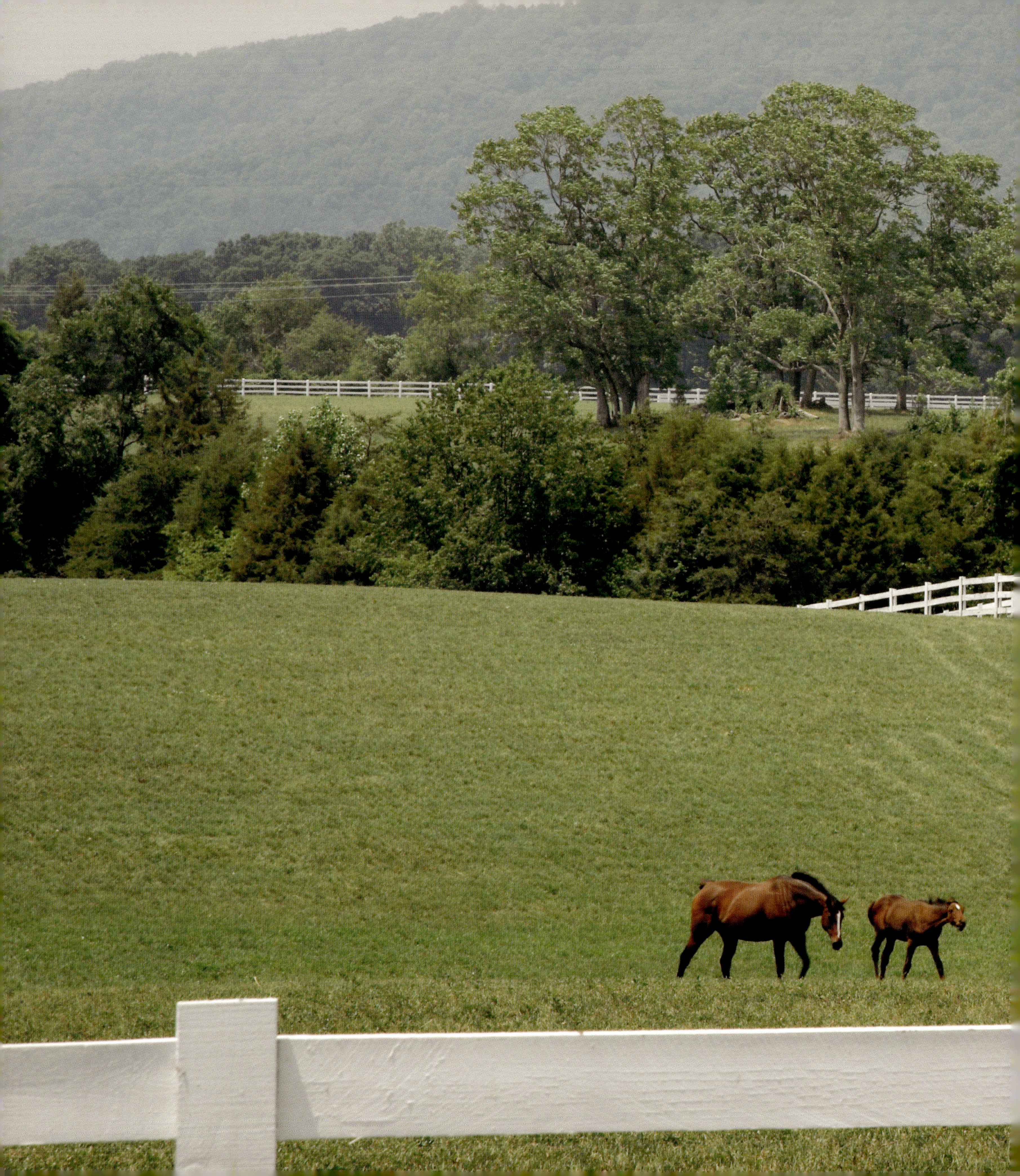

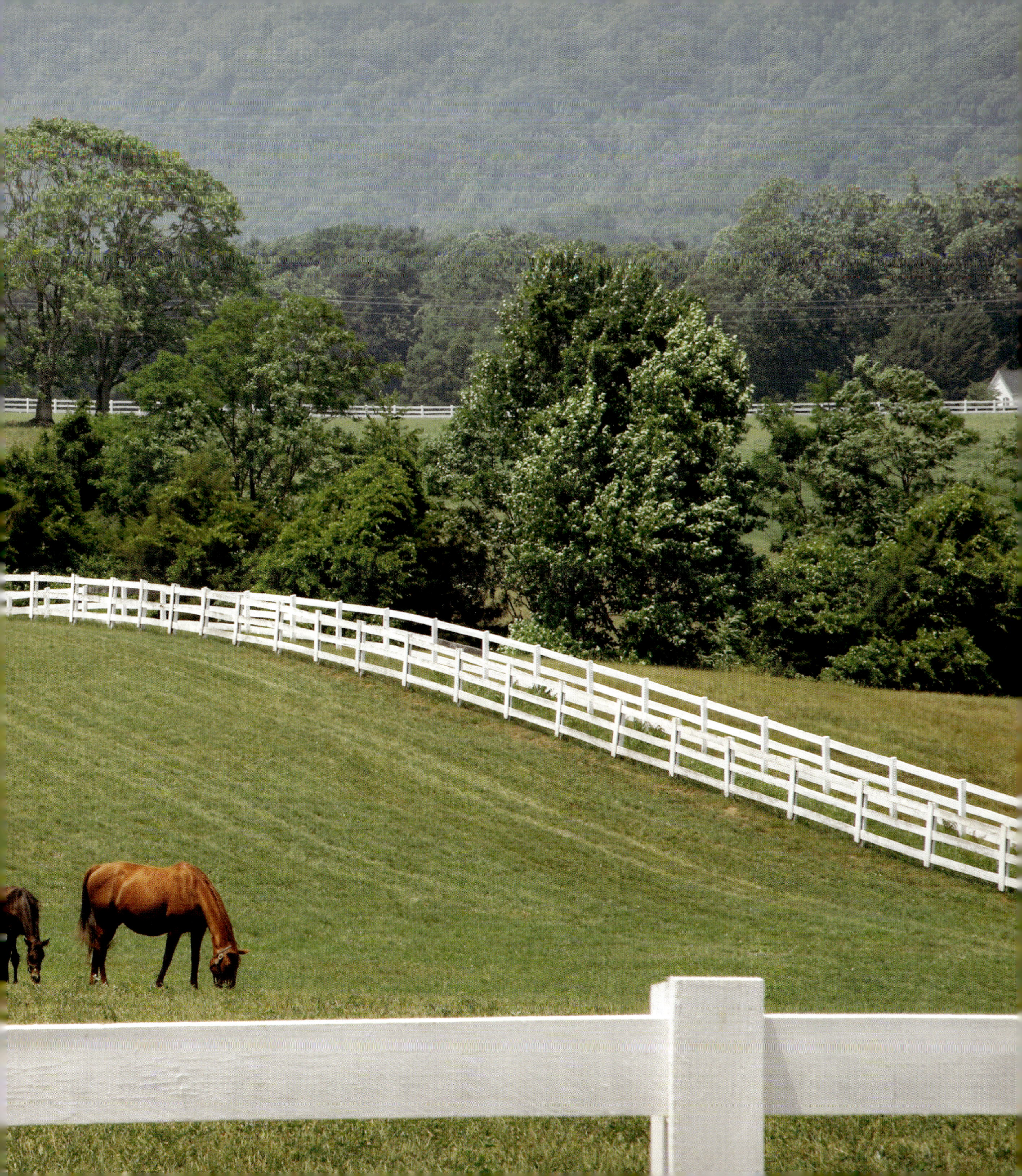

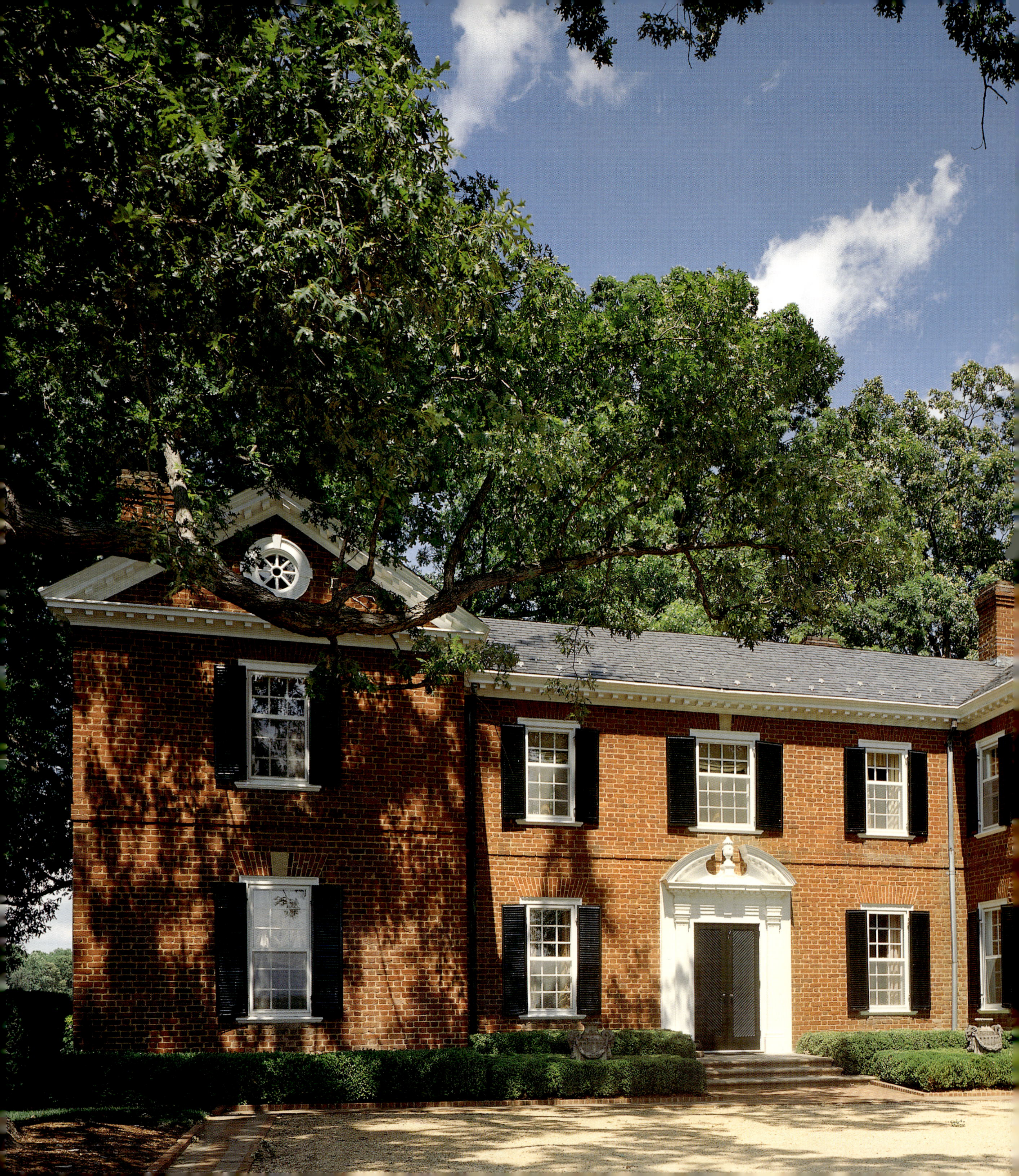

WHILTON

Original frame structure, 1914; Eugene M. Bradbury, architect
Brick veneer, additions and remodel, 1936; Milton Grigg, architect
House remodel, 1988, potting shed complex, 2004; Edward Eichman, architect

Whilton, with its elegant Georgian-style manor house, magnificent formal gardens, and picturesque stucco and limestone potting shed, is a 350-acre working cattle farm. It is the realization of a goal for the owners, a couple who decided to live their dream sooner rather than later. The husband vowed to own a farm in Virginia someday while a graduate student at the University of Virginia, and the wife, who had grown up foxhunting, longed to return to the country life. Twenty years ago they moved from New York and created new lives in the Virginia countryside, a change they have never regretted.

Whilton was built in 1914 for Algernon Craven and is well-situated on flat pastoral land to the west of Charlottesville. It was designed by architect Eugene M. Bradbury and built as a two-story frame structure. In 1936 it received a complete remodeling by the well-known restoration architect Milton Grigg. He clad the house in brick veneer to transform it into the Colonial Revival style for then owner Gordon Buck. He also enlarged the structure with additional rooms to either side of the original building to create architectural symmetry and remodeled the interior with the inclusion of a spectacular sweeping staircase in the entry hall.

When the current owners purchased Whilton in 1988 they hired Charlottesville architect Edward Eichman to update the house with another remodel.

LEFT *The centerpiece of Whilton, a 350-acre farm in the bucolic countryside outside Charlottesville, is its Georgian-style manor house. The house's elegance is complemented by the magnificent gardens that surround it. The fifteen acres of landscaping have been the inspired work of the current owner for over twenty years.*

LEFT AND OPPOSITE *The entry foyer sets the tone of refinement. The restored woodwork of the curving staircase reinforces the detailing of the patterned wallpaper. Furnishings include an eighteenth-century French gilt mirror over an eighteenth-century English mahogany hall table. A small woman's "pannier" chair sits beside an eighteenth-century French candlestick stand. Green-black in the antique marble flooring and a pair of Chinoiserie lamps adds drama to the space.*

FOLLOWING PAGES *The luxurious living room was created by enclosing a back porch. Lit only by candlelight, the room is imbued with the sensuality and subtlety of eighteenth-century European elegance. Interior designer Suzanne Rheinstein of Hollyhock & Associates in Los Angeles has featured the exquisite silk window treatments at the series of arched French doors. Furnishings include a nineteenth-century painted hatbox, a strié velvet ottoman surrounded by Regency side chairs with their original paint, and an eighteenth-century Venetian sofa. There is also a collection of rare early-nineteenth-century French papier-mâché and dragée boxes used for sweets or pills.*

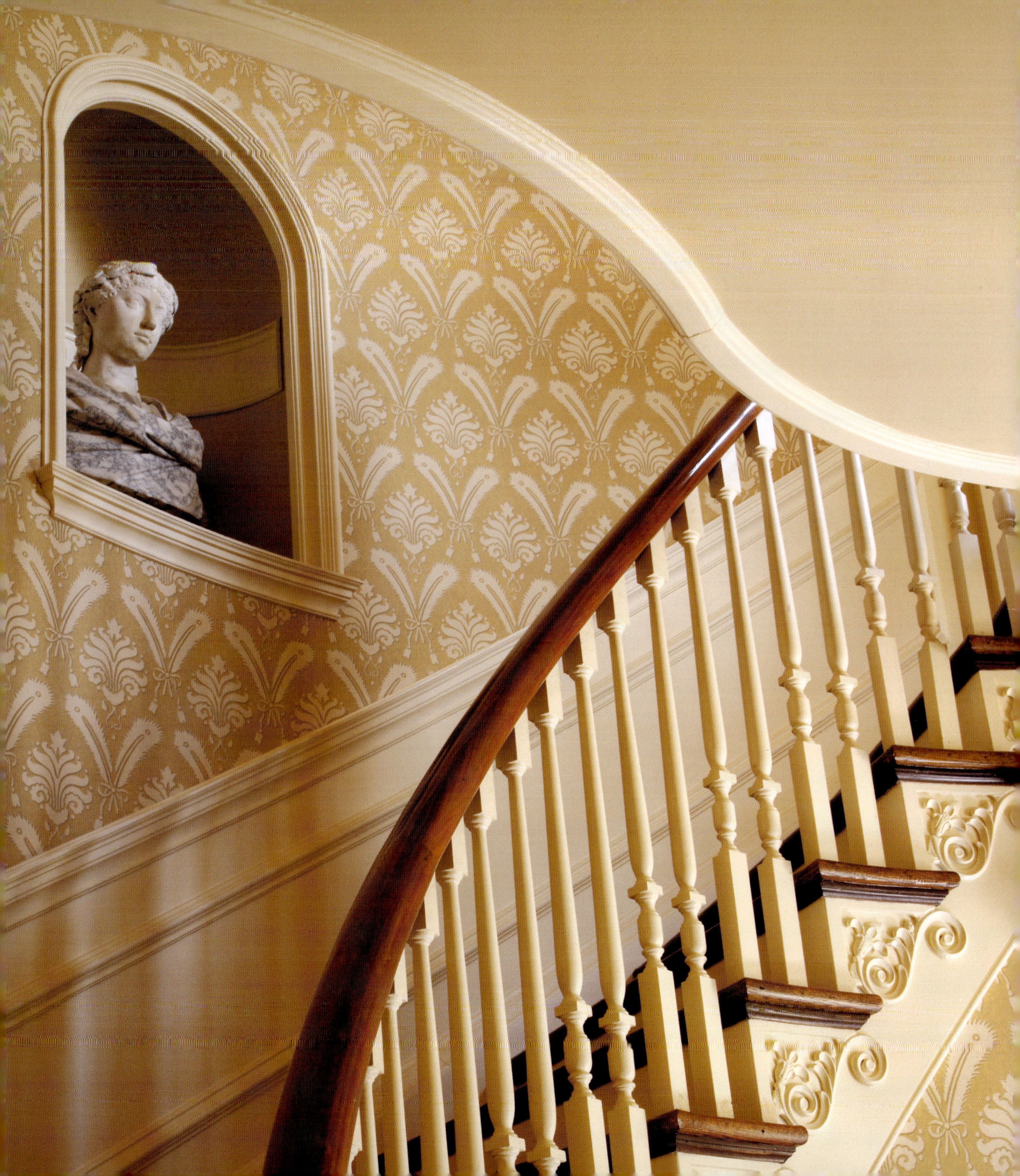

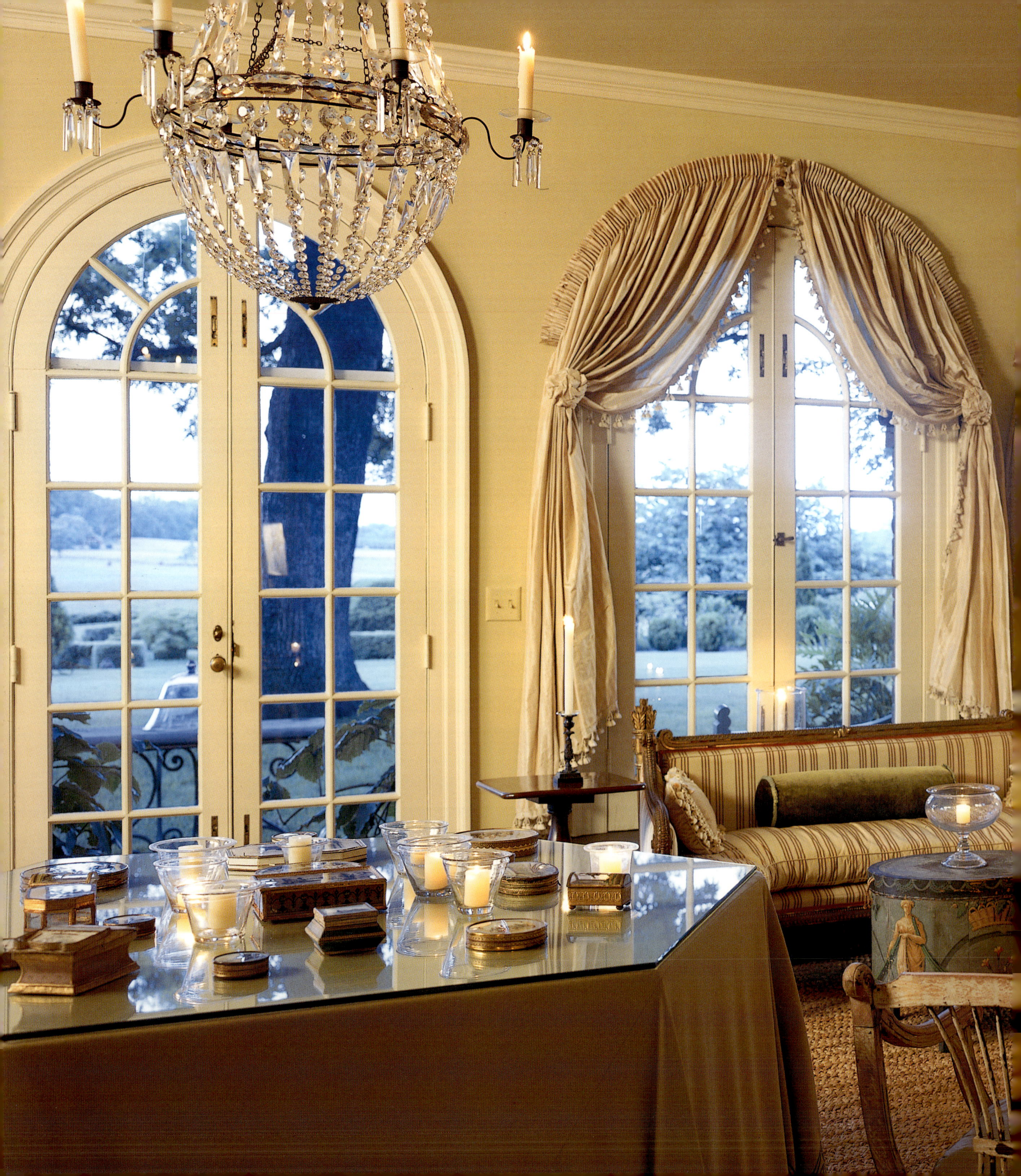

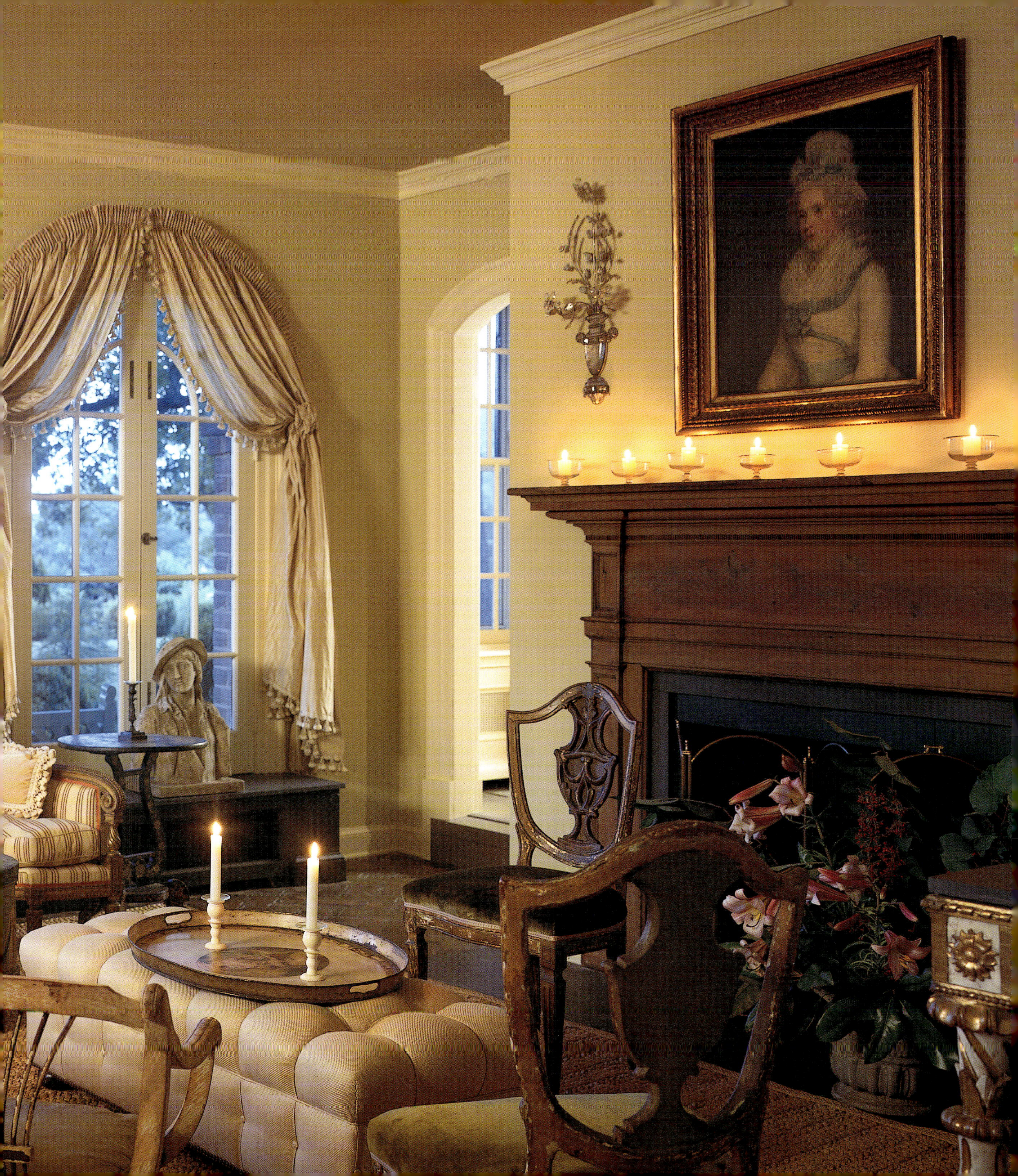

LEFT A warm palette of muted tones was used in the sitting room. Subtle, complex hues are found in the patterned cotton drapery and upholstery fabric as well as the wall color and in the early-nineteenth-century Chinese wallpaper panels. An eighteenth-century Swedish painted side table stands below it.

OPPOSITE Contributing to the house's uniqueness are its finely crafted woodwork, generous room proportions, extended ceiling heights, and decorated entrances. The library's substantial door-surround with its broken-pediment and the finely carved mantel and chimney breast with its surrounding engaged fluted pilasters are particularly noteworthy.

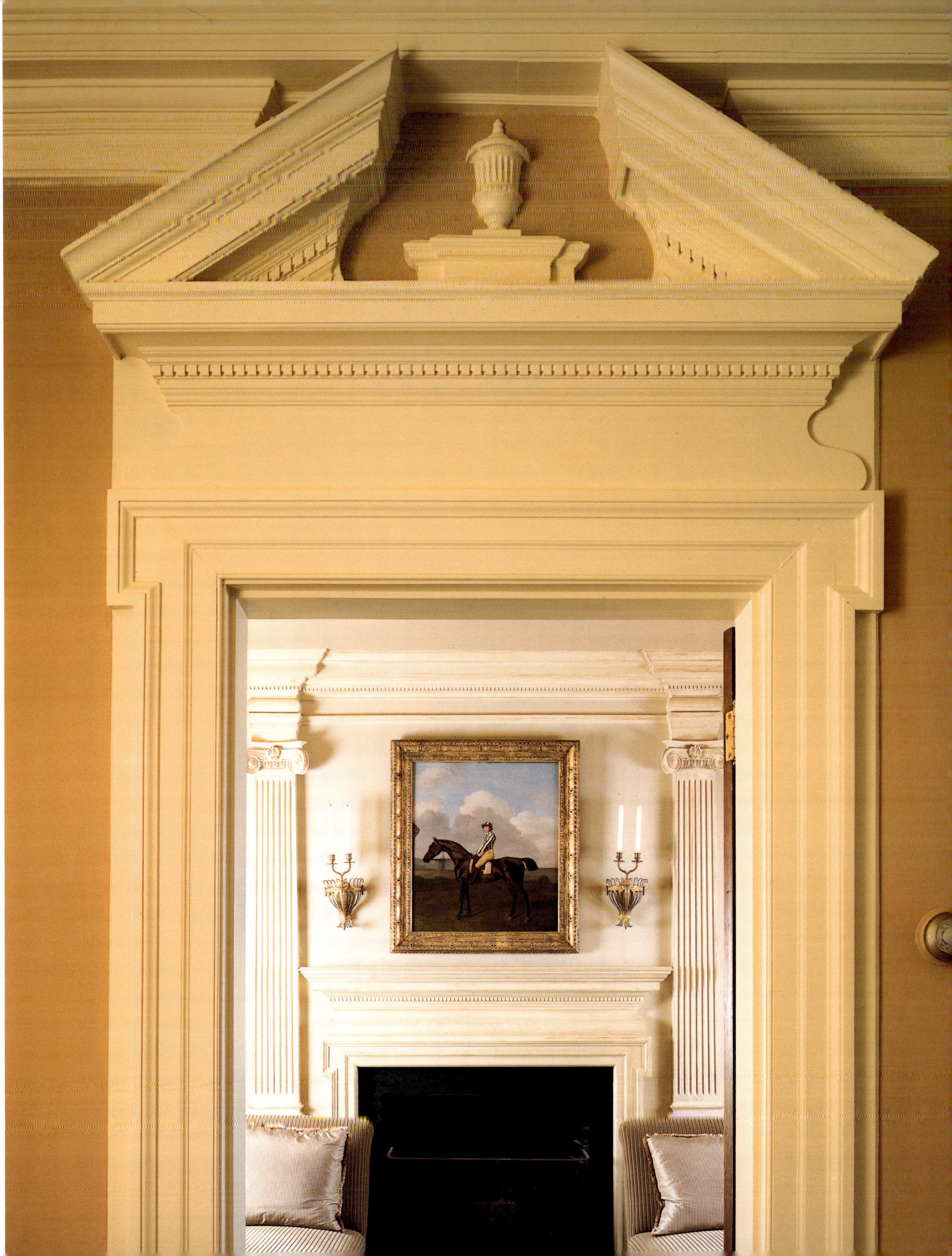

ABOVE *The formal dining room's beautiful woodwork complements the delicacy of the room's furnishings that include an eighteenth-century crystal chandelier, six eighteenth-century English and four eighteenth-century Swedish chairs with original paint, a pair of mirrored sconces, an ornate gilt mirror, and the mahogany dining table.*

OPPOSITE *A serpentine hallway that leads from a door in the entry to the dining room was hand painted by Savannah fine artist Bob Christian to resemble the eighteenth-century French wallpaper of Dufour et Cie. This example of fine artistry is representative of the detailed perfection found throughout the house.*

With his keen understanding of traditional style, Eichman was also re-enlisted to design the spectacular potting shed complex in 2003. Its theatricality and pure lines make it a splendid addition to the exuberant and colorful gardens that surround it.

Suzanne Rheinstein, an interior designer in Los Angeles and good friend of the wife, created a fresh interior that reflects the relaxed but luxurious mood of a French country house. Rooms were designed with eighteenth-century painted country furniture with silk and linen fabrics for upholstery and draperies, surfaces embellished with faux bois work and other special textural treatments, and candle light used wherever possible to heighten the feeling of a different time and place.

Extensive gardens, created with an artist's eye toward color, design, and texture, cover fifteen acres. They are varied and lush and include formally planted areas, small secretive spaces that feature sculpture, walled garden "rooms," an allée of October Glory maple trees that leads to the stables and riding ring, and color-themed gardens in yellow, yellow variegated, orange and apricot, and chartreuse, among others. With characteristic energy and enthusiasm the owner has dedicated herself over the past twenty years to her pride and passion of gardening. Invigorated by the free exchange of knowledge about gardens and life, she shares her

FOLLOWING PAGES *The transformation of Whilton's 1988 remodel included a spacious new kitchen and mudroom. The room is furnished with a large early-nineteenth-century country French farm table, and a family piece, the early nineteenth-century walnut and cane high chair (at left). The portrait over the mantel is from the eighteenth-century. A striking element is the set of ceramic mortars and pestles.*

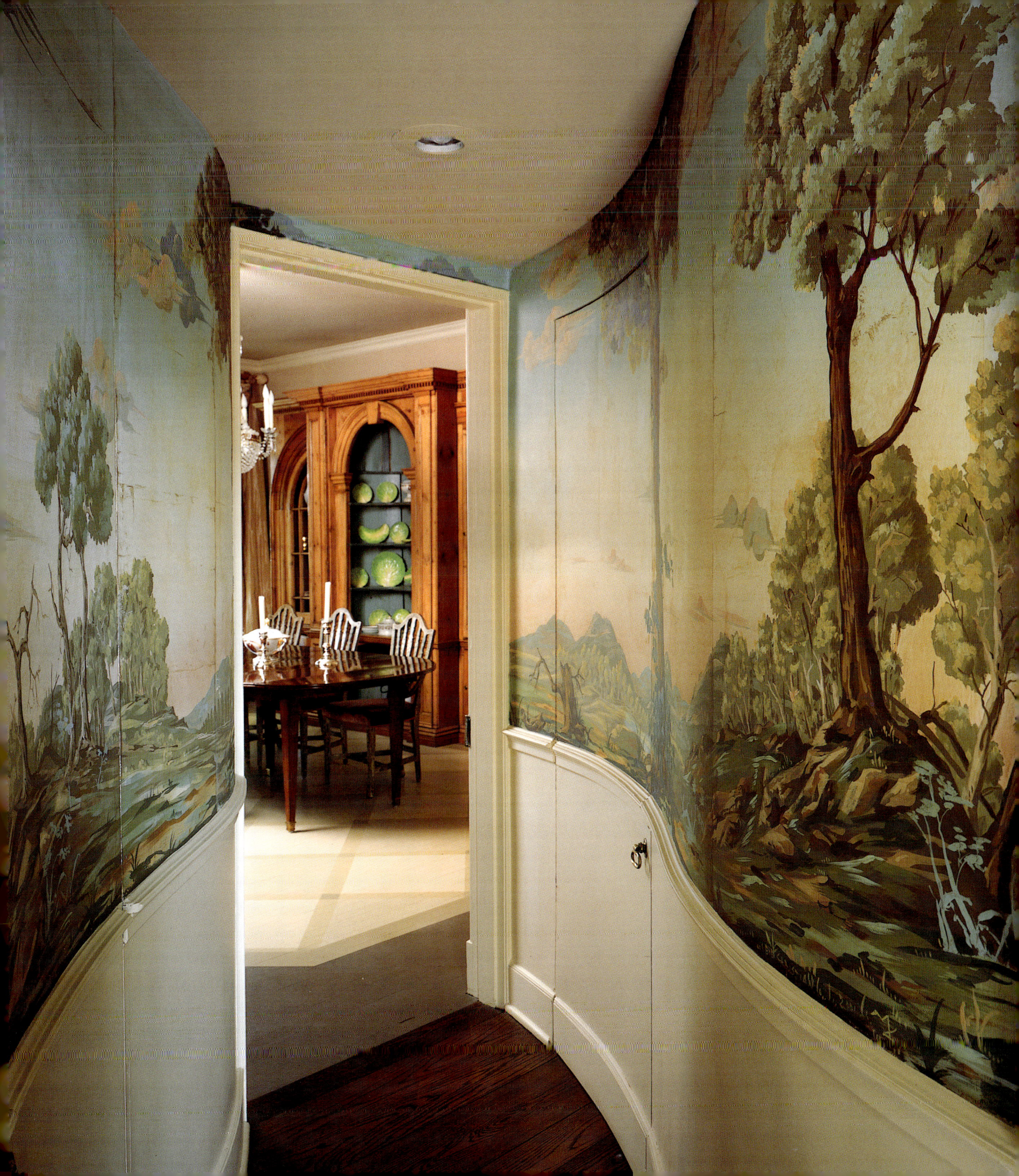

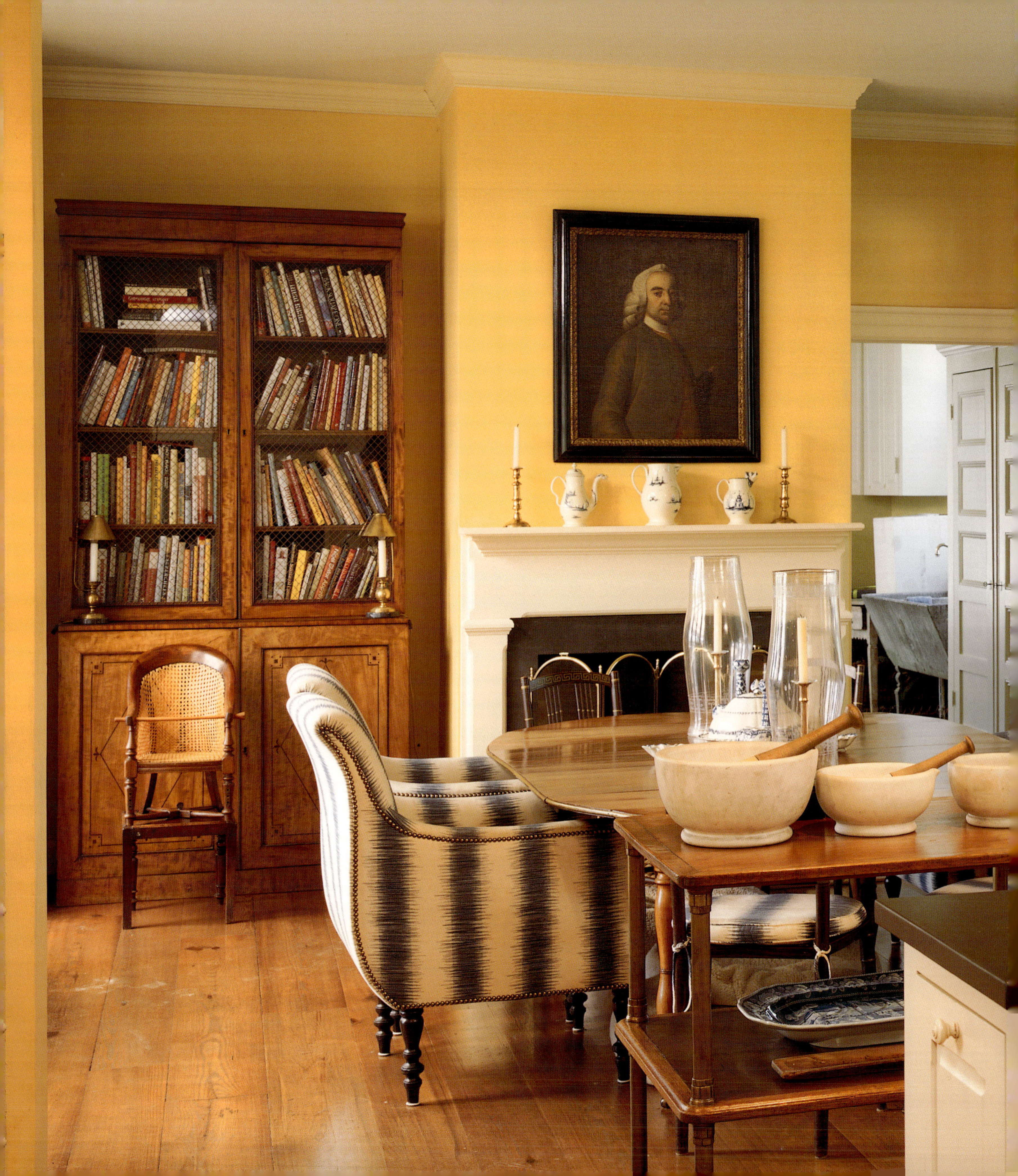

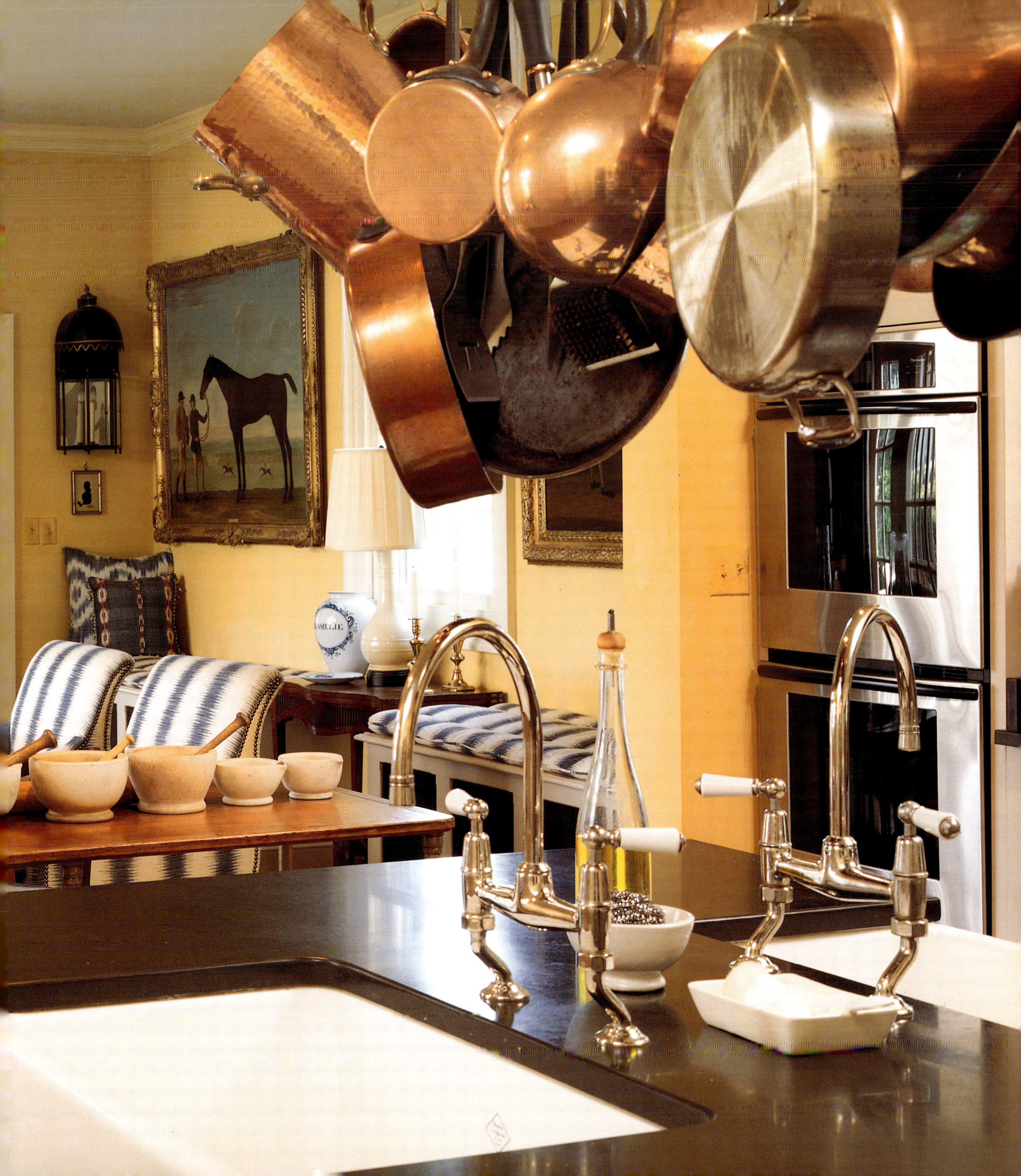

ABOVE AND RIGHT *The gardens at Whilton are visited by small groups of garden enthusiasts from all over the United States as well as other countries. From the house a sweeping lawn reaches to the manicured boxwoods that delineate some of the spectacular garden "rooms." Sculpture, classical urns, a fountain, a lead-roofed gazebo, and a classically designed pool house anchor the diversely planted areas. Gardens include a boxwood parterre that encloses two large clipped shaped yews with a Japanese maple in the center and fourteen theme gardens that feature shade plants, grasses, or one color for plantings. A 2004 potting shed and conservatory complex has space for an office, a propagation room, and greenhouses that protect tender plants during the winter.*

FOLLOWING PAGES *Toward the southern end of the gardens an allée of maples guides a path to the barn and stables. Over a stone wall is the "yellow garden," which is entirely devoted to yellow-flowering plants.*

work with the many friends and guests, small garden clubs, and international visitors who frequent her gardens each year. As an outreach to the larger gardening community she also serves on the board of directors of The Garden Conservancy, an organization that promotes small, specialized gardens throughout America.

The gardens are a mammoth job, never ending, always a work in progress. But that is exactly why the owner loves gardening. "It's like life," she explains. "It's the process that is important, not so much the final result—because that always changes."

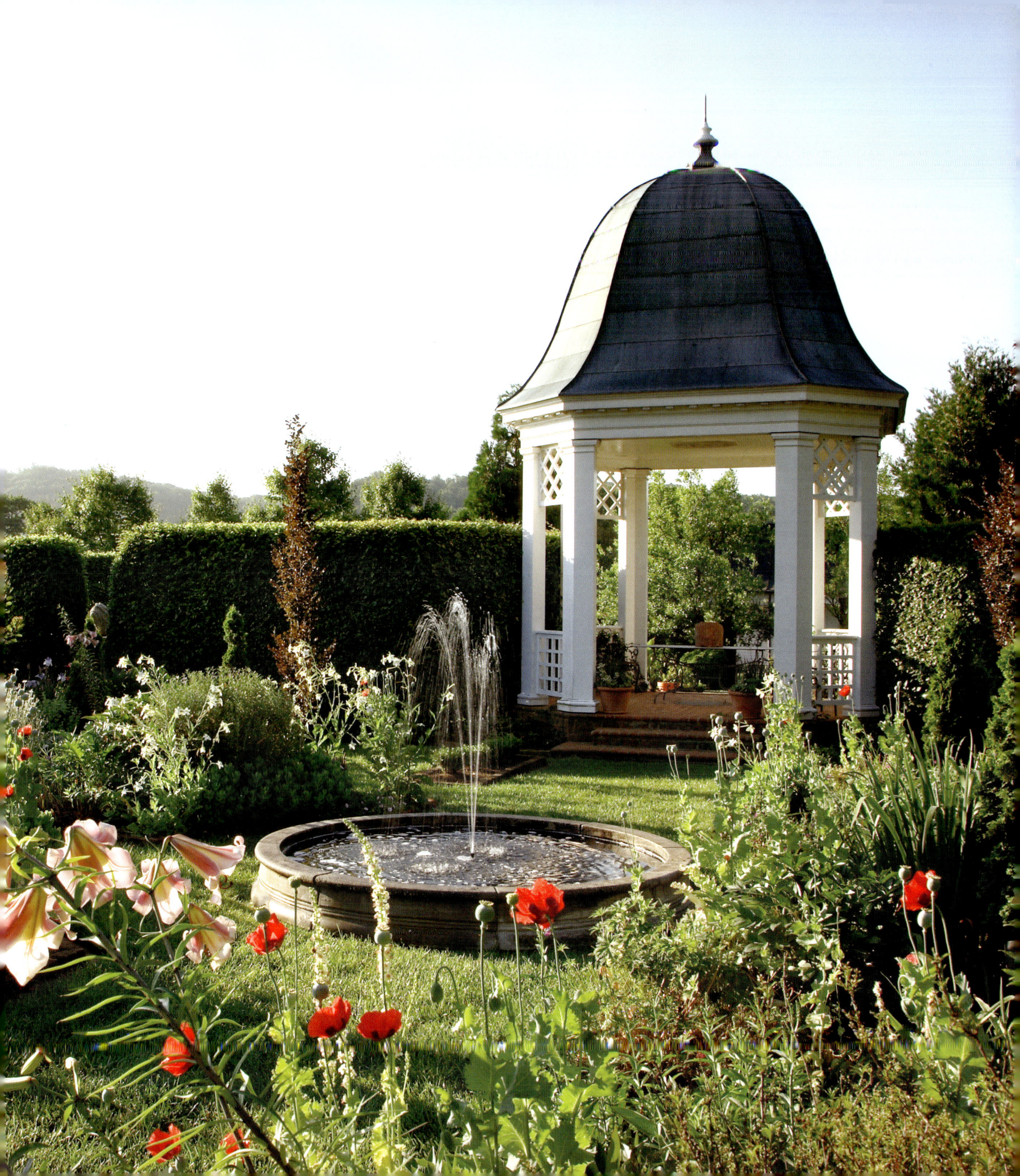

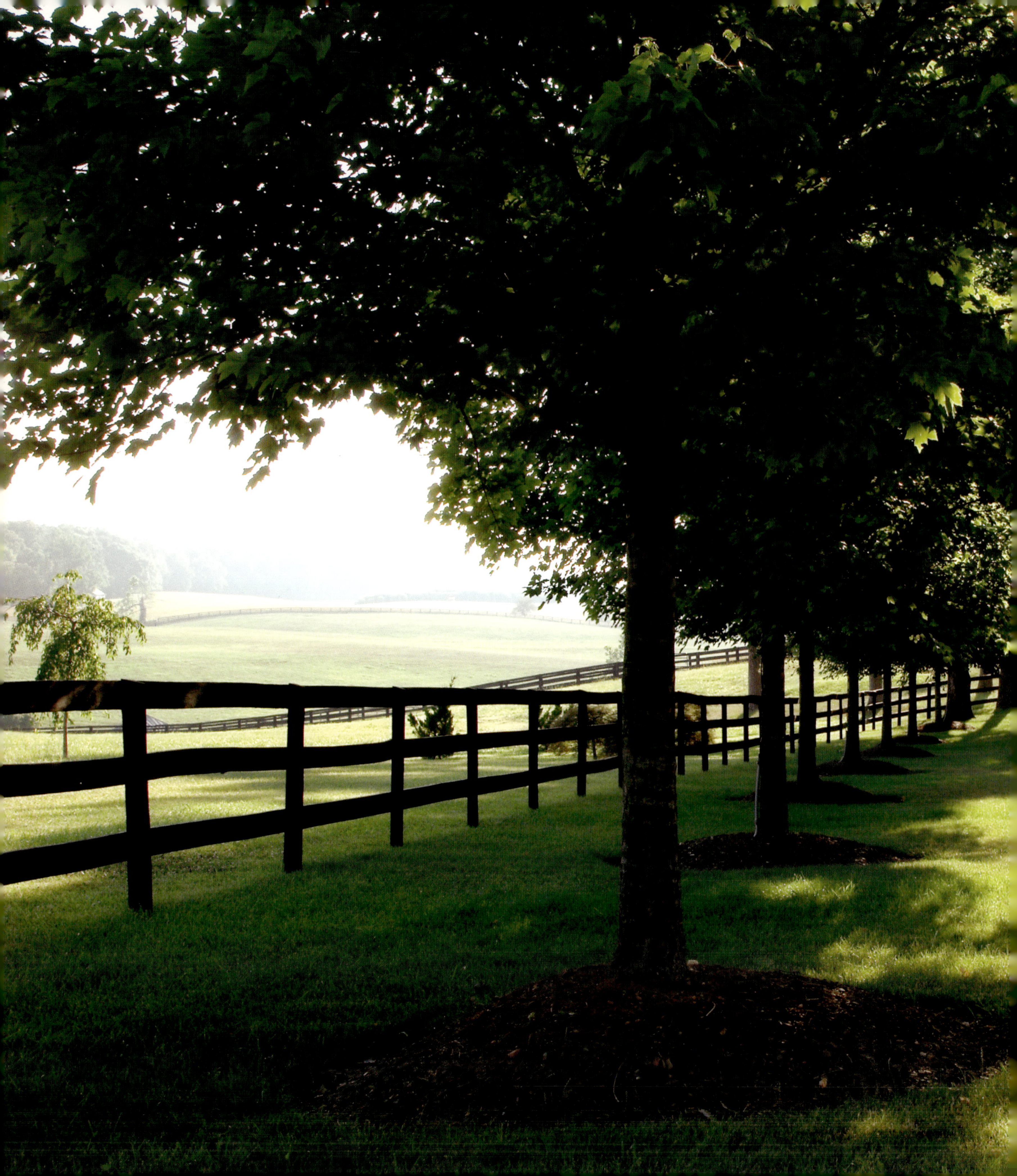

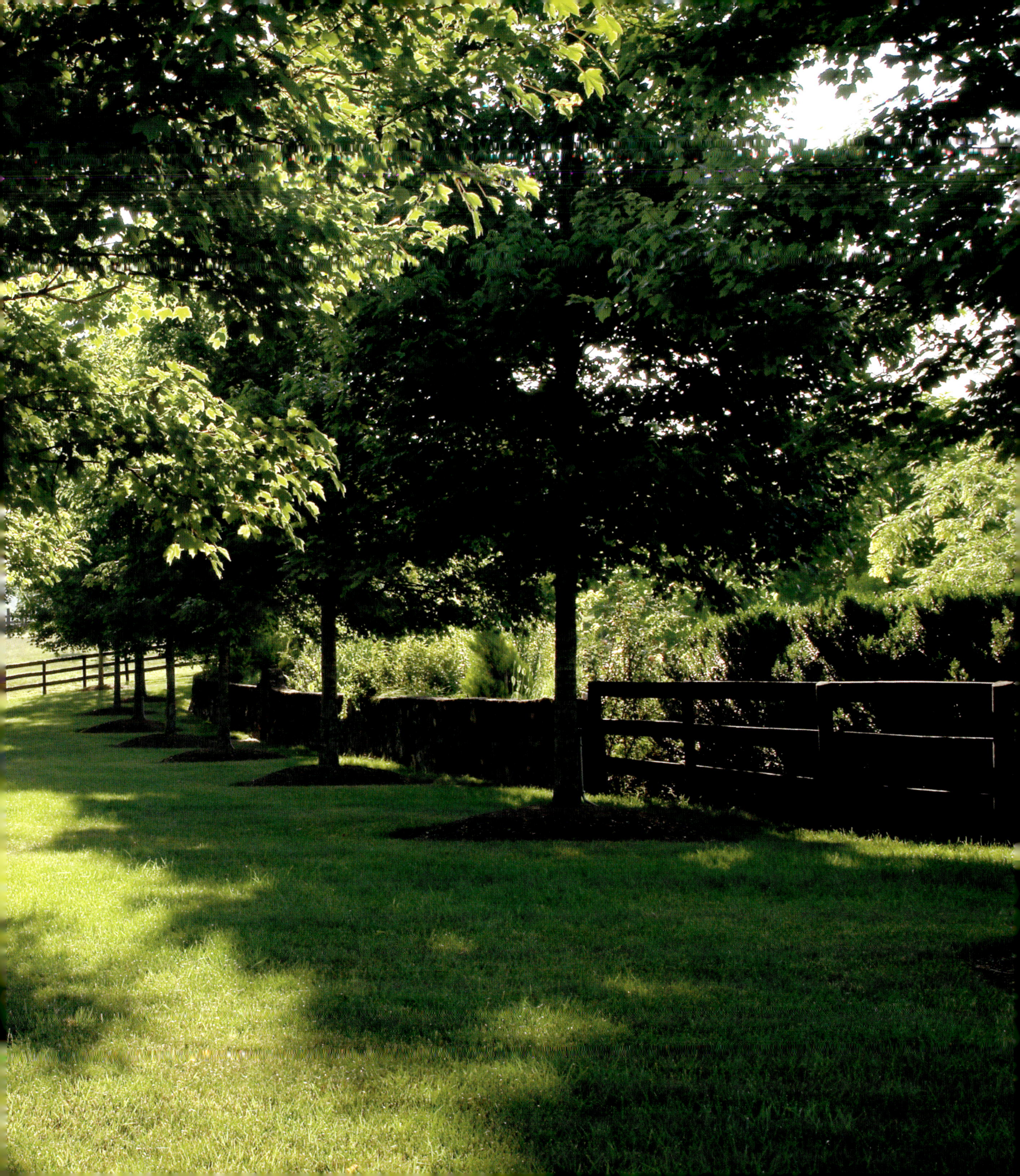

FARM IN NORTHERN VIRGINIA

Original barn complex, c.1920
Remodel and additions, 1986

Over the past twenty years the owner of this farm in northern Virginia has transformed an equestrian complex of barns built in the 1920s into a showplace home. The former hay and horse barns, stables, foaling and wash stalls, and tack room are now the civilized and elegant rooms of the main house, guest cottage, and ancillary galleries. When she acquired the property of sixty acres in prime Virginia hunt country, the owner, who lived for many years in England, intended that the transformation include architectural design that respected the farm's history. The original barns' vernacular charm was retained in the updated design with resurfacing in mellow-colored stucco, using local fieldstone for paths, stairs, and building details, restoring wood trim, and adding a metal roof with bird stops to the entire complex. Additional space came from enclosing the original horse barn's overhang in the front of the building to create a new central hallway and gallery. The back of the house was extended out onto a new, covered porch. A large addition at the rear includes an enfilade, a paneled den, a game room, and the magnificent library, designed in Palladian scale with a 16-foot-high coved ceiling.

Among the splendors that fill the house are the fine collections of English and American art, English, German, and French porcelain, and exquisite eighteenth-century furnishings. But the crowning glory of the interiors, and the owner's particular passion, is the

RIGHT *This farm in northern Virginia is an equestrian complex of barns built in the 1920s that included hay and horse barns, stables, foaling and wash stalls, and a tack room, that was transformed in the 1980s into an elegant country home. Set in 60 acres of Virginia hunt country, the main house is surrounded by hillsides of imaginative, lush gardens.*

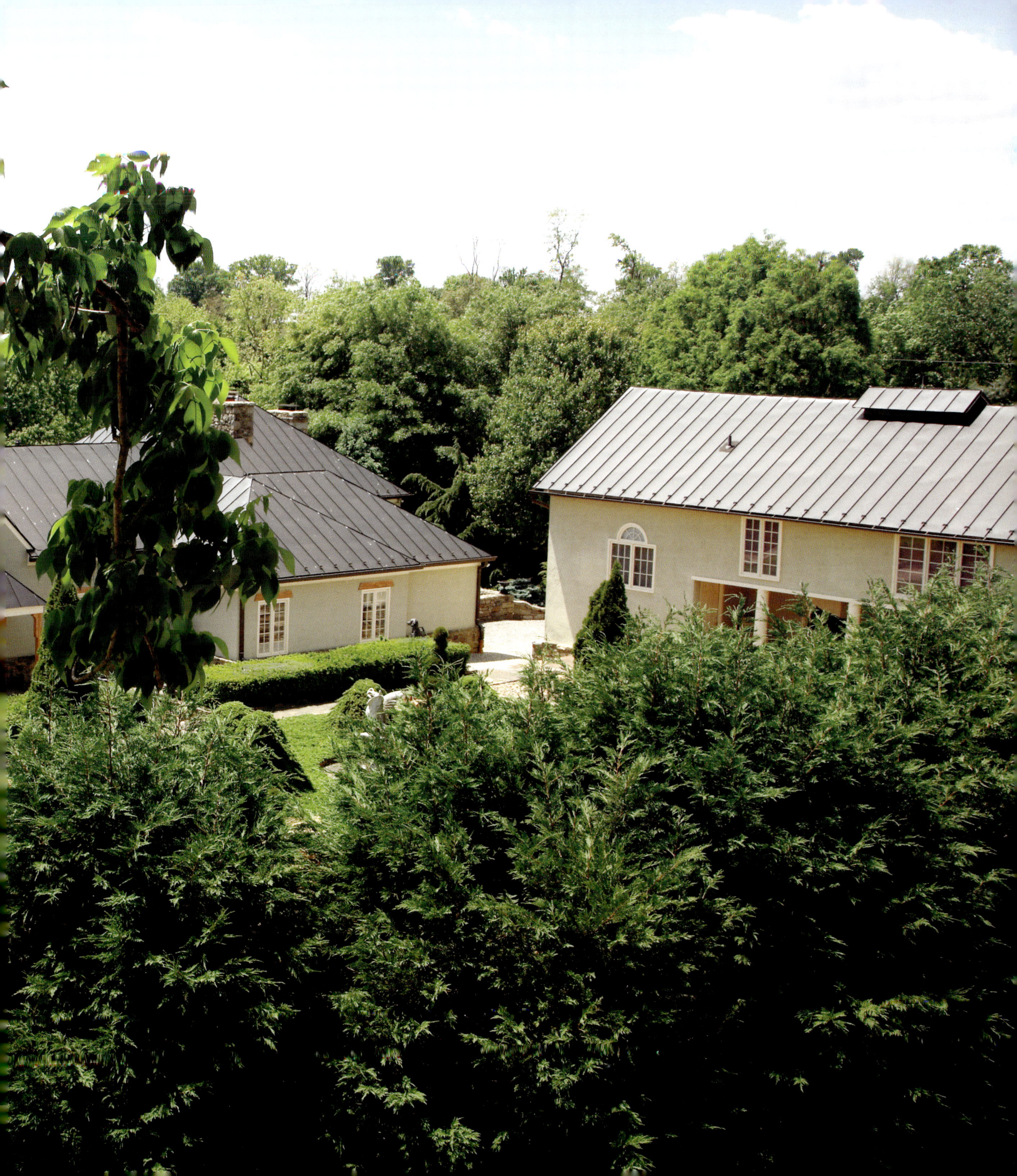

The library, an addition to the back of the house, is a modern take on Palladian grandeur. Its 16-foot-high coved ceiling is in perfect proportion to the room's dimensions. The owner's passion for rare books and manuscripts is evident in the wall of shelves that displays them at the far end of the room. Fine collections of English and American art, English and European porcelain, and pristine eighteenth-century furnishings fill the room.

228   FARM IN NORTHERN VIRGINIA

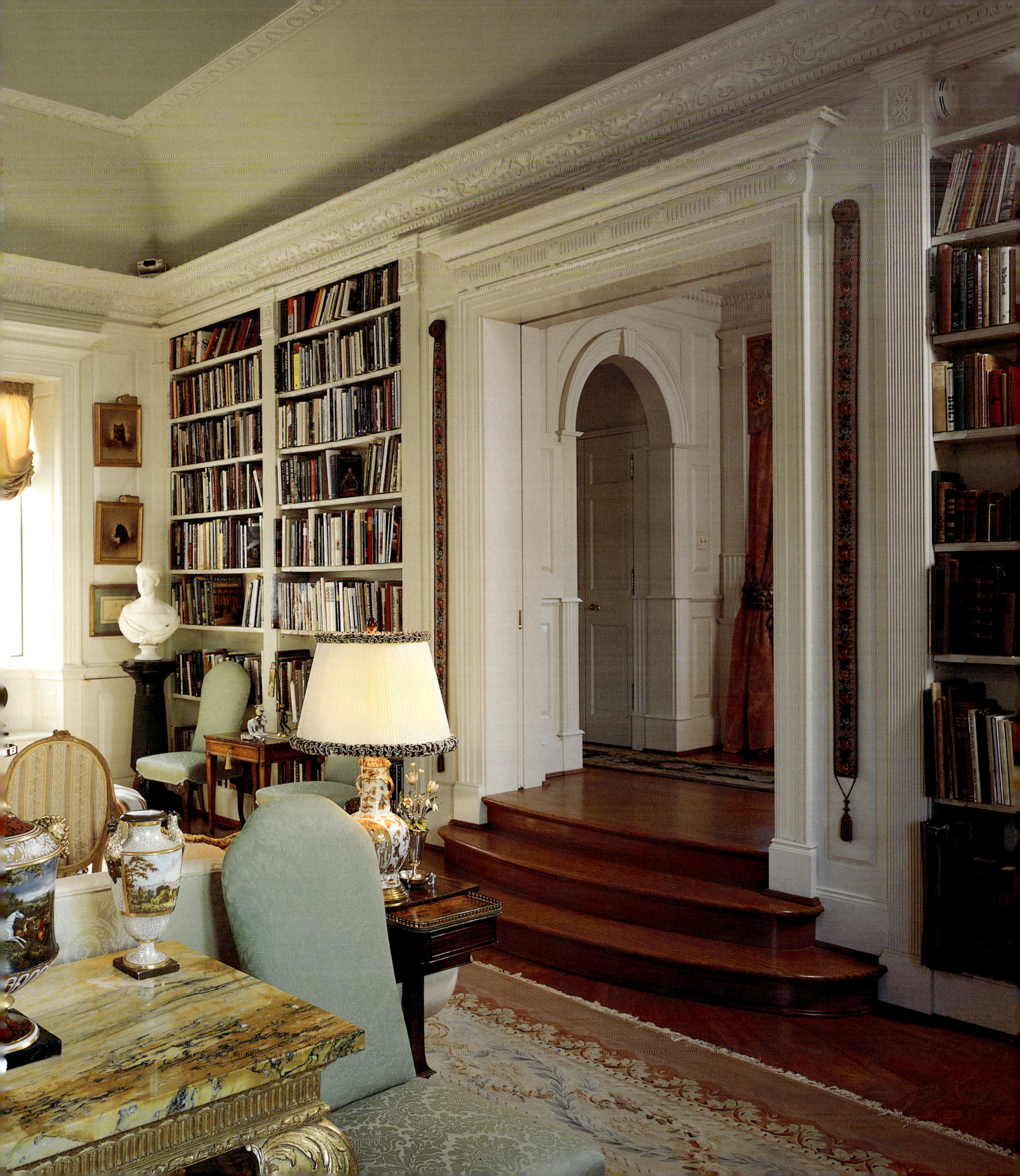

ABOVE AND RIGHT *The paneled den leads to the enfilade that connects the library to the main house. In the enfilade, a Chippendale cabinet displays fine English, French, and unusual German porcelain figures, while comfortable seating in the den includes an unusual eighteenth-century wing chair and a contemporary sofa displaying fine lace pillows designed by the owner. The original oil in back of the wing chair is c.1900 by Gaspar Latoix.*

FOLLWING PAGES *The hall is the original porch of the barns and has been transformed into the entry hall and gallery. Fine antique furnishings, bronze sculptures, and paintings are among pieces of the owner's fine collections of sporting art. Nineteenth-century English paintings include the hounds running by John Gifford, the coaching scene at the end of the hall by C. D. Rowlands, and the equestrian painting on the right wall by Henry Hall. Bronzes are nineteenth-century French pieces that include the jockey and horse by da Dassage and the large greyhound by P. J. Mene.*

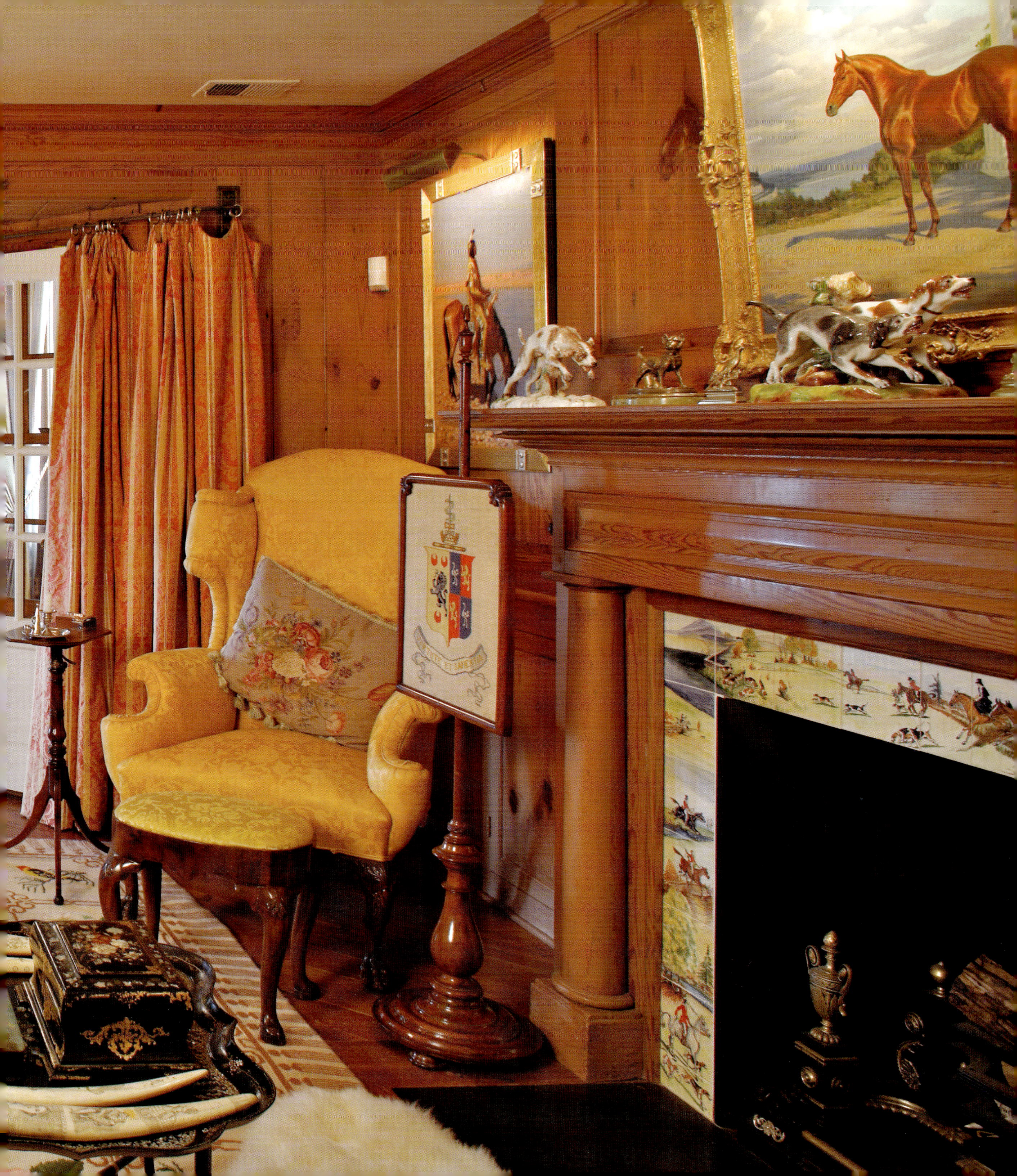

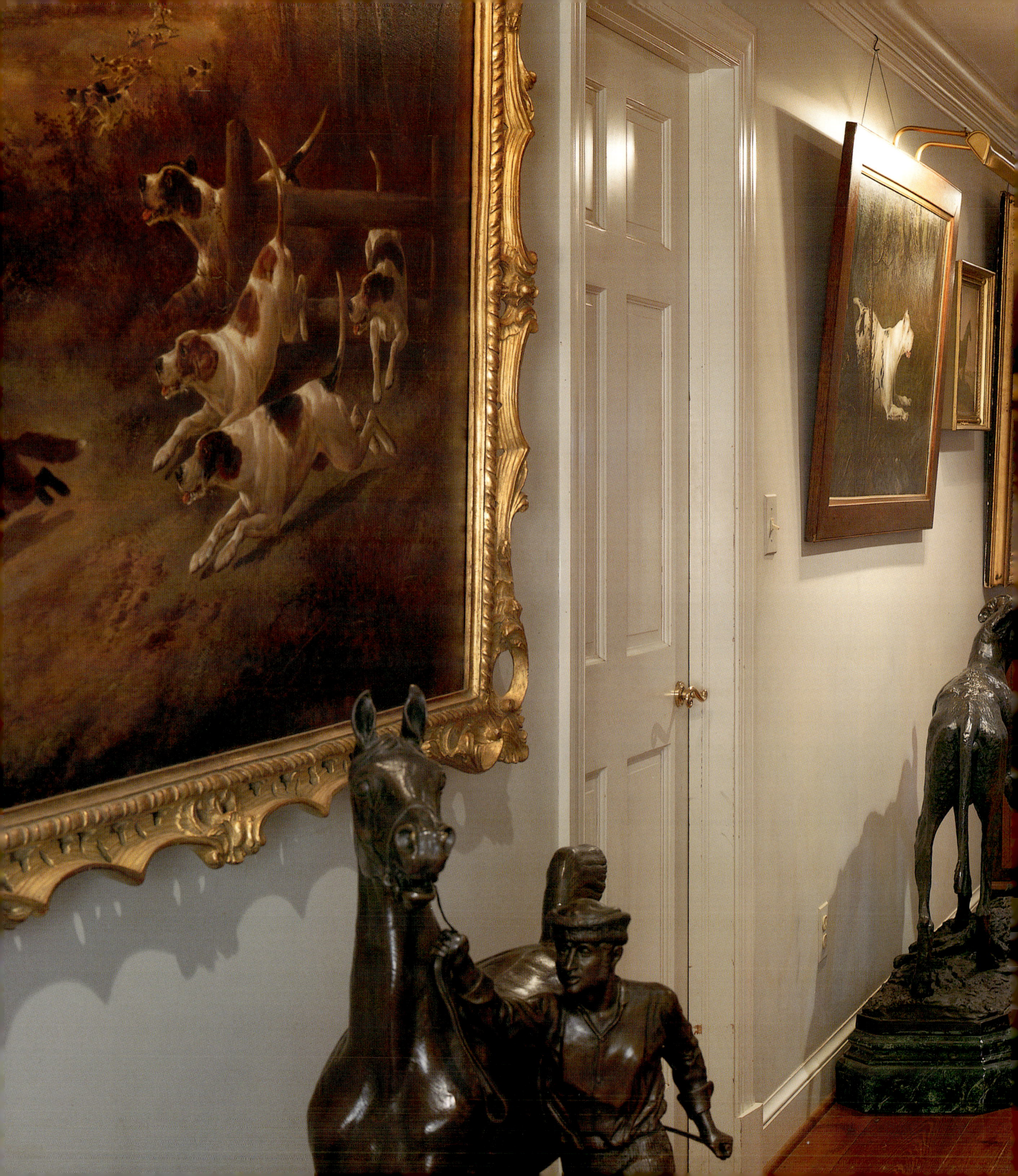

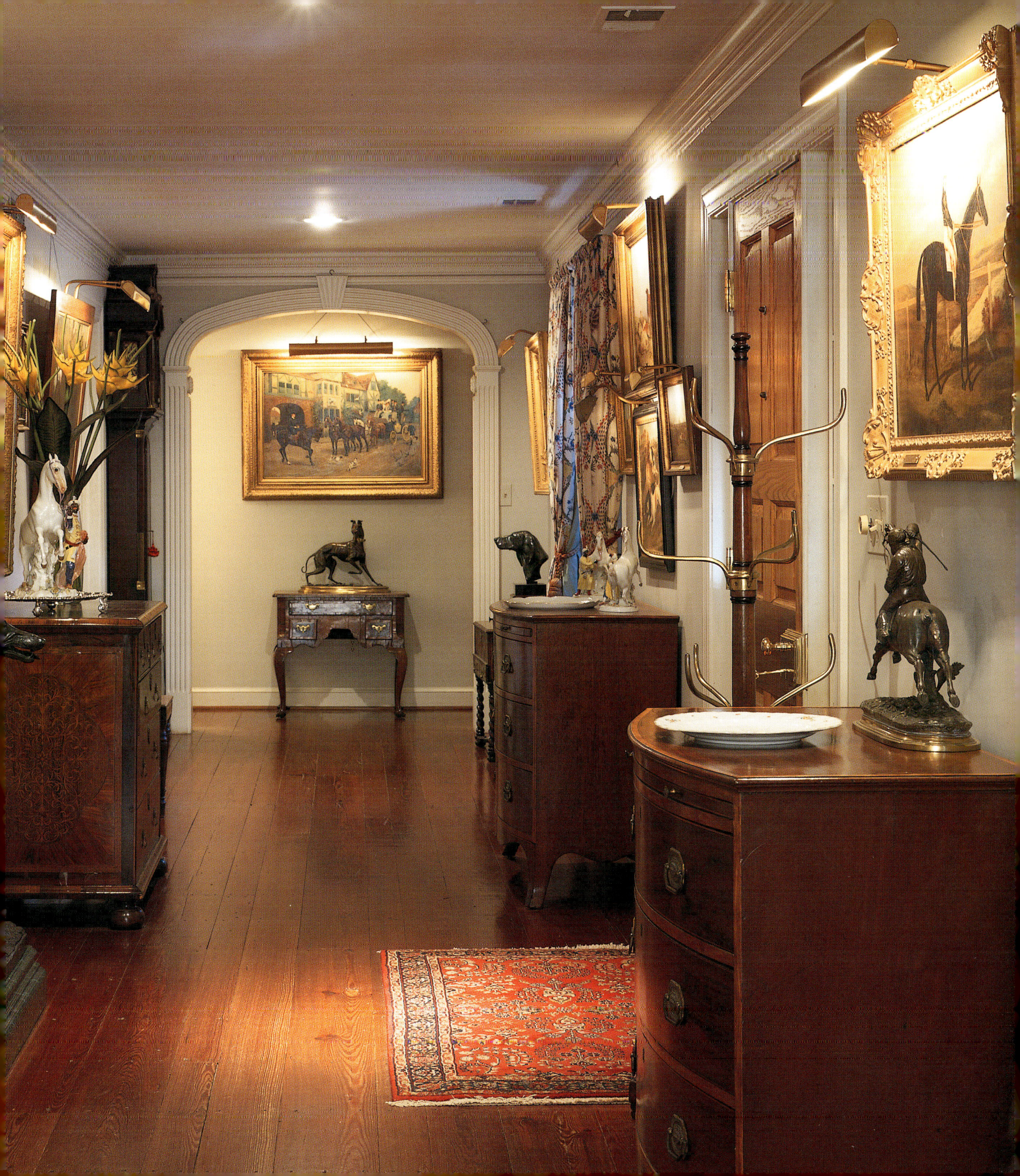

A centerpiece of gold-rimmed yellow and blue Chamberlain Worcester porcelain and a pair of ornate silver candelabra are exquisite on the eighteenth-century English mahogany dining table that seats twenty. An arrangement of Meissen plates is displayed on the far wall. The nineteenth-century Scottish painting above the mantel is by Patrick Nasmyth.

world class collection of rare books, about which she is impressively knowledgeable. Included among these antiquarian manuscripts are seventeenth-century volumes as well as later publications bound in richly tooled leather decorated with fine gilt work.

The owner's most expressive and creative work, however, has been the landscaping of forty acres with a series of spectacular gardens where once there were only overgrown hillsides. The gardens are a personal statement of passion and creative energy and after twenty years they are still evolving. Grand or intimate, gardens with statuary, natural rock formations, and themes of foliage are seamlessly woven together to present one spectacular idea on a grand scale. One of the striking individual features is a whimsical topiary fox chase of oversized leafy riders, hounds, and fox that is filled with motion, bursting forth from a curtain of tall, dense evergreens, weeping Norway spruce, an imposing backdrop. The owner's reference to the area's celebrated equine sport has special meaning, as she is a former master of foxhounds of a Virginia hound pack. Although the different gardens vary in their formality, scale, and use of rare or indigenous plantings, a strong sense of wholeness and consistency pervades the estate. From the great outcroppings of slate that form the focal point for the lower yard, to the pavilion and equine statuary that border the pastures, to the vegetable garden, mosaic marble patio, and teahouse on the upper grounds, the landscape of the estate is majestic and exuberant.

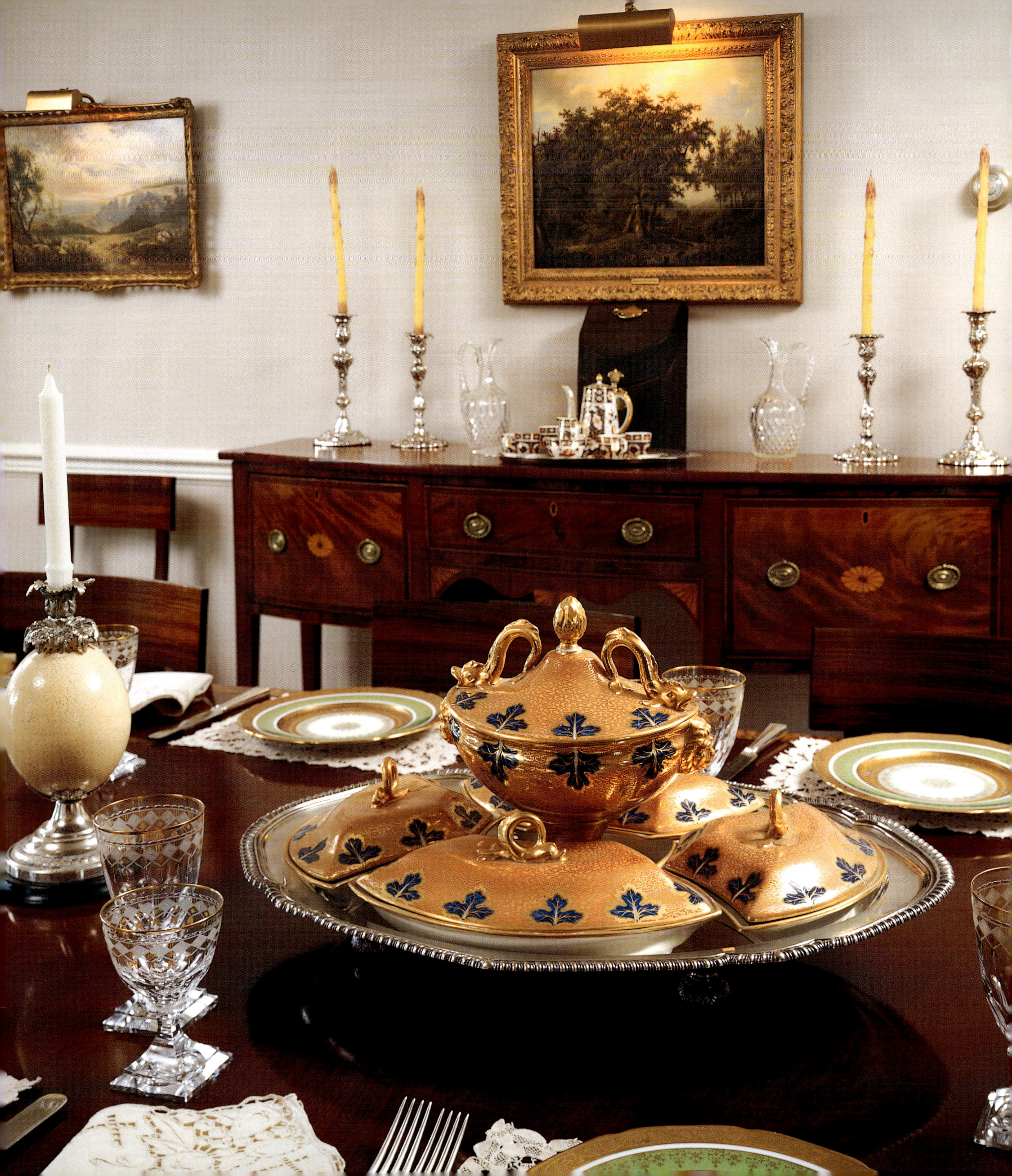

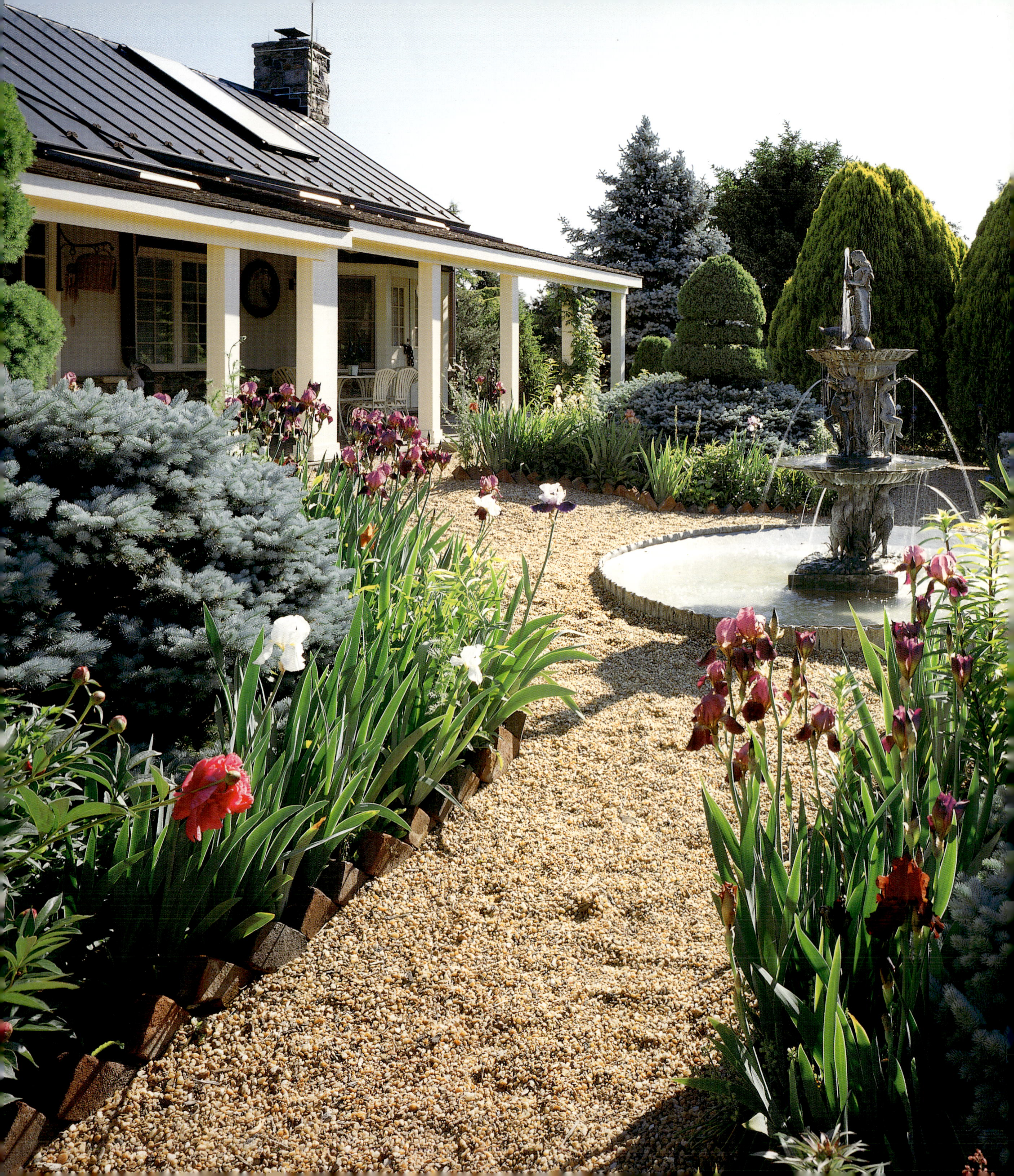

A back porch that was added in the 1980s remodel features a trompe l'oeil ceiling of the sky. The immediate garden features a fountain surrounded by irises and mature plantings that include four substantial arborvitae trees.

LEFT *Pastures in the distance form a backdrop for stone sculpture in the lower garden. An English stone pavilion is flanked by stone horse heads on stands. Rhododendrons flourish.*

BELOW LEFT *A large natural fieldstone outcropping is a spectacular sculptural piece in the lower garden. Stone steps bordered by clipped hedges lead up to the formal gardens and the house. The landscape includes a weeping Blue Atlas cedar that drapes over the outcropping and variety of conifers and two well-established apple trees, one over a hundred years old.*

238 FARM IN NORTHERN VIRGINIA

RIGHT *A reflecting pond with whimsical sculpted fish waterspouts and an allée of DeGroot's Spire guide the view to one of the gardens' many pieces of ornamental statuary.*

BELOW RIGHT *A metal teahouse with decoratively painted oriental figures that spin in the wind was adapted from a larger version found in Sweden. Antique Chinese millstones have been made into seating at the far end of the lawn.*

FOLLOWING PAGES *In a lower garden a small pond formed from the hillside waterfall is flanked by eighteenth-century stone statuary representing the four seasons. Cascading from the row of arborvitae are American and English boxwoods shaped into spheres surrounding the lawn and
a bank planted with Rosa rugosa. Nineteenth-century traditional black iron urns complement the elegance of the formal statuary.*

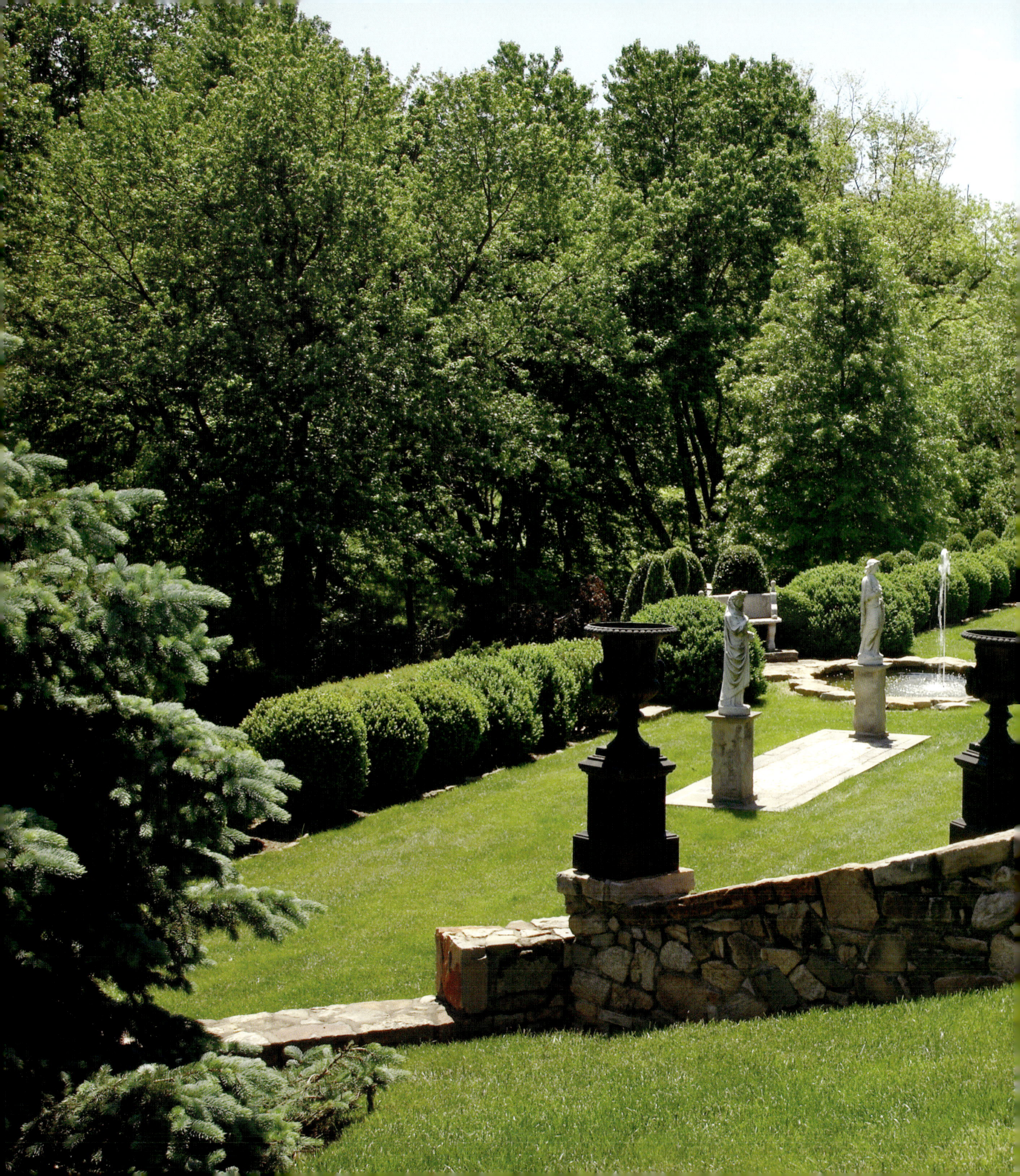

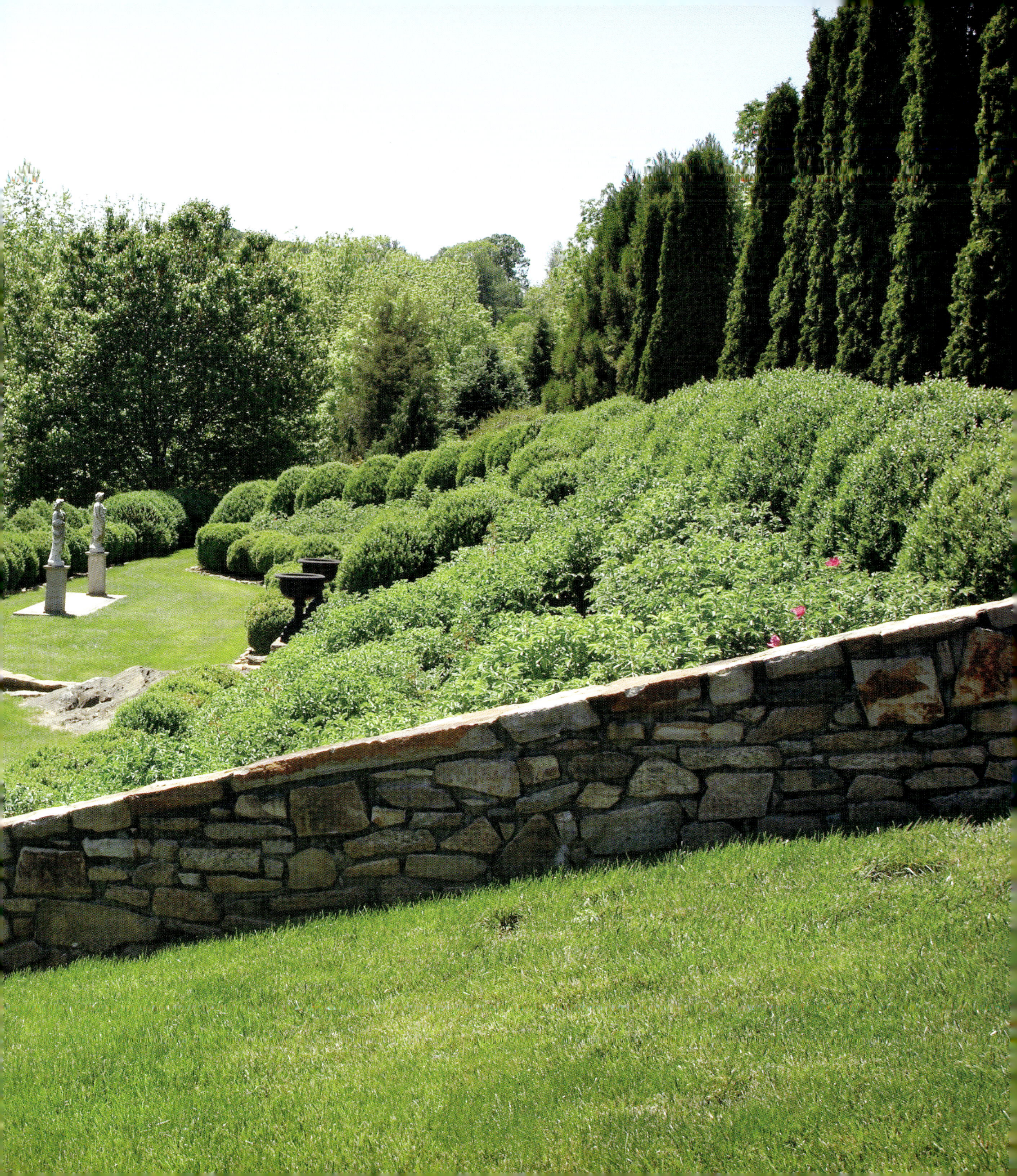

HENCHMAN'S LEA

Residence of Mrs. G. F. Steedman Hinckley
Main house, 1941; Henri de Heller, architect
Breakfast room addition, 1992; Albert P. Hinckley, Jr., architect

Henchman's Lea is an outstanding example of the American Revival architecture popular during the 1930s and 1940s. Current owner Mrs. G. F. Steedman Hinckley's parents-in-law moved the family to Virginia in 1940 and created this working farm that would allow them to enjoy the beauty of Virginia rural life. This included foxhunting, which ultimately resulted in Col. Hinckley becoming the master of the Old Dominion Hounds for 25 years. They sited their house on a rise that overlooks hills and woodlands reaching to the Blue Ridge Mountains and used fieldstone gathered from the property for its construction.

The Georgian-Revival style Henchman's Lea has a stately entrance with carved-wood columns, a layered door-surround, and a substantial broken pediment. The house is protected from roaming cattle by a ha-ha, a sharp drop in land created when an upper lawn is banked by a wall.

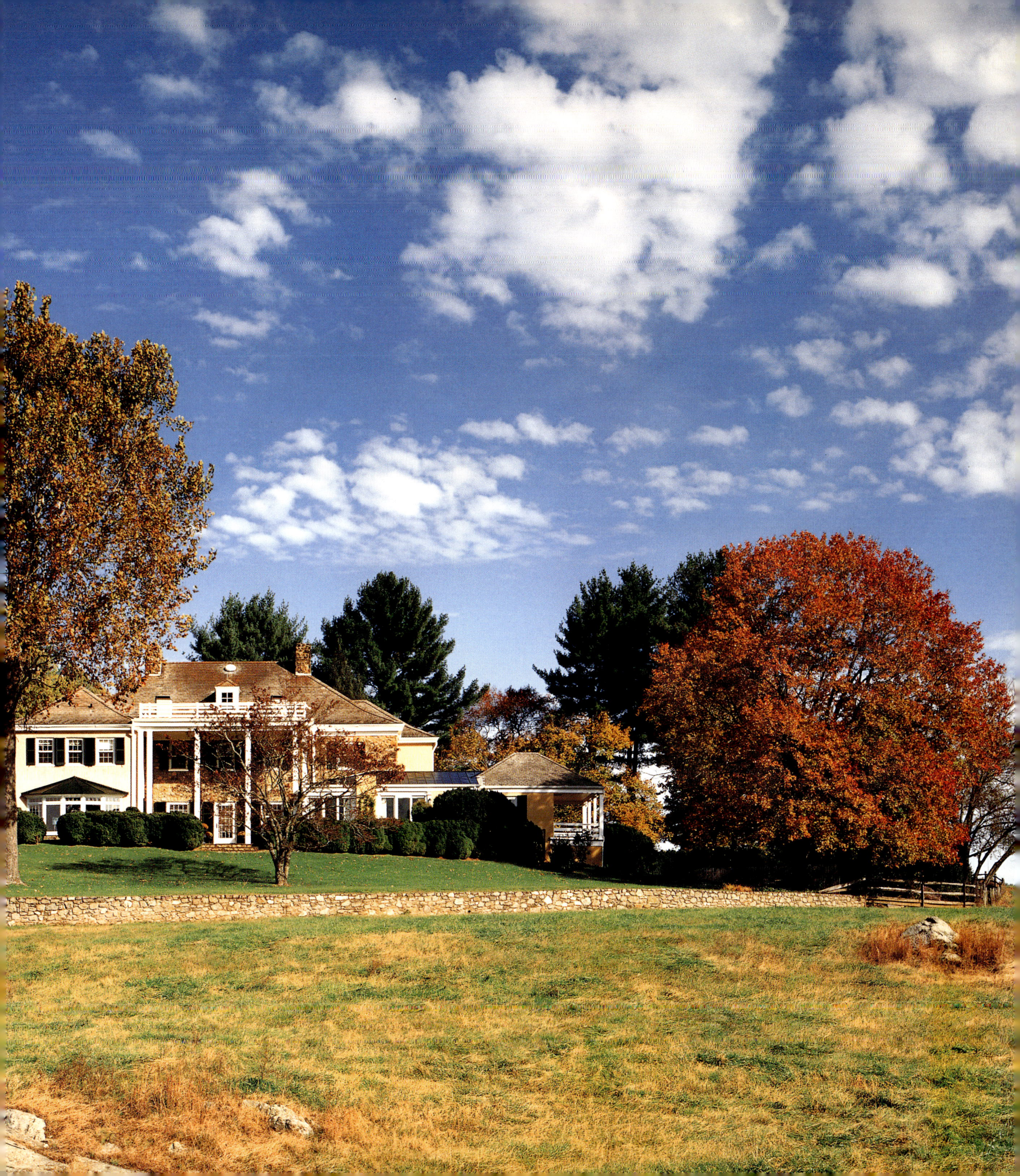

ABOVE *In the front hall the long line of a pendant lantern complements the upward sweep of the graceful curved stair rail. Another elegant form is the arched window.*

OPPOSITE *The owner and the local designer and trompe l'oeil artist Dana Westring completely updated the house in warm tones inspired from the colors in the vintage curtains that hang in the living room. A portrait of Colonel Albert P. Hinckley, the owner's father-in-law and a former master of the Old Dominion Hounds, hangs above the English oak mantel that is in the manner of Grinling Gibbons. Among the fine antique furnishings in the room are a pair of American fancy chairs of early-nineteenth-century design and a boule side table with marquetry of tortoise and brass inlay that sits beside the fireplace.*

Still a working farm, a majority of the land has been put into a conservation easement to protect and preserve its beauty for the future.

The house was designed by Henri de Heller, a Swiss architect then living in Warrenton, whose residential work also includes a house in Switzerland built for Audrey Hepburn. Heller's refined taste is evident in the plan, scale, and ornamentation of Henchman's Lea. The entry foyer is lit by a Palladian window halfway up a graceful curving stairway and separates the public spaces on the first level of the house. A magnificent living room represents the best of Revival-style interiors with its substantial cornice, high ceiling, and good proportions while a bay window the full width of the room enhances the space with a panoramic view of the spectacular countryside. Altogether, the serene setting, the skillful design, and use of evocative native materials give Henchman's Lea solidity, elegance, and grace.

The livability of the house was greatly increased in 1992 when the owner, together with local designer and trompe l'oeil artist Dana Westring, completely updated the interiors and Warrenton architect Albert P. Hinckley, Jr., the owner's brother-in-law, remodeled the southern section of the house, giving interior access to the lower level, transforming a former sitting room into an office for the owner, and adding a spacious, light-filled breakfast room. The house was brought back to life with a palate of warm tones for the paint colors and complementary upholstery fabrics, inspired by the subtle hues in a set of vintage draperies that the owner particularly liked that hang in the living room today. For the dining room, a more dramatic approach succeeded with deeper, richer tones of the same warm color palate.

Architect Albert Hinckley, Jr.'s elegant and functional design for the new breakfast room incorporates beautiful exterior stone walls of the 1940 design, high ceilings, shades of white in tile, paint and woodwork, and a series of tall glass doors that open the space to sunshine and wide vistas of the countryside to create a bright, cheery atmosphere. Hinckley, known for creating well-balanced designs with impeccable detailing that convey a sense of drama and joy, approached the project with his natural sense of style, and because he had grown up in Henchman's Lea, worked with a unique advantage. The house has become vibrant once again. With tasteful design and a gracious owner, it has seen four generations of the Hinckley family raised, and continues to be filled with friends and family enjoying hunt breakfasts and holiday celebrations.

FOLLOWING PAGES *The library is a repository for the family's myriad books including many on fox hunting, family photos, and fox hunting memorabilia. The room is the epitome of a "den"—full of the warmth of wood, leather, and earth-toned fabrics.*

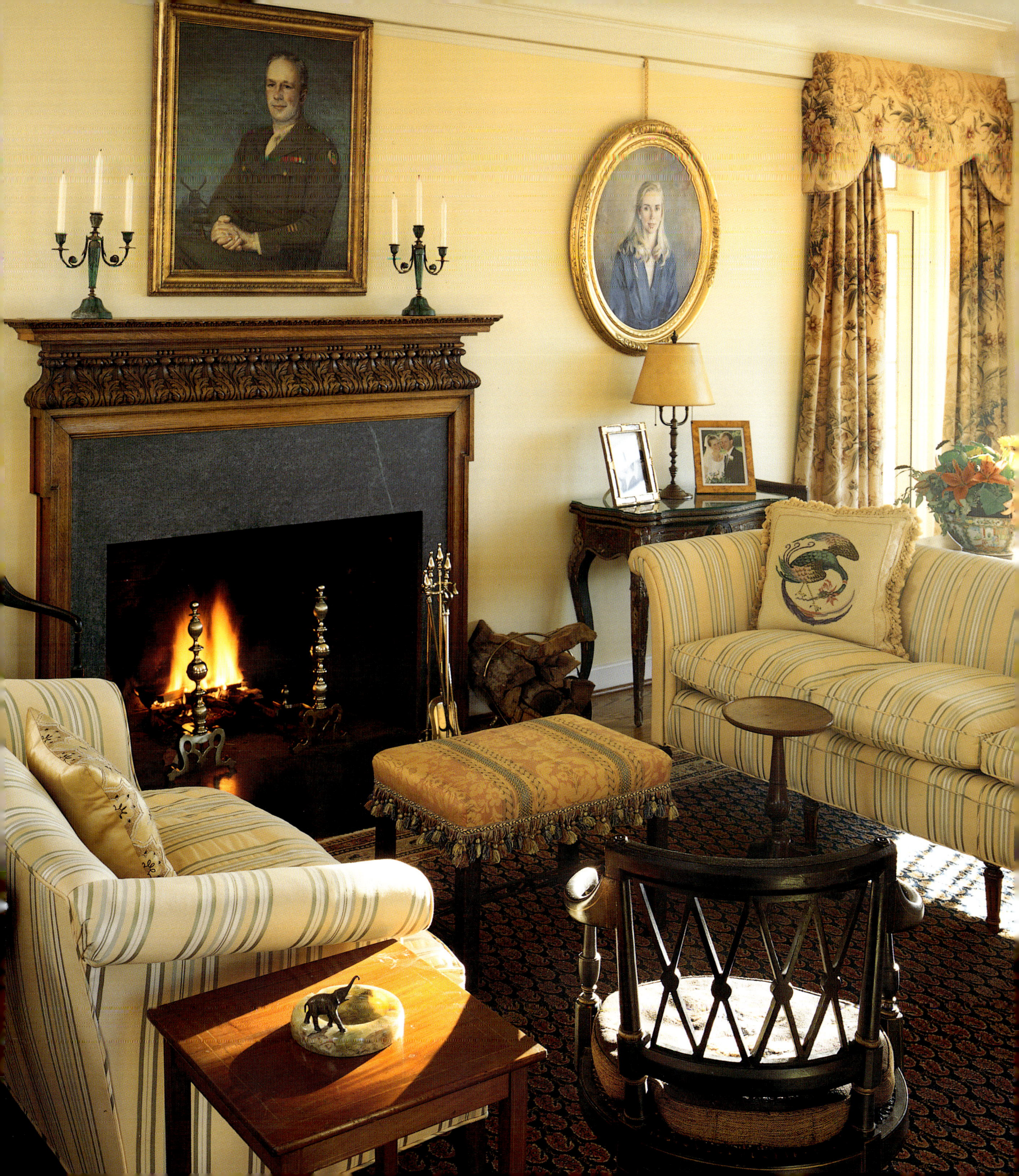

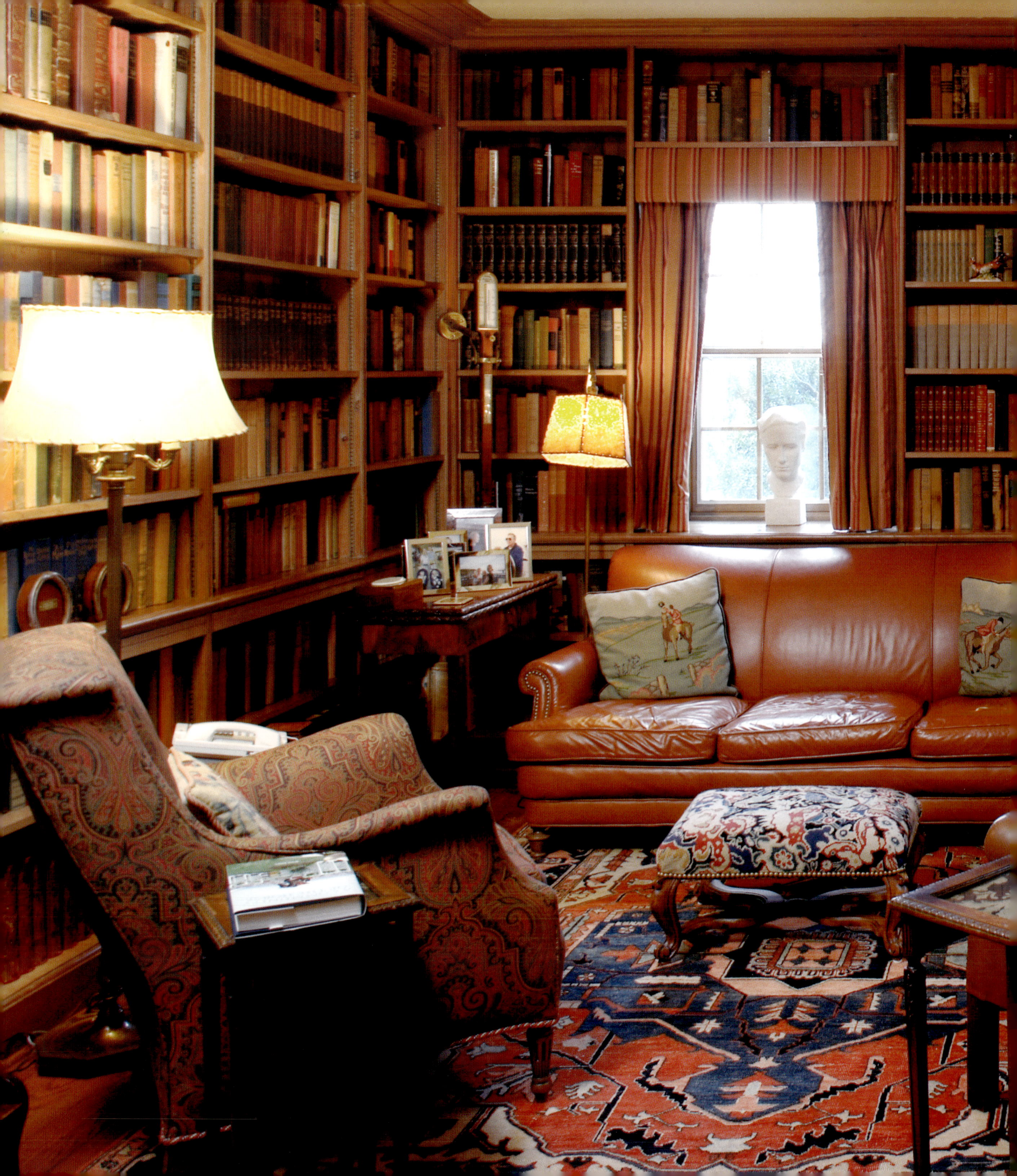

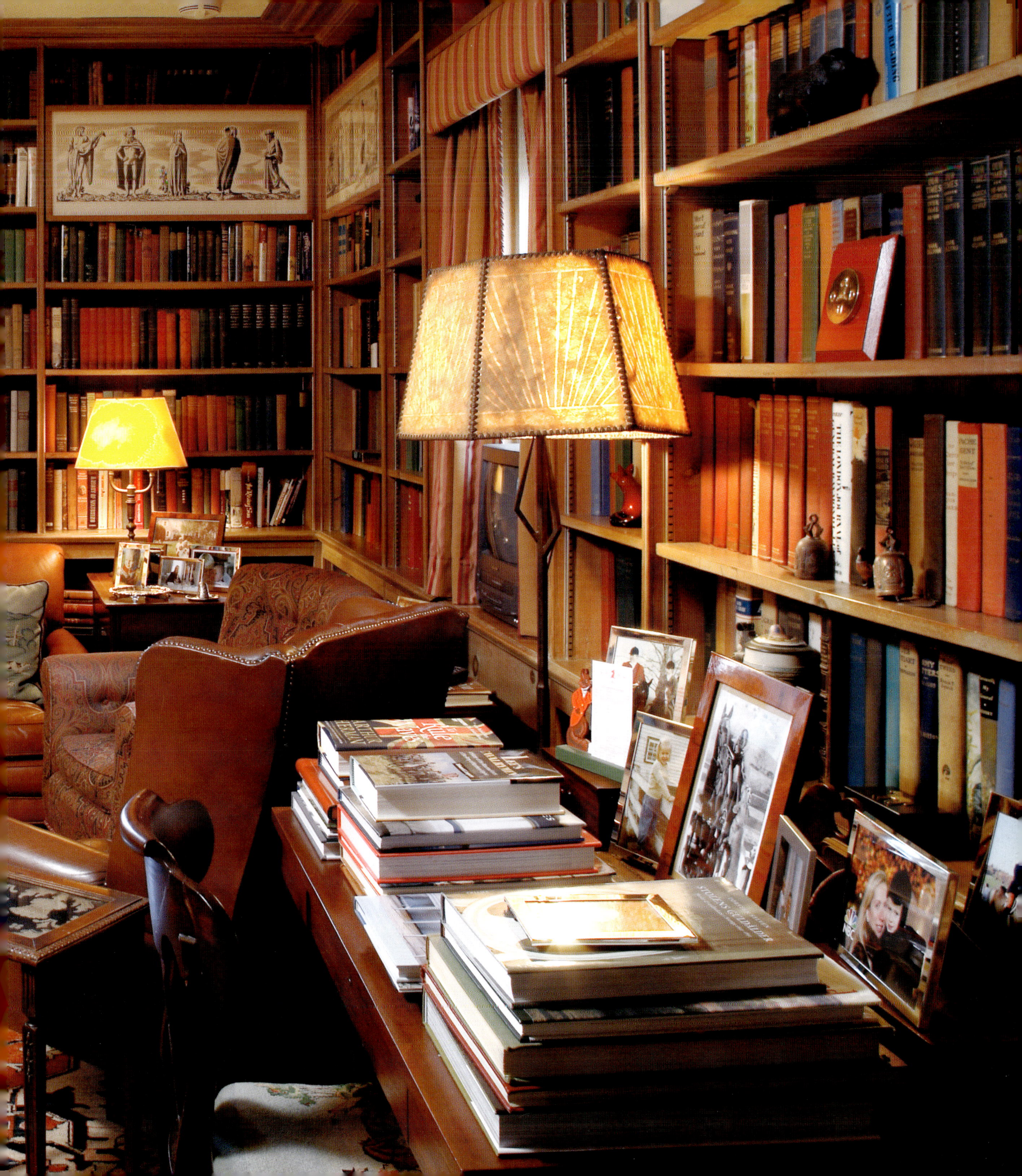

TOP AND ABOVE *The well-lit breakfast room was created by Warrenton architect Albert P. Hinckley, Jr., when he remodeled the southern portion of the 1941 house. The room incorporates a fieldstone wall of the main house and slate floors that complement the plain white glazed tiles of the fireplace in the style of a Swedish stove. A clever design for the adjacent area provides natural light from a skylight for the stairs from the lower level.*

RIGHT *A three-pedestal English mahogany dining table that seats fourteen or provides the space for a huge hunt breakfast buffet, mahogany Chippendale side chairs, and a Sheraton sideboard that displays a collection of silver, are reflected in the pair of tall mirrors that flank the fireplace.*

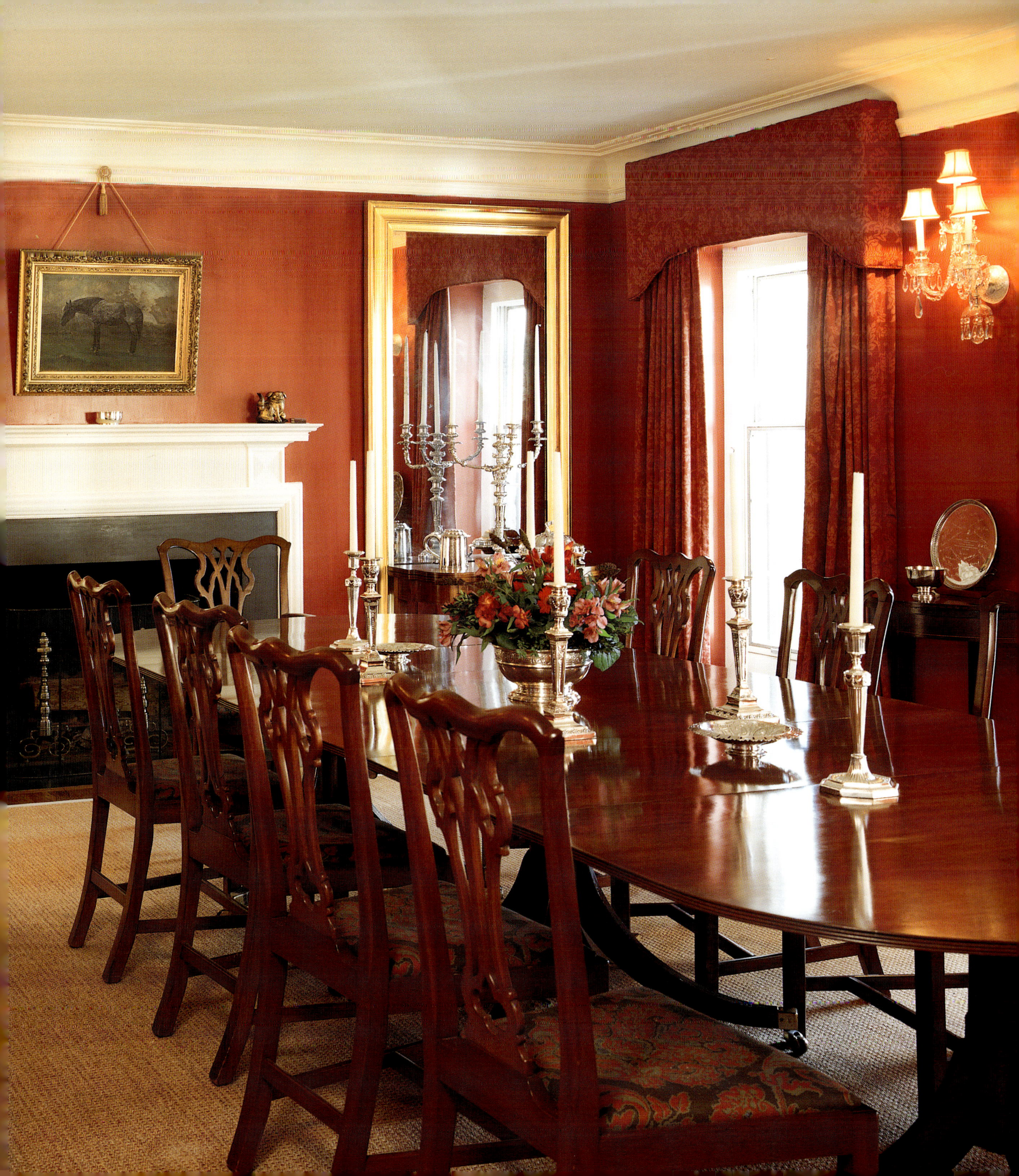

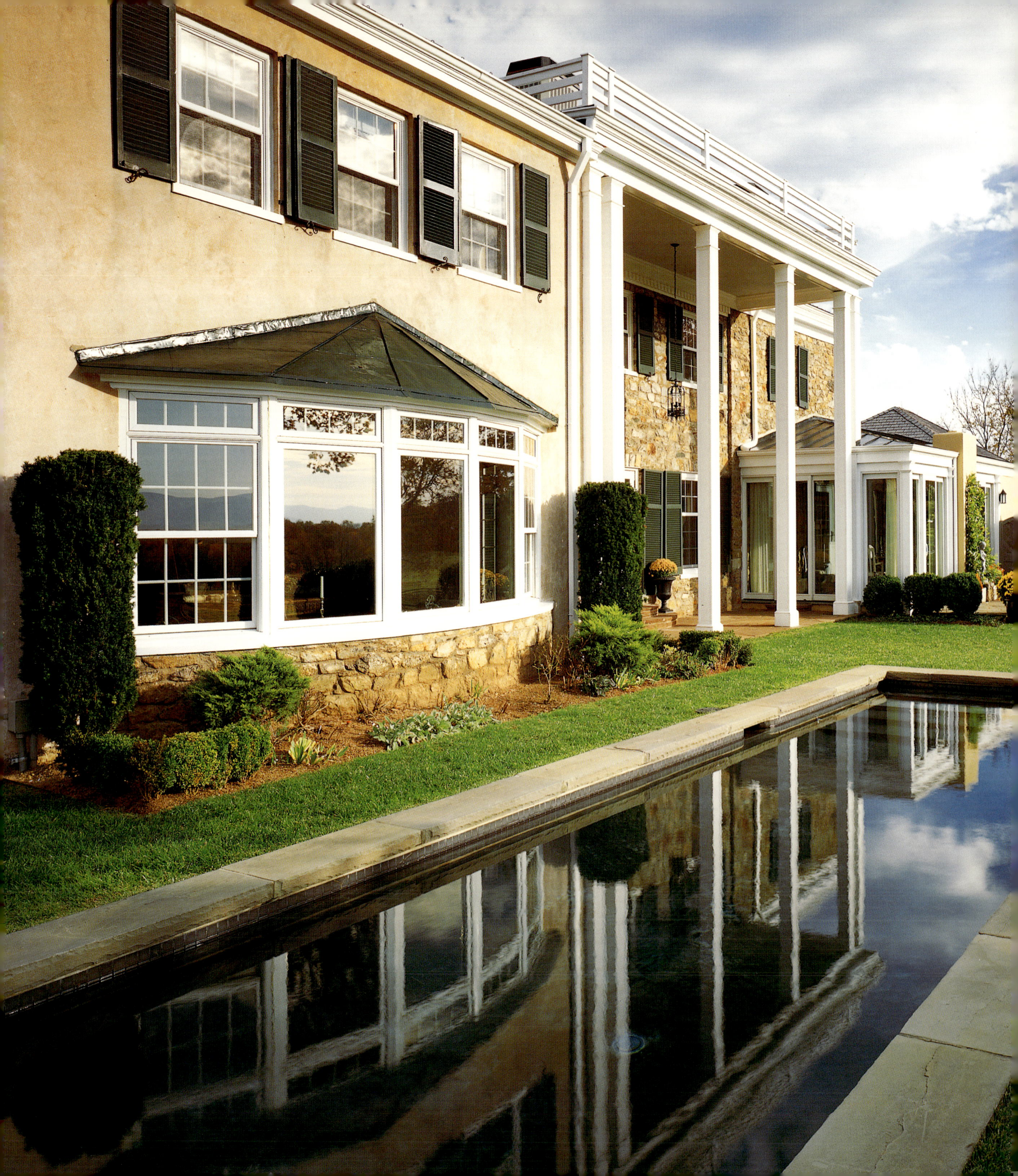

A bay window above the lap pool and the multitude of tall glass doors in the breakfast room allows for the enjoyment of beautiful vistas encompassing the farm's protected lands and the distant Blue Ridge Mountains.

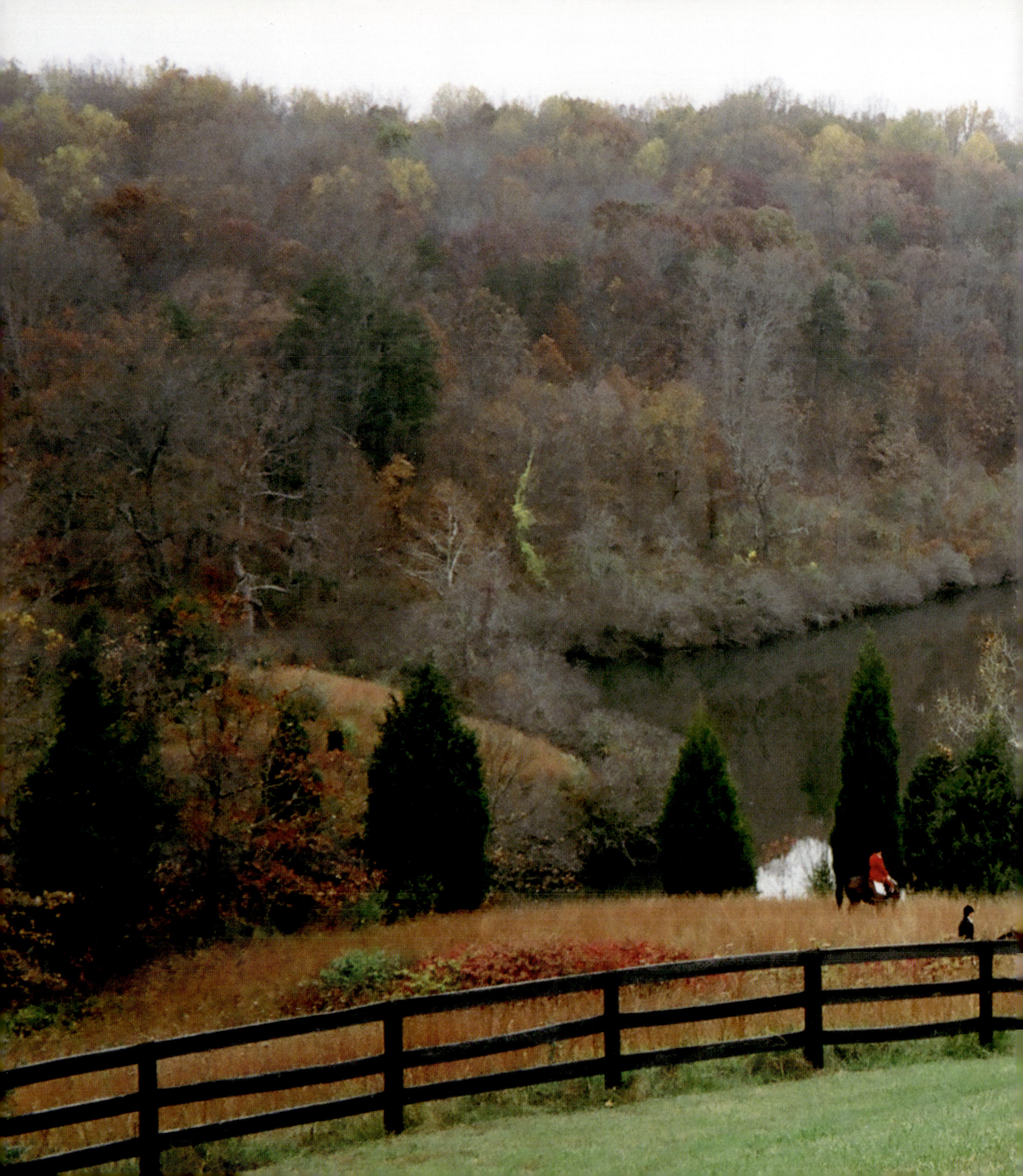

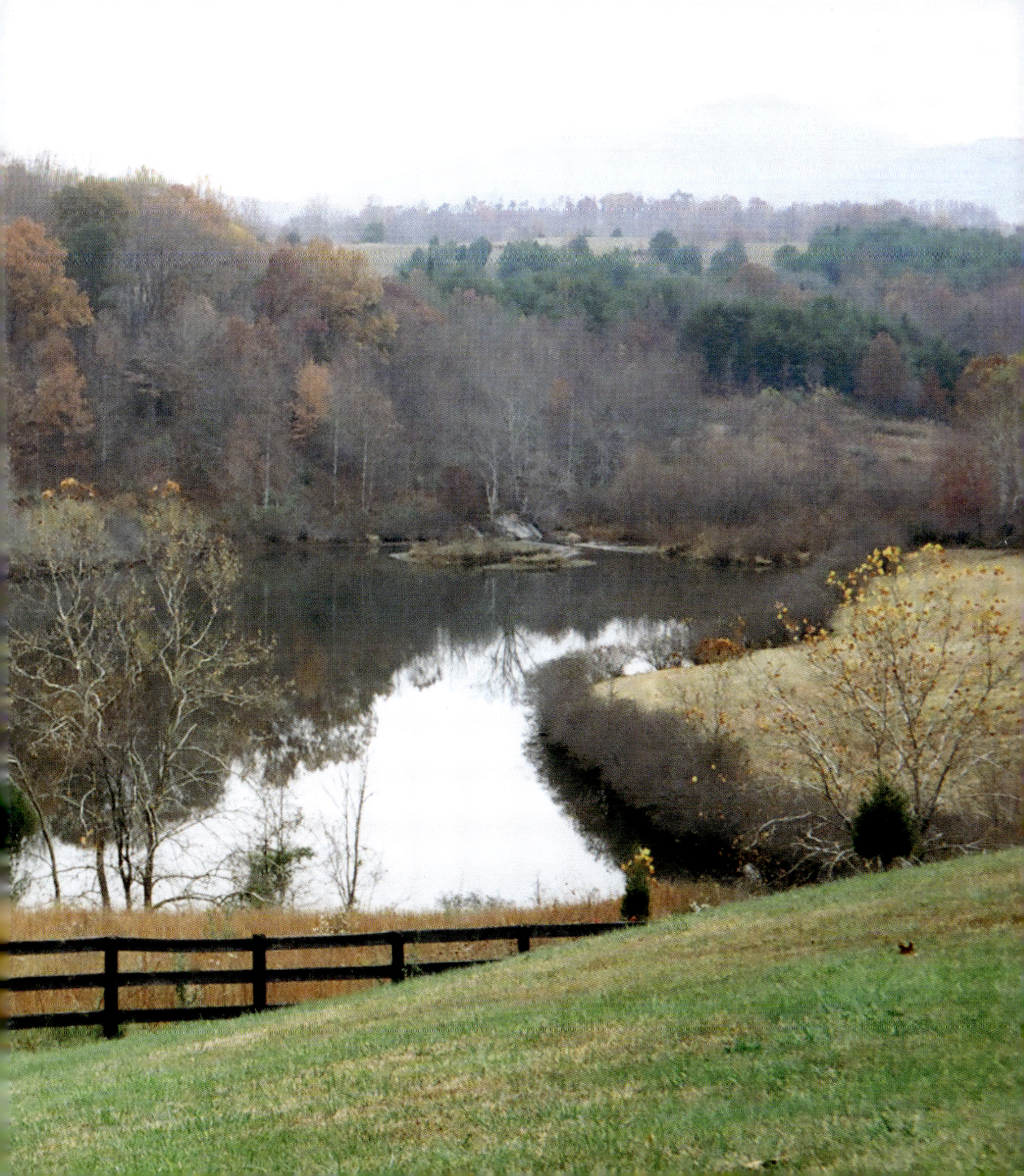

ACKNOWLEDGMENTS

Many people contributed to the creation of this book and I thank them for their guidance and good will, and for making the process a pleasure. First of all, I thank photographer Paul Rocheleau not only for his outstanding and evocative images but, as well, for his great personality, warmth, and charm. It was a pleasure to work with him. I thank editors David Morton and Douglas Curran at Rizzoli for their continued support, good cheer, and suggestions. And I thank designer Abigail Sturges, whose beautiful work I always appreciate, and her assistant Gerrit Albertson. I thank my husband David Pashley for his love and care. And I thank all of the owners of these beautiful Virginia houses for their hospitality and knowledge. I appreciate how they all truly care to preserve the treasures of their houses and land.

Special thanks to Rick Stoutamyer, antiquarian and bookseller, who knows practically everyone in the Middleburg area and who made many introductions on my behalf, lent me books from his extraordinary private collection, shared his knowledge and enthusiasm of the area, and was always willing to answer questions.

I am indebted to Mr. K. Edward Lay, Cary D. Langhorne Professor Emeritus of Architecture, University of Virginia, for his knowledge and kindness.

Thanks also to helpful friends who made introductions for me and shared their knowledge of the Piedmont's history, including Nancy Parsons, president of the National Sporting Library, Jean Perin in Middleburg, Terry Whittier in Keswick, Betsy Manierre in Middleburg, Anne Coyner in Upperville, Louisa Woodville in Middleburg, Cheryl Hanback Shepherd, architectural historian in Warrenton, Elaine Burden in Middleburg, Lucia Henderson in Berryville, Sandra Forbush in Flint Hill, Dale Lindsay in New York, Diana Braak in Clarke County, and Bucky Slater in Upperville;

Also the following:

Albemarle Charlottesville Historical Society: Margaret M. O'Bryant, librarian and head of reference resources
Aldie Mill, Aldie: Brenda Bruce Branscome, mill manager
American Bird Conservancy: Paul Salaman, International; Gavin Shire, Washington D.C.; Judy Szczepaniak, The Plains
The Ashby Inn, Paris, Virginia
Tommy Beach, architect, Upperville
John and Gloria Carswell, Snohomich, Washington
Cricket Bedford, realtor, Thomas & Talbot Real Estate, Middleburg
Charlottesville and Albemarle County Historical Society, Charlottesville: Margaret M. O'Bryant, librarian, head of reference resources
Clarke County Historical Association, Berryville: Jennifer Lee, executive director
Anne Coyner, Upperville
Marcia Cronan, Delaplane
Culpeper Historical Museum, Culpeper
Equutopia Riding Academy, Remington: Cleo van Zelst, owner, instructor
Cindy Ewing, mural artist, Clearbrook
Farmington Country Club, Charlottesville: Carol Minetree, public relations director; Elisa Bricker, communications coordinator
Stephanie Fassold, Florist, Lavender Green, Paris, Virginia
Fauquier and Loudoun Garden Club, Upper Fauquier and Loudoun Counties
Norman M. Fine, editor, "Covertside," Millwood
Dan Frisch, architect, New York
Denis Fuze and Barbara Lamborne, Lovettsville
The Garden Club of Virginia, Richmond
The Garden Conservancy, Cold Spring, New York
James Gordon, Gordon Construction, Berryville

Goose Creek Bridge Foundation, Middleburg
Albert P. Hinckley, Jr., architect, Hinkley Shepherd Norden, Architects, PLC, Warrenton
Robert Jennings, R J Photo Images, Morgantown, Pennsylvania;
Thomas Katheder, LakeBuena Vista, Florida
Keswick Hunt Club, Keswick
Kinross Farm: Neil Morris, trainer; Chris Read, jockey
Corey Kitzke, head gardener, Castle Hill, Keswick
K. Edward Lay, Cary D. Langhorne Professor Emeritus of Architecture, University of Virginia, Charlottesville
Douglas Lees, Photographer, Middleburg
Leesburg Garden Club (The), Leesburg
Library of Virginia, Richmond
Calder Loth, senior architectural historian, Virginia Department of Historic Resources, Richmond
Masters of Foxhounds Association of North America, Millwood
Ann Miller, historian, Virginia Transportation Research Council, Charlottesville
Montpelier, James Madison's Montpelier, The Montpelier Foundation: Peggy Seiter Vaughn, director of communications
Morven Park, The Westmorland Davis Memorial Foundation, Inc., Leesburg; Cathy Hill, director of development
The Mosby Heritage Area Association, Middleburg
Museum of Hounds and Hunting North America, Morven Park, Leesburg
National Sporting Library, Middleburg: Nancy Parsons, C.E.O. and president; Elizabeth Manierre, art curator; Lisa Campbell, librarian; Louisa Woodville, director of communications
National Steeplechase Association, Fair Hill, Maryland
Oakland Green Bed and Breakfast, Lincoln: Jean Brown, innkeeper
Orange County Historical Society, Orange: Marianne Hurd, research assistant, Office Administration
Jean Perin, Jean Perin Interior Design, Middleburg
Piedmont Environmental Council: Christopher Miller, president; Douglas Larson, vice president; Eve Fout, president of the board of directors
Red Fox Inn, Middleburg
Barclay Rives, Keswick
Barbara Robinson, designer, Santa Barbara
Sara Salaman, ProAves Colombia, Warrenton
The Shaggy Ram, Middleburg: Joanne M. Swift, owner; Howard Halberson, Chuck Hunter, Anne-Marie Walsh, staff
Shenandoah Stone & Masonry, Upperville; Jonathan Fickling, sales manager; Carl Stohl, stonemason, foreman
Cheryl Hanback Shepherd, architectural historian, Millennium Preservation Services, Warrenton
John and Roma Sherman, Paris, Virginia
Susan Shipp, Designer, Upperville
Sarah Smith, Sara Smith Interiors, New York, New York
Kim Stoutamyer, Marshall
Rick Stoutamyer, Stoutamyer Fine Books, Middleburg
Swofford, Don A., F.A.I.A., principal, DASA plc, Architects, Planners & Conservators, Charlottesville
Thomas Balch Library, Leesburg
Phillip S. Thomas, Thomas & Talbot Realty, Middleburg
Virginia Historical Society, Richmond
Virginia Museum of Fine Arts, Richmond
Westmoreland Davis Foundation, Morven Park, Leesburg
Dana Westring, trompe l'oeil artist, Marshall
Winmill Carriage Museum, Morven Park, Leesburg; Leona Heuer, curator;
Terry Whittier, Keswick.

RESOURCES

Abramson, Rudy. *Hallowed Ground: Preserving America's Heritage.* Charlottesville, Virginia: Thomasson Grant & Lickle, Inc., 1996

Baker, Norman L. *Valley of the Crooked Run: The History of a Frontier Road.* Delaplane, Virginia: Norman L. Baker Publisher, 2001

Britton, Rick. *Albemarle & Charlottesville: An Illustrated History of the First 150 Years.* San Antonio, Texas: Albemarle Charlottesville Historical Society, Historical Publishing Network, 2006

Brown, Stuart E., Jr. *Virginia Baron: The Story of Thomas 6th Lord Fairfax.* Berryville, Virginia: Chesapeake Book Company, 1965

Campbell, Lisa. "Before George Washington Helped Found a Nation, He Was A Foxhunter" in *The Chronicle of the Horse* magazine. Middleburg: The Chronicle of the Horse, Inc., September 20, 2002

Doran, Michael F. *Atlas of County Boundary Changes in Virginia, 1634–1895.* Iberian Publishing Co., 1987 and Athens, Georgia: New Papyrus Publishing Co, 2003

Edward 2nd Duke of York, ed. W.A. and F. Baillie-Grohman. *The Master of the Game.* London; Chatto & Windus, 1909

Havighurst, Walter. *Alexander Spotswood: Portrait of a Governor.* Williamsburg, Virginia: Colonial Williamsburg, Inc., 1967

Heath, Susan, David Pashley, and Faren Wolter. *Managing Land in the Piedmont of Virginia for the Benefit of Birds and Other Wildlife.* Warrenton, Virginia: American Bird Conservancy and Piedmont Environmental Council, 2006

Irving, Washington. *The Complete Works of Washington Irving: Life of Washington Vols. I and II.* New York: Thomas Y. Crowell & Co., 1855

Jones, Mary Stevens, (edited and compiled by). *An 18th Century Perspective: Culpeper County, Virginia.* Culpeper, Virginia: Culpeper Historical Society, 1976

Lay, K. Edward. *The Architecture of Jefferson Country: Charlottesville and Albemarle County, Virginia.* Charlottesville and London: University Press of Virginia, 2000

Loth, Calder, ed. *The Virginia Landmarks Register Fourth Edition.* Charlottesville, Virginia: The University of Virginia Press, 1999

Mackay-Smith, Alexander. *The American Foxhound 1747–1967.* Millwood: The American Foxhound Club, 1968

———. *American Foxhunting An Anthology.* Millwood: The American Foxhound Club, 1970

Magazine of Albemarle County History, The, vol. 52, Charlottesville, Virginia: Albemarle County Historical Society, Inc., 1994

Mead, Edward C. *Historic Homes of the South-West Mountains Virginia.* Bridgewater, Virginia: C.J. Carrier Company, 1962; originally published J.B. Lippincott Company, 1898

Moore, John Hammond. *Albemarle: Jefferson's County, 1727–1976.* Charlottesville, Virginia: The Albemarle Charlottesville Historical Society, 1976, 1986

O'Neal, William B. *Architecture in Virginia: An Official Guide to Four Centuries of Building in the Old Dominion.* New York: Walker & Company, Inc., 1968

Page, Thomas Nelson. *Social Life in Old Virginia: Before the War.* Sandwich, Massachusetts: Chapman Billies, Inc., 1984; first published, 1892

Rawlings, Mary. *Ante-Bellum Albemarle: Historical Sketches.* Charlottesville, Virginia: Albemarle County Historical Society, 1974

Rodes, Ruth. *Culpepper, My Heritage: The Ancestors and Descendants of Mary Alberta Coiner and Edward Thomas Rodes.* Harrisonburg, Virginia: Park View Press, Inc., 1982

Rouse, Parke, Jr., *Virginia: The English Heritage in America.* New York: Hastings House Publishers, 1966, 1976

Schell, Eugene M. *The Guide to Loudoun: A Survey of the Architecture and History of a Virginia County.* Leesburg, Virginia: Loudoun County Chamber of Commerce and Potomac Press, 1975

———. *Culpeper: A Virginia County's History Through 1920.* Culpeper, Virginia: The Culpeper Historical Society, 1982

Stephenson, Richard W. (Selected and with an introduction by). *The Cartography of Northern Virginia: Facsimile Reproductions of Maps Dating From 1608 to 1915.* Fairfax County, Virginia: History and Archaeology Section, Office of Comprehensive Planning

Stephenson, Richard W. and Marianne M. McKee, eds. *Virginia in Maps: Four Centuries of Settlement, Growth, and Development.* Richmond, Virginia: The Library of Virginia, 2000

Thomas, Arthur Dicken, Jr., Ph. D. and Angus McDonald Green, editors. *Early Churches of Culpeper County, Virginia: Colonial and Ante-Bellum Congregations.* Culpeper, Virginia: The Culpeper Historical Society, 1987; Appendix 4: reprint of "Milton Gregg & Joseph Oddenino" by Richard Guy Wilson, Ph. D. in the Charlottesville Daily Progress Sept. 21, 1982 "Our County and the Arts Issue"

Warrenton Antiquarian Society, The, ed. *Jericho Turnpike: The Storied Route of Foxhunting from New York to Virginia.* Warrenton, Virginia: The Warrenton Antiquarian Society, 2005

Wayland, John W. *The Washingtons and Their Homes.* Berryville, Virginia: Virginia Book Company, 1944, 1973

Williams, Kimberly Prothro, ed. *A Pride of Place: Rural Residences of Fauquier County, Virginia.* Charlottesville and London: The University of Virginia Press, 2003

Wilson, Richard Guy, ed. *Buildings of Virginia: Tidewater and Piedmont.* New York: Oxford University Press, 2002

Woods, Rev. Edgar. *The History of Albemarle County in Virginia.* Bowie, Maryland: Heritage Books, Inc., 1901, 1989

INDEX

Adells, Errol, 130
Aldie Mill, *13*
Alken, Henry, 109

Bateman, William, 150
Beach, Tommy, 91, 92, 95
Bishop, Molly, 74
Blassic, Kay, *22*
Bonheur, I., 92
Bradbury, Eugene M., 211
brick construction, 17–18
Brown family, 32, 35, 37–38
Buatta, Mario, 104, 110
Buck, Gordon, 211
Burwell family, 122, 124
Byrd, Charles, 122

Carter, George, 138
Casanova Hunt, *22*
Castle Hill, *40–49*
Chapel Hill Farm, *114–123*
Cheatham, Daphne, *105*
Christian, Bob, 218
Chronicle of the Horse, 26
Civil War, 18, 26. *See also* Mosby, John Singleton
Clagett, Jean, 150
Clark, Jeanne Fendley, *22*
coaching drives, *24–25*
Covertside, 26
Craven, Algernon, 211

da Dassage, 230
Donovan, William "Wild Bill," 115
Dulany, John Peyton, 66
Dulany, Richard Henry, 63, 65–66

Earle, Maude, 104
Edgewood, *90–101*
Eichman, Edward, 211, 218

Fairfax, Thomas 6th Lord, 12–13, 15
Farmington Country Club, *18*
Farm in Northern Virginia, *22–23, 226–241*
Fassold, Stephanie, 94
Fendley, Joyce, *22*
Fitzgerald, F. Scott, 66
Fletcher, Robert, 158, 160, 164
Forbush, Gus, 166, *172*, *172*
Forbush, Sandra M., 166, *170*
    paintings, *150, 170, 172, 188, 193*
Foshay, Mr. and Mrs. William W., Jr., 176, 183
Foxhall Farm, *166–175*
foxhunting, *2–3, 8–9*, 15, 18–20, 22, *28–29*, *172*
Frisch, Dan, 186
Frishmuth, Harriet, 122

Gifford, John, 230
Goose Creek, *13*
Greenville, *176–185*
Grigg, Milton, 211

Hall, Henry, 230
Hardwick, Gunther, 83
Haynes, Will, *26*
Heller, Henri de, 244
Henchman's Lea, *242–253*

Herring, John Frederick, Sr., 150
Hewitt, Mark, 116
Hickory House, 6, 27, *102–113, back cover*
Higginson, A. Henry, 19
Hill, Robin, 84
Hinckley family, 242, 244, *244*
Hoisington, Gaylord, 22
hounds, *8–9*, 15, 18–19
Howe, George L., 122
The Hunt Country of America (Slater), 162
Hunt Country (Piedmont of Virginia)
    architecture, overview, 16–18, 20, 22
    foxhunting tradition in, 15, 18–20, *28–29*
    geography and history, 10–16
    horses, importance of, 22, 25–26
    towns of, 26
Hytla, Ms. Douglas, *172*

International Foxhound Match (Great Hound Match, 1905), 18–19

Jefferson, Thomas, 17–18, 19
Jennings, Joe and Karen, *24–25*
Johnson, Robert, 22
Jones, Tommy Lee, *22*

Kerfoot family, 130
Keswick Hunt, 194
Keswick Stables, 53, *58*, 59
Kinross Farm, *146–157*
Kinross Training Stables, 146, *154, 156–157*

Lafayette, Marquis de, 15
Latoix, Gaspar, 230
Lawrence, Col. and Mrs. Clark J., 48
Lewis, Fielding, Jr., 116, 122, 127
Lincoln (Virginia), 32
Llewellyn, *124–133*
Loveridge, Clinton, 84

Madison, James and Dolley, 16
Manierre, Betsy, *28*
Mars, Jacqueline B., *25*
McCarty, William R., 80
Mellon, Paul, 10, 90
Mene, P. J., 230
Midway Plantation, 196
Monticello, *17*, 17–18
Montpelier, 16
Morison, Nat and Sherry, 61, 65–66
Morris, Neil, 146, *155*
Morrowdale Farm, *196–209*
Morton, Jeremiah, 178, 183
Morven Park, *20–21*
Mosby, John Singleton, 26, 80, 102, 158
Munday family, *196–209*
Munnings, Alfred, 150
Murphy, Jeff, 26

Nall, Wallace, 26, 74
Nasmyth, Patrick, 234
National Sporting Library, *10–11*, 25, 26

Oakland Green Farm, *32–39*
Ohrstrom, George L., Jr., 30
Ohrstrom, George L., Sr., 10
Old Dominion Hounds, *2–3*, 166, *172*, 172, 242
Old Keswick, *front cover, 50–59*

Orange County Hunt, 70
Ovoka Farm, *134–145*

Page, Judith Walker, 53, 54
Page, Mann, 53, 54
Paris (Virginia), *14–15*
Perin, Jean, 91, 92, 95, 97, 101
Piedmont Environmental Council (PEC), 28, *31*, 191
Piedmont Fox Hounds, 63, 66, 160, 162
polo matches, *28*
Proprietary of the Northern Neck, 12
Pullman, Tessa, 10

Quakers, 32, 35

Ray, Marcia, 84
Read, Chris, *26*, 146, *155*
Red Fox Inn, *30*
Reuling, Frank H., Jr. and Tressa Borland, 124, 130
Rheinstein, Suzanne, 212, 218
Rives family, 40, 44, *45*, 48
Rodes, Thomas Layton, 196
Ross, Mr. and Mrs., *118*
Rowlands, C. D., 230
Ryan, Greg, 26

Sagart, Vincent, *28*
Scassa, Roli, 183
Seven Springs Farm, *80–89*
Slater family, 158, 160, *160*, 162, *162*, 164
Smith, Alexander Mackay, 10
Smith, Harry Worchester, 19
Smith, Sarah, 116
Steeplechase racing, *26*, 146, 153, *154–155*
Stovin, Charles J., 143
Stubbs, George, 150

The Tannery, *70–79*
Thomas, C. Reed, 143
Thornton Hill Hounds Point-to-Point (2006), *26*
Thoroughbred breeding, 53, 58, 102, 110, *112–113*, 146, 153

University of Virginia, *19*
Upperville Colt and Horse Show, 66, 162

Valley of the Crooked Run, *142–143*

Walker, Mildred Thornton, 50
Walker, Thomas, 15, 46, 48, 50
Washington, George, 15, 138, 142
Washington, Warner, II, 124, 127
Welbourne, *60–69*
Westring, Dana, *105*, 244, *244*
West View, 1, *158–165*
Weymouth, George A. "Frolic," *25*
Wheeler, Larry, 170, 172
Whilton, *210–225*
White, Robert, 70
Wiley family, 26, 186, *188*, *189*, 191, 194
Wolfe, Thomas, 66
Woodlawn, *186–195*
Wyeth, Jamie, 109

Young, John and Margaret, 143

256

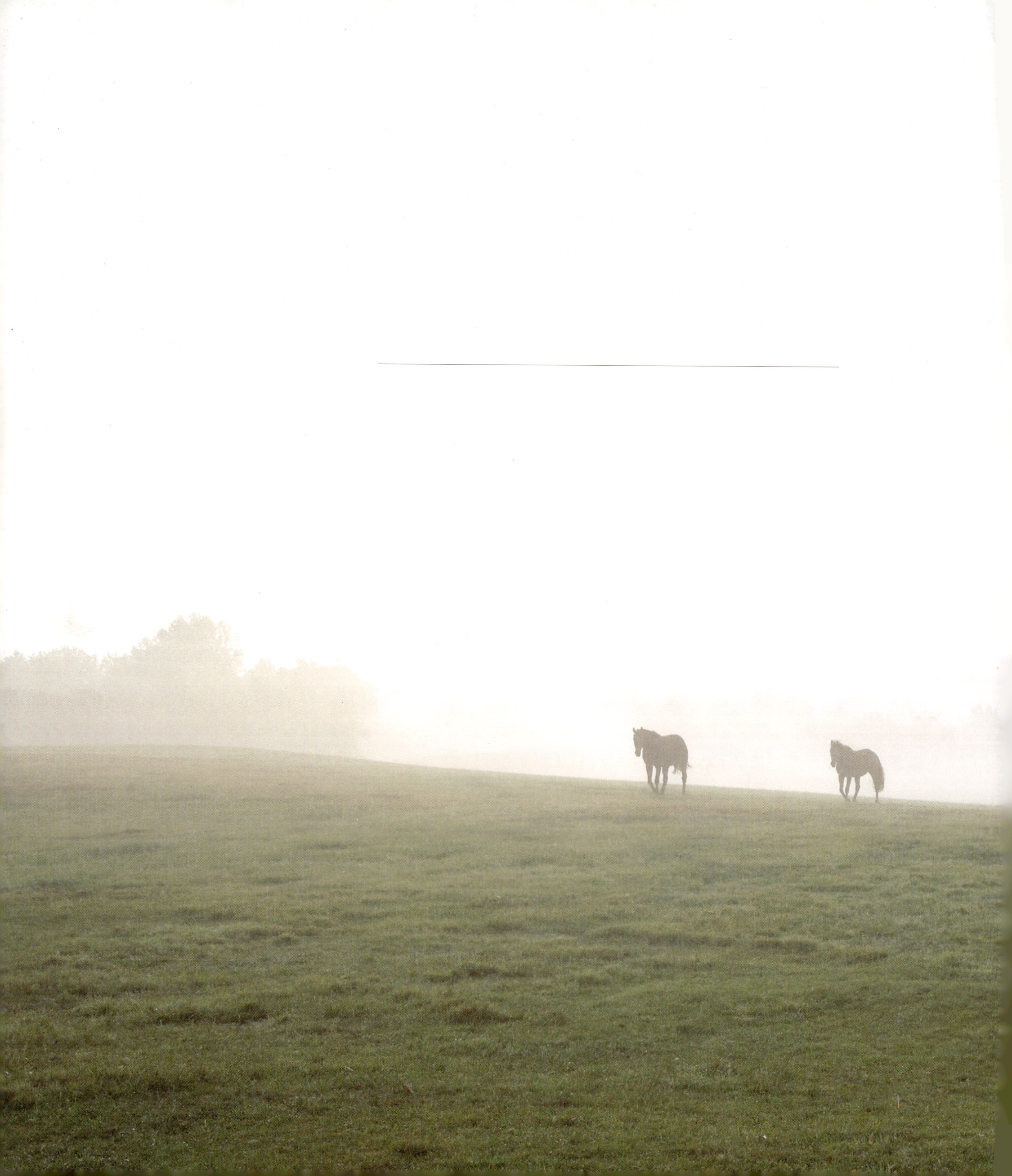